THE HARROWSMITH
COUNTRY LIFE
BOOK OF GARDEN SECRETS

THE HARROWSMITH COUNTRY LIFE BOOK OF GARDEN SECRETS

A down-to-earth guide
to the art and science of growing
better vegetables

By Dorothy Hinshaw Patent &
Diane E. Bilderback

CAMDEN
•HOUSE•
PUBLISHING

Camden House Publishing, Inc.
A division of Telemedia Communications (USA) Inc.

Library of Congress Cataloging-in-Publication Data
Patent, Dorothy Hinshaw.
The Harrowsmith country life book of garden secrets : a down-to-earth guide to the art and science of growing better vegetables / by Dorothy Hinshaw Patent & Diane E. Bilderback. – 1st ed.
p.   cm.
Rev. ed. of: Garden secrets. © 1982.
Includes index.
ISBN 0-944475-14-0
1. Vegetable gardening.
I. Bilderback, Diane E.   II. Patent, Dorothy Hinshaw. Garden secrets.   III. Title.
SB321.P375   1991
635 – dc20   90-25759
                                                        CIP

Edited by David Belknap
Designed by Eugenie S. Delaney
Cover photograph by Rosalind Creasy
Black-and-white line drawings by Elayne Sears
Photo credits: William D. Adams, p. 114 (top), p. 115, p. 226, p. 232 (bottom); Walter Chandoha, p. 118, p. 229 (bottom); Rosalind Creasy, p. 113 (bottom), p. 117, p. 119 (top), p. 228; Thomas E. Eltzroth, p. 116 (bottom), p. 120 (top), p. 230-231, 232 (top); Turid Forsyth, p. 229 (top); Jerry Howard/Positive Images, p. 113 (top), p. 119 (bottom); Dwight R. Kuhn, p. 114 (bottom), p. 116 (top), p. 120 (bottom), p. 225, p. 227.

Camden House Publishing, Inc.
Ferry Road
Charlotte, Vermont 05445

First Camden House Publishing Edition, 1991

Trade distribution by
Firefly Books Ltd.
250 Sparks Avenue
Willowdale, Ontario
Canada M2H 2S4

Printed and bound in Canada by
D.W. Friesen & Sons
Altona, Manitoba

To our families,
whose patient understanding during our long working hours
made this book possible.

ACKNOWLEDGMENTS

First and foremost, we wish to thank David Bilderback, Diane's husband, for reading and commenting on the entire manuscript, even when it meant staying up until two in the morning to meet a deadline. His scientific training in botany and his experience as a fellow gardener have been invaluable to us. Besides lending a hand with the editing and playing the devil's advocate, he helped find sources of information, assisted as our scientific advisor, and took care of the Bilderback children while Diane was off writing and researching.

In the process of working on the book we consulted with scientists having various specialties. We would like to thank them for their time and patience in answering our questions: Dr. Nancy Callan, Western Agricultural Research Center, Montana State University, Corvallis (seed moisturization and bio-priming); Dr. Michael Dickson, New York State Agricultural Station, Geneva (beans); Dr. Robert Dwelle, School of Agriculture, Washington State University, Moscow (potatoes); Dr. Calvin Lamborn, Rogers Brothers Seed Company, Nampa, Idaho (peas); Dr. H.J. Mack, Department of Horticulture, Oregon State University, Corvallis (beets); Dr. Edward J. Ryder, United States Agricultural Research Station, Salinas, California (lettuce); Dr. Philipp Simon, Department of Horticulture, University of Wisconsin, Madison (carrots); Dr. William L. Sims, extension vegetable specialist, University of California, Davis (tomatoes); Dr. Paul G. Smith, Department of Vegetable Crops, University of California, Davis (peppers); Mark Tappen, Rogers Brothers Seed Company, Nampa, Idaho (corn); and Dr. Ronald E. Voss, vegetable crops specialist, Cooperative Extension, University of California, Davis (onions). In addition, special thanks are due to Dr. Sims for reading and commenting on the tomato chapter for the first edition of the book and to Dr. Dwelle for reading and commenting on the potato chapter for both editions.

We also want to thank Sandra Taylor of Camden House for her encouragement during the preparation of this revised edition and David Belknap for his patience and helpful editorial suggestions.

CONTENTS

Introduction 10

Chapter 1 The Secret Life of Seeds 16

Chapter 2 Understanding Plant Structure 30

Chapter 3 The Care and Feeding of Your Garden Soil 56

Chapter 4 Nurturing Plants throughout the Season 64

Chapter 5 Lettuce and Spinach: Abundant Garden Greens 84

Chapter 6 The Versatile Cabbage Family 100

Chapter 7 Onions and Their Allies 140

Chapter 8 Radishes, Beets, Swiss Chard, and Carrots:
Colorful Root Crops and Greens 172

Chapter 9 Potatoes: Those Tasty Tubers 194

Chapter 10 Beans and Peas: The Generous Legumes 214

Chapter 11 Corn: The Oddball Crop 252

Chapter 12 Tomatoes: America's Garden Favorite 272

Chapter 13 Peppers: From Sweet Bells to Red-Hot Pods 290

Chapter 14 Cucumbers, Melons, and Squash: Rambling Cucurbits 306

Seed and Plant Suppliers 335

Vegetable Varieties 336

Glossary 340

Further Reading 343

Index 344

INTRODUCTION

When we first begin to garden, most of us learn the basics from a knowledgeable friend or a gardening book. We accept what we are told and don't ask why things are done a certain way. But after gaining some experience gardeners often become daring and want to experiment. Our experiments can, however, get us into big trouble when we don't understand the reasons behind the basic gardening practices we've been following. Without this knowledge we don't know which methods can be changed without bringing disastrous results.

This gardening book is very different from any you've ever read. Instead of merely giving you instructions on how, when, and where to plant your vegetable crops, we will usher you into the exciting world of your garden to help you see things you've never noticed before and to show you how your plants function and why they sometimes behave in strange or frustrating ways. We strongly believe that when you really understand the biology of your plants, you will be a far better gardener than if you were to follow the instructions in a book blindly without understanding the *whys* behind the *hows*. And when you know something about the factors that can influence your crops for better or worse, you'll be able to deal more effectively with gardening problems and to experiment more creatively with gardening methods.

Unfortunately, there are many gaps in our knowledge of garden plants. We would like to be able to tell you why radishes get hot when temperatures rise and what chemical makes lettuce bitter. It is frustrating not to be able to state exactly what day lengths will make some popular onion varieties bolt. But these and many other aspects of vegetable crops remain mysteries and will stay that way until someone chooses to investigate them. You will see as you read this book that we know the most about crops such as corn and potatoes, which are grown extensively on a commercial scale. Plants such as kale, kohlrabi, peppers, and radishes, which are not of great economic importance, have been slighted by researchers. For this reason our book is necessarily uneven in its coverage; we can explain to you only those phenomena that have been studied.

Our sources of information are varied. We have combed the scientific literature for writings illuminating the biology of vegetable plants, and much of our information on major crops came from government publications based on research carried out at state universities such as the University of California–Davis. We also used several books summarizing the scientific information about certain crops, as well as more general works such as *Evolution of Crop Plants,* edited by N.W. Simmonds (New York: Longman, Inc., 1986).

In this book we start by talking about plants in general, examining how they awaken to life from seeds and how they develop into full-fledged, mature, productive plants. Next we turn our attention to the garden itself and show you what goes on in the soil at root level and how you can create the best possible environment for your plants. A chapter on the most effective cultural techniques for you to follow all season long will help you avoid the common mistakes that are the downfall of many gardeners.

With all that background information in mind, we go on to consider each of more than twenty common garden crops. We give you pointers on choosing varieties; specific growing conditions (in terms of temperature, light, day length, nutrients, and water) that will help or hinder your crop; storing the crop; how to save your own seeds (where applicable); and pest and disease problems you're likely to encounter. Finally, we provide a glimpse at what sort of breeding research is being done for each crop to give you a preview of what new varieties you can expect in the seed catalogs of the future. By the time you've finished the book, you will have a new appreciation of your plants as living things as well as a better understanding of how to make them do their best for you. We hope you enjoy yourself in the process.

To set the stage for what follows, we start out by explaining a few key concepts that will be referred to throughout the book.

Days to Maturity

When a seed catalog advertises that a particular variety of corn or radish takes only sixty-eight days or twenty-five days to mature, what does this mean? Where we live, in Missoula, Montana, we average slightly more than ninety days of continuously frost-free weather in the growing season. But that doesn't mean we can have success with every crop that's listed in catalogs as taking fewer than ninety days to mature. Unfortunately, many of our frost-free days are quite cool, averaging less than 50°F over each twenty-four-hour period. In the case of a crop such as corn, temperatures below 50°F will halt growth, whereas temperatures above 50°F will allow the corn to grow. Up to a point the higher the temperature, the faster the corn will grow.

Some scientists and some seed catalogs use the measurement *degree days* for determining days to maturity of certain crops. Since 50°F is the critical point for corn growth, any daily temperature average above this point will earn degree-day units—one unit for each degree that the average temperature is over 50°F. For instance, if the average temperature for four days was 60°F, this would count as forty degree-day units (ten units for each day). Just how many units a corn plant must amass to reach maturity varies a bit among varieties, but to give you some idea, scientists have calculated that 'Golden Cross Bantam' sweet corn takes about 1,875 degree-day units to reach maturity. You can see that corn will mature faster under warm temperatures than under cool ones—just two days averaging 80°F will count for sixty degree-day units, whereas four days at 60°F would produce only forty degree-day units. This phenomenon accounts for the difficulty we have growing sweet corn varieties that are rated at more than sixty-eight days to maturity, even though there are more than ninety frost-free days in Montana. There just isn't enough heat on many of those days to make the corn grow.

With all crops seed sellers have to assume particular climatic conditions when they calculate days to maturity, whether they use degree days as a measure or something else. If you have cool summers with average temperatures below 65°F to 70°F, your crops generally will mature more slowly than the catalog's predictions lead you to believe. To guarantee that you'll be able to harvest a crop, you must select the fastest-maturing varieties. Remember that we are talking about *average* daily temperature, not maximum. Our average temperature here in a mountain valley can be low even on a day when the maximum reaches 95°F. The maximum temperature lasts only a couple of hours, and the nighttime temperature almost always drops below 60°F, even in the height of summer. A coastal area with less of a difference between daily maximum and minimum temperatures may allow crops to grow faster than they do here, even if the maximum never exceeds 85°F. And if you have very hot weather—temperatures in the 90s or above 100—crops that do well in the heat may mature more rapidly than the catalogs predict.

Because days to maturity may not be calculated in the same way, listings in catalogs from different companies are not necessarily comparable. Before you order your seeds, do a little comparing of the catalogs you have on hand. Find a common variety that most catalogs offer, and check the days to maturity given in each catalog. You may be surprised at the wide range you find. You might want to crosscheck a few more common varieties to get a feel for which catalogs tend to give a shorter time to maturity than others. Also be sure to note whether the time given is from direct seeding in the garden or from transplanting. Some crops, such as carrots and radishes, are always given from seeding, whereas others, including broccoli and peppers, are generally given from transplanting.

Varieties and Microclimates

Wherever possible in this book we recommend particular varieties of crops for different regions of the country. Each broad geographic area has its own climatic variations, however, and even within a small area the variations among microclimates can be significant. This concept can even extend into the garden itself. One area of the garden may be protected from the wind by a fence, and another part may be shaded by a large tree for part of the day. Since frost tends to settle in low spots, you may find that some parts of your garden will become frosted, while just a foot away the plants will be untouched.

For all these reasons variety recommendations must be taken with a grain of salt. 'Early Cascade Hybrid,' an early tomato variety with a supposedly sweet flavor, was sour and tough when grown in more than one Missoula garden. The 'Dutch Treat' pepper, however, grows beautifully here but was panned by a midwestern gardener in a magazine article.

We also have found that crops or varieties that grow well for one gardener may be a real problem for another. For example, Diane grows beautiful cucumbers, squash, and corn, but Dorothy has trouble with all three. When Dorothy is happily eating her way through a mound of peppers, Diane may be carefully rationing out a few ripe fruits. There are always the exceptions to the general trends, however, such as the year Diane's pepper plants were loaded with 'Colorado' chilis while Dorothy's crop was modest. 'Early Girl Hybrid' tomatoes consistently ripen first and taste better in Dorothy's garden, while Diane has had better luck with 'Burpeeana Early Hybrid.'

We could go on and on, but the point is that the best recommendation for a particular variety is that it grows well for you in your garden. But a year with unusual conditions can result in a disappointing crop or no crop at all. For this reason we always plant more than one variety of almost every crop we grow. Since there is no such thing as a typical growing season in our valley, we plant different varieties in the hope that at least some will be successful.

Warm and Cool Places

Here and in other books you are often directed to put germinating seeds, or to store harvested crops, in a warm or a cool place. What exactly do these terms mean? For our purposes, a warm place should stay between 75°F and 85°F as much as possible. You can probably find some warm spots in your home without much trouble. For instance, if your water heater is in a closet, the temperature there is likely to be warm. A cupboard above a wall oven, especially a gas oven with a pilot light, is another warm place.

If you lack these warm spots in your home, you can resort to the space on top of the water heater, but you must be careful. Many water heaters get quite hot on top, as friends of ours can testify. They lost all their newly planted seeds because the water heater got so hot that it cooked them! To be safe, place the containers holding your newly sown or just-germinating seeds on cake racks on top of the heater. Keeping this buffer zone between the heat source and the seeds should ensure that it won't get hot enough to kill them.

Those of you with wood stoves know that it is toasty warm in the vicinity of the stove. You could locate your germinating seeds near the stove (not on it), but only after measuring the temperature to determine the best distance. Since wood stoves produce dry heat, be especially careful about keeping the soil moist.

If you have a window that gets direct sun, you can place your freshly sown seeds by the window during the day and move them to the warmest part of the house at night.

Lettuce and spinach are two crops that germinate best under cool conditions (60°F to 65°F). Cool locations can be found in an unheated closet or cupboard that shares an outside wall. Basements also tend to be cool, as long as you are careful not to put the seeds near a furnace or water heater.

When we talk about cool storage conditions for harvested crops, we're referring to the 32°F to 40°F temperature range. Many of the crops you'll be carrying through the winter, such as acorn squash, beets, cabbage, carrots, onions, and turnips, require a cool, but not freezing, location for the longest storage life.

A root cellar, of course, is the ideal location. Those of you who aren't lucky enough to have access to one can improvise by storing your vegetables in a basement window well that has a 6-inch layer of insulating leafy mulch strewn on the bottom and a board set over the top to keep out the elements and hungry animals. An attic, breezeway, or unheated room are other possible options. In a house that's heated by a wood stove, check the closets on the north side of the house—they may be just the right temperature. Dorothy has had good results storing her onions in her unheated garage along the wall that's attached to the house. Following these suggestions, pull on your detective's cap and sleuth around your house to find the nooks and crannies that will provide cool storage conditions.

Chapter 1

The Secret Life of Seeds

Have you ever picked up all your garden seed packets and realized that you are holding an entire garden in your hands? The seed is one of nature's miracles, for it stores the essence of its kind in the smallest of spaces. Seeds from different crops often look very much alike. You probably could not tell the difference between cauliflower, broccoli, and cabbage seeds if you mixed them together in your palm, for they are very similar in size, shape, and color, resembling so many tiny deep brown to black specks of dirt. But what differences you see when these members of the cabbage family have grown up!

The dissimilarity between seeds of unrelated plants is usually quite obvious. Tawny carrot seeds, with their characteristic oval shape and lengthwise ridges, don't look anything like the wrinkled, relatively large khaki-green seeds of the pea plant. Beet seeds, with their brownish coloring and crinkly surface, may remind you of a breakfast cereal and appear downright humble compared to sleek, shiny jet-black bean seeds.

Despite the vast array of seed shapes, colors, and sizes, in terms of actual growth habits, there are only two basic types of seeds produced by two quite different types of plants: dicots and monocots. Most garden crops are dicots. If you look closely at a large dicot seed, such as a shelled peanut, you will see that it can be split into two halves, or cotyledons (also called seed leaves). They contain nourishment for the young plant as it germinates. Hidden between the seed leaves is a tiny plant embryo that will grow into the mature plant. The seed leaves

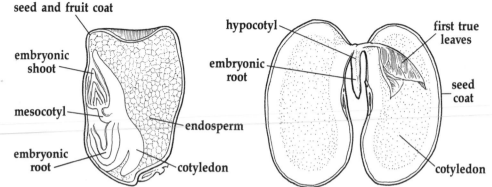

Seed Structure: The seed of a dicot plant, such as the bean seed on the right, can be easily separated to reveal the embryo nestled between two seed leaves (cotyledons). The corn seed on the left, a monocot, has only one cotyledon, along with a large endosperm containing stored food.

and the embryo are surrounded by the seed coat, which protects them from environmental extremes that, for example, cause them to dry out and from mechanical damage to their delicate tissues.

The monocot is exemplified by a corn seed, which cannot be split in two. Corn, onions, and grasses are monocots and have only one cotyledon. Most monocots store food for the young plant as endosperm tissue, which lies outside the embryo rather than entirely within the cotyledon itself. Corn stores almost all the nourishment for the young plant as protein and carbohydrates (sugars and starches) in its endosperm. The sugar in the endosperm is what gives corn its sweetness. Onions have much less endosperm than corn and store food both there and in the cotyledon. As you'll see in this chapter and the one that follows, there are other important differences between monocots and dicots besides their seeds.

The Best Way to Store Seeds

Within each seed is all the information it needs to develop into a productive garden plant—if you treat it right and plant it properly. Treating seeds right begins with proper seed storage. Many of us stow our seeds haphazardly in a box or bag and leave them in the basement for the winter. Diane also used to use this method, but an experience early in her gardening career made her mend her ways. For years, her long-lasting seeds survived just fine in the basement. But her luck ran out one spring when all her stored seeds germinated very poorly. Something was different about that winter; probably the weather, and thus the basement was much damper than usual. Whatever the reason, Diane had to replant many crops, losing valuable time and money in the process.

If you've ever had a similar experience, you've already learned the hard way that the most important factor in the survival of stored seeds is moisture. The drier your seeds are kept, the longer they will last. Ideally, storage humidity should be only about 4 to 6 percent. Cool temperatures also help, but dryness is the key to success. Increases in humidity and temperature lead to more rapid degeneration of the stored food and genetic information within the seeds. This in turn decreases the chances that the seeds will complete their complex germination process.

A reliable way to store your seeds is to enclose them in an airtight container with some silica gel or other type of drying crystals and set the whole container in a cool (but not humid) place, such as an unheated attic. Most hobby shops sell kits for drying flowers that include an airtight container and crystals. For a less expensive setup, use recycled glass jars with screw-on lids or airtight plastic containers and add a tiny packet of powdered milk to act as the desiccant. Making these packets is easy; just layer four tissues on top of each other and heap 2 tablespoons of powdered milk in one corner. Roll up the tissues, draw the long ends together, and secure them with a rubber band. If your seeds will be in storage for a while, replace the packet every six months or so.

How long seeds last in storage depends not only on storage conditions but also on seed type. Tomato seeds will remain viable for five or more years under favorable conditions, while onion seeds rarely survive more than a year even under the best circumstances. Sometimes old seeds will germinate but will produce inferior plants. One friend of ours grew 'Yellow Globe' onions two years in a row from the same seeds. Both years she started the seeds indoors, so their early growing conditions were similar. The first year the plants flourished, but the second year they grew very slowly. The seeds apparently had been weakened in storage, although they were still capable of germinating. Perhaps the stored food inside the seeds had deteriorated and thus the young plants did not get that vital early boost to their growth.

Testing for Germination

If you read your seed packets carefully, you will see that some seed companies provide germination information for the seeds they sell. A well-labeled packet should give the year the seeds were packaged and the expected percent of germination. Companies germination-test their seeds by placing them between layers of damp absorbent paper and leaving them in special germination chambers for a specified number of days. Then they count the number of germinated and ungerminated seeds to arrive at a percentage. Germinating the seeds on paper is much easier than planting them in soil, and the paper method usually gives a higher percentage of germinated seeds for the company to advertise. When seeds are planted in the ground, the young plants must push their way through the soil. The weaker seedlings can usually germinate on damp paper but may not make it in the garden.

It is easy to test your own seeds for germination. Place at least ten of them between layers of moist paper towels and keep them damp. (Be careful not to waterlog them.) Wait a few days after the first seeds germinate and then count them. If seven out of ten seeds germinate, your germination rate is 70 percent. If the germination rate is less than 50 percent, you should get new seeds.

Other conditions also can make the germination rate of seeds planted in your garden considerably lower than the rate given on the packet and the rate indicated by your home test. Seed companies often sort out the larger seeds for selling. These seeds make a good showing in germination tests but may have a harder time pushing through the soil because of their larger cotyledons. In addition, bacteria, insects, and fungi can attack the seeds or seedlings before they break through the soil. A friend of ours was very puzzled when bean seeds that had germinated perfectly well for her in damp paper towels never sent shoots above the soil when planted in the garden. Finally, after her second or third try, she couldn't resist digging some of them up to see what had gone wrong. She discovered that the seeds had rotted before the cotyledons had appeared—victims of harmful organisms in the soil.

What Seeds Need to Germinate

There are many theories on how to determine the best time to plant. Some gardeners go by the phases of the moon, while others gear their planting to coincide with the blooming or budding of certain key plants in the area. But the most effective method is to put your seeds in the ground when the soil temperature is right for germination of the crop you wish to grow. Many garden supply companies offer soil thermometers, which are a worthwhile investment. You simply plunge the thermometer into the soil to the depth at which the particular seeds are to be planted, then compare the temperature that registers to the best temperature for germination of that seed. (Germination temperature is listed in the "Vital Statistics" box at the beginning of each crop chapter later in this book.) If you start your seeds indoors, try to keep them at the optimum temperature. Some crops, such as onions and peas, will germinate over a wide temperature range. Others, such as beans, require a temperature within a very narrow range.

The seeds of some cool-weather crops such as lettuce and spinach will refuse to germinate at high temperatures. The warmth induces dormancy in the seeds rather than stimulating germination, as it would with eggplant or pepper seeds. One summer Diane planted spinach seeds during the hot August weather and mulched them with only a light covering of grass clippings. She also piled up her old spinach plants in a shady corner for future composting. She waited and waited for her seeds to germinate, but only two seeds in the entire 100-foot row pushed their way up! When she got around to moving the old spinach plants to add them to the compost pile, she found hundreds of tiny spinach plants beneath them. The seeds she had so carefully planted in the hot sun with their shallow mulch cover had gone dormant, but those that had fallen under the cool pile of plants had germinated perfectly. For this reason, if you want to start lettuce,

GERMINATING SEEDS BETWEEN PAPER TOWELS

In several chapters we recommend germinating seeds between layers of paper towels. Here are some tips for doing this successfully:

- Use only white or off-white unbleached towels; there is always the possibility that dyes in colored towels may kill the seeds.

- Use a brand of towel that is advertised as being strong when wet; you don't want towels that will disintegrate before the seeds have germinated.

- Use a ball-point pen to label each towel (before wetting it) with pertinent information such as the variety and date.

- Dampen the towels thoroughly; they should be wet but not dripping. The fine spray from a plant mister does a good job of providing just enough moisture. If the towels get too wet, gently squeeze out any excess water.

- Sprinkle seeds on one half of a towel, then fold the other half over to make a seed "sandwich."

- Layer several of these sandwiches in a casserole dish or glass pie plate. Alternate the position of the corners of the sandwiches as you layer them so that you can get to one layer at a time by lifting up a corner. Cover the dish loosely with wax paper.

- Put the container in a place where you expect the temperature to stay within the germination range for the crop you are sprouting. Be sure to check every two days to make sure the towels haven't dried out and to see whether the seeds have begun to germinate. If the towels are getting dry, use the plant mister to moisten them or sprinkle 1 tablespoon of water at a time over the pile (to avoid saturating the seeds).

spinach, or parsley during the summer, plant the seeds indoors or in a cool, shady corner of the garden to ensure that they will germinate properly.

The temperature at planting time affects not only germination of the seed but also later stages of the plant's development. If you sow pea or lettuce seeds in cold soil, the resulting plants will flower and form their own seeds earlier than if the original seeds had been planted in warm soil. This is fine for peas because earlier flowering means earlier peas for picking. But you don't want lettuce to bolt—flower and go to seed—early if you can avoid it.

Light also can affect seed germination. Most vegetable seeds germinate best in darkness, but some (including many varieties of lettuce and some celery) may require light for germination. Light affects not only the garden seeds you plant so carefully but also weed seeds. Many weed seeds will germinate only in light. That is why your garden may sprout into a lush weed patch after you have painstakingly tilled it. Your tilling brings the weed seeds to the soil's surface where they germinate in the light.

Temperature affects weeds, too. They may go dormant if the weather gets too hot, but when the soil cools again, you may end up with a fresh crop of weeds.

Some weeds, such as the British weed called fat hen and the American pigweed, produce two types of seeds. One type has a normal seed coat and will germinate easily. The other type has a hard seed coat that must be weakened by a scratch before it will come to life. Every time you conscientiously cultivate your garden, some of those hard-coated seeds are scratched by small rocks in the soil and then germinate. No wonder weeds are so hard to get rid of!

Seeds also need oxygen to germinate. If they are sown in water-logged soil or are planted so deep that sufficient oxygen cannot reach them, they will just sit there and rot. One year that happened to Dorothy's cucumber seeds. She planted them too deep in heavy clay soil, in valleys rather than in hills, and then watered them too much. Not a single seed germinated. In the "Vital Statistics" box at the beginning of each crop chapter, you will find the proper planting depth for each type of seed; follow these guidelines carefully.

Although temperature, light, and oxygen are important to seed germination, the most important factor is adequate moisture. Water-logged seeds will not germinate, but neither will dried-out ones. A lettuce seed planted at the proper temperature near the soil's surface, where it will receive the right amount of light and oxygen, will not germinate if it does not get enough moisture. That's why it is sometimes difficult to germinate lettuce seeds and others with similar requirements. They need light (so they should be scattered on the surface of the soil or planted very shallow), but they also need to stay moist. This can be a tricky combination to achieve during a warm, sunny spring.

In the garden a thin layer of light mulch such as grass clippings can help keep these seeds moist while letting in the necessary amount of light. In the house seeds such as lettuce, snapdragons, and runnerless strawberries can be germinated by sprinkling them on top of the soil, watering them gently, and placing the container in a plastic bag on a bright windowsill. The plastic cover will act as a miniature greenhouse, letting in light but retaining plenty of moisture. If you use this technique, be sure you have sterile potting soil so that you don't have trouble with mold. If mold does form, loosen the plastic so that the atmosphere inside your "greenhouse" dries out somewhat.

The Seed Coat's Role in Germination

The seed coat that surrounds the living seed sometimes does more than just protect it. The seed coats of many plants contain chemicals that inhibit germination of the seeds. This keeps them from germinating too early or when only briefly exposed to moisture. Some gardeners who are interested in rapid germination soak and wash their seeds to get around these germination inhibitors. Some types of peppers, such as jalapeños, may germinate more rapidly if soaked

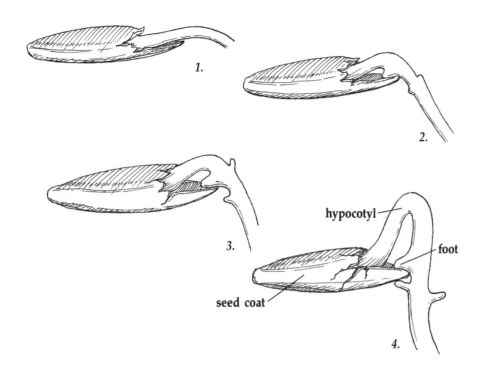

1.

2.

3.

hypocotyl

foot

seed coat

4.

Seed Coat Removal: During germination the cucumber produces a unique foot on its stem that catches onto the seed coat and pulls it away from the emerging cotyledons. The removal process begins as shown at the top left and progresses as the foot becomes fully developed (bottom).

in a couple of changes of lukewarm water before planting. Beet and chard seeds also have a germination inhibitor; these strange-looking lumpy "seeds" are not really seeds at all but dried-up fruits of the plant, each of which contains several seeds. (That's why beets and chard always need to be thinned.) The hard fruit covering contains a germination inhibitor, but if you soak the seed (fruit) over-night, it will absorb too much water, and you will still have poor germination.

Seed coats play other important roles in the lives of plants. They regulate how much oxygen, water, and light the seeds receive. You may have planted beans or corn in soil that was very moist but cool and were dismayed by subsequent poor germination. The seed coats of these crops can allow water to rush into the seeds too quickly, as with beets. This rapid water uptake can damage the tender cell membranes, permanently harming a young seedling so it grows slowly or preventing germination altogether. This process has been termed imbibitional shock, or soaking injury. Soaking injury can occur at any time with some crops, but cold temperatures make it worse.

To avoid soaking injury, you can allow the seeds of sensitive crops such as beans, beets, and corn to soak up water gradually before planting them in the garden. This method is called seed moisturization. One way to do this is to place them in moist vermiculite for eight to sixteen hours before planting. An easier method for most home gardeners is to place damp paper towels on a sheet of wax paper, sprinkle on the seeds you want to hydrate, and roll up the towels with the wax paper on the outside. Leave the seeds inside the paper for eight to six-teen hours at room temperature, then plant them. Don't let them sit for more than nineteen hours, or the delicate seedling root may begin to penetrate the seed coat, and you could damage it during planting.

How Seeds Germinate

The uptake of water is the first stage in seed germination. But just because your seeds swell with water does not mean they are alive. Water uptake is a passive process that even dead seeds will undergo. This water uptake can generate a surprising amount of force. A friend of ours was sprouting some wheat seeds for eating and put too many in the jar, which she covered with a screw-on lid. The next day, when she went to rinse the seeds, she found that the force of the swelling seeds had cracked the jar!

After a seed has swollen with water, the tiny embryo inside begins to grow. It sends a chemical message (a hormone) to the part of the seed where food is stored (the endosperm in monocots such as corn and the cotyledons in dicots such as beans), which directs cells in the storage area to produce enzymes. These enzymes digest the stored food and make it available to the embryo.

The tiny, delicate embryonic root is the first part of the new plant to break through the seed coat. It grows straight down, guided by the force of gravity, into the soil. It makes no difference which way the seed is planted, as the root will always grow downward. Then the stem and leaves begin to grow. Once a corn seed begins to germinate, the leaves, covered by a protective sheath, grow straight upward toward the surface, leaving the old seed behind in the soil. With beans the stem elongates, pushing the cotyledons and true leaves to the soil's surface. The young bean stem looks like an upside-down J when it breaks through the soil, with the cotyledons and true leaves pointing downward as part of the hook. As soon as the seedling breaks through into the sunlight, the stem straightens out, exposing the leaves.

You can easily distinguish the cotyledons from the true leaves on beans and other seedlings. The cotyledons are thick and spongy with stored food. They also

Corn Germination: The leaves of the developing corn plant emerge from the soil in a protective sheath, leaving the old seed behind in the soil.

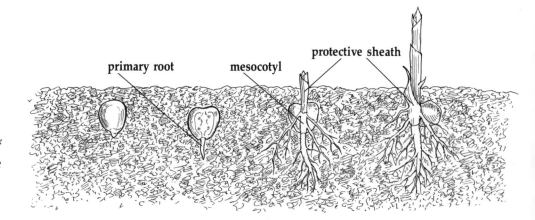

primary root   mesocotyl   protective sheath

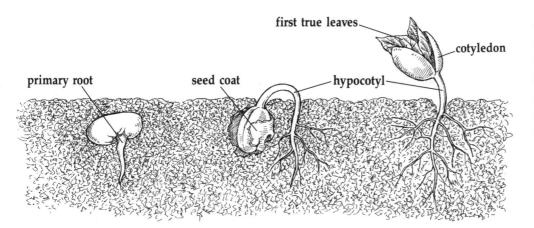

first true leaves
cotyledon
primary root
seed coat
hypocotyl

Bean Germination: The new stem of the bean elongates and pushes the cotyledons and true leaves to the surface of the soil. The stem and leaves, bent like an upside-down J, break through the ground and become upright.

are shaped differently from the first true leaves, which are miniature versions of the leaves that will be produced by the plant throughout its life. Although bean cotyledons do photosynthesize to produce some food for the young plant, they continue to nourish it primarily with their stored food.

The seed leaves of peas remain in the soil as the young plant grows, while tomatoes send their cotyledons up into the sunlight to manufacture food for the plant before the first true leaves are visible. It is important to leave the seed leaves alone, since they are, in one way or another, providing food for the young plant.

Some young seedlings discard the old seed coat from the cotyledons. This occasionally presents a problem, especially with peppers and some watermelons. With these crops, the seed coat may not come off and will hold the tips of the cotyledons together. The small true leaves become imprisoned between the cotyledons and cannot expand. When this happens, you can try to remove the old seed carefully without damaging the seed leaves or the true leaves. Cucumber seedlings have a special little foot on the stem to push off the old seed coat. As the cotyledons bend out of the seed coat, this foot catches on the coat and levers it off.

When an onion seed germinates, the old seed is carried aloft on top of the single, long green cotyledon. The tip of the cotyledon is buried in the endosperm of the seed, gleaning nutrients from it. For this reason you should leave the hard black head of the onion seedling alone for fear of pinching off its supply of nourishment.

What Makes Hybrid Seeds So Special?

It seems that more and more varieties of garden vegetables are called hybrids. Have you ever wondered just what hybrid seeds are? You also may have questioned why they are so expensive and whether they are worth the extra cost. Gardening books caution against saving seeds from hybrid plants, but do you know why?

Hybrid seeds are produced by crossbreeding two different parent strains of a particular plant species. Each of the parent strains has been bred to itself for so many generations that it is very uniform genetically. These two uniform strains, which are quite different from each other, are cross-pollinated to produce the hybrid seeds. Growers experiment with different crossbreeds to find out which ones result in good crop plants. Hybrids are very consistent in their characteristics, such as size and time to maturity, because the genetic make-up of each hybrid plant is almost identical to that of every other plant resulting from the same crossbreed.

It takes a lot of time, space, and labor—all of which cost money—to maintain the parent strains that are crossbred to obtain hybrid seeds. In addition, the flowers of one parent strain generally must be hand-pollinated with the pollen of the other strain to ensure uniform hybrid seeds. This can be a very labor-intensive process. For example, when hybrids of vegetables with perfect flowers (containing both male and female organs) are wanted, the anthers (pollen-producing parts) of the flowers that will be the female parents may need to be removed. Doing this guarantees that the plant will not pollinate itself but will receive only the pollen from the male parent to complete the desired crossbreed.

Before the advent of corn plants that do not produce pollen, hybridizing corn offered summer employment for many teen-agers who lived near big seed growers. Each corn plant has its own male flower (the tassel) and female flower (the ear with its silks). The normal course of events is for pollen from the tassel to drift down and find its way to the silks or to be carried by the wind to the silks of near-by plants. Seed growers intent on making a crossbreed needed to control which pollen did the pollinating, so they had their hired helpers remove the tassels on the female parent plants so that they could not spread their pollen and pollination would be done by the male parent plants.

Hybrid varieties often are worth the extra cost. Many hybrids mature earlier than the standard, open-pollinated varieties. For example, some hybrid varieties of corn and tomatoes mature several days earlier and yield more consistently than the standard ones. If you live in a short-season area and want to grow corn or tomatoes, you may have no choice but to plant early-maturing hybrid varieties. The quality and quantity of the harvest also might convince you to buy hybrid seeds, for many hybrids have a better flavor and a higher yield than standard varieties. Disease resistance is another important trait built into many hybrids, which is a boon to organic gardeners.

If a hybrid does not offer any overwhelming advantage over a more traditional strain, you probably should buy nonhybrid seeds. Then you can save your own seeds from year to year and not have to depend on commercial sources. If you save seeds from hybrid plants, the genetic traits from the two parent strains will be all mixed up in the second generation, and your plants will be variable and unreliable. Seeds from nonhybrid plants produce a more predictable crop, and if you carefully save seeds from the best plants in your garden, you will eventually

THE MAKING OF A HYBRID VARIETY

All plants carry two units of inheritance, called genes, for each genetic trait—one derived from the female parent and one from the male parent. The genes determine the flavor of the produce, the height of the plant, the time to maturity, and all other characteristics that make up the plant. This chart shows what happens when hybrids are produced. Each set of letters—AA, Bb, Cc, and so on—represents one pair of genes.

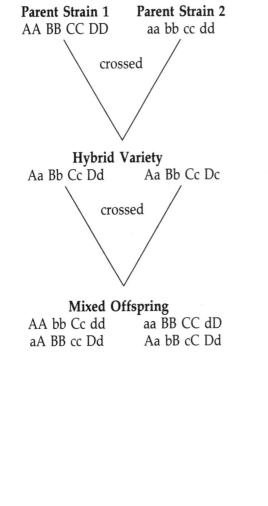

Parent Strain 1   **Parent Strain 2**
AA BB CC DD   aa bb cc dd

crossed

Hybrid Variety
Aa Bb Cc Dd   Aa Bb Cc Dc

crossed

Mixed Offspring
AA bb Cc dd   aa BB CC dD
aA BB cc Dd   Aa bB cC Dd

Parent strains are inbred for generations so that they are genetically uniform. The individual plants within each strain have an almost identical genetic make-up, and both genes for each trait also are identical (AA, aa).

When plant breeders cross the parent strains, the hybrid offspring receive one gene for each trait from each parent (Aa, Bb). Since plants of each parent strain are essentially identical, all the offspring are almost identical.

When hybrid plants are allowed to go to seed, the pollination that occurs as a matter of course introduces an incredible variety of combinations of genes and thus of traits. This diagram shows only some of the potential combinations of only four gene pairs. There are actually thousands of genes in each plant, so you can see that the variety of possible combinations is almost infinite. That's why when you sow seeds taken from hybrid plants, you can never be quite sure what will come up.

have seeds that are especially adapted to your growing conditions. In the long run you could end up with strains that are even more reliable and more productive than the hybrids you can purchase. Similarly, a local seed company or one located in a climate much like your own will provide nonhybrid seeds that are better adapted to your garden than a company that grows and saves seeds under different conditions.

We encourage gardeners to buy from local seed companies as much as possible. Besides having better adapted seeds, these companies often are the sole source of many unique varieties. These varieties may have valuable traits such as disease resistance, ability to germinate in cold soil, or drought tolerance. When small seed companies go out of business, the unique genetic combinations that make some varieties special are lost.

The disappearance of heirloom vegetable varieties has become a source of worry for many people concerned about the need to maintain genetic variability in the crops we grow. The more traits breeders have to choose from in their work, the easier it is to develop varieties that can meet goals such as disease resistance, tolerance of adverse conditions, and early yield. But when good hybrids come along, growers can too readily abandon older varieties and grow only new ones, which can lead to disaster.

Corn is probably the best example of this problem, since commercial growers of field corn all want to raise the varieties that will give them the best yield in the shortest time. Perhaps the ultimate example of the perils of genetic uniformity in corn is the epidemic of corn blight that destroyed a large part of the United States' corn crop in 1969. Ironically, the problems that year were due to the breeding of hybrids rather than to the inbreeding of standard varieties. A few years before, corn breeders had discovered a gene that resulted in male-sterile corn plants—plants that produced no pollen. These plants were very convenient for breeders, for they made tedious detasseling of corn for hybridization unnecessary. This gene, called the T-type cytoplasm gene, had been incorporated in 70 to 90 percent of all hybrid corn varieties by 1969. That year a mutant strain of the fungus causing corn blight arose, and it proved to be especially devastating to plants with T-type cytoplasm. Since most of the corn being grown in the United States carried the gene for T-type cytoplasm, by 1970 the new blight strain had spread to every state east of the Rockies, and the corn crop was devastated.

That near-disaster alerted corn breeders and other observers of the nation's food supply that it is imperative to keep corn more diversified to avoid the perils of inbreeding. The incident focused attention on the need to establish seed banks where breeders can store and propagate hundreds of corn varieties (as well as varieties of other crops). Ideally, when problems with one strain develop, the breeder should be able to turn to the seed bank to find genes that will confer disease resistance or other desirable traits on the variety with which he or she is working.

Because beans have been around for such a long time, there are almost countless variations on the basic bean. Most of these strains are not available to home gardeners via commercial channels, and in many cases they have been kept alive only because one individual lovingly and carefully saved seeds and replanted them year after year. At best this is a tenuous existence. What happens when that individual dies or is unable to continue gardening? Often the answer is that that particular bean strain dies out. Fortunately, many people have become concerned about the accelerating loss of these heirloom varieties and the need to preserve genetic variety for future breeding efforts.

One man dedicated to preserving heirloom bean varieties is John Withee. With the help of many home gardeners and farmers, Withee has collected more than twelve hundred strains of beans. In 1981 he donated samples of his entire collection to the Rodale Research Center in Maxatawny, Pennsylvania, and to Kent Whealy, founder of Seed Savers Exchange. Both the Rodale Research Center and Whealy, with the help of concerned gardeners across the country, are working to increase the store of seeds in the collection to ensure the preservation of each strain. If you are interested in joining in the effort to maintain the diversity of heirloom vegetables and want to participate in a growers' network to save and propagate heirloom seeds, write to Seed Savers Exchange, RR3, Box 239, Decorah, IA 52101. In 1990 the membership fee was $25 and included the *Seed Savers Yearbook,* summer edition and harvest edition. In this nonprofit organization, heirloom seeds of many common garden vegetables are traded among gardeners committed to saving and propagating nonhybrid varieties.

Chapter 2

Understanding Plant Structure

E ach part of a plant—root, stem, leaf, and flower—plays a unique role in its life. Understanding the special functions of the different plant parts can make you a better gardener because you will be better able to meet the needs of your crops. Let's start from the bottom and examine each part of the plant to find out just what is going on as the plant grows, matures, and provides you with food.

***

Roots

P lant roots may be hidden in the soil where you can't see them, but that doesn't mean you can afford to ignore them and their needs. Many gardeners and even some scientists have an "out of sight, out of mind" attitude toward roots, especially inedible ones. But roots are very important, as they provide most of the mineral nutrition, water uptake, and support for the plant. Roots are vital to the nutritional content of our food, too, for they mine the soil and bring biologically important minerals into the plant and thus into the food chain.

The Many Shapes of Roots

Just like leaves and flowers, roots come in different shapes and sizes. Many plants send one fleshy primary root deep into the soil with only a few small side roots. Beets, carrots, rutabagas, and turnips have these big, succulent taproots, which we enjoy eating. A taproot enables a plant to probe far into the ground for minerals and water. Since the fat root acts as a storage organ for moisture, plants with taproots can withstand drought better than plants with shallower fibrous roots. Taproots also store food to fuel the plant's growth. When you bite into a crunchy carrot stick, the delicious, sweet flavor comes from the sugars the plant has stored in the taproot. The long taproot also anchors the plant in the soil so that it isn't easily uprooted. If you've ever had the tops break off carrots when you tried to pull them up, you know how well taproots function as anchors. Because their taproots extend so far down, crops such as carrots and daikon radishes should be planted in the part of the garden where the loose, crumbly topsoil is deepest.

Other plants, such as beans, cabbages, and peas, have shallower, more branched root systems. Since the surface of the soil dries out first, these plants need more frequent watering than do those with deep taproots. Corn and potatoes differ in having underground stems from which many small roots grow. Like cabbages and peas, corn and potatoes need plenty of water because their roots are shallow. These plants sometimes have problems remaining upright because their underground structure may not be extensive enough to stabilize their aboveground growth. Corn plants have special prop roots that are supposed to help the plant stand up straight, but they don't always do the job. One hot summer day Diane watered her corn very heavily in the morning, and that afternoon a gusty thunderstorm raged through her garden. When the storm was over, Diane and her husband were alarmed to see all their corn plants lying flat on the ground. They rushed out and carefully straightened up each stalk, giving it a stronger anchor by heeling the soil up against it. It was tedious work, but it paid off when the corn recovered to produce an abundant crop.

Proximity to other plants is an important factor in how a plant's root system develops. Competition with nearby plants can force a plant to send its roots downward instead of sideways or may inhibit root growth altogether. Since the topsoil is richer in minerals than the deeper subsoil, crowded, deep-probing plants will be smaller and will yield fewer fruits than if they were not so close together. If you've ever planted your garden near the edge of the lawn, you've probably seen firsthand a good example of root competition. Crop plants growing near the lawn will be weaker than those situated in the center of the plot because the very vigorous grass roots ramble underground and absorb nutrients and water, stealing them right out from under your crop plants.

Branching roots can cover an amazingly large area. This is to the plant's advantage, for the greater the root surface area, the more minerals and water the roots will absorb to fuel growth. One patient scientist grew a rye plant in a box of soil 12 inches square and 22 inches deep and measured the roots when the plant was four months old. He found that the total length of the roots, not counting the tiny root hairs, was 387 miles. When he added in the lengths of the root hairs, he estimated that the grand total was 7,000 miles! This provided the modest little rye plant with a root surface area of 7,000 square feet.

While the shape and extent of the roots are vitally important to the growth and ultimate yield of vegetable plants, you never see advertisements for new varieties with the heading "New, Larger Root System Makes This Variety Need Less Fertilizer and Yield More." In the case of some corn hybrids, however, this is just what the copy should say. Corn hybrids often have more fibrous lateral roots in comparison with their inbred parents and so are more efficient at absorbing phosphorus and nitrogen. This efficiency results in much greater yields. Tomato and bean varieties with larger, more fibrous roots also can absorb more phosphorus and yield more than plants with smaller roots when this element is in short supply. Unfortunately, most plant breeders do not look at the root system, so root improvement often isn't a breeding goal unless they are dealing with a root crop.

When a plant grows uncrowded in loose, organically rich soil, its roots can spread out naturally to develop plenty of surface area for the absorption of water and minerals. But if the roots have to force their way through heavy clay or compacted hardpan, or if they have to compete with invasive roots of weeds or grass, they cannot extend to their natural size and will not be able to nourish the plant adequately. Roots also will grow toward the source of water. Thus if plants are sprinkled lightly but often, their roots will be concentrated near the surface and will not be able to bring enough water to the stem and leaves when the top layer of soil dries out. Less frequent but thorough watering will allow the water to soak down deep into the ground, encouraging deeper roots that will be able to extract water from the lower levels of the soil even when the top few inches are dry.

How Roots Do Their Job

If you've ever tested your seeds to find their germination rate, you've seen how delicate a seedling's first little root looks. But appearances are deceiving, for this tiny, pale appendage is incredibly strong and resilient. It breaks out of the seed coat and thrusts its way down into even the heaviest clay or the rockiest soil, pushing aside soil particles and even small pebbles and finding its way around more resistant obstructions. How can such a tiny bit of tissue accomplish this arduous task? First, the tender tip of the root is protected by a tough group of cells called the root cap, which shields the growing cells from damage by stones or hard dirt particles. The root cap cells often produce a slimy lubricating substance that helps the growing root ease its way through the soil. These cells also play a role in orienting the root's growth. They contain tiny starch grains that respond to gravity and settle to the lowermost side of the cells. This build-up of grains tells the root to grow with gravity.

Behind the cap is the actively growing region of the root. After being formed rapidly by cell division, the new root cells just a few millimeters behind the dividing tip begin to elongate. These elongating cells help propel the tip through the soil.

Inside the Root: The root cap is the thimble-shaped mass of cells that directs growth and protects the actively dividing cells in the root tip. The epidermal cells, with the aid of the root hairs, function to extract from the soil minerals and water that will be transported to larger roots and to the shoot by the xylem. The phloem cells are located outside of the xylem.

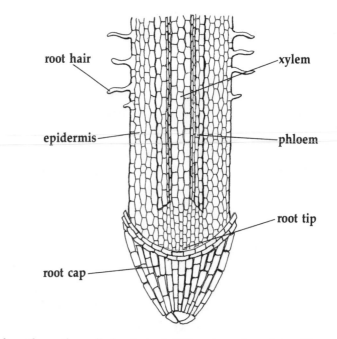

After they lengthen, the cells begin to fulfill various functions. The outer, or epidermal, cells absorb minerals and water from the soil. Many of them form tiny extensions called root hairs, which probe between soil particles to extract water and minerals. Because these root hairs are so delicate and their job so important, you must make every effort not to disturb the soil around the roots when transplanting. Each individual root hair functions for only a few days to a few weeks. Its job is then taken over by newly formed root hairs closer to the growing tip.

How long a root can actively absorb nutrients can be of critical importance if vital nutrients such as nitrogen become limited. An efficient plant will continue to absorb nutrients throughout the growing season. For example, one study showed that one variety of field corn stopped absorbing nitrogen after the ears began producing silks, while another, higher-yielding variety continued to soak up this vital nutrient as the kernels filled out the ear. When the scientists looked at the root systems, they found that the more efficient hybrid had a greater root mass and continued developing roots throughout the growing season.

Besides careless transplanting, any setback that slows root growth, such as allowing the soil to dry out or not replenishing soil nutrients, will decrease the number of root hairs and thus the capacity of the roots to absorb water and minerals. This can hinder your plant's growth considerably.

Locked within the central part of the root are the vital plant transport systems, the xylem and the phloem. Like the circulatory systems of animals, the xylem and phloem carry nutrients and fluids throughout the plant. The xylem exists in many plants as an X-shaped cluster of tubes in the center of the root. It carries minerals and water from the root to the rest of the plant. The phloem consists of bundles of tubes nestled between the arms of the X and carries food manufactured in the leaves to the root cells for maintenance and storage.

Between these transport tubules and the outermost layer of root cells are various other kinds of cells. Some of them divide to enlarge the root or to form other roots. Others store food and are able to concentrate the dilute minerals found in the soil and pass nutrients on to the xylem.

When it comes to gathering nutrients, most plants can count on help from some friends in the soil. Bacteria and fungi growing in tandem with the roots assist by extracting minerals from the soil. In the case of bean and pea roots, the bacteria actually convert nitrogen gas into a form that the plant can use. Although scientists already know a great deal about the beneficial bacteria associated with legumes such as beans and peas, they are just beginning to learn about many other fascinating relationships between plant roots and bacteria and fungi. For instance, bacteria associated with the roots of corn and tomatoes may use vitamins and other nutrients in the roots to manufacture plant hormones that stimulate growth.

In some plants fungi can replace the root hairs entirely. The plant provides the fungus with food, and the fungus sends its filaments into the soil to extract minerals and water for the plant. These relationships are called mycorrhizal associations and occur in plants such as peppers and onions. Researchers have found yield increases when they add these fungi to the soil at planting time.

One way that mycorrhizae help plants is by providing them with phosphorus. In one study, peppers inoculated with mycorrhizae needed only one-quarter to one-half as much phosphorus from the soil as uninoculated plants. Mycorrhizae also help the soil structure by holding the smallest bits together with their tangled cellular strands.

As research uncovers more and more information about such interactions between soil microorganisms and plants, the importance of building and maintaining a healthy soil is becoming apparent. Mycorrhizae are probably an important factor in the success of organic gardens, where beneficial soil organisms thrive. Because the fungi act in concert with the plants, the latter take fewer nutrients from the soil in an organic garden than they do in a chemically managed one.

Stems

Gardeners often regard stems merely as a place to hang the leaves. But stems are the indispensable main arteries of the plant, as they carry vital substances to and from the roots, leaves, and flowers. Stems play a big role in orienting leaves toward the sun, making sure that the plant is an efficient solar collector. When a plant is shaded, the stem responds by developing long internodes (the stem lengths between the leaves), and it continues to grow in this manner until the plant reaches sunlight. With some crops, such as asparagus and kohlrabi, the stem is the edible part of the plant. And who could do without the most popular of all underground stems, the potato? To help you appreciate the importance of stems, we'll take a closer look at their structure and how they help plants to grow and develop.

The Stem Tip and How It Grows

All plants have a region of actively growing cells at the tip of the stem. This apical tip is the main part of the aboveground plant, where cell divisions take place and new stem and leaves are formed. This tip is usually protected within a small bud of developing leaves. If you expose the stem tip and examine it closely, you will see a tiny, rounded dome with minute bumps around its edge. These bumps are the very beginnings of leaves that form at regular intervals below the dome. When the apical tip grows and leaves are produced, new secondary growth sites are spawned above each leaf. These potential growth sites are called axillary buds. Just below the leaf-forming area of the dome is the region where cells divide to form more of the stem and then elongate to lengthen it.

Before true leaves and axillary buds form, the young plant depends entirely on this tiny, delicate tip for its growth. For this reason, you must be careful not to damage the growing tip of a young plant. Diane has had the unfortunate experience of observing firsthand what happens when the stem tip is disturbed. One spring her inquisitive two-year-old son got into her tomato seedlings and carefully pinched off the cotyledons from some plants and the first true leaves and stem tips from the rest. She kept the plants to see what would happen. Those stripped of their cotyledons recovered after a while and grew normally, but those with no true leaves and no stem tips withered away.

Other menaces besides two-year-olds can threaten vulnerable growing tips. In the course of transplanting, it's very easy to damage your seedlings through careless handling. Never pick them up by their stems. Instead, gently hold one

Monocot and Dicot Shoots: If you look closely at a growing plant, you can identify a few of its parts. The node is the place where leaves and buds arise and is distinctly swollen in monocots (right). The internode is the area between two adjacent nodes, and on the dicot shown on left, you can spot axillary buds tucked in the leaf axils. The apical tip can be found in the terminal bud at the top of the shoot and brings about the elongation of the shoot.

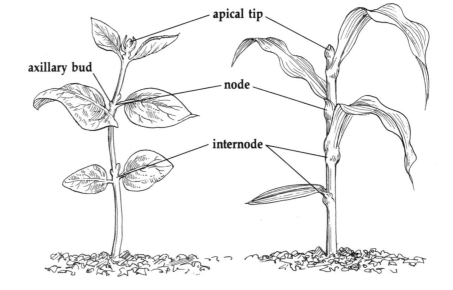

apical tip

axillary bud

node

internode

cotyledon between your thumb and first finger and support the plant with your hand or a spoon nestled under the roots. Also try to keep as much soil around the roots as possible.

Even if you are careful in your handling, frost, drought, or insects can damage the growing tip. You can sidestep these spoilers by not planting out too early, sheltering your young plants from any late frosts, watering them well, and keeping close tabs on the insect population in your garden. Tend your young transplants carefully at this vulnerable stage so their growing stems remain healthy and vigorous.

Why Stem Length Is Crucial

The length of stem between the leaves is called an internode. How a plant looks is determined by the length of its internodes. A plant with long internodes will be tall and thin like corn or long like winter squash vines. If the internodes are very short, the plant will be short like beets or spinach. Each type of plant has an optimal length for its internodes, but conditions in your garden, such as too little light, too high temperatures, or improper nutrition, can interfere with normal growth and cause the internodes to be much longer than usual. A plant in this condition is spindly and likely to fall over in a high wind.

The length of a plant's internodes also can affect its fruits. For example, if you grow your tomato plants under low-light conditions and they grow tall too quickly, the roots cannot keep pace with the tops and will not develop enough surface area to provide the large amounts of nutrients and water that the plant will need later when it produces fruits. When the root system is inadequate, the plant responds by producing fewer flowers than it would if the stem were not so long. The result is fewer tomatoes. Because sun-loving plants grown in low light yield fewer fruits, it is important when you start such plants indoors to give them as much light as possible.

If you watch some of your plants' internodes carefully, you'll know when harvest time is about to begin. A cauliflower plant ready to flower produces less growth hormone, causing the plant to form short internodes. The stem between the newly forming leaves shortens, resulting in a tight rosette of leaves. Cabbage does the same thing but won't flower until the following spring. Thus when the internodes start to get shorter, look for a tiny cauliflower or cabbage head within the rosette of leaves.

Watching your plants' internodes can give you further clues about the onset of the harvest. In the case of beets or spinach, a hormone causes the plant to form long internodes when it is about to bolt, or flower. Since these crops are often tough and not as tasty when their internodes are long, an observant gardener will finish harvesting the remaining portion of the crop at the first sign that the internodes are getting longer. The same hormone that causes the internodes of plants such as spinach or beets to lengthen before flowering affects other plants

A FEW WORDS ON AXILLARY BUDS

If you look closely at a plant, you can see the axillary buds as tiny bumps just above the spot where the leaves join the stem (the leaf axil). Most axillary buds remain tiny and untested, their potential for growth untapped. This is because the apical tip of the plant produces a hormone that inhibits their growth. But once you remove the apical tip, you remove the inhibiting factor, and the axillary buds sprout forth.

Diane saw this happen in her cold frame early one season when a cutworm snuck inside and ate the tops of some of her tomato seedlings. Luckily, the hungry invader left the first set of true leaves untouched, and new stems eventually grew from the angles between the leaves and the stem. What the worm did, of course, was destroy the apical tips. But because the leaves with their axillary buds were left on the plant, the removal of the inhibiting hormone freed them to grow, resulting in tomato plants with two main stems. When you pinch back your flower plants or house plants to make them bushier, you are doing the same thing the cutworm did – removing the apical tips so that the axillary buds can grow.

The effect of the apical tip is different in different plants. The axillary buds of a naturally bushy plant grow because the stem tip does not have a strong influence on the axillary buds. In indeterminate tomato plants, the axillary buds begin to grow when the main stem is about a foot long. By then, not enough hormone has reached the axillary buds to have an effect. In Brussels sprouts, the inhibiting effect of the apical tip disappears as the plant matures, allowing the axillary buds to develop into tasty sprouts.

during normal growth. Bush beans, dwarf peas, and bush squash produce less of this key hormone, so their internodes are short. If you were to spray these bush varieties with a hormone solution, they would grow long and viny, just like their full-size relatives.

A Look Inside the Mature Stem

If you cut across the stem of a dicot and look at the exposed surface, you can see that the outer ring of tissue appears quite different from the center. The central pith is a food storage area, while the outer vascular area transports nutrients and water throughout the plant. Enveloping this ring of tissue is the cortex, which contains photosynthetic, storage, and support cells. The outermost covering of the stem is the epidermis, which may be waxy as in cabbage or hairy as in tomatoes. The main functions of the epidermis are to slow water loss, prevent infections, and reduce mechanical injury to the important transport system in the stem.

The pith is the tender, succulent portion of the stem of many plants. Its cells have thin, delicate walls and are packed with stored food. The vascular area is

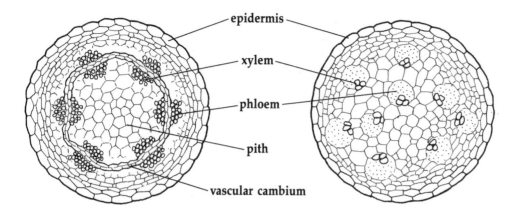

epidermis

xylem

phloem

pith

vascular cambium

Stem Cross Section: The vascular bundles of a dicot stem (left) are arranged in a circle around the pith. Monocots (right) have a random distribution of vascular tissue and lack a vascular cambium, which lies between the xylem and phloem in each bundle of a dicot.

tougher than the pith **due** to the thick-walled transport cells **and** fibrous support cells it contains. The next time you enjoy a succulent piece of broccoli, remember that it is the enlarged pith that makes every bite so delectable. Cookbooks that tell you to peel away the outer layers before preparing this vegetable are instructing you to peel away the tough vascular area, leaving the tender pith for you to enjoy.

The water- and mineral-transporting xylem and nutrient-carrying phloem form the vascular area encircling the pith of the stem rather than forming an X as in the roots. Both of these tissues have special cells that help support the upright stem. Between the xylem and the phloem is the vascular cambium, which produces new xylem and phloem cells. The older a stem, the more of these transport and support cells it has, and the tougher it is. This explains why the succulent stems of your tomato seedlings become tough and woody by season's end.

Some of the cells of the cortex clustered around the outside of the vascular tissue have chlorophyll in them and perform photosynthesis. This accounts for the green color of the stem. Other outer cells form fibrous strands of tissue that help support the plant.

What can you expect to find inside the stem of monocots such as corn and onions? Monocot stems contain the same kinds of tissues as dicots, but the tissues are arranged differently. Instead of seeing the xylem and phloem concentrated in an area surrounding the pith, you will find them scattered throughout the pith in structures called vascular bundles. Although they're organized differently, the xylem and phloem in both types of plants perform the same important role of transporting water and nutrients.

The Stem's Transport System

While most plant tissues play their vital roles during life, xylem cells are able to function as transport channels only after they have died. While they are alive, the cells lengthen and develop thick, sturdy walls with tiny holes through which water and minerals penetrate. When they die, the ends of many xylem cells disappear, leaving behind tiny hollow tubes. Think of these tubes as microscopic water pipes connected end to end.

For a long time scientists didn't understand how water defied gravity and moved all the way from the roots to the leaves of plants. After all, some sequoia redwood trees are over 350 feet tall! Now we know that the evaporation of water from the leaves provides the pulling power that brings the water up through the stem. The leaves of one plant, when added all together, have an enormous surface area from which water is always evaporating. The suction force produced by this constant evaporation is estimated to be minus thirty times the pressure of the atmosphere (minus because it is a pulling power, like a vacuum, as opposed to the push exerted by the atmosphere) and can result in water being pulled up through the stems of some plants as fast as 30 inches per minute.

The structural support that the xylem gives the plant also is vital, for it keeps the plant upright so that its leaves can be exposed to sunlight. Plants grown indoors, where the wind never blows, produce fewer xylem cells and are less sturdy than plants grown outdoors. In fact, the stems of wind-blown plants are thicker than those of protected plants. Plants jostled by the wind also have shorter internodes, which is an asset since stocky plants are sturdier than spindly ones. You can take advantage of these features by growing seedlings in a cold frame, where the young plants can be exposed to the wind on sunny days when the frame is open. This will help them develop into strong, sturdy plants that are not likely to topple over in a storm. Seedlings grown indoors will have a harder time adjusting to the weather conditions in the garden and will be more likely to suffer damage from winds or heavy rain soon after they have been transplanted.

The phloem, which differs from the xylem in several important ways, carries the nutrients manufactured in the leaves during photosynthesis throughout the rest of the plant. The photosynthetic process produces carbohydrates (sugars), and thus the sap that flows through the phloem is a 10 to 25 percent sugar solution. Some plant pests have found ways to tap into the phloem, much as people tap the phloem of sugar maple trees in the spring. The champion phloem feeder is the aphid. Aphids have long, hollow, needlelike mouths that they use to penetrate the stem of a plant and pierce the phloem. The sap is under pressure, so the aphid doesn't even need to suck. It just sits there as the sap flows into its body.

Scientists have used aphids in some studies of phloem tissue. As soon as the aphid's mouth is embedded, they cut the rest of the insect off, leaving only the tiny hollow stylet (piercing mouth part) through which the phloem flows. Then they collect and analyze sap samples and use radioactive tracers to find out where and how fast materials circulate in the phloem. It appears that nutrients can move up or down within the phloem, but usually the lower leaves produce food that is transported to the roots, and the upper leaves make food for the stem tip and young leaves. Fluid moves through the phloem much more slowly than through the xylem, generally at a rate of less than 1 inch per minute.

Phloem transport cells are long and narrow and have end walls pitted with tiny holes. The phloem cells are butted up against each other to form transporting tubes, but unlike the disappearing ends of xylem cells, the end walls in the phloem cells remain intact, and all materials must pass through minute holes in the walls. If you cut through a stem, special microscopic fibers block these holes, preventing the plant from "bleeding" to death. This reaction can save a plant's life, but it makes it difficult for scientists to study phloem in action, since these transport channels must be cut to see them well.

Partly for this reason, scientists still don't know exactly how transport in the phloem occurs. They do know that the sugars manufactured in the leaves first move into spaces between the cells, then into specialized transfer cells next to the phloem. From there the sugars move into the phloem cells themselves. The transfer process requires energy and is quite selective. For example, in sugar beets sucrose is given preferential transfer over other sugars, and the minerals nitrogen, phosphorus, and potassium are transported, but calcium, iron, and boron are not.

Certain environmental factors can adversely affect the phloem. One reason that beans grow well only during warm weather is that cold inhibits movement of materials through the phloem. If the temperature drops too low, fewer nutrients will be moving, and your bean plants will grow slowly at best. The phloem of crops such as sugar beets is not affected by the cold, and the plants will grow even in cool weather. These plants can, however, be damaged or even killed when bacteria, fungi, or viruses block the phloem, resulting in a girdled stem. One strange potato disease is caused by a fungus that restricts flow through the phloem. Sugars accumulate in the aboveground portion of the stem, and the plant responds by producing potatoes there instead of underground.

Aphids, squash bugs, and other sap-feeding insects can transfer diseases from one plant to another through their feeding activities. If a squash bug feeds on an infected plant and moves to an uninfected one, it will transmit the disease-causing organisms to the healthy plant when it inserts its stylet. Once this happens, the disease can spread throughout the plant by way of the phloem.

Anything you do to restrict the flow of materials in the phloem, such as tying tomatoes or cucumbers too tightly to stakes, will slow the plant's growth or stop it altogether. To avoid this problem, use soft materials such as strips of cloth or pieces of old nylon stocking to tie up your plants instead of string or wire.

Leaves

Leaves are vital to plants and equally important to the gardener. They contain structures called chloroplasts, which manufacture food for the plant. When we pluck tender greens from the garden, these leaves also provide nourishment for us. In addition to being a source of sustenance for both plants and humans, leaves are a good indicator of the plant's health. If they are wilted, we assume that the plant needs water. If the plant lacks nutrients, the symptoms appear first in the leaves. But there's a lot more going on inside these structures than meets the eye.

Leaf Development

As we have seen, leaves first form as tiny bumps on the growing tip of the stem. They grow by cell divisions that first make them longer and then make them wider. At this stage they are still very small and may be hidden by the larger leaves surrounding the stem tip.

Soon the leaves undergo a growth spurt, and the cells get larger as each develops into a specialized structure to perform its specific function. This early stage of leaf growth and development can be affected by environmental conditions. For example, one year when Diane's grandmother's garden was hit by a light frost in May, all her green beans had just two or three leaves. After the frost the next two leaves to appear were very long and narrow like shoestrings. Her grandmother feared that a terrible virus must be attacking the beans, but when the next leaves were normal, she realized that the frost had stopped the development of the leaf margins. Another year Diane's tomato plants were similarly affected, and the leaves that developed immediately after the frost were twisted and misshapen. The rest of the leaves grew normally, however. So don't despair if you have a few misshapen leaves after a cold snap. If the plants aren't obviously damaged, probably only a few leaves will be affected and the plants soon will resume normal growth.

Leaf development also can be affected by nutritional stress. A potassium deficiency makes young tomato leaves wrinkle and carrot leaves curl. If the leaves on your young plants look strangely misshapen when there has been no cold weather, look for a mineral deficiency in your soil or call your county extension agent (see Glossary) and enlist his or her aid.

Examining the Leaf Surface

The upper and lower surfaces of a leaf have a waxy coating called the cuticle, which is produced by the outer layer of leaf cells. (This outer cell layer is called the epidermis, just like our skin.) The cuticle helps slow the loss of water from the leaf. Some plants, such as cabbages, have a very prominent cuticle. That is why water will form in droplets on a cabbage rather than wet the leaves. If you rub a cabbage leaf, sometimes you can remove the waxy layer. Then water will wet the leaf instead of beading up. Air pollution can damage this important waxy layer. For example, scientists have found that table beets grown in Los Angeles have widely separated bumps of wax instead of waxy sheets covering the leaf surface. Such leaves can be damaged through the increased loss of moisture from the unprotected parts.

Many plants, such as tomatoes and turnips, have tiny hairs on their leaves. These hairs can perform very different functions on different plants. The hairs on some leaves are dense enough to create an air space around the leaf, slowing water loss, especially on windy days. The hairs of sunflowers and possibly other plants reflect ultraviolet light, helping prevent too many of the damaging rays from entering the leaves. Leaf hairs also can frustrate insect pests. Some varieties of wheat are resistant to the cereal leaf beetle because their leaf hairs deter the female beetles from laying their eggs. If the females do persist, the eggs dry out and die. And even if some eggs hatch, the dense hairs make it difficult for the larvae to get at the leaves to feed.

Some leaf hairs are connected to glands that manufacture chemicals. These chemicals affect insects in various ways. Some tobacco leaf hairs secrete poisons that paralyze the legs of aphids and kill them. The leaves and stems of wild potatoes have a thick covering of hairs. If one hair is touched by an aphid, the hair releases a clear liquid. On contact with the oxygen in the air, this liquid is transformed into an insoluble black substance that coats the aphid's legs. As the aphid explores the plant, it triggers more and more hairs until it is immobilized by the black material, eventually starving to death.

How Leaves Monitor Water Loss

The epidermal cells that cover the leaf are flat and translucent so that light can penetrate the leaf. These cells have tough walls that resist injury. Scattered among the epidermal cells are tiny openings called stomata. The stomata are vital to the leaf, for they regulate the amount of water loss and allow carbon dioxide to enter the leaf. The carbon dioxide is then transformed into sugars during photosynthesis. There are many more stomata on the shaded, lower leaf surface than on the sunnier upper side. This helps minimize unnecessary water loss.

If you look at the lower surface of a leaf with a magnifying glass, the stomata look like tiny mouthlike openings. The "lips" are two sausage-shaped guard cells attached to each other at both ends. The stomata open and close in response to the amount of water present in the leaf. The inner side of each guard cell is thicker than the outer side. When the cell is full of water, the pressure pushes against the more flexible outer wall and makes the guard cell bow outward, causing the stomate (singular of stomata) to open. When there is not enough water in the guard cell, it becomes deflated. This closes the stomate, keeping water inside the leaf but also keeping the important carbon dioxide out.

Since plants need carbon dioxide for photosynthesis and photosynthesis is absolutely vital to growth, it's easy to see that a plant with closed stomata won't grow very well. If a plant isn't getting enough water and starts to wilt, the stomata will close, slowing water loss. But photosynthesis also will slow, producing less food for the plant and ultimately less for you. Potatoes provide a dramatic example

Stomate Action: When water is abundant, pressure on the elastic outer wall of the guard cells forces the stomate open (left). When the guard cells dry out, they deflate and cause the pore to close (right), drastically reducing water loss.

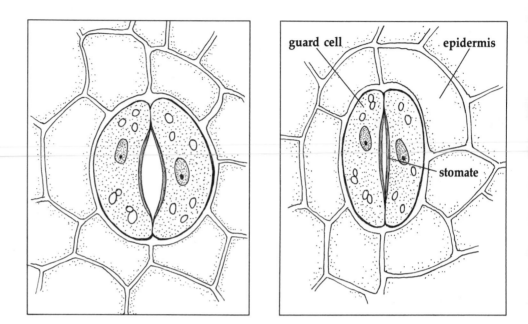

of what water stress can do to a plant. Potatoes grown with an erratic water supply will be irregular in shape, with constrictions along their length marking the parts of the tuber that were forming during periods of water stress.

What Goes On Inside the Leaf

Underneath the upper leaf epidermis in dicot plants is a layer of tall, rectangular cells. These palisade cells are packed with chlorophyll-laden chloroplasts and are very active in photosynthesis. Although scientists have studied the palisade cells of only a few plants, they have found that the epidermal cells have the ability to concentrate vital sunlight in the palisade layer, much as a lens does in a camera. The light in this layer of cells is actually greater than that on the outside of the leaf surface, increasing the opportunity for light-driven photosynthesis.

The palisade layer is very sensitive to environmental conditions. Leaves of many plants will produce two layers of palisade cells when grown in bright light. In shade, the same leaves will produce only one layer of cells. That is why leaves grown in the shade generally are thinner than those grown in the sun. Potato leaves vary a bit from this general rule. Leaves on plants grown in the sun have only one palisade layer, but the cells are longer and have more chloroplasts than the palisade cells in shade-grown leaves.

Even after the leaf is fully formed, it can still respond to the level of sunlight it receives. If there is not much light, the chloroplasts will line up so that their broad surfaces are facing the sun. If the sun is very bright, they will move so that their narrow surfaces face the sun and less light will hit them. They can even flatten against the side walls of the cell to decrease their exposure to even brighter sunlight.

Because the leaves are so responsive to light conditions, it is important to grow your seedlings in the strongest possible light. Leaves that develop only one palisade layer under weak light can never produce another after they have formed. These leaves will die and fall off when you move the plant to a sunnier location. You can minimize damage to plants grown in low-light conditions by gradually exposing them to the sun.

Even though it is chlorophyll's job to absorb sunlight, too much sun will destroy it. That explains why leaves of plants that you have moved outside abruptly turn white. In effect, these leaves are sunburned. Thus you must take care to expose your plants gradually to the sun. In so doing, pigments called carotenoids will form in the leaves. These pigments protect the chlorophyll from the bright sun and keep it from breaking down all at once. This gives the chlorophyll level time to decrease gradually. (This decrease is necessary because a plant grown in full sun needs less chlorophyll to do the job than one grown in the shade.)

Cells aren't the only structures that play a part in the activity inside the leaf. Air spaces are just as important as cells. Within the lower part of the leaf are widely scattered, irregularly shaped cells (which also contain chloroplasts). The spaces between these cells are filled with air, which allows for the crucial exchange of carbon dioxide and oxygen that occurs during photosynthesis. The area above a stomate is clear of cells, providing a space in which the exchange of gases can take place.

Besides the photosynthetic cells, the leaves of many plants contain other specialized cells. Spinach leaves have cells that contain crystals of calcium oxalate. This is the substance that makes your teeth feel coated when you eat a lot of spinach. Bolted lettuce leaves have specialized cells containing bitter chemicals that give the lettuce a bad flavor, while corn leaves have bubble-shaped cells that make the leaves fold when they are under water stress. If you ever see your corn

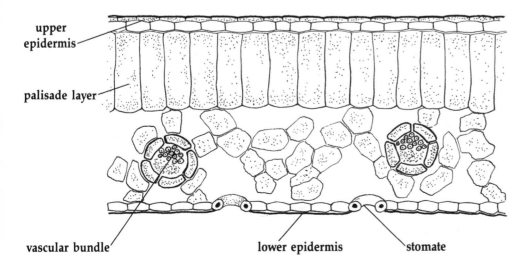

upper epidermis

palisade layer

vascular bundle

lower epidermis

stomate

Leaf Cross Section: The vascular bundles inside the leaf are embedded in a layer of loosely arranged spongy cells. The rectangular palisade cells are sandwiched between the upper and lower epidermis. The stomata are located in the lower epidermis here, but they can appear on both epidermal surfaces.

WHAT IS PHOTOSYNTHESIS?

Without photosynthesis, life on earth wouldn't last very long. Photosynthesis provides the stored energy that, along with oxygen, most living things need for survival. Plants are the ultimate solar energy converters, using the energy from the sun to manufacture energy-rich carbohydrates, which are a form of food for the plant. Several plant pigments are capable of trapping the sun's energy and using it to fuel chemical reactions, but the usual ones are forms of chlorophyll, the green pigment responsible for the most familiar plant color.

Just how the plant captures the energy of the sun is a complex process that we do not yet completely understand. What we do know is that when light hits pigment molecules within the plant chloroplast, these molecules become excited. Chlorophyll molecules and other yellow, red, or orange pigments (called carotenoids) collect the solar energy and pass it on to particular chlorophyll molecules, providing those reactor molecules with enough energy to cause some of their electrons (extremely tiny, negatively charged particles) to escape. When that happens, the reactor molecules must replace their electrons; they do so by splitting water molecules into hydrogen and oxygen, picking up stray electrons in the process.

The splitting of water into hydrogen and oxygen requires light energy, but the next step in photosynthesis can occur in the dark. (Don't be fooled into thinking that your plants close up shop when the sun goes down!) The hydrogen from the water is combined with carbon dioxide to form sugars and other carbohydrates, while the oxygen from the water is released into the atmosphere through the stomata in the leaves. This release of oxygen is an important step, for almost all the oxygen in the air came originally from the photosynthetic activities of plants. During this stage of photosynthesis, the open stomata let in the carbon dioxide necessary to keep the entire process going.

leaves folded in half the long way, water them immediately.

If you examine a leaf closely, the pattern formed by the veins is usually visible. You must use your imagination, however, to see the xylem and phloem that lie within the veins. In monocots such as corn and onions the veins are parallel, whereas in dicots the veins branch out into a fine network much like the capillaries in our bodies. As the veins branch, they get smaller and smaller until they are barely visible. Cells that are photosynthesizing often have a vein running right beside them, and no active cell is very far from one of these branches. The plant's vascular system transfers water and other nutrients from the xylem to the cells, while the phloem picks up the food produced by photosynthesis, largely the sugar sucrose, and distributes it to other parts of the plant.

The Bridge between Stem and Leaves

Next time you're in the garden, pause for a minute and examine a plant closely to see how the leaves are attached to the stem. If the plant is a dicot, the leaves will be attached to a stalk called a petiole. Monocot leaves are attached directly to the stem. Some plants, such as celery and rhubarb, have very large petioles that we eat. The petiole carries the vascular system to the leaf (some of the "strings" you find in a celery stalk are nothing more than bundles of xylem and phloem) and helps orient the leaf toward the sun. A hormone made by the leaf moves to the darker side of the petiole and makes that side grow faster than the light-exposed side. This results in the elongation we see as the leaf grows.

Leaves also may move in response to the daily light-dark cycle. One night Diane ventured into her garden and was upset to see all the leaves of her bush beans hanging down. She thought they needed water badly, but the next morning the leaves had perked up and were back in their normal position. Since that episode she has learned that bean leaves go through especially dramatic movements, drooping down at night and rising up during the day. No one knows for sure why this happens, but one appealing idea is that leaves drawn closer to the stem at a vertical angle will lose less water than those held up in a horizontal position.

Flowers

Like many vegetable gardeners, you may find that you have developed a love-hate relationship with flowers. At the same time you are watching anxiously for the first female squash or cucumber blossom to arrive announcing the fruit to come, you are cringing at the sight of a flower stalk developing on a spinach or lettuce plant, for that signals the end of the edible harvest and the onset of seed production. Many factors affect the flowering and setting of fruit and seed from those flowers. When you understand some of the things that influence flowering, there is much you can do to take advantage of nature.

Keep in mind that flowering is a complex process that varies from crop to crop. Although there's been much research on the phenomenon of flowering, scientists often are discouraged to find that the more information they uncover, the more there is to be learned. As a gardener, you can help by keeping your own records of how the different varieties you grow respond to environmental conditions such as day length and then communicating that information through letters to the editor of your favorite gardening magazine or through exchanges with garden club members. Sometimes seed companies provide information concerning the varieties they carry, so queries to them can be helpful.

What Makes a Plant Flower?

Many factors affect flowering. Nutrition is one cultural characteristic that often plays a role. For example, tomatoes grown in soil deficient in nitrogen or phosphorus will flower much later than those with adequate mineral supplies. In contrast, potatoes will be slow to flower and form tubers if they are grown in nitrogen-rich soil. The looseness of the soil is another factor. Radish plants grown in compacted, heavy soil are likely to flower without first producing a radish.

Many garden plants must reach a certain stage of maturity before they flower. Beans, corn, and peas grow quickly in warm weather and thus reach the blooming stage earlier during an uninterrupted stretch of warm weather than they would if their growth had been held in check by a brief cold spell. And plants grown in rich soil will be bigger and stronger when they get to that critical flowering stage than ones grown in poor soil.

Environmental factors affect the flowering time of some crops more than stage of maturity does. Many gardeners, especially in northern areas where spring is often cold but day length increases rapidly as summer approaches, have had the discouraging experience of watching their tiny spinach plants bolt when they have only a few small leaves. Like wild animals that produce their young only at certain times of the year, plants such as spinach flower and produce seeds best at certain times. These sensitive plants perceive day length and respond to it by flowering when daylight lasts a particular number of hours. Although this can be very frustrating for you, the system has its advantages from the plant's point of view. Unlike temperature, day length is one environmental cue that does not vary from year to year. Whereas a plant that responds to temperature can be thrown off by a mild winter and bloom too early, a plant that responds to day length will stay on schedule.

As you can see, temperature and day length can conspire against your best efforts in the garden. To be able to work around these two environmental factors and raise a good crop, you need to understand what you're up against. The next three sections tell you how your garden crops respond to these stimuli and how you can outsmart them.

How Temperature Affects Flowering

Plants react to warm temperatures because all their metabolic processes depend on enzymes. Up to a point, the higher the temperature, the faster the enzymes work and the faster the plants grow. Conversely, at lower temperatures most enzymes slow down and so does plant growth. Through this basic effect on growth rate, temperature influences the flowering time of almost all plants. However, each enzyme has a temperature at which it works best. Enzymes of cool-weather crops such as broccoli and radishes have lower optimum temperatures than those of warm-weather crops such as beans and corn. Above the optimum temperature, enzyme activity slows down again.

Temperature also can affect flowering in other ways. For example, most tomatoes flower when they have twelve or more internodes. But if a young seedling is exposed to night temperatures of 43°F to 50°F, it will begin to flower when it has only four to ten internodes. Not only will the plant bloom earlier, but all the flower clusters will have more blossoms than they would have had without the cold temperatures. If you want early tomatoes, you should expose your young tomato plants to low nighttime temperatures (but not so low that your plants freeze). You might not get as large a crop, but you can start eating fresh garden tomatoes before your neighbors.

Cold temperatures have still other effects on flowering. When swollen and just germinating beet, lettuce, or pea seeds remain in cold soil for a couple of weeks, the plants that eventually emerge will flower sooner than they normally would. This might be an advantage with peas, especially if you have a short spring followed by a hot summer, but it is a distinct disadvantage in growing beets and lettuce. (For more details on these crops, refer to chapters 5, 8, and 10.) Onion sets also will be affected by cold temperatures. If the sets are kept in cold storage (below 35°F), they will bolt rather than form bulbs once they are planted.

The process in which cold stimulates early flowering is called vernalization. The Russian word for the process means "making like spring grain," for it was first discovered by Russian researchers studying winter rye and wheat. They found that by planting these crops in the fall, the farmer can get a head start on spring, since the crops will grow more quickly to the stage where they produce grain.

Brussels sprouts, cabbages, carrots, celery, and some varieties of beets require two growing seasons before they flower. Plants with a life cycle that spans two seasons are called biennials. Like wheat and rye, these plants are vernalized by cold temperatures and will flower during the next growing season. Sugar beets that have never been exposed to a cold winter and are kept warm will keep growing and never flower. If you garden in the extreme South, you'll have a frustrating time trying to grow your own seeds of plants such as table beets. Because it never gets cold enough in the winter for vernalization, your plants will never flower. You might want to experiment with lifting your biennials and storing them for some weeks in a cool location to see if the plants can be "fooled" into blooming when you plant them out again.

The apical tip of the plant is especially sensitive to cold temperatures. In areas where the mercury dips down low in the winter, the apical tip may be killed by the cold temperatures. This will keep the plant from blooming the following spring, even though the rest of the plant may survive the cold. If you garden in a cold-winter area, you will have to buy commercially grown seeds for these plants unless you can devise a way to prevent your plants from freezing. One way to get seeds from your biennials is to lift the plants before the ground freezes, store them in a root cellar or other cool location, and replant them in the garden come spring. Or you can "put them to bed" in the fall by covering them deeply with leaves and adding a layer of plastic to anchor the leafy mulch. When it warms up in the spring, just uncover them and watch for signs of flowering. An especially cold winter, however, might kill the apical tips of even such protected plants.

How Day Length Affects Flowering

Let's go back to the problem of small spinach plants forming flowering stalks instead of leaves. Spinach blooms when there are long days and short nights. But how does the plant keep track of day length? Spinach and many other plants perceive the length of night and day through a pigment in their leaves called phytochrome. Phytochrome changes chemically in response to light, and the changes in the phytochrome result in the production of plant hormones that are involved in initiating flowering. The whole process is very complicated and has different results in long-day and short-day plants.

Light doesn't have to be as strong as the sun to affect the phytochrome of spinach plants. Those of you who garden in the city or other areas lighted at night may have had trouble growing beets, lettuce, radishes, spinach, and turnips without their bolting. If the lights are strong enough, they can affect the light-sensitive pigment in the leaves of short-day plants and make them flower much faster than they ordinarily would.

Bolting of dill, radishes, and spinach actually requires two conditions. First, the plants must have been growing for a certain number of days. After that, exposure to just one long period of light will trigger the flowering hormone. For example, many spinach varieties require about thirteen days of growth before they will respond to a long-day, short-night period. Once the plants have been exposed to one twelve-hour day, nothing you can do will stop them from flowering.

Many gardeners in Montana wait until May 1 or later to plant their spinach. By the time it comes up, the days are already almost twelve hours long. All that those plants need to bolt is their thirteen days of growth. Hapless spinach plants like these may bolt when they have as few as three or four true leaves. The gardeners complain that "you just can't grow spinach here" and give up. But if they and other northern gardeners planted their spinach and radishes earlier, around April 1, they could harvest a reasonable crop in mid-June. Another alternative is to plant such crops in late July or early August when the days are getting shorter. Or you can wait until mid-August and plant one of the spinach varieties designed for overwintering. Southern gardeners who plant spinach in the fall don't need to worry about bolting, as the days are getting shorter and are never long enough to trigger bolting.

Certain varieties of beets, lettuce, garden peas, and turnips have a somewhat different reaction to day length. They must be exposed to a particular total number of daylight hours before flowering. This could mean many short days or fewer long days. In addition, they must have reached a certain stage of maturity to respond to daylight at all. This sort of situation has different consequences for the gardener. If you're a northerner who plants beets, lettuce, or turnips in the early spring (late March or early April), you risk having these crops bolt when they are fairly small in response to the long days of May and June. However, if you wait until June to plant these crops, you will find that they are too immature to respond to the long days and will grow bigger and yield more before bolting than would seeds planted in April. If you frequently run into trouble with these plants, keep an eye out for varieties listed in catalogs as being slow to bolt.

Since you want peas to bloom early and beat the heat, the situation is reversed with them. Plant your late-flowering varieties early so they will respond to the long days of May and June by flowering and producing before the hot weather hits.

Just as there are plants that flower under long-day, short-night conditions, there are those that bloom during short days and long nights. Some varieties of corn, soybeans, sugar cane, and sunflowers fit into this category. Varieties of many short-day crops have been developed with different day-length requirements. This can be very important for gardeners in certain regions. For example, some soybean varieties flower best when they receive about twelve hours of daylight. If they get more than that, flowering decreases in proportion to the increasing hours of light until no flowers are produced in twenty hours of light. A northern gardener would reap a poor harvest from these soybeans. Plant breeders have developed soybean varieties adapted to the North, but some of them are very specific, growing well only in an area within 50 miles of a particular latitude. The point to remember if you want to grow soybeans is that the variety you select must be bred to produce at your latitude.

Not all garden plants are as temperamental as those just discussed. In fact, some are not the least bit sensitive to day length. Some varieties of corn, cucumbers, Jerusalem artichokes, kidney beans, peas, and tomatoes are unaffected by hours of light and dark. These varieties are referred to as being day-neutral.

Day Length and Temperature Combined

Day length and temperature sometimes act together to influence flowering. Low-temperature vernalization of the spinach variety 'Nobel,' for example, will shorten the day-length requirement for flowering from fourteen to about eight hours. Planting this variety in the North in early spring, when the seeds might take a long time to germinate in cold ground, would result in young plants that bolt very quickly. Obviously, 'Nobel' should not be grown for a spring crop in the North. It is much more suitable as a fall crop in the South.

Some varieties of lettuce grown at low temperatures are unaffected by day length. When exposed to high temperatures, however, they will respond to long days by sending up seed stalks. This accounts for the shorter than usual spring lettuce-growing season that northern gardeners experience if there are hot days in May or June.

Beet varieties that bolt easily are more subject to flowering when it is cool than when it is warm. Luckily, most of the commonly carried beet varieties are bolt resistant.

Map of Day Lengths: This map gives a rough estimate of the hours of daylight on the longest and shortest day of the year for each latitude. The longest day occurs at the summer solstice (June 21 or 22), and the shortest day occurs at the winter solstice (December 21 or 22).

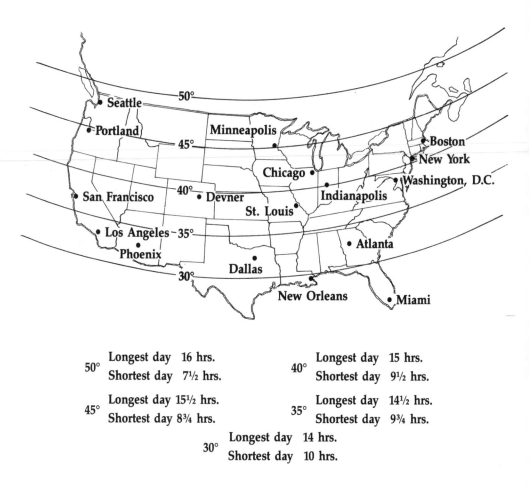

	Longest day	16 hrs.		Longest day	15 hrs.
50°	Shortest day	7½ hrs.	40°	Shortest day	9½ hrs.

	Longest day	15½ hrs.		Longest day	14½ hrs.
45°	Shortest day	8¾ hrs.	35°	Shortest day	9¾ hrs.

	Longest day	14 hrs.
30°	Shortest day	10 hrs.

Even though temperature and day length can have profound effects on garden crops, you'll find very little specific information in gardening guides or seed catalogs about which varieties fit into which categories. This is where home gardeners can help out. By keeping good records of how your crops respond to different conditions each year, you can share valuable information with other gardeners. For example, if you plant several varieties of lettuce and one consistently bolts before the others, it is probably reacting to the temperature and day-length conditions of your area. Or if you have several hot May days one year and some lettuce varieties bolt early and others do not, you may have discovered which varieties are especially sensitive to high temperatures in the spring.

To help you get a rough idea of your area's day lengths at different times of the year, we have provided a map that shows day lengths at the summer solstice (June 21 or 22) for different latitudes. At the spring (March 21 or 22) and fall (September 21 or 22) equinoxes, day and night are just about twelve hours long at all latitudes. For more exact day-length information, consult your local newspaper or weather bureau.

Flowers and Their Variety

The visually pleasing variety of flower colors, shapes, and sizes is certainly easy to spot in the garden. But flowers vary in other ways that aren't as visible to the eye but are more important to the vegetable gardener. Some flowers are perfect—that is, they have both male and female parts. Peas and tomatoes, for example, have perfect flowers. Some garden crops have flowers with only male or female parts; these are known as imperfect flowers. In some cases, as with asparagus and spinach, the male and female flowers are on separate plants. One year when Diane, early in her gardening career, was slow in pulling up her bolted spinach, she noticed that some plants had lots of seeds and others had none. The reason for this is that only the female plants produce seeds. Other crops with imperfect flowers, such as corn and squash, have male and female flowers on the same plants.

If you examine a perfect flower such as a buttercup, you can easily distinguish the different parts. Underneath the familiar petals is a circle of green petal-like sepals. The sepals protect the flower bud before it opens. In the center of the flower is a cluster of pistils or one large pistil; this is the female part of the flower. The pistil has a long stalk called the style topped by a rounded end called the stigma. The stigma has a sticky surface to which pollen adheres when the flower is pollinated. Around the pistil or pistils is a circle of stamens. The stamens are the male parts of the flower. Each stamen is made up of a stalk called the filament and an oval structure sitting atop the filament called the anther. The anther contains the pollen.

The flowers on the crops in your garden are variations of this simple type. In tomato flowers, the anthers are all fused together so that they form a tube around the pistil. Beans and peas have perfect flowers, but the petals on each flower are not all the same. All the flowers on a cucumber or squash plant look much alike at first glance, but you can tell the male and female flowers apart by examining

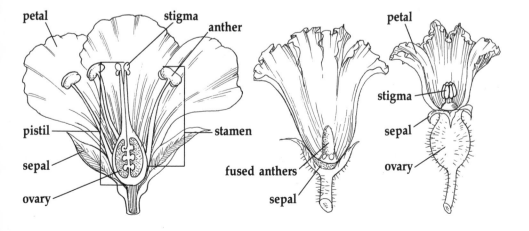

Perfect and Imperfect Flowers: A perfect flower (left) has the anthers and stigmas in the same flower. Plants with imperfect flowers, such as squash, have separate male (center) and female (right) flowers on the same plant.

them closely. The female flower has a nubbin that resembles a miniature cucumber or squash at its base, while the male flower has only a slim stem. Also, the female flower has a stigma in the center, while the male flower has a fat tube with a convoluted top; this consists of the fused filaments and anthers.

Pollination and Fertilization

While flowers come in different colors and shapes, the processes of pollination and fertilization are basically the same in all garden plants. Pollen grains are transported from the anthers by wind or animals such as bees or hummingbirds onto the sticky surface of the stigma, pollinating the flower. Once they've alighted, the grains begin to grow, forming long, microscopic tubes that push their way through the style. At the base of the style is the ovary, where the egg cells lie. A growth hormone (auxin) from the pollen grains causes the ovary to begin to enlarge once it is pollinated, even before fertilization occurs. For this reason, a heavily pollinated squash fruit will grow faster than a lightly pollinated one (one that hasn't been visited by bees).

When a pollen tube approaches an egg, its tip bursts, releasing two sperm cells. One of these fuses with the egg cell to produce the beginnings of the embryo. The other fuses with a cell next to the egg; the resulting cell develops into the endosperm, which nourishes the seedling during germination. The twin action of these sperm cells fusing with female cells to form the embryo and the endosperm means that fertilization has taken place.

Many things can go wrong with pollination and fertilization that will affect your crops. If the temperature is low (below 55°F), for example, tomato pollen tubes will grow so slowly that the flowers sometimes will drop off before fertilization has occurred. If the temperature is too high, flowers also may drop off. Water stress can affect pollen so that it won't germinate and grow when it lands on the stigma, so you must be sure that your plants are getting enough water while flowering and setting fruit.

Fruit Growth and Ripening

The fruits we so look forward to eating from our vegetable plants – cucumbers, eggplants, peppers, squash, and tomatoes – are the thickened ovary walls that develop around the seeds. At first the fruit develops by cell division, with little discernible growth, so you don't see the fruit enlarge very much. But the rest of the growth process is accomplished by cell expansion, which can happen very rapidly – so rapidly, in fact, that during this period your zucchini can swell to the size of a giant club almost overnight. After the cells expand to their final size, they assume their ultimate roles as the fruit ripens. In a tomato that is ripening, for example, several changes take place. The fruit changes from green to red, it softens, the seeds develop, and, most importantly, the flavor changes dramatically.

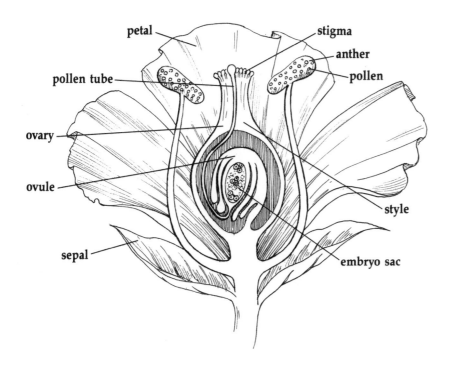

petal — stigma — anther — pollen — pollen tube — ovary — ovule — sepal — style — embryo sac

Pollination and Fertilization of a Flower: Pollen from the anther is transferred to the stigma, where it will germinate and form a pollen tube. The pollen tube grows down the style to the embryo sac, where it releases two sperm cells. One sperm will unite with the egg to form the zygote, which develops into the embryo. The other fuses with two polar nuclei to form the endosperm.

While plants in your garden are developing fruits, you should keep them well watered and well nourished. The fruit is almost completely dependent on the rest of the plant for its food and water. A fruit that lacks a specific nutrient may take it from the rest of the plant, weakening it. Don't crimp or bend the area where the fruit is attached to the stem, as this could damage the phloem and xylem, which transport food, minerals, and water to the fruit. This point of attachment is highly specialized for rapid and efficient transport of materials to the developing fruit.

Toward the end of their ripening phase, most fruits undergo a dramatic rise in respiration rate. Because cold slows respiration, putting fruits in the refrigerator will slow their ripening. Some fruits, such as peppers, will ripen more slowly in a plastic bag than when exposed to air. This is because the plastic keeps out oxygen and holds in carbon dioxide, thus slowing respiration. Each fruit has its optimal storage conditions. For example, some long-lasting cucumber varieties can be stored for only fifteen days at 41°F but will last for sixty-five days at 55°F. At room temperature, they will last about fifty days. We give information about storage conditions for each of the crops discussed later in the book.

Chapter 3

The Care and Feeding
of Your Garden Soil

Garden soils are a little bit like thumbprints—no two are exactly alike. It's important for you to understand the characteristics of your soil, for its physical composition will determine to a large degree how early in the season you can plant and whether your growing crops will receive enough water and air at root level. Remember that healthy plants mirror a healthy soil—and you have a say in your soil's health.

Basic Soil Types

All soil is made up of three basic types of particles—sand, silt, and clay—in varying proportions. A given soil generally will have more of one component than another, and the presence of this component in large quantities determines the soil's characteristics.

Take a stroll out to your garden and pick up a handful of soil. Look at it critically, rubbing it between your fingers. If it's a sandy type, you'll be able to distinguish the particles with the naked eye. Sandy soil feels grainy and gritty and falls apart when you try to squeeze it into a ball. Gardening in sandy soil is a challenge, for the large sand particles encourage water and soluble nutrients to flow through rapidly, often before the roots have a chance to absorb them. This nutrient leaching means that sandy soil is often deficient in calcium, nitrogen, phosphorus, and potassium. On the plus side, this soil does dry out and warm up early in the season, so it's possible to get started early with spring crops. Later in the season, however, the soil will have little water in reserve for the plants to draw on.

A soil laden with silt particles will have a fine, powdery texture like flour and the silky feel of talcum powder. Silt particles are much smaller than sand particles, so you won't be able to see them with the naked eye. Although silt is an important component of soil, soil with too much silt will have some of the same characteristics as a sandy soil.

If your soil inspection reveals rock-hard lumps under dry conditions or sticky, rubbery, greasy clumps under moist conditions, the soil is composed mostly of clay particles. When you squeeze a ball of this soil together in your hand, it forms a sticky, dense mass that won't fall apart easily. Clay soil is slow to absorb water, but once it becomes wet, it is very slow to dry out. It usually stays too cold and wet in the early spring for the gardener to hope for much luck with early-season crops. But clay can be a boon at the other end of the season, when it stays warmer longer than lighter soils, encouraging good fall crops. You must be careful not to work clay soil when it is still very wet, or rocklike clods that are nearly impossible to break apart may form. There is little nutrient leaching in this type of soil.

If your soil looks as though it's made of various-size crumbs that mold together in a ball when you squeeze them but fall apart easily when you poke the ball with your finger, you have a loamy soil. In general, loam consists of approximately 40 percent sand, 40 percent silt, and 20 percent clay. This ideal soil retains water well but is loose enough to allow the excess to drain away. There's seldom a problem with nutrient loss through leaching.

⚓

How Soil Texture Affects Plant Growth

Each of these soils behaves differently, and a look at what goes on underground will point out those differences. The particles of sand, silt, and clay, along with any organic matter that is present, form the texture of a soil. These components, plus any rocks and pebbles that may be present, also determine the soil's pore size. Pores, or empty spaces, between the soil particles are essential to provide channels for water and air to reach plant roots. Actually, plant roots don't grow in soil; they grow in the spaces between particles. For roots to have room to grow and access to air and water, about half the soil volume should consist of these pores.

The size of the spaces is important in determining how well the soil will store water and how efficiently it can conduct water up from the lower soil levels as the upper layer dries out. If the pores are too large, as in a very sandy soil, water will run through quickly and be lost to your garden. If the pores are too small, as in clay soils, the water will move slowly. Clay soils can store as much as eight times more water than sandy soils, but much of this water doesn't benefit the plants because it is stuck to the walls of the tiny pores. As the surface soil dries out, water from below moves upward very slowly, which explains why clay soil

STARTING A NEW GARDEN

What if you've bought a new home and want to start a garden, but all you have is a thick green lawn or a patch of weeds? How do you go about turning this piece of land into a productive vegetable plot?

The best time to begin a new garden is a year before you want to plant. Mark out the garden area in the spring or early summer and cover it with black plastic, using rocks along the edges and in the middle of the plastic to hold it down. By mid-August the plants that were growing there should be dead. Use a full-size rototiller to break up the ground and incorporate the dead plants into the soil. That gives you a head start on a garden with lots of organic material.

After tilling the ground, rake it smooth and plant a cover crop. The cover crop will protect your new garden from erosion during the winter and add organic matter to the soil when tilled under in the spring. The best cover crop is a legume such as clover, which will add nitrogen to the soil. But if you live in the North, you may not have enough time for legumes to grow sufficiently before winter. Rye, wheat, or rye grass work well as cover crops in the North. Your county extension agent or local nursery should be able to advise you about the best cover crops for your area.

In early spring, as soon as the ground has thawed and dried out somewhat, till under the cover crop. If the growth is thick, you may need to run the lawn mower over the garden area before tilling to break up the foliage. You also might add a source of nitrogen, such as a layer of well-rotted manure, before you till.

Wait about two weeks, then take samples of your soil for testing. Contact your county extension agent about having the soil tested to find out if it's deficient in vital nutrients or suffers from a pH imbalance. When you get the results back, the county extension agent can give you advice on how to correct any imbalances. Be sure to ask for organic sources of any deficient nutrients.

Once your new garden is under way, you'll have to be especially diligent about weeds for the first year or two. If you let them mature and go to seed, you'll be battling them forever. Be sure to dig out weeds such as quack grass and thistles that multiply through underground rhizomes. You can minimize weeding by using a black plastic or organic mulch.

takes so long to dry out. In a loamy soil, with the proper balance of sand, clay, and silt, the pores are the right number and size to facilitate the movement of moisture through the soil. Water in a loamy soil is available as the plants need it, with little delay. The water can be pulled toward the surface from quite deep down, much as water is pulled up through plant stems by the evaporation of water from the leaves.

Soil pores do more than regulate the movement of water. They also hold air, which is probably the most important element for plant growth. The amount of oxygen in the soil controls how fast the roots respire. This respiration is very important, as it provides the roots with the energy they need for growth and mineral uptake. Finely textured soils with tiny pores will not come close to providing the amount of oxygen a growing plant needs, and the consequences can be alarming. If the roots are starved for oxygen, their growth slows, upsetting the well-being of all parts of the plant. In addition, insufficient oxygen slows the production of hormones within the plant, further disrupting the plant's functioning. In water-logged soil where oxygen is scarce, microorganisms that produce toxic substances can multiply and cause your plants to wilt or grow more slowly.

Since pore size plays such an important role in determining how much water and air your plants receive, and hence how well they grow, you should take steps to remedy a soil with extremely small or large pores. The key to balancing pore size is organic matter. If your garden soil is predominantly clay, the addition of organic matter such as compost, peat moss, or shredded leaves will loosen it up and increase the pore size, enhancing both air and water circulation. You also can work in some sand to help unlock the tiny clay particles and create more spaces. In a sandy soil organic matter will work its magic by improving the soil's water-holding capacity. The spongy bits will soak up and hold water in the root zone, where it's needed. Pieces of organic matter also will decrease the pore size by filling in some of the large spaces between the grains of sand.

Humus is the key to the success of an organic garden. Humus is difficult to define, but it consists of the remains of living material left after microorganisms have done their work of decomposition. The humus particles are a complex mixture of many chemical substances, but they are smaller than the organic particles that have yet to be broken down. A good garden soil should have a humus content of 5 percent or more. When you add material from a mature compost pile, you are adding humus to your soil. Covering your garden with a 1 to 3 inch layer of compost is a good guideline to follow. The humus will provide nitrogen and improve soil texture.

Soil Nutrients

We've indicated that nutrients such as nitrogen are vital to your plants' health, but why? What benefits do these chemicals bestow on your garden?

The most important nutrients—the ones all your crops need in abundance to grow well and produce—are nitrogen, phosphorus, and potassium. Other elements, such as boron, calcium, and magnesium, are needed in smaller quantities, and their availability is rarely a problem, especially in organic gardens. But if we feel that a lack of one of these nutrients could result in problems for your garden, we will mention it in the appropriate crop chapter.

Nitrogen is an essential nutrient for plant growth. Without adequate nitrogen, plants are stunted and have pale, sickly leaves. When nitrogen is in good supply, plants grow quickly and mature rapidly, with healthy dark green foliage. Too much nitrogen can stimulate plants to grow too quickly, resulting in weak, watery tissues that are easily damaged by wind and frost. Excess nitrogen also can delay flowering. Organic gardeners needn't worry about an oversupply of nitrogen, however. Blood meal, bone meal, fish emulsion, and poultry manure all provide nitrogen.

Scientists believe that a lack of phosphorus inhibits cell division, a prerequisite for growth. If plants have an inadequate phosphorus supply, they stop growing and fail to mature. Phosphorus also helps plants to fight diseases and is vital for strong roots and fruit development. If your plants have a phosphorus deficiency, the undersides of their leaves will turn purple. Sources of phosphorus include bone meal and ground phosphate rock.

Potassium is needed for the vital process of photosynthesis. It also aids in resistance to disease, cold weather, and drought. An adequate supply of potassium can offset an overabundance of nitrogen by conferring disease resistance on the overstimulated plants. Plants suffering from insufficient potassium may have yellow streaks or spots on the leaves, or the leaf margins may appear scorched. Good sources of potassium include compost, granite dust, greensand, manure, and plant residues.

Nutrient Availability

All the nutrients in the soil aren't just free-floating, amorphous bodies waiting to be sucked in by a hungry plant root. An intricate choreography is going on all the time in which nutrients are changed from forms that are unacceptable to plants into forms that can be readily assimilated. For example, soil phosphorus is locked up in insoluble compounds, and soil potassium is bound up in mineral form. As is, neither of these nutrients is in a form that allows it to be taken up by plant roots and put to use. Organic matter is the key that unlocks these nutrients and makes them available. In the case of phosphorus, the organic matter promotes active colonies of soil bacteria to secrete acids that spur the breakdown of the insoluble phosphorus compounds into a form that plants can use. As for potassium, plants in moist soils can take up more potassium than those in drier soils. But soluble potassium can be leached away quickly, so organic matter also acts as a sponge to hold the soluble potassium where the roots can get to it.

In soil lacking organic matter, nitrogen can be leached out very quickly, depriving plants of its benefits and possibly contaminating the ground water or nearby waterways. But particles of organic matter in the soil help hold on to nitrogen, keeping it available longer. In addition, the slow breakdown of organic material produces a gradual release of nitrogen instead of the sudden flush provided by chemical fertilizers.

Soil type and texture also affect how available nutrients are to plants. Clay particles and organic matter act like magnets, holding minerals on their surface so the minerals aren't washed away. When plant roots absorb some of the soluble minerals from the soil water, minerals attached to the clay or organic particles are released to replenish the mineral content of the water. If your soil is lacking in organic matter, clay content, or both, it won't retain minerals very well. Overall, organic matter is better than clay particles at holding minerals, and it will release the minerals back into the soil water more readily than clay.

Using Fertilizers in the Garden

We are convinced that overdependence on chemical fertilizers leads to a self-defeating cycle. When you use chemical fertilizers, nutrients are available to your plants for only a short time. Only a portion of the minerals are held by the soil particles, while the rest are washed away. If you continue to use *only* chemical fertilizers year after year, the natural processes of erosion, water movement, and plant growth use up whatever organic matter was in the soil to start with. Each season there are fewer organic particles in the soil to retain the minerals you add, so you have to add more and more fertilizer each year to sustain the plants' growth. As the organic material decreases, your soil becomes subject to erosion because there are fewer microorganisms producing humus. You find that you have to water more frequently because there is less organic matter to absorb water and hold it in the root zone. Perhaps worst of all, chemical fertilizers make the soil more and more acid and promote salt build-up to the point where your plants may actually have trouble growing.

Organic gardeners avoid this unpleasant cycle by using compost, manure, rock powders, and other organic materials to boost the soil's fertility. One possible drawback of organic fertilizers is that most of them are very slow acting. If you start out with poor soil, most organic fertilizers will not get your plants off to a fast start. You can make up for this lag between application and availability by adding slow-acting fertilizers to the soil well before you plan to plant so that the nutrients will be there when needed. For example, slow-release potassium fertilizers such as granite dust and greensand are best applied in the fall for spring crops and in the spring for fall crops. This rule also applies to the application of slow-release phosphorus fertilizers such as phosphate rock and bone meal.

Some organic fertilizers release their nutrients at a relatively fast rate. These should not be applied too early, or all the nutrients will be leached away. Quick-release fertilizers should be applied right before planting for best results. Relatively fast-acting potassium sources include green plant residues, seaweed, and wood ashes. (A word of warning: Wood ashes burn seeds, stems, and root hairs of young plants on contact. To avoid any mishaps, work the ashes thoroughly into the top 8 inches of soil before planting.) Fast-acting nitrogen sources include dried blood and fish emulsion. If you take the time to understand the mechanics of nutrient availability and apply organic fertilizers so that they will release nutrients when needed, you'll seldom have to make supplemental feedings during the season, since there won't be any nutrient deficiencies to remedy.

Many organic gardeners say that pests leave their crops alone but bother those of neighbors who use only chemical fertilizers. Although many people have been skeptical of this claim, two scientists from Cornell University decided to test it. They grew collards in two plots, one fertilized with manure and the other with chemical fertilizers. They found that flea beetles much preferred the chemically fertilized collards over those grown with manure.

Why pH Is Important

You've probably heard it a thousand times: keep the soil pH between 6.5 and 7.0 for most common vegetable crops. But what are the consequences if your garden soil strays outside those boundaries?

A soil that's too far to the alkaline side of the pH scale (above 7.5) will lock up most of the trace elements so that they are unavailable to the growing plants. Acutely alkaline soil will go so far as to break apart humus and result in a toxic level of salt.

In overly acid soil (below 5.0) phosphorus is in a form that cannot be absorbed by plant roots. Calcium, magnesium, and potassium also tend to leach out of this type of soil. Even earthworms are turned off by too high an acid level and will move on to a more agreeable pH environment. And if you're growing any members of the cabbage family, your plants are more likely to be plagued by club root.

Soil tests are a sure-fire way to assess your garden's pH status. You can buy a simple pH-testing kit at your garden supply store. To combat alkaline soil, work in cottonseed meal, leaf mold, peat moss, pine needles, sawdust, or wood chips. Test the pH in several weeks and keep adding material as needed until you've arrived at the desired range. To remedy an overly acid soil, use bone meal, clamshells, dolomitic limestone, ground eggshells, oyster shells, or wood ashes. Liming material works best when spread on top of the soil after working it. If you mix the liming substance into the soil, it is likely to leach out too quickly. Different crops have different pH preferences, and these are noted in the "Vital Statistics" box at the beginning of each crop chapter.

Chapter 4

Nurturing Plants throughout the Season

G ardening presents many pitfalls along with its abundant rewards. When you understand the rationale behind common garden practices, you can avoid many of the problems that can plague the naive gardener. We know because we've been there!

When Diane first began to garden, she was told to harden off her indoor-grown tomato plants before setting them outside. She decided that since the plants had been grown in a very sunny west-facing window, two days of hardening off, with two hours outside the first day and four hours outside the second day, would be enough. She gave the plants their abbreviated hardening period, then planted them out in the garden and congratulated herself on her efficiency. She was horrified when all her plants lost every single leaf! If she'd been told why gradual hardening off is so important, she would never have made such a foolish mistake.

In this chapter we discuss the reasons behind hardening off and some other common gardening tasks, such as starting seeds indoors, transplanting, watering, fertilizing, and mulching. This should help you understand why some things must be done in a certain way.

Microscopic Farming: How to Compost

W hen you make an active compost pile, you are farming on a microscopic scale, feeding countless microorganisms and worms that break down complex organic material into a simpler form, just as a rancher feeds his or her cows and chickens. And just as such animals need a balanced diet to be healthy, microorganisms in the soil need a balanced supply of carbon- and nitrogen-containing organic material.

These microorganisms function most efficiently and do their quickest work when given about thirty times more carbon than nitrogen. If they get too much carbon and not enough nitrogen, as on a diet of sawdust or dried leaves, they can't decompose the pile very fast, and it may be years before you get a rich humus. If they are fed a diet high in nitrogen, such as too much fresh grass clippings, they grow too quickly and form ammonia from the extra nitrogen. Not only does your compost pile smell awful, but much of the nitrogen is lost as the ammonia gas escapes out of the pile and into the air. If you have a stinky compost pile, you have fed your microorganisms too much nitrogen and are simply wasting it.

Organic materials that have little nitrogen but lots of carbon (more than one hundred times as much carbon as nitrogen) include paper, sawdust, and wood. Straw, cornstalks, and some types of leaves also can have a high carbon-to-nitrogen ratio. These need to be mixed with materials containing a lot of nitrogen for the best decomposition. Some high-nitrogen sources include alfalfa, fresh (not rotted) manure, grass clippings, fruit or vegetable trimmings, and young legumes such as sweet clover, white Dutch clover, mammoth red clover, and Austrian winter peas. The best way to compost materials is to make a mix of different organic materials. For example, if you have a lot of leaves, you can mix them with alfalfa hay or manure.

Besides the right proportions of carbon and nitrogen, your compost pile needs air and water. A lack of air will encourage less desirable microorganisms. These bacteria take much longer to do the job and give off an unpleasant rotten-egg odor in the process. You should water your pile often enough to keep it as moist as a wrung-out sponge, and you should turn it about once a week to make sure it has enough air.

There are many ways to build a good compost pile. Alternate thick layers of dry, carbonaceous material with thinner layers of high-nitrogen material. For example, use a 6-inch layer of hay or kitchen wastes and a 2-inch layer of manure, topped off with a thin layer of soil. You can compost in just about any container—a plastic garbage can, wood bin, or concrete-block bin—or in an open pit or just a pile on the ground. A simple way to compost is to dig a hole 8 to 12 inches deep and big enough to contain the day's kitchen wastes, spread out the material, and cover it with several inches of soil. During the summer, these piles will decompose in about a month; of course, they will take longer in winter.

Earthworms: The Gardener's Friends

By developing a good garden soil, you encourage the activity of earthworms. An acre of rich soil may contain 12 tons of earthworms, which move a hundred tons of material to the surface in one year. A garden rich in worms must be rich in organic material, for this is the earthworm's food. It eats its way through the earth, passing the soil through its body and partially digesting it, leaving castings that are rich in plant nutrients. Besides enriching the soil, earthworms aerate it by crawling through it. Their tunnels help water as well as air move into the soil more easily and provide easy channels for root growth. These creatures also mix the soil by moving the lower soil up to the surface and the rich organic material from the surface down below, where it can benefit the plant roots.

Burying plant remains and composting encourage these gardener's helpers, as does mulching. One reason mulch mysteriously disappears during the season is that earthworms come up at night and carry it down into their burrows. Chemical fertilizers and pesticides can kill earthworms, which is yet another reason to avoid these products.

Getting a Head Start

There are many reasons for starting some of your crops indoors. Because of a limited outdoor growing season, few gardeners have the luxury of seeding all their crops directly in the garden. In our short Montana summer, crops such as peppers and tomatoes wouldn't have a long enough period of warm weather to mature if we seeded them outdoors.

Even some of those crops that you might be able to grow easily during your regular outdoor growing season will do better if started inside, away from the heat of summer or the bugs that might eat them. If a fall crop of lettuce is what you're after, you'll get better germination indoors in a cool place than in the hot, dry soil found in most gardens in midsummer. In our gardens here in Montana, we find that starting our broccoli inside gives it time to grow big enough to withstand the annual onslaught of flea beetles, which can demolish the young seedlings of direct-seeded broccoli. Southern gardeners also may be able to outsmart insect pests by starting especially vulnerable crops inside.

Whatever your reasons for planting indoors, you must grow your plants under the right conditions, or they will be sickly and yield poorly. Factors such as light, moisture, planting depth, soil, and temperature must be monitored carefully if you want to grow sturdy, healthy transplants.

Choosing the Right Container

The first decision you must make about planting seeds indoors is what type of container to use. Your choice may be governed primarily by cost, for commercial pots can be very expensive. You can recycle milk cartons, Styrofoam egg cartons, yogurt cups, and other similar containers, but you should be aware of some disadvantages to using these. Most recycled containers come with no drainage holes, so before you start planting, you must make your own by puncturing the bottom of the container. If you are using egg cartons, use only Styrofoam ones. The cardboard kind will disintegrate after a few waterings. Another point to remember is that the compartments in egg cartons are so small that they are useful only for very small plants. Use them for starting crops such as peppers and tomatoes, which will be transplanted into larger individual containers while very small, or lettuce seedlings, which can be transplanted to the garden while still little.

Purchased containers may add to your gardening expenses, but they do offer some advantages. Square plastic pots and peat cube planters are designed to fit closely together so they take up a minimum of space. This is especially important if greenhouse or cold-frame space is at a premium. They often come with trays to hold them together as a unit, which is useful when you start to harden off seedlings and are shuttling them outside and inside every day. In addition, the initial cost of these containers can be offset by the fact that you can use them for many years. Diane has used plastic six- and four-compartment pots for three to four years. To extend their life, she washes them and puts them away out of the sun as soon as they have served their purpose for the season.

Some containers can affect how your indoor garden grows. Pots that breathe, such as those made from fiber or peat, do well in an enclosed area such as a greenhouse or on a windowsill. They do not work well in an open cold frame because they dry out much too quickly. Clay pots also breathe, but they do not dry out as fast. If you plan to grow your plants in a cold frame that is open on sunny days, plant your seeds in clay, plastic, Styrofoam, or waxed containers (such as milk cartons or yogurt cups) or in wooden flats. This will cut down on water loss through evaporation.

If you use paper-based containers such as fiber pots, you will need to use a soil richer in nitrogen than if you plant in plastic containers. The microbes that break down wood products such as paper require a lot of nitrogen, as well as carbon, to fuel their work. The wood fiber provides them with a carbon source but has little nitrogen, so the microbes will pull nitrogen from the soil into the container, leaving less for the growing plants.

Many gardening experts recommend starting crops that are especially sensitive to transplanting, such as cucumbers and squash, in biodegradable peat pots so that the pots can be planted in the garden right along with the plants. However, we've found that setting peat pots right in the soil retards the growth of these temperamental crops, for their roots often have a hard time breaking through the pot. We've had much better luck using plastic, Styrofoam, or waxed containers. Before transplanting, water the seedlings so that the soil in the pot is slightly damp and will not crumble away from the roots. Then tap the pot lightly to loosen the mass of roots and soil, gently slide the plant and soil out of the container, and carefully place them into a watered hole. The roots are hardly disturbed and can grow right into the soil without first having to break through a tough peat pot.

Gardeners who use peat pots with good results have a few secrets that ensure their success. Right before planting, they make a couple of vertical tears in the sides of each pot so that the roots can grow through. When they set the pots in place, they make sure the rims are completely buried, or they trim off the part of the pot that protrudes. If the top of the old pot sticks out above the soil, it acts like a wick, carrying water up out of the ground and away from the plant's roots.

Individual peat cubes bound by plastic netting also can restrict root growth when they're set in the garden. If you use these, be sure to clip off the netting just before you transplant so the roots can grow freely.

If you start your seeds in a small container such as the cavity of an egg carton or a compressed peat pellet that swells with water, be sure to transplant your seedlings before their growth is slowed by the cramped quarters. If this happens, the plants will not produce as big a crop as they would have if their growth pattern hadn't been retarded.

When a plant's roots are crowded, the shoot, or aboveground portion, outgrows them. The root system is then too small to supply nutrients and water to the whole plant. When you water the plant, the small root system will absorb all the water that it can, but this will not be nearly enough to satisfy the requirements of the aboveground growth. The shoot will quickly use up all the available water and start to droop unless you water again soon.

Frequent waterings leach nutrients out of the soil. Therefore, plants with crowded roots are in double jeopardy—prone to both water stress and nutrient deficiencies. Unfortunately, both problems will persist after you transplant the seedlings into the garden. The roots will have a hard time catching up to the aboveground growth, so these top-heavy plants will always be more susceptible to problems than well-balanced ones, especially when they begin to bear fruit and there are heavy nutrient and water demands on the roots.

One way to grow sturdy, problem-free transplants is to follow this basic rule: keep plants in containers at least as deep as the plants are tall, especially during the first six weeks of growth.

Potting Soils for Seedlings

Choose your potting soil carefully. Soil for seedlings must be very light and loose so that their small, fine roots can grow freely. A planting mixture that drains well is vital in the limited confines of a container, but it also must be able to hold enough water and air to keep the plant roots healthy.

The soil that works so well out in your garden isn't necessarily the best choice for your containers. Ordinary garden soil is too heavy to use in a pot or flat, as seedlings will be hampered by the lack of air spaces and inadequate drainage. With some effort, however, you can prepare your own potting soil mixture. First, spread your soil in a shallow layer in a foil baking pan and set it in a 140°F oven for one-half hour. This heat treatment will kill damping-off spores and other disease organisms but will not harm beneficial microorganisms.

Once you've pasteurized your soil, you should lighten it by adding soil conditioners such as builder's sand, peat moss, perlite, and vermiculite. There are almost as many home potting soil formulas as there are gardeners, but one simple, successful mix contains 1 to 2 parts pasteurized garden soil, 1 to 2 parts organic matter (fine compost or peat moss), 1 part vermiculite or sand, and a little steamed bone meal (a good source of phosphorus).

Pasteurizing soil for growing mixes is fine for small batches, but if you do much indoor planting, you'll find yourself spending a lot of time and energy preparing enough garden soil. And besides, the hot soil can really smell up your house! Many gardeners buy their potting soil at a garden center instead.

How do you choose a good potting soil? In some areas, gardeners can purchase organic potting soil that's rich in crumbly humus and devoid of chemical fertilizers. In others, gardeners may be able to purchase premixed bags of potting soil already containing conditioners such as peat moss or vermiculite. All these gardeners have to do is pour the mix into containers and plant their seeds. Unfortunately, most of us do not have much choice when it comes to purchasing potting soil. Usually only a few brands will be available in a given geographic area. Some of the potting soils on the market are too heavy to use alone, so you must lighten them up, just as you would with soil from your garden.

You may encounter some problems with commercial soil, so watch your young seedlings carefully as they grow. If you find a brand of soil that performs well, stick with it. Most brands claim to be sterilized, but many contain viable damping-off spores and weed seeds. Some commercial potting soils contain harsh chemical fertilizers, and some are deficient in basic nutrients.

The most common problem is a lack of adequate phosphorus. You can avoid this problem by adding bone meal or phosphate rock to the soil at the same time you are blending in soil conditioners such as sand or vermiculite. If you don't add any extra phosphorus to the soil and you notice that the undersides of your seedlings' leaves are turning reddish purple, that's a sure sign that they aren't getting enough phosphorus. A good dose of fish emulsion at the concentration recommended on the container will restore your plants to good health.

If the leaves of your plants have an anemic, pale green tone instead of a healthy, deep green glow, they're experiencing a nitrogen deficiency. You can remedy the situation by administering a dose of manure tea or fish emulsion. If you keep your plants in the same soil for more than four weeks, you should feed them fish fertilizer or manure tea anyway to keep them well nourished.

Any nutrient deficiency that develops while the plant is young can seriously affect its ultimate yield. But if you correct a deficiency as soon as you notice it and give seedlings a nutrient boost at the four-week mark, your plants won't disappoint you at harvest time.

Starting the Seeds
A general rule for planting seeds indoors is to plant them as deep as they

are wide. Remember that some crops, such as lettuce, require light for germination, so you should press the seeds gently into the soil with a very light touch. After planting your seeds, moisten the soil with lukewarm water and put the container in a place where the temperature is as close as possible to the ideal for germination of that particular seed. The best temperature is listed in the "Vital Statistics" box at the beginning of each crop chapter.

If your planted seeds are at the right temperature and they haven't begun to germinate in the time listed for that crop, your seeds could be too old, and you may need to replant with a fresh batch of seeds. (Before you go to the trouble of replanting, pretest the seeds for germination as described in chapter 1.) Old seeds sometimes take longer to germinate than new ones, so don't give up right away. Old eggplant and pepper seeds are notorious for taking their time. They may take a week or more longer than the expected time. If they haven't germinated by then, however, they may be too old to produce healthy plants. With most other crops, if no seedlings have emerged by three days after the maximum germination time, you should replant to play it safe. Also, if the temperature is lower than ideal, the seeds may take quite a bit longer to sprout.

Be sure to keep your seeds moist but not sopping wet while they are germinating. If they are too dry, the embryos will not be able to break out of the seed coats. If they are too wet, they won't be able to "breathe" and thus won't grow. Many gardeners create an "incubator" by covering their flats or pots loosely with plastic while the seeds are germinating, taking care that the plastic doesn't rest directly on the soil's surface. If the seeds have been adequately watered, the plastic will hold in enough moisture for successful germination. Watch for any signs of mold or fungus growing in such covered containers, and be sure not to overwater. If any problems do develop, prop open the cover to allow air to circulate and dry out the soil a bit. After the young plants push their way up, remove the plastic and place the flat or pot in bright light. Never place the containers in the sun while they are covered with plastic, or the contents will fry.

If you do not use a plastic cover, you will probably have to water your seeds more often. Water very gently so you don't disturb the seeds and use warm but not hot water. Hot water can kill the embryos, and cold water can cool the soil, slowing germination.

The most serious problem that can cause trouble with tender young seedlings is damping off. The seedlings emerge from the soil and look fine. Then one day you check on them, and they have keeled over and died. Damping off is caused by a fungus that lives in the soil. When seedlings are crowded or are living in a very humid environment without enough fresh air, damping off can devastate them. That's one reason we warn you to be careful when using plastic to create incubators for your seedlings. If you use high-quality potting soil, keep your seedlings in a cool, well-ventilated place, and give them good drainage, you are less likely to be bothered by this common problem.

The Best Environment for Growing Seedlings

The most common mistake gardeners make when growing seedlings indoors is to give them too little light and too much warmth. Outdoors, when the temperature increases, so does the intensity of the sunlight. Most plants grow best under these increasing proportions of light and heat. When you grow your plants in a heated house, however, you can upset the balance between increase in temperature and increase in light intensity, and your plants may become spindly.

For example, if you have seedlings in a sunny window, the combination of heat from the house and solar radiation coming through the window can bring the air temperature around the plants up to 80°F. Outdoors at this temperature the plants would be in full sunlight. But on the windowsill, they are only getting the portion of the sunlight that passes through the glass, considerably less than the full amount. Under these conditions not only does the top of the plant grow too fast, but the roots, which grow best in cool soil, grow too slowly, and the balance between the roots and the rest of the plant is upset. In addition, the leaves, which are receiving less than maximum light, produce many chloroplasts, which are packed with chlorophyll. When such a plant grown this way is planted outside in the garden, the leaves absorb so much sunlight that they self-destruct. The chlorophyll is destroyed, and the leaves turn white and fall off.

If windowsills are such iffy places to get seedlings off to a good start, why do so many gardeners put their growing plants there? The most likely answer is for the sake of convenience. For gardeners who are concerned about the health and well-being of their plants, we recommend using a cold frame. A cold frame provides the best possible growing conditions for seedlings. Unlike a greenhouse, it allows you to expose them gradually to the sun, wind, and temperature extremes they will encounter when planted out in the garden. You can place your seedlings in the cold frame as soon as they are up. On sunny days raise the top so that the plants receive the natural ratio of temperature to sunlight. In colder parts of the country protect your plants from freezing nights with a heat source. We run an electric soil-heating cable under pots and flats containing our frost-sensitive plants. Not only does this protect them from frost, but it also keeps the roots from getting too cold, and it doesn't cost very much.

A variation on the cold frame is the solar growing frame. This superinsulated structure is designed to collect the solar energy available during the day and with the help of a folding shutter, release this stored heat to the growing plants steadily throughout the night. The solar growing frame is a real boon to gardeners who live in cold-winter regions, for it allows them to grow greens throughout the winter, as well as to start their seedlings in spring. Do-it-yourselfers can find plans for building one of these frames in the book *Rodale's Solar Growing Frame* edited by Ray Wolf (Emmaus, PA: Rodale Press, 1980).

Capitalizing on the insulating properties of the earth's nearly constant temperature (about 50°F), Diane dug a deep hole next to her house and attached a cold frame to the south foundation wall. The soil on the other three sides of

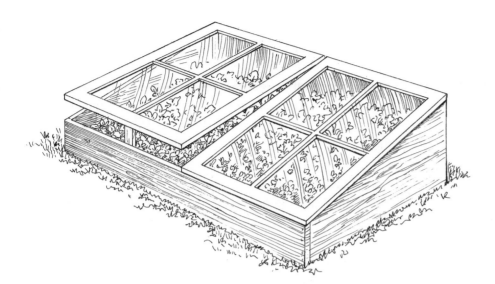

Cold Frame: A cold frame provides the best environment for growing seedlings, as it allows them to adapt naturally to garden conditions when transplanted in the garden. Raise the lid on hot days to prevent the build-up of heat in the frame.

the frame helped to keep it warm.

For those of you who don't have the time or skills to build a cold frame, most seed companies and gardening supply companies carry lightweight, easy-to-construct cold frames. Most come with a solar-powered vent that opens the frame automatically when the temperature inside becomes too warm. This feature is worth its weight in gold because most gardeners cannot open and close their frames every few hours as the temperature changes.

Any cold frame offers several advantages at this early stage of the gardening season. For one thing, your garden plants are out of the house, so they don't occupy all your window space and compete with your house plants. When you open the frame on sunny days, the plants will be exposed to unfiltered sunlight and to fresh air. Every time the breeze shakes the plants, it helps stimulate the stems to become stronger and thicker. The air circulation also makes the plants lose water more quickly, which stimulates the roots to grow. Plants grown in an open cold frame need no hardening-off period, so you are relieved of the chore of hauling your plants out of and back into the house.

If you have a greenhouse, you can provide better lighting for your plants than they will get inside the house. But if you can't open up the greenhouse to let unfiltered sunlight shine on your plants, you will still have to harden them off, although it should take less time than for house-grown seedlings. One problem with greenhouses is the heat that can build up inside on sunny days. Excessive heat can result in spindly plants, so if you don't have a good ventilation system in your greenhouse, you may end up with a crop of inferior seedlings.

House-grown plants and some greenhouse-grown plants may need supplemental light beyond the sunlight they receive. Tall and spindly plants with long internodes need more light. Fluorescent fixtures provide the most natural light and are cheaper to run than incandescent ones. Special grow-light tubes are available for fluorescent fixtures, although you may find that a combination of the less expensive cool white and warm white tubes works just as well.

Don't keep your plants under artificial lights for more than fourteen hours a day. Plants need darkness as well as light to grow properly. Timer switches that turn the lights on and off are inexpensive and easy to install, and they save you the bother of having to remember yourself. Hang the light fixture 3 to 4 inches above the tops of the plants and check the plants daily to make sure no leaves are too close to the hot bulbs. Raise the fixture as necessary to keep the leaves from getting scorched (a task made easier by an adjustable fixture).

Although a windowsill is not the best environment for raising transplants, many gardeners make do with such a location year after year with good results. If you don't have access to a cold frame or a greenhouse, keep the following points in mind. First, give the transplants as much light as possible, and if you can't provide supplemental light as described above, lower the temperature in the room to around 65°F. Never let it go above 75°F, or your plants will be spindly. If possible, turn the heat down at night to between 50°F and 55°F. The plants won't grow as fast, but they will be stronger and better balanced. A sturdy plant on the small side with a strong root system that is large enough to support the top growth will outproduce a larger, spindly plant whose top outgrew its roots.

Seedlings grown in a sheltered environment such as a windowsill or greenhouse need to be gradually acclimated to the outdoors so that they can withstand the increased light exposure, buffeting winds, and wide temperature swings that will be their lot in the garden.

Hardening Off

Hardening off young plants is the process of increasing their resistance to drought and decreasing their efficiency at gathering sunlight. As they are slowly exposed to increasing amounts of sunlight and cooler air, the chlorophyll content of the plants' older leaves, which are adapted to the filtered light of the indoor environment, gradually decreases. This decrease is necessary so that they won't absorb light at such a high rate, as too much sunlight will destroy the leaves. At the same time, the new leaves that form grow thicker, with two layers of sunlight-gathering palisade cells to make good use of the extra light.

As your carefully tended indoor plants are given more outdoor exposure, the waxy cuticle of their leaves thickens, affording them more protection from the generally drier conditions to which they'll be exposed in the garden. Decreasing the amount of water you give the plants stimulates their roots to grow so the seedlings won't be water stressed after transplanting. Exposure to the wind also induces structural cells to grow in the stem. These help the plant to endure heavy winds without falling over or snapping.

All these adaptations take time, so you must be patient. If your plants have been grown entirely inside and are weak and spindly, they will require a long, gradual hardening-off period. Hardening off will take from one and a half to three weeks depending on the plants' condition. The following recommendations are based on our own experience.

TIMETABLE FOR HARDENING OFF

	First Day	Second Day	Third Day	Fourth Day	Fifth Day	Sixth Day
In full sunlight						
Spindly plants	½ hour	¾ hour	1 hour	1½ hours	2¼ hours	3½ hours
Sturdy plants	1½ hours	2½ hours	3½ hours	5 hours	6 hours	7 hours
In light shade*						
Spindly plants	1 hour	1½ hours	2¼ hours	3½ hours	5 hours	3 hours in sun
Sturdy plants	2½ hours	3½ hours	5 hours	6 hours	7 hours	7 hours in sun

* Receiving reflected or indirect sunlight only for the first five days.

The first day, place weak plants in direct sun for no more than half an hour. Slowly increase the time in the sun over the first week until they are out for about four hours (see the box "Timetable for Hardening Off"). From then on, increase the amount of sunlight by about an hour a day until the plants are outside all day long.

If your plants are sturdy and have been receiving filtered direct sunlight for about four hours a day indoors, you can give them one and a half hours of full sun or two to two and a half hours of filtered (shaded) sun the first day outside. Try to put the plants out during hours when they would not be getting sunlight inside; this will help them adjust faster. For example, if the sun doesn't strike their window until noon, do your hardening off in the morning if possible. If the plants are in a southeast window, harden off in the afternoon if you can. Each day, increase the time outside by an hour until the plants are out all day. The last few days before transplanting you can leave them outside overnight if you like. This saves you the trouble of carting them in and out, and some people think it helps them adjust that much better to conditions outdoors.

Keep in mind that the weather can interfere with even the most carefully managed hardening-off schedule. If it is snowing or unseasonably cold when you plan to begin the process, you will have to wait until conditions improve. If hail or heavy rains descend while your tender young plants are outside, you will have to bundle up and rescue them from the inclement weather and then pick up where you left off when the sun comes back out.

During the early stages of the hardening-off period, water your plants once a day, and always keep an eye out for wilting, especially on hot days. If your plants do wilt, take them inside and water them right away. As hardening off progresses, you want the plants to develop strong roots and to become used to drier conditions, but you don't want to stress them. Encourage this acclimatization by gradually decreasing the amount of water you give the plants. The last few days before transplanting, water them as little as possible short of letting them wilt. If it is windy when you begin hardening off, protect your plants from the wind for the first few days until they begin to get stronger and more accustomed to dryness. You can place your seedlings on the leeward side of a building or tree to protect them from the wind as long as it isn't shady there. Or you can place low barriers such as old fruit boxes between your plants and the prevailing wind.

If your seedlings are growing together in a flat, you must take an additional step to prepare them for transplanting. Two or three days before you plan to transplant, cut the soil into blocks about 3 inches square or larger around each plant (just like cutting a sheet cake). In this procedure, known as blocking off, delicate root hairs and the root ends are cut off as you draw a trowel or other sharp tool through the soil mass. You are actually lessening the transplant trauma by inflicting some of the inevitable damage early and giving the plants a chance to recover before being transplanted.

Transplanting to the Garden

When your plants have finally become accustomed to being outside for a full day, they are ready to be transplanted. Time your hardening off so that the plants are ready when it is safe for them to be in the garden. Hardy crops such as broccoli, cabbage, and lettuce can be set out quite early, even before the last expected frost. Tender, more cold-sensitive crops such as eggplants, peppers, and tomatoes must not be set out until after the last frost. Check with your county extension agent for the proper planting time in your particular area.

For final transplanting, pick a calm, cloudy day if possible. If this isn't convenient, transplant in the evening so the plants can start adjusting under the cover of darkness. Transplanting will be less stressful to your seedlings if they are not exposed to the hot sun or drying wind right away. Granted, it's hard to find the perfect day, for even on a cloudy day the wind can be very drying and cause your transplants to lose water faster than their disoriented roots can pull it up. As long as you don't transplant under the blazing midday sun and follow our tips on how to minimize root damage, your seedlings should recover quickly.

It's important to realize that no matter how careful you are, the roots probably will sustain some change during transplanting. To minimize this damage, have the soil in the pot moist enough so that it will hold together around the roots when you pull out the root ball. Soil in plastic pots should be very moist but not soaking wet, whereas soil in fiber pots should be a bit drier. If you are using peat pots through which the roots are growing, soak the pots thoroughly and tear the sides in several places before setting them into the garden.

Dig the hole deep enough so that the root mass will sit slightly below the soil's surface. Leaving a shallow depression around the base of the plant will allow water to collect there so it can soak slowly down to the root mass.

If your soil is poor or compacts easily, dig the hole an inch or so deeper and a couple of inches wider than the root ball. Then mix some compost or pre-moistened peat moss thoroughly with the soil you dug out of the planting hole. Add some of this fortified soil to the bottom of the hole and use the rest to cushion the sides and top of the root ball once the plant is in place. The roots need loose, fertile soil that they can penetrate easily and from which they can absorb nutrients for the growing plant. Soggy soil tends to compact around the roots and hampers their nutrient and water uptake. If your garden soil is very wet, delay planting until the soil dries out and loosens up a bit.

It's never a good idea to set your plant into a bone-dry hole. If your garden is dry, or if the day is very hot, windy, or both, be sure to water the hole thoroughly before you set in the plant.

To get the plant out of its pot easily, tap the sides soundly with the blade edge or handle of a trowel or run a knife around the inside edges of the pot. Once you've loosened the root ball, cup one hand over the soil's surface, with your fingers cradling the stem. Tip the pot upside-down and gently shake or tap it until the plant is released. Set the plant into the hole at once, fill in the gap between the hole and the root ball with soil, and tamp the soil down firmly, remembering to leave a depression around the base of the plant. Water generously right away. At this point water stress is the worst enemy your young plants face. If the wind comes up or the sun comes out, or if the transplants wilt, turn on a soaker hose or sprinkler so that the plants receive constant moisture for a couple of hours. Alternatively, you can cover them with a row cover (described later in this chapter) or prop boards, shingles, or window screens alongside your transplants to create a sheltered, shady haven. Keep a close eye on your transplants for the first few days and water them when they show any sign of wilting.

If you have done a careful job of hardening off, your new garden should begin to grow well soon after transplanting. But if your plants are not completely acclimated to garden conditions and some leaves turn white and fall off, don't despair. Even when Diane's tomato plants lost every single leaf in her misguided attempt to speed up hardening off, they grew new ones and eventually produced tomatoes. Her crop surely would have been earlier and more abundant, however, if she had heeded the voice of experience and hardened them off gradually. Careful hardening off and transplanting may seem like a lot of trouble, but in the long run your plants will thank you by giving you generous yields of high-quality produce.

How to Water Effectively

There's an art to making sure your plants get enough water throughout the season. Too many gardeners still go by the hit-or-miss method, turning on the spigot when they think of it—oblivious to the fact that the garden needed water several days ago or that perhaps it doesn't really need any for another couple of days. In the first case, the plants will be water stressed, and that condition could adversely affect the ultimate yield. In the second case, water is being squandered needlessly and may even saturate the soil to the point where it interferes with plant growth. Here are some pointers to help you undertake an effective watering regimen in your garden.

Knowing your soil type is very important, for it will determine how you water. You should never overwater clay soil because it will hold too much water next to the plant roots and, in essence, drown them. If you have a sandy soil, you don't have to worry about overwatering because the excess water will just drain through the ground. Whatever your soil type, you should water just until the soil is thoroughly moist but not soggy.

Besides wasting precious water, overwatering will leach minerals into the subsoil and out of the reach of most roots. In contrast, when too little water percolates down through the root zone, the result is slow growth or the demise of your plants. Not only do the plants need the water itself, but water also carries vital minerals from the soil into the plant. When water is in short supply, important nutrients become scarce as well. Frequent light watering that moistens only the top layer of soil encourages the roots to grow near the soil's surface. There they are subject to drying between waterings and are vulnerable to perishing under drought conditions. In addition, they will not probe deep enough to extract minerals from the entire depth of the topsoil.

In general, the best way to determine if your garden needs watering is to dig down about 3 inches. (Important exceptions are explained in the individual crop chapters.) If the soil at this depth is dry and won't stick together, it is time to water. Also watch your plants for signs that they need water. On a hot day some wilting is normal in the afternoon. For example, if you go out to the garden and see your cucumbers drooping, don't panic. Their leaves have been giving off water faster than the roots can pull it up from the soil. There may be plenty of water available in the soil, but the plants just aren't getting it quickly enough. In most cases, they will regain their perky appearance by morning. However, if you notice that your plants are wilted in the morning, get water to them right away. That's a sure sign that there's not enough water in the soil for the plants to take up.

If your soil is loamy, you should water at least an hour so that the soil is deeply soaked. A sandy soil needs to be watered for less time at more frequent intervals, and a clay soil will need only infrequent watering.

Whatever your soil type, the best watering method probably is drip irrigation. Drip irrigation delivers the water right to the roots where it is needed. Little water is wasted through evaporation, and the rate of application is slow enough for any soil type. There are two methods of drip irrigation: (1) long tubes with holes at each plant or (2) long tubes with tiny holes all along their length. Drip systems that are buried under the soil or under a mulch such as black plastic or straw will save even more water, as there is less evaporation.

If you choose a different type of watering method, make sure it is appropriate for your soil type. For instance, if your soil is sandy, you could use an overhead sprinkler, but you wouldn't want to use flood irrigation. It would take up to four times as much water to flood-irrigate a garden with sandy soil as it would to use an overhead sprinkler, and flood irrigation also would leach a lot of the nutrients out of the soil.

If your soil is clay, you should use a sprinkler that delivers water as fine droplets, such as a soaker hose, rather than large drops. Large drops would beat the soil and compact it, slowing root growth and mineral uptake. In addition, they would not be absorbed as well as fine droplets, which are more evenly distributed. With clay you also must make sure that the water doesn't puddle up on the surface. If it does, slow the rate of application.

Unmulched soil that forms a crust also needs a sprinkler with fine droplets. Using a hoe during weeding helps break up the crust, but if your weeds are gone and a crust has reformed, hoe it again so that the water can penetrate more easily.

Mulches

Most gardeners are familiar with the often-touted benefits of mulching, especially when organic materials are used. Almost every gardening book carries the following refrain: an organic mulch will conserve soil moisture; deter soil erosion; supply nutrients and humus as it breaks down; thwart weed growth; regulate temperature extremes; and keep the harvest clean and free of mildew, mold, and rot. But they don't tell you the hidden character traits of each kind of mulch that will appear only with time and can spell trouble if you are caught unaware. Here's a run-down of the more commonly used mulches and some well-kept secrets we thought you'd like to know.

A number of mulches fall into the category of nitrogen robbers; these are organic materials rich in carbon such as dry alfalfa hay, shredded corncobs and cornstalks, sawdust, and straw. When such mulches are used, bacteria steal nitrogen from the soil to fuel decomposition of the mulch, leaving less nitrogen for the plants and sometimes leading to a serious deficiency. To avoid a potential deficiency, apply substances high in nitrogen, such as blood meal, compost, manure, or soybean or cottonseed meal to the soil before mulching. Or you can compost the carbonaceous nitrogen robbers with the nitrogen-rich materials and apply the resulting mixture as a compost mulch.

Grass clippings are usually available in abundance, but they also can cause a host of problems if not used correctly. Clippings that have started to go to seed will introduce a new crop of unwanted plants, so avoid them at all costs. Fresh clippings can compact down, blocking soil aeration and causing water to run off instead of soak in. Besides giving off an objectionable odor, they also have the nasty habit of being a breeding haven for flies and gnats. To avoid this unpleasantness, compost the clippings briefly or combine them with fluffier materials such as compost or wood chips. Also be careful of your source and make sure the lawn that yielded the clippings wasn't treated with herbicides that can harm your garden plants. If you're not sure, play it safe and compost the clippings before applying them to the garden.

Unshredded leaves soon compact into a sodden mass in the garden after a few waterings. Shred them before applying or mix whole leaves with straw or wood chips to lighten their texture.

Fresh manure should never be used as a mulch, as it will burn your plants. Use only well-composted manure and be aware that with prolonged use, excess salts can build up and hordes of weed seeds will be introduced to the garden.

Newspaper is another readily available mulching material. Be sure to use only the black-and-white pages, not the Sunday comics or the coated glossy paper that is used in magazines and newspaper supplements. As the latter types of paper break down, they release substances that are harmful to soil microorganisms. Newspaper is a nitrogen robber, so add blood meal or another good source of nitrogen to your garden before mulching with newspaper.

Peat moss makes a very agreeable mulch—until you let it dry out. In its dry state, it is easily carried off by the wind and is almost impossible to remoisten, as the water will just run off the surface. Before spreading peat moss, give it a good soaking in its bag and let it sit overnight. During the growing season keep the garden well watered so that the mulch doesn't have a chance to dry out.

You may have a bountiful supply of sunflower seed hulls, but it would be a big mistake to use them in your garden. These hulls contain a chemical that will leach out into the soil and stunt or even kill growing plants.

Besides organic mulches, many gardeners use black, clear or white plastic, or other reflective mulches in combination with row covers. Black plastic raises the soil temperature about 10°F and also acts as an effective weed-control device. For the greatest temperature increase, use clear plastic. This mulch will not control weeds, however, and you must be careful that the soil doesn't get too hot. White or silver-colored mulches are handy in the South, where cooling the soil may be necessary. These reflective surfaces also help deter pests such as aphids, leaf miners, and thrips. Since these pests often spread viruses and fungal diseases, controlling the pests also will help control the diseases.

When mulching, be aware of the following problems:
• Don't jump the gun and mulch with organic material too early, or the soil will stay cool long into the season, delaying the planting of heat-loving crops such

as eggplants and peppers. Wait until the soil temperature reaches 78°F when you measure it 3 to 4 inches below the surface.

- Never mulch dry soil; water will have a hard time penetrating the layer of mulch to reach the soil. Wait for a rainfall or give the garden a thorough soaking before you apply the mulch.
- If you use a dense mulch, keep it a few inches away from the bases of your plants to avoid fungus problems.
- Mulching may encourage slugs in wet climates. You can control them by placing a board or plank on the path during the night and lifting it up in the morning. Many slugs will have taken refuge there, and you can pick them off and remove them permanently from your garden.

Row Covers

Row covers are a tremendous help to gardeners limited by a short growing season and to those who want to get a head start on growing heat-loving vegetables. Transplants grown with a combination of row covers and plastic mulch yield much earlier than those grown without these aids, and often the total yield is much greater. For example, total yields of cucumbers and melons often increase by 30 percent or more. But row covers aren't just for altering the microclimate around your plants. They also can be used to protect crops from hungry cucumber beetles, flea beetles, and other chewing pests that can spread diseases.

Row covers come in three different forms: clear plastic, fabric, and polypropylene. Since the temperature can soar under clear plastic covers, most have tiny holes or slits to let the air circulate and decrease the temperature on hot days. Even so, these covers work best if removed on clear, warm days and

Row Covers: Row covers allow gardeners to extend the season at both ends by helping protect plants from extremes of weather. They also are useful for warming heat-loving plants such as peppers in cooler climates. When plants are small, the covers can be left with slack (right) to give the plants room to grow.

replaced at night. The temperature under such slitted clear plastic film can increase as much as 23°F on a sunny day! These covers also must be supported with wire hoops to prevent burning of the growing tips of the plants.

Because of such problems, most gardeners use fabric or polypropylene row covers. In addition, these covers are so light that they float on the growing tips of the crops. Be aware, however, that the growing tips of peppers and tomatoes can't take even the pressure of these light-weight materials, so any type of row covers for these crops should be held up by hoops.

Row covers come in varying weights and porosity. The heavier, less porous ones provide more frost protection (they maintain a temperature 2°F to 10°F higher than the outside air) but tend to overheat. The lighter, more porous varieties often are used to protect against insects. Since the row covers must be securely anchored by soil, so that no insects can get to the plants, these covers must allow good air circulation, or the plants will get too hot. You might have to try several types of covers before you find one that suits your needs, or you might want to start out with a heavier cover in the spring and replace it with a lighter one when the weather starts to heat up.

Allow plenty of growing room under the row covers, or they can damage the plants and slow their growth. If you are using the covers for insect control, place 2 inches of soil along the edge and leave any excess material in a fold down the middle of the row. If you are not concerned with insects, remove the covers when temperatures get into the 90s.

Proper use of row covers can increase yields, but if they are left on in hot weather, they can decrease yields. For example, beans and tomatoes will drop their blossoms when the temperature gets too high, and although the plants will look fine, you won't get much of a crop. We give more information on using row covers in the chapters dealing with specific crops.

Soil Solarization

If you are having trouble with weeds or are finding that your plants are plagued by a particular disease, you might want to give the affected part of your garden a rest for the season and try soil solarization. This simple technique consists of moistening the soil and covering it with a clear sheet of plastic. It is important to minimize the air space between the ground and the plastic to keep the temperature as high as possible. Leave the plastic on for one to two months during the hottest time of the summer. The temperature under the plastic soars, killing harmful fungi such as club root, damping-off fungi, fusarium wilt, verticillium wilt, and some disease-causing nematodes. Even when soil diseases are not present, soil solarization can increase yields. Some scientists feel that the heat causes a shift in the soil microorganism community to more beneficial fungi, such as mycorrhizae, that are not killed by the heat.

There's nothing worse than watching your gardening efforts undermined by the dark forces of nature—encroaching lawns, tree roots, and rhizomatous weeds. Here are some tips on how to defeat these perpetrators.

When you carve a garden out of an area that was formerly a lawn, you're setting the stage for fierce competition between the roots of your crops and the grass roots that remain along the edge of the garden. Grasses are among the most sapping of plants, and you may notice that the garden plants close to the grassy border are smaller and feebler than plants growing toward the center of the garden plot. Even if several inches of bare dirt separate the edge of the lawn and the first garden row, the grass roots are wending their way underground toward your crops. You can resign yourself to the fact that the plants on the outskirts of your garden won't be as vigorous, or you can dig up a sort of no man's land, a 12-inch band in which you replace the sod with mulch. This area can serve as a neat-looking path that runs around the garden and will protect your garden plants from the grass roots.

Tree roots are another garden nemesis that can wreak havoc with growing plants. These tenacious subterranean venturers ramble far and wide to pull in enough nutrients and water to fuel the tree's growth. Most gardening guides recommend that you locate your garden outside the drip line (the circular area on the ground that corresponds to the area covered by the farthest-reaching branches, where most of the tree roots are concentrated). That way you can avoid most of the interference from roots, and your garden won't be drained of water and nutrients. But trees that sprout from the roots, such as aspens, poplars, and willows, send their roots 15 to 20 feet beyond the drip line, where they lie very close to the surface. If you must share your gardening area with such trees, you will be supporting two crops—your food plants and your trees! With this in mind, you will have to water more often, give midseason supplementary feedings, and increase the level of organic material in the soil.

Rhizomatous weeds such as Canadian thistle, morning glory, and quack grass are the bane of many a gardener's existence. It often seems that no matter how hard you try to get rid of them, they regroup and come back twice as strong. Your best plan of attack is hand-to-hand combat. You must pull them up by the roots and try to extricate the entire underground rhizome system by which they multiply. If you leave even a tiny piece of one rhizome in the ground, the weeds will grow with renewed vigor. A friend of Diane's learned this the hard way when she had her garden rototilled. She did not remove the quack grass prior to tilling and was appalled afterward by the almost overwhelming increase in the weed population. The rototiller had just chopped up the rhizomes and distributed them all over her garden, making the problem much worse than it had been before.

Dealing with Persistent Nuisances

Chapter 5

Lettuce and Spinach: Abundant Garden Greens

Lettuce and spinach are especially satisfying crops to grow, for they can supply that eagerly awaited first taste of fresh greenery in the spring. Both grow rapidly and easily in the home garden, and the quality of the homegrown product is far superior to what you can buy in the supermarket. Both lettuce and spinach can even be overwintered in many areas for an extra-early spring crop, long before most other vegetables are even in the ground. A good stand of lettuce or spinach can put the gardener in the enviable position of having to enlist friends and neighbors to help eat up the harvest. Not everyone ends up with an excess of greens, however, for some gardeners have trouble growing these tasty crops. All that's needed is an understanding of their biological clocks for anyone to succeed with these leafy greens—even in problem areas.

Lettuce is an ancient crop. We know it was grown by the Egyptians sixty-five hundred years ago, for drawings of romaine-type lettuce appear on the walls of Egyptian tombs. By the time of the Greeks, there were at least three types of lettuce. Spinach was tamed at a much later date. Spinach comes from southwestern Asia and wasn't familiar to Europeans until after Roman times. While lettuce and spinach belong to two different plant families, they are alike in so many ways that they must have lived under very similar conditions in the wild.

Lettuce (*Lactuca sativa*) belongs to the sunflower family (Compositae). This is one of the largest plant families and includes other familiar plants such as chrysanthemums, dandelions, goldenrod, and salsify. The genus name, *Lactuca*, means

---

VITAL STATISTICS

Family:
Compsitae—lettuce
Chenopodiaceae—spinach

Species: *Lactuca sativa*—lettuce
Spinacia oleracea—spinach

Soil: Very rich organic soil, heavy or light

pH: Lettuce—5.8 to 7; 6.5 to 7 optimum
Spinach—6 to 6.5

Soil temperature for germination: Lettuce—35°F to 80°F
Spinach—35°F to 75°F
For both crops, germination rates decrease at higher temperatures

Air temperature for best growth: Lettuce—73°F daytime; 45°F nighttime
Spinach—60°F to 65°F daytime; 40°F to 45°F nighttime

Seed viability:
Lettuce—1 to 6 years; generally 2 to 3 years
Spinach—3 years

Seed germination:
Lettuce—3 to 7 days
Spinach—6 to 12 days

Seed planting depth:
Lettuce—from ¼ inch to top of soil
Spinach—½ inch

"latex" in Latin and refers to the milky, bitter white sap produced by special cells in lettuce plants. This is the liquid you see oozing from the stem when you cut or pick large leaves of leaf lettuce. Some species of *Lactuca* are always bitter. Cultivated lettuces usually produce the bitter chemical only when they become overmature or bolt, although some varieties become bitter in response to hot weather.

Spinach (*Spinacia oleracea*) belongs to the goosefoot family (Chenopodiaceae). Several other edible plants also are members of this family, such as beets, Swiss chard, and that tasty, wild spinachlike plant, lamb's-quarters.

Both these greens deserve their reputation as healthy, low-calorie foods. Spinach is especially rich in vitamin A. It also contains large amounts of vitamin C and thiamine. While spinach is often thought of as a good source of iron, there is controversy about how available the iron actually is to your body. Lettuce also has few calories but is not as rich in vitamins as spinach. Different types of lettuce vary considerably in vitamin content (see the box "Lettuce Nutrition"). Homegrown leafy greens are far superior to store-bought ones. Diane's kids love to go out to the garden and pick fresh leaves for a snack. People aren't the only ones that love greens. During the early spring and late fall, Diane's family must compete with the deer for these crops. If they decide to be selfish and not share, they erect a tent of chicken wire over the greens to keep the deer away.

The Best Soil for Growing Greens

The title of an article in the February 1978 issue of *Organic Gardening* magazine summarizes the key to successful spinach (and lettuce) growing: "And Now a Word from the Spinach King: Manure!" It tells of a gardener, Glenn Munson, who ordered manure to spread on his garden. But the mucky ground entrapped first the manure spreader and then the rototiller. Munson finally gave up trying to spread the manure and just scattered spinach seeds over the area, even though there was a higher concentration of fresh manure in the top soil layer than he would have liked. He didn't expect much of a harvest, but as the season progressed, he started to feel like the accidental hero of *Jack and the Beanstalk*. He ended up with his best spinach crop ever! The plants grew quickly, producing lots of tender leaves that gave him repeated pickings.

Most garden crops would have expired in such nitrogen-rich, salty soil, but both lettuce and spinach tolerate mineral salts, and both require abundant nitrogen for the rapid growth that gives a tender, early harvest. Lettuce isn't quite as salt tolerant as spinach and won't germinate well in very salty soil. If you consistently have trouble germinating lettuce seeds in your garden even when the conditions seem appropriate, salty soil may be the culprit. Gardeners in regions with salty soil should try starting seeds in prepared potting mix and transplanting lettuce seedlings into the garden instead. The transplants should do just fine as long as

LETTUCE NUTRITION

Just because they're all green doesn't mean that different types of lettuce contain the same amounts of vitamins and minerals. To highlight their differences and show you how they compare nutritionally,* we have broken down the four major nutrients per 100-gram serving of the four main lettuce types.

	Vitamin A	Vitamin C	Calcium	Iron
Butterhead	970 IU†	8 mg‡	35 mg	2.0 mg
Crisphead	330 IU	6 mg	20 mg	0.5 mg
Looseleaf	1,900 IU	18 mg	68 mg	1.4 mg
Romaine	1,900 IU	18 mg	68 mg	1.4 mg

* Daily Requirements:	Vitamin A	5,000 IU	† International units
	Vitamin C	60 mg	‡ Milligrams
	Calcium	800 mg (25 and over)	
	Calcium	1,200 mg (under 25)	
	Iron	300 mg	

you haven't chosen a salt-sensitive variety such as 'Bibb,' 'Grand Rapids,' 'Prizehead,' 'Red Salad Bowl,' or 'Ruby.'

Because of their relative salt tolerance and need for abundant nitrogen, lettuce and spinach are ideal crops to grow in an area that you might have over-manured. But if your garden is low in nitrogen, work manure into your lettuce and spinach beds before planting to avoid a disappointing harvest. If you use well-rotted manure, such as the kind you can buy in bags, be sure to add plenty to the soil (1½ pounds per square foot).

Potassium is another important nutrient for lettuce and spinach, for it speeds their growth, enabling them to mature while the weather is still cool and days are short. On the cellular level, potassium regulates the opening and closing of stomata as well as the rate of water retention. In this way it controls how rapidly photosynthesis takes place. When you make sure there is plenty of potassium available to these leafy crops, you're ensuring that they'll grow quickly and retain enough water to fill out the crisp, fleshy leaves. Two good sources of potassium are granite dust and wood ashes. Just remember that wood ashes are faster acting than granite dust, so they are effective when used close to planting time. Granite dust should be applied the fall before spring planting to give the nutrients time to break down. If your soil is acid, the wood ashes will sweeten it, but be careful not to get the soil too alkaline; lettuce likes soil between pH 6 and 7, while spinach prefers pH 6 to 6.5. Peat moss or pine needles will lower the pH if it gets too high.

Both lettuce and spinach have fibrous root systems that are not especially deep; most of their roots grow in the first foot of soil. For this reason, both crops need plenty of water throughout the growing season. Lettuce roots are not as efficient at nutrient uptake as those of some other garden plants, which is one reason why

THE LOWDOWN ON SALTY SOIL

Soil is salty when it contains an excess of calcium, magnesium, or sodium ions. Organic gardeners usually encounter salty soils with excess sodium ions. Salty soils are mainly a problem of dry areas, especially in the arid West. Rain tends to wash salt deep into the soil, but if there isn't enough rain, the salt stays near the surface where plants grow. Salty irrigation water can compound the problem by adding still more salt to the upper soil layers.

Manure is a chief culprit in adding salt to soil. Poultry manure contains more salt than do other types because the excretory wastes from the kidneys of birds are mixed with the digestive wastes from their intestines, creating an especially salty blend. Steer manure from feedlots where cattle are confined to a small area also can be very salty because it contains urine as well as manure. These types of manure should be applied in moderation.

Scientists can measure the soil's sodium content by passing an electric current through it to see how well the current is conducted. The more salt in the soil, the better the current will pass through it. Unfortunately, the equipment used in this test is so expensive that it's virtually inaccessible to home gardeners. But don't despair; if you suspect that your soil has too much salt, there are affordable ways to check it. Contact your county extension agent or local soil-testing laboratory about having a soil sample analyzed.

Why is salty soil so harmful to your plants? Excess salt hampers growth in several ways and can lead to the untimely demise of your plants. Plants have a hard time coping with excess salt because it interferes with their ability to take up water. In addition, since sodium ions are water soluble, they eventually end up inside the plant, carried along with the water the plant absorbs. If massive amounts of sodium build up in a plant's tissues, they can kill it.

Plants do, however, have ways of coping with the influx of sodium. Plant cells contain systems called sodium pumps that do just what their name suggests: they remove sodium from the cells. One kind of pump deposits sodium ions outside the cell; the other kind pumps it into the large central vacuole (which functions as a sort of garbage dump) inside the cell. These sodium pumps require energy to do their job, so they deprive the plant of energy it could use for growth and crop production. And there is a limit to how much sodium the cells eliminate depending on the salt tolerance of the species.

Some plants have very efficient sodium pumps and can tolerate a fair amount of sodium in the soil. Garden crops in this category include beets, broccoli, lettuce, spinach, and tomatoes. Other plants are very sensitive to sodium and will grow poorly in even weakly salty soils. Beans, carrots, onions, and radishes all have a low salt tolerance. If you've accidentally overmanured your soil or the salt level has risen for some other reason, try growing the more tolerant vegetables until the salt level has decreased. Watering heavily can help leach the salts out of the growing range of the roots.

lettuce requires such rich soil to grow well. Young lettuce rootlets are the most efficient part of the root system at calcium uptake. Head lettuce stops producing these rootlets about two weeks before the plants mature, however, so many varieties of head lettuce are susceptible to calcium deficiency, resulting in burnt-looking leaf tips.

Nighttime temperatures above 65°F and high humidity also help encourage tip burn, as head lettuce can have the same problems of mineral transport to the inner leaves as cabbage (see chapter 6). Some types of lettuce, such as 'Imperial' and 'New York', are more susceptible to tip burn than resistant varieties such as 'Great Lakes.' The best preventive measure you can take is to make sure your soil has enough calcium to begin with; bone meal is a reliable source. Succulent, young growth is most susceptible to tip burn, so don't give your plants an extra shot of nitrogen fertilizer late in the season when they have few of the young rootlets that absorb calcium. Also, try to keep the soil uniformly moist. If it's too late for preventive measures and you see your plant's leaves starting to get brown at the tips, you can slip a paper bag over the plant, as described for cabbage, and with luck halt the browning process. Diane hasn't had any tip burn since she started growing lettuce under row covers. Although tip burn is a concern with lettuce, spinach does not have this problem.

The Best Conditions for Seed Germination

Lettuce and spinach may be among the easiest and quickest crops to grow, but if you don't provide them with the proper conditions from the moment you plant the seeds, you're setting yourself up for a disappointing harvest. Both lettuce and spinach seeds will germinate over a wide temperature range (35°F to 75°F for spinach; 35°F to 80°F for lettuce), but the germination rate falls off dramatically at the higher temperatures. At 70°F only 50 percent of spinach seeds will germinate; lettuce does the same thing at 80°F. Such high temperatures induce dormancy in the seeds, which makes sense from the plant's point of view. The seeds have a built-in detector that allows them to germinate for the most part when conditions for their survival will be best. Thus the seeds often won't germinate when the weather is warm because the plants would be faced with trying to grow in the summer heat.

The age of lettuce seeds is another influence on germination. Seeds taken from plants that have just flowered often will not germinate under *any* conditions for a couple of months or more. This also is a natural protective measure. It ensures that the growing season after germination will be long enough so that the new plant will have time to flower and produce seeds of its own. If lettuce seeds germinated in the early fall, the new plants probably would not have time to flower and set seed in the few weeks remaining before frost set in.

If you want to grow a fall crop of lettuce or spinach, you can fool the seeds into germinating. During hot summer days the easiest way is to start the seeds in pots indoors if your house is air-conditioned or place the pots in a cool basement. You also can plant them outside and mulch them lightly, watering them with cold water every afternoon. The purpose of these cool baths is to keep the soil temperature down; in hot weather there's little chance that you'll oversaturate the soil, since it tends to dry out quickly. This method will work if your area has hot days but cool (50°F to 65°F) nights that will help keep the soil temperature low.

If you have warm nights or don't want to be bothered with watering the seeds every afternoon to keep them cool, try pregerminating them on moist paper towels. Slip the moistened, seed-laden towels into plastic bags and set them in the refrigerator for three to five days before planting. After five days germination will have begun within the seed coat, causing the seeds to swell a little, but the root won't have broken out yet. You can even plant these seeds in 90°F soil. They will complete germination with no trouble because the cool, moist pretreatment released the seeds from their dormancy.

Spinach seeds can be planted ½ inch deep, but lettuce seeds should be placed no deeper than ¼ inch deep. Some lettuce varieties require light to germinate. If the seeds are too deep, light will not reach them, and they won't germinate. Other lettuce types will germinate in darkness, but they will come up more quickly if given light. For these reasons it is always best to cover lettuce seeds only lightly with soil.

In addition to light, lettuce seeds need plenty of moisture to germinate properly. An easy way to keep lettuce seeds moist and yet expose them to some light is to sow them right on the soil's surface and then cover them with a mulch of grass clippings. A thin scattering of grass is best, but if it is very sunny and dry, you can make the layer as deep as 1 inch.

Starting Seeds Indoors

Both lettuce and spinach can be started indoors to get a jump on the growing season. But since they can be planted outside so early, it is usually easier just to start them directly in the garden. If you are determined to get a head start, plant two to three seeds each in small pots at the proper planting depth. When the seedlings have developed two true leaves, thin to one seedling per pot.

It's important to remember that lettuce and spinach require cool daytime temperatures for good growth. They also need strong light, so a cold frame is their best early home. Warm temperatures or low light will slow their growth. When this happens, lettuce will turn bitter, and spinach won't produce large leaves when planted in the garden. If you have a cold frame or protected area outside where you can put the plants during the day, you will be able to harvest lettuce and spinach two to four weeks earlier than if you'd planted directly outdoors. This lead time could make all the difference to gardeners who live in areas with hot summers that come on early or who want to harvest a good crop of spinach before long days make the plants bolt. Just remember, when you transplant them into the garden, place them at the same depth as they grew in the pots, or they will rot. After Diane transplants them into the garden, she uses row covers to keep them growing vigorously.

In very rich soil spinach plants can be set 4 to 6 inches apart in the row. Over-crowded spinach will produce small plants with only a few large leaves. Loose-leaf lettuce needs to be at least 8 inches apart, while head lettuce should be spaced about 1 foot apart to allow plenty of room for proper heading. The inefficient roots of crowded head lettuce plants aren't able to absorb enough nutrients if they are competing with one another. Very crowded plants won't head up at all. When red lettuce plants are crowded, they won't color well, for their energy will go into growing, with little left over for production of their attractive red pigment. If you aren't using wide rows, spinach and compact lettuce varieties such as 'Deer Tongue' and 'Tom Thumb' can be grown in rows as close as 1 foot apart, while head and other large lettuce varieties require 2 feet between rows.

Because both crops depend on fast growth for success, it is imperative to keep lettuce and spinach well thinned and to keep the weeds down. Lettuce seeds are tiny, making it very easy to plant too thickly. If you do, you must thin right after the plants come up. Mixing sand in with seeds will help you sow it more thinly. Spinach seeds are larger and easier to handle, so you have better control over the spacing. Even so, you may want to plant more closely than the final 4- to 6-inch spacing and thin the rows as soon as the plants have developed two true leaves. The thinnings are a special treat to eat in salads, barely steamed and served with a little butter, or blended with chicken broth and canned tomatoes for a delicately flavored soup.

Some Tips on Growing Greens

Many gardeners have been disappointed by tiny spinach plants that bolt or lettuce leaves that become bitter before reaching their mature size. Both problems result from the response of the plants to day length, temperature, or a combination of the two. Both lettuce and spinach will bolt in response to days that are fourteen to sixteen hours long.

In the past, when breeders were developing new varieties, early-bolting plants were destroyed in an effort to select plants that would hold in good condition longer. However, lettuce seeds are now produced in a rather contrived way that doesn't allow for selection against early flowering. Young lettuce plants grown commercially for seeds are treated with gibberellic acid, a plant hormone that makes

The Effects of Day Length and Temperature

them flower while still small. This allows seed growers to protect against diseases such as lettuce mosaic virus (which is seed borne) and to harvest the seeds under controlled conditions (if a large lettuce seed stalk is hit by heavy rain or high wind, most of the seeds can be lost). But it means that the plants' natural tendency to bolt quickly or to hold their leaves in good condition is not apparent, and home growers have no way of knowing how likely their plants are to go to seed early.

In warm weather lettuce or spinach will respond faster to long days than if the weather is cool. Many gardeners think the hot weather itself makes these crops bolt, but the heat only accelerates the long-day response. The difference between lettuce and spinach is that spinach requires long days to bolt, while lettuce will flower with or without long days; they just make it bloom earlier than it otherwise would. Once lettuce is mature, it won't be long before it blooms, no matter what the environmental conditions. But if it is exposed to hot weather and long days, your lettuce will be doomed to a short, bitter life.

Lettuce and spinach are both so sensitive to long days that they should not be grown near yard lights or streetlights. Even though these artificial light sources are weak compared to the sun, they will fool the plants into responding as they would to long days. If you raise lettuce or spinach under artificial lights indoors for later planting outdoors, keep this in mind and don't give them more than twelve hours of light. You cannot compensate for weak light by giving them a longer day length.

Plants have ingenious ways of monitoring day length. Lettuce and spinach perceive light by way of a chemical, phytochrome, in their leaves. Phytochrome is activated by light and triggers a signal to move from the leaves to the apical

Spinach Bolting: When spinach begins to bolt the leaves become more spear shaped (left). Not long afterward the plants will be in full flower (right).

tip of the plant. When enough of the signal has been received by the apical tip, it starts to produce flower stalks and buds instead of just leaves. If you carefully pick the largest and oldest leaves of your spinach and leaf lettuce as the plants grow, you can delay bolting by reducing the flowering signal going to the apical tip.

Before we learned about this phenomenon, Diane always kept the older leaves on her spinach picked, while Dorothy left the biggest, dirtiest, toughest leaves in place, thinking that they would help the plants grow more quickly with their photosynthesis. Despite leaving those big leaves to help the plant grow, Dorothy's spinach always bolted disappointingly early. By keeping all the older leaves carefully picked, however, Diane was unwittingly removing the flowering signal and preventing its build-up in the apical tip. This helps account for her great success with spinach, even here in Montana, where long days come on fast and hot spells often hit erratically during the spring. Using this method, Diane has been able to keep harvesting tender, tasty spinach until the end of June or the beginning of July. If you want to extend your spinach harvest, be sure to pick the leaves faithfully every few days, gathering all that are large and fully expanded.

If you apply this method to lettuce, you can extend your harvest by only about a week, since the plants will bolt when mature under any conditions. In any case the older lettuce gets, the more bitter latex there is in the leaves, making it unpalatable even before it bolts. The exception to this rule is the looseleaf variety 'Green Ice,' which doesn't turn bitter until the flower stalk starts to elongate. As long as you keep the leaves picked, you can enjoy this variety for a few extra days.

You can tell when your spinach and looseleaf lettuce are about to bolt by watching the shape of their leaves. As the spinach plant prepares to bolt, its leaves change from a rounded to a pointed, arrowlike shape, and the internodes grow longer, making the leaves farther and farther apart. Lettuce leaves become narrower and smaller as the plant begins to bolt. Head lettuce develops a bulge at the top, signaling the emergence of the seed stalk—if it can break through the head.

Overwintering for Early Spring Greens

Both lettuce and spinach can be started four to six weeks before the first expected fall frost and overwintered in the garden for an especially early spring harvest. With a mild autumn, you can even get a significant harvest of leaves before the cold weather shuts down plant growth.

Spinach can take cold weather easily in stride when slowly acclimated. Even week-old seedlings can survive below-freezing temperatures, and unmulched plants of some varieties can tolerate 23°F. But in most parts of the country, spinach needs some protection to survive the winter. In our gardens properly mulched spinach has lived through −30°F nights.

To overwinter spinach, mulch the plants so that they are completely covered as soon as the ground has frozen. Dorothy favors unshredded leaves for a loose mulch that doesn't pack down on the plants under winter conditions. For over-wintering pick varieties such as 'Cold Resistant Savoy,' 'Giant Winter,' and 'Winter Bloomsdale,' which are specifically designed to be grown this way. The versatile variety 'Tyee' also is good for overwintering.

While spinach can survive winter in most parts of the country, lettuce is less hardy. Large plants with lots of succulent growth won't even survive freezing. Young lettuce, however, can take some frost. If you live where the climate is mild, you can overwinter lettuce by covering it with ventilated plastic or row covers or by growing it in a cold frame. To overwinter lettuce in the garden, cover it completely with mulch as soon as the average temperature drops to 40°F. Bitterness can be a problem with overwintered lettuce, so you should pick your varieties carefully. Some reliable varieties for overwintering are 'Arctic King,' 'Oak Leaf,' 'Prizehead,' 'Winter Density,' and a new variety called 'Valdor.'

If you live in a part of the country with hot summers and mild winters, you'll have the most success with lettuce and spinach if you grow them during the winter. Where there's a chance of occasional winter frosts, be prepared to protect large lettuce plants with blankets, plastic sheets, or row covers to prevent frost damage. Once lettuce has been nipped by frost, the leaves rot easily, and you will have a hard time keeping the plants alive.

Lettuce Varieties

Lettuce comes in a dizzying number of varieties, many of which have become available in the past ten years. The selection of looseleaf lettuces has widened to many colors and textures. It is probably the most popular for home gardens, for the leaves are especially tender and can be harvested at any time. This type of lettuce doesn't form a head; in its place a rosette of leaves unfolds, with new ones constantly developing in the middle. Looseleaf lettuce matures more rapidly than other types, producing big plants within forty to fifty days of planting. Looseleaf varieties are among the hardiest and most heat-tolerant lettuces. 'Garnet,' a red-tipped lettuce, has a crisp texture, while 'Biondo Lisce' is tender. The new dark red leaf lettuces such as 'Red Sails' and 'Red Salad Bowl' add a lovely accent to summer salads.

Much progress in developing new varieties of head lettuce also has been made. Head lettuce used to be difficult to grow in home gardens. For example, 'Great Lakes,' the old standby head lettuce, is prone to bitterness. Now some of the varieties that commercial growers raise are available to home gardeners. 'Ithaca,' which was developed for the eastern United States, is resistant to bolting and will grow even in hot temperatures. Here in Montana 'Ithaca' produced sweet, succulent heads one summer after three weeks with daytime temperatures in the 90s. 'Salinas,' also called 'Saladin,' is another fine variety developed for the cooler conditions found along the Pacific coast. 'Mission' is heat resistant and matures in only seventy-four days. 'Vanguard' is a large, dark green crisphead that is so tolerant of heat that it can grow successfully in desert areas. It also is resistant to tip burn. Still, head lettuce is more sensitive to growing conditions and tip burn than leaf lettuce. It needs especially fertile soil and consistent watering.

Butterhead, or Boston, lettuce forms a loose head with dark green outer leaves and cream-colored inner leaves. Butterheads deserve their name, for these varieties produce especially tender, fragile leaves that almost melt in your mouth. Butterheads take sixty to seventy-five days to form heads, but you don't have to wait that long to harvest; you can always steal a few individual outer leaves from the plants as they grow. A nice selection of butterheads is available, from the standard 'Buttercrunch' to tiny 'Tom Thumb' and the red-tinged 'Pirat.'

Romaine, or cos, lettuce forms a loose head of upright, crisp leaves with a thick, juicy middle rib. This is the traditional type used for a Caesar salad. It takes about seventy days for most romaine varieties to mature. 'Parris Island Cos' is a standard romaine type. 'Winter Density' is not only good for overwintering, but it also will thrive when planted in the spring or early fall.

In recent years, a new type of lettuce has come to the United States from Europe. These continental varieties are crisp like iceberg or romaine but also sweet and juicy. The plants start out like a looseleaf variety but mature into more compact heads. They are bolt resistant as well. 'Canasta' is a red-tinged French type that is resistant to tip burn and can be grown from spring through fall. 'Anuenue' looks similar to an iceberg lettuce when mature but is more heat resistant and not as tricky to grow.

Here are some tips for choosing the right lettuces for your garden. Order from catalogs that give you specific information about the conditions under which each variety grows best. Decide when you want to grow lettuce and choose accordingly. For example, 'Bibb' will grow well during cool spring weather, but if you want to have butterhead lettuce into the summer, you're much better off planting the heat-tolerant variety 'Buttercrunch.' For fall butterhead lettuce French varieties such as 'Brune d'Hiver' are a good choice. The same differences exist among the other lettuce types, and a good catalog will steer you in the right direction.

If your soil is really salty, choose an especially resistant variety such as 'Climax,' 'Parris Island Cos,' or 'Wintergreen.' If you get hot weather early, avoid varieties that bolt easily, such as 'Black Seeded Simpson,' 'Red Salad Bowl,' and 'Ruby.' Choose instead a resistant variety such as 'Prizehead' or 'Salad Bowl.'

Growing and Saving Your Own Lettuce Seeds

Saving seeds from looseleaf, butterhead, or romaine lettuce is a snap. Before we tell you how to do it, we'll fill you in on a little lettuce flower biology. If you let a lettuce plant go to seed, it will send up a very long stem with many flowering branches. The flowers resemble dandelions, only smaller. Each "flower" is actually made up of many tiny flowers, and what look like the petals are actually bracts, which are more akin to leaves. The petal-like bracts surround a cluster of true flowers, called florets. Each group of bracts encircles ten to twenty florets, each with one tiny, thin petal. The anthers of the floret are fused into a tube through which the stigma must grow when the floret opens. Since the pollen is released from the anthers as the stigma grows through, most lettuce is self-pollinating. For this reason, if you want to save seeds from a nonhybrid variety of lettuce, you needn't isolate it from other varieties.

To save seed from looseleaf, butterhead, or romaine lettuce, just let a plant or two go to seed and keep an eye on the stalk as the flowers fade. When the seed head begins to dry, bend it over a paper bag and shake it so that the seeds fall into the bag. All the seeds do not ripen at the same time, so you should shake the seeds off every other day or so over a seven- to ten-day period. Separate the good seeds from the debris by pouring the contents of the bag from one container to another in a slight breeze or in front of a fan. The air current will whisk away the light debris, leaving you with the seeds.

Store the seeds in a cool, dry place. Remember that if you want to use seeds that are less than two to three months old, you will have to put them in the refrigerator for several days to break their dormancy.

If you want to collect seeds from head lettuce, let the head mature and then incise the top with a cross design about 3 inches deep. This will allow the seed stalk to break out of the wrapper leaves and emerge from the top of the head.

Collecting Lettuce Seeds: To collect seeds from looseleaf, butterhead, and romaine lettuce, bend the mature seed head over a paper bag and shake the head gently to release the seeds into the bag. For head lettuce make a cross-shaped cut in the top of the head so the developing seed stalk can make an easy exit.

If you don't make the cuts, the seed stalk is not likely to get out and will grow around in circles inside the head.

It is strange that, despite their other similarities, lettuce and spinach are so different in their pollination strategies. While lettuce is almost always self-pollinating, spinach is almost always cross-pollinating. We say almost always because occasionally a spinach plant will have both male and female flowers. Such a plant can self-pollinate.

Spinach Varieties

Spinach varieties vary widely in how quickly they respond to hot weather and long days, how tolerant of cold they are, and how long they take to reach maturity, so read catalog descriptions carefully to match your crop to your climate. Varieties that are slow to bolt are best for spring or early summer harvests, while cold-tolerant varieties do best for overwintering. While some spinach varieties have smooth leaves, most have deeply crinkled, savoyed leaves. The savoyed leaves are the result of slow growth of the leaf veins compared to the rest of the leaf. A deeply savoyed leaf has more surface area than a leaf that isn't savoyed if the two are the same size. This means that savoyed varieties produce more food per unit of space in the garden. A disadvantage of savoyed leaves is that they can hold dirt in the wrinkles and take more effort to clean. If you grow savoyed spinach, mulch it carefully from the time the plants are small to keep the leaves free of grit and mud splatters.

'Hybrid No. 7' is a popular, fast-growing spinach for early spring planting. This variety also is good for fall planting in mild climates. Since it bolts easily in warm temperatures, be sure to plant it early in the spring or after the hot weather is over in the fall. 'Melody Hybrid' is another good, fast-growing spinach suited to the same conditions as 'Hybrid No. 7,' but it is slower to bolt. 'Hybrid No. 7' holds its leaves higher off the ground than 'Melody,' so it stays cleaner. When Diane grew these two side by side, she thought that 'Hybrid No. 7' was producing better because more leaves were visible. But when she harvested a test patch, she found that both produced equally well.

'America' is a good variety to grow when the weather gets warm, while 'Winter Bloomsdale' is good for overwintering. The newer variety 'Tyee' is one of the best spinaches yet developed. It grows quickly and is resistant to bolting. Like 'Hybrid No. 7,' 'Tyee' grows upright, producing cleaner leaves. 'Tyee' can be grown in spring, summer, fall, or winter, so if you don't want to be bothered with different varieties for each season, 'Tyee' is perfect for you. Diane did find, however, that 'Tyee' didn't grow well when temperatures were low one spring (the average daily highs were in the 50s).

Gardeners in the Southwest should keep an eye out for a new variety, 'Fall Green,' developed at the Arkansas Agricultural Experimental Station. 'Fall Green' is resistant to many diseases and is winter hardy in Arkansas. It is suitable only for fall planting.

Saving Spinach Seeds

Unlike most garden crops, spinach has separate male and female plants. Commercially produced spinach seeds will give you mostly female plants; seed companies select for them because they bolt a few days later than male seeds. If you want to save spinach seeds, you will have to let a patch flower to ensure that some pollen-bearing male plants are included. The wind will carry pollen from the males to the females.

Since spinach flowers are wind pollinated and need not attract insects, they are quite inconspicuous. The petals are greenish brown, and the flowers are borne on long stems that grow up from the center of the plant. It is difficult to tell the sexes apart until they set seed; only female plants will provide you with seeds. Once your plants have bolted and the flowers have dried up and turned brown, just gather the seeds from the elongated stalks, clean away the debris, and store the seeds in a cool, dry place.

Lettuce and Spinach Problems

Spinach is rarely bothered by pests and diseases. Like other cool-weather crops, however, it can suffer from downy mildew. If this is a problem in your garden, choose resistant varieties such as 'Dixie Savoy,' 'Hybrid No. 7,' 'Melody Hybrid,' or 'Tyee.'

In addition to tip burn, which we've already discussed, a few other diseases and pests may attack your lettuce. Lettuce rot first appears as a rotting of the lowest leaves, then spreads through the rest of the plant. Moist conditions foster this disease, so one preventive measure is to hill up the rows to encourage drainage. Downy mildew and mosaic virus plague lettuce, but you can avoid them by using row covers with the edges covered by soil (see chapter 4). If these diseases are a problem year after year, try to rotate your lettuce crop, never planting it in the same spot two years in a row.

Smog also can damage lettuce. The oxidants in smog, such as ozone and nitrates, can damage the outer leaves. If this happens to your plants, don't throw out the heads; the inner leaves still make fine eating. Boston is susceptible to ozone, while romaine and 'Black Seeded Simpson' are somewhat resistant. 'Prizehead' is resistant to ozone and at least one damaging nitrate. In addition to damaging the outer leaves, ozone can delay heading of lettuce.

Cutworms and slugs will nibble on the succulent shoots of your plants if you let them. To deter cutworm attacks, place a loose cardboard collar around each plant as it germinates or when transplants are set out. You can keep slugs at bay by putting a thick ring of coarse sand, sawdust, or wood ashes around each plant; the coarse material will damage the slugs' soft underbellies.

Breeders of both lettuce and spinach are continuing to search for varieties that are more resistant to bolting and to develop more hybrids that give a uniform crop. Varieties resistant to fungal and viral diseases are another research goal. Because lettuce is an important crop in smoggy Southern California, many researchers are studying the effects of air pollution and acidic fog on lettuce and are developing resistant varieties. Lettuce is likely to be a premier space crop as well, grown in spaceships to feed the crews on their long journeys. Lettuce is ideal for this use, as it produces quickly, is mostly edible, and provides plenty of fiber, minerals, and vitamins.

Wild lettuce species have been used to improve cultivated lettuces. 'Calmar' and 'Valverde' have had genes for downy mildew resistance introduced from a species of wild lettuce, while 'Vanguard' is a cross between *Lactuca sativa* and a wild lettuce. The wild lettuce genes help give 'Vanguard' its dark green color and crisp texture.

Lettuce and Spinach Frontiers

Chapter 6

The Versatile Cabbage Family

VITAL STATISTICS

Family: Cruciferae

Species: *Brassica oleracea*

Soil: Slightly heavy loam that retains moisture

pH: 6.0 to 7.5 for all crops except cauliflower, which prefers 6.5 to 7.0

Soil temperature for germination: 45°F to 85°F for all crops except cauliflower, which needs a minimum of 55°F

Air temperature for best growth: 60°F to 65°F optimum

Seed viability: 3 to 4 years

Seed germination: 4 to 20 days

Seed planting depth: ½ inch

All of the crops assembled under the name *Brassica oleracea* provide perhaps the best examples in the plant kingdom of how people can influence the genetics of living things to fit their own needs. There are many examples of this in the animal kingdom. The dachshund, with its short legs and long body perfectly adapted to pursuing badgers down holes, and the greyhound, sleek, racy, and fast as the wind, are descendants of the same wild ancestors. People simply stepped in and started selecting traits that they wanted, directing the breeding to arrive at two different dogs.

In the same fashion we have influenced the genes of one plant species, *Brassica oleracea*, to provide us with a great variety of crops. Over the course of hundreds of years we have selected brassicas for leaves growing tightly together to form a head, until we arrived at the vegetable we know as cabbage. We have encouraged certain plants to form a tasty, vitamin-rich, loose crown of leaves, resulting in the present day crops of kale and collards. We have induced the stems of other brassicas to swell into delicious crunchy bulbs, which became known as kohlrabi. We have persuaded the flower buds to grow into tender and tasty clumps of broccoli and cauliflower. And finally, when we managed to coerce the axillary buds into forming tiny, tender heads of their own, Brussels sprouts arrived on the scene.

The fact that all these tasty crops belong to the same botanical species means that they are able to cross-pollinate. (As a matter of convenience, all of these variations often are lumped together as "cabbage family," although they are not a family in the true botanical sense of the term. They are also known collectively as cole crops or cabbage crops, names we will use interchangeably throughout this chapter.) They are less closely related to other familiar garden crops in the same plant family, Cruciferae, such as mustard, radishes, and turnips.

All crucifers contain bitter chemicals called glucosinolates, but these have been tamed down to a palatable level in the cultivated varieties. They are still present, however, and give radishes their tang and mustard its zing. Certain types of cabbages contain varying amounts of these substances, which accounts for the subtle differences in flavor. Mild spring varieties possess less than the more robust-flavored fall storage types, while red cabbages with their mellow taste have the least.

Cole crops originated in the Mediterranean area, with kale probably the first type to be tamed some two thousand years ago. Next in line as a cultivated crop was heading cabbage. By the fifteenth century Europeans were already growing kohlrabi and cauliflower. Broccoli came along later and was raised almost exclusively in Italy, while Brussels sprouts were developed in Belgium in the mid-eighteenth century. Today these assorted crops are very popular in the Western world and occupy up to 30 percent of the agricultural land in European countries. Broccoli is still a favorite in Italy, as well as in the United States, while cabbage is especially favored in Eastern Europe.

As a group, the cole crops are a dieter's dream. They tend to be high in vitamins and very low in calories. For example, one stalk of cooked broccoli will give you more than your daily vitamin A requirement, nearly four times your vitamin C allotment, 33 percent of your required riboflavin, and 15 percent of your necessary vitamin B_6, all for 47 calories! Kale does an even better job than broccoli in providing you with certain vitamins. One cup cooked gives you a little more than twice your daily requirement of vitamins A and C. Of course, all these vegetables have an even higher vitamin count when eaten raw. All cole crops are packed with vitamin C, but as we'll learn later, *when* you harvest them and *how* you store them can have a considerable effect on their vitamin C content. Including cole crops frequently in your diet has been shown to decrease your risk of colon and other cancers. They also are a good source of fiber. For example, a ½-cup serving of broccoli provides 2.2 grams of fiber.

How Cole Crops Grow

If you've ever bought plants labeled "broccoli" at a nursery and ended up with cabbage, it's probably because all cole crops start out with a pair of heart-shaped seed leaves that look identical. As their true leaves begin to appear, you can start to detect some differences. Young cabbages have rounder leaves than baby broccoli, and kale seedlings tend to be a darker green than the others. With all of them, however, the first few leaves have longer petioles than later ones. With cabbage in particular, the progressively shorter petioles eventually lead to the formation of the head.

These cole crops have four distinct stages of growth. First comes the initial growth stage, when the plant sends stem and leaves above ground. Next, the outer leaves expand. During the third stage, the outer leaves develop into nutrient storage areas for the fourth and final stage, the development of the edible crop.

The third stage has a direct effect on the abundance of the harvest. Scientists have studied this stage extensively in cabbage, and their findings can almost certainly be extended to at least some other cole crops as well, since removal of the outer leaves will lead to small broccoli heads and buttoning cauliflower. During the third stage of growth, nitrogen, phosphorus, and potassium from the soil are stored within the outer leaves. As the cabbage head forms, these nutrients are shuttled quickly from the older, outer leaves into the phloem, which carries them to the newly forming leaves inside the head. Because the head forms so rapidly, the roots are unable to pump minerals fast enough to keep up with the expansion going on above ground. When scientists deprived cabbage plants of nitrogen during the second and third stages of growth, small heads resulted even though plenty of nitrogen was provided during the actual heading stage. There's a lesson in this for home gardeners: it is important to grow cole crops in a rich soil from the very beginning, or the crops will be puny. Even a dose of fast-acting fish emulsion given when the final crop is developing won't help.

Cole Crop Basics

While each of the cole crops has its own peculiarities, they do share some common traits. Whether it's a full head of cauliflower or a fat bulb of kohlrabi you're after, you need to master the fundamentals before you can expect a good crop. In most of North America, many cole crop varieties can be grown from seeds sown directly in the garden. But most gardeners are in the habit of starting their plants indoors and transplanting them out later, which involves tending them carefully and hardening them off in the interim.

Why go to all that trouble? The main reason is that cole crop seedlings offer an attractive feast for a great variety of insects, with hungry flea beetles being especially abundant early in the season at a time that coincides with peak seeding activity. We have both tried direct-seeding some cole crops in the spring, only to see the lovely, heart-shaped seed leaves transformed into fine green lace by flea beetles. Rarely do such chewed-up plants get beyond the seed-leaf stage; they just gradually disappear. If you've ever tried direct seeding and have been discouraged by an onslaught of flea beetles, try mixing some turnip seeds in with your cole crop seeds to act as a decoy crop. Flea beetles seem to prefer turnip leaves to those of cabbage. To compensate for losses due to hungry insects, plant three or four seeds in a group at the final spacing recommended for adult plants. When the seedlings have grown, thin each clump to leave the strongest plant. Starting cole crops indoors is safer, however, since four- to six-week-old transplants can take a little chewing and still grow into healthy, productive plants.

A good way to grow your own cole seedlings is to use the compact plastic six-packs popular with commercial nurseries. They take up little space but give your plants enough room to get off to a good start. Fill the depressions with a potting soil that's not overly rich in nitrogen. Too much nitrogen will promote spindly, top-heavy growth, which makes the seedlings hard to transplant properly. Plants raised on a high-nitrogen diet also turn out to be less hardy. Put two seeds into each compartment (or other individual containers), thinning to the strongest seedling after they begin to grow. For speedy germination, put the containers in a warm place, up to 85°F. As soon as the seeds have germinated, move them to a cooler place; cole crops germinate quickly in warm soil but do not grow very well in it. If possible, keep the air temperature no warmer than 68°F and no cooler than 45°F.

If you take the safe route and start your plants indoors, when it's time to transplant the seedlings, don't be disturbed if their long, thin taproots are slightly damaged. While most taproot plants are set back considerably if the root is injured during transplanting, this is not true for members of the cabbage family because their taproot eventually becomes a fibrous root system. Although the root system is fairly shallow, few roots grow in the first 2 inches of soil, so it is safe to cultivate cole crops lightly at any stage. For instance, cabbage roots can extend as far as 78 inches down, but 70 to 80 percent of the roots are concentrated in the top 8 to 12 inches of the soil.

The roots of cole crops seem to be less efficient than the roots of squash or tomatoes and need evenly moist soil to function at their best. Even though potatoes also have a fibrous root system, theirs is more efficient at water uptake, so they need less moisture than the cole crops. In the same garden the potatoes, squash, and tomatoes may be thriving while the cole crops are dying of thirst. Make sure the cole crops never get the chance to become water stressed. Diane has found that slightly water-stressed cole crops take on a light blue hue before they wilt, unlike well-watered plants, which are a dark green.

Cover the young transplants with row covers to speed growth in a cool growing season or for early harvests. Remove the covers when the temperature gets above 70°F to prevent bacterial rotting and overheating.

Seed-Saving Pointers

If you want to save seeds from your cole crops, you must do so carefully. As we mentioned before, all of them can cross-pollinate. As a further complication, each flower on a plant must be pollinated by pollen from a different plant.

Therefore, to get reliable seeds that will produce plants of the same type as the parents, you must have more than one plant of, say, broccoli in bloom at one time but no other cole crops flowering at that time. Any cole crops blooming within a quarter of a mile of yours are potential pollinators, so even pollen from your neighbors' gardens can spoil your seeds. When one cole crop pollinates another, their offspring can be weird indeed. When friends of ours went on vacation a few years ago, some purple cabbage that hadn't headed properly went to seed at the same time as the overwintered kale in their garden. The cabbage seed heads shattered before their return, and the next year, tall, leafy red monsters cropped up unexpectedly.

If you do save your own seeds, wait until they turn brown inside the yellowed pods before collecting them. Don't wait too long, though, or the pods may break and scatter the seeds on the ground. If you can't pay close attention, tie a square of cheesecloth over the seed head to catch the seeds in case the pods shatter. If the seeds are wet when harvested, dry them in a warm place.

Cole crop seeds are especially sensitive to storage conditions. All these crops have such small seeds that their stored food is easily broken down when improperly stored. If they are kept in a warm, humid place, they may not even last until the next spring. Stored at temperatures well below freezing, however, these seeds may last more than ten years. The best way to store them is to put them in a waterproof container with powdered milk or silica gel and set them in the freezer. *Do not* store kohlrabi seeds this way, however; cold temperatures will vernalize them, and you will get bunches of yellow flowers instead of succulent stems! The safest place for kohlrabi seeds is in a cool closet or basement.

General Problems with Cole Crops

While each cole crop has its own particular problems, they all are bothered by most of the same pests and diseases. Perhaps the most annoying problem is the array of hungry green caterpillars, such as the cabbage looper, that may descend on your garden. While they will attack any and all cole crops, the caterpillars are likely to bother some more than others. For unknown reasons, red cabbage is less popular with voracious caterpillars than green varieties. Broccoli is a favorite, but fortunately, it can thrive and provide you with an abundant harvest even while it's serving as a feeding ground for caterpillars.

Luckily, some very effective organic controls can eliminate the caterpillar problem. By using row covers as soon as plants are set in the garden, you can eliminate most of the aboveground insects. The covers must be in place (with the edges buried in the soil) throughout the season to work effectively. If the humidity is high during the growing season, use the lightest or most porous row covers that you can find so that you won't lose your crop to bacterial rot, which flourishes under such conditions. Another control is simply to plant early in the growing season so that your crop matures before most pests are active. You can hand-pick caterpillars, of course, or you can get the *Trichogramma* wasp to do the dirty work for you. These parasites lay their eggs on the caterpillar, and the wasp larvae kill the caterpillar by feeding on it. You can buy these wasps through your local organic nursery or through the mail from advertisements in gardening magazines.

One of the best means of caterpillar control is a preparation made from the naturally occurring bacterium *Bacillus thuringiensis* (BT for short). BT turns the caterpillars into mushy dark brown blobs. It is sold under several different names, including Biotrol, Dipel, and Thuricide.

Even with attempts at control, you'll probably end up with a few caterpillars hidden in the nooks and crannies of your broccoli and cauliflower. A twenty-minute soak in cold, salty water after harvesting should drive them out without affecting the flavor of your produce.

Club root is a fungal disease that attacks the roots of all cole crops, rendering them unable to take up nutrients and water. It deforms the roots so that they take on an enlarged, club-shaped appearance. If your soil becomes infected with club root, keep the pH above 7.2 to help control it and don't plant any cole crops in the affected area for at least two years. Any disease that affects one of these closely related plants can attack the others, so always consider them as a group when planning any crop rotation scheme.

After this brief introduction to cole crop culture, it's time to turn our attention to the particular needs of the individual crops. Our cabbage family profile will cover cabbage, kale and collards, Brussels sprouts, kohlrabi, cauliflower, and broccoli.

CABBAGE

Cabbage is a very popular home garden crop. It grows well at various seasons in different parts of the country and stores well for a considerable time after harvesting. But cabbage has a few quirks, and knowing something about them will help you to grow the biggest, healthiest heads in your neighborhood.

We have already said that all cole crops need a balanced soil from the beginning, and cabbage is no exception. Because cabbage is a mass of leaves, you might be inclined to grow this crop in extremely nitrogen-rich soil. That would be a mistake. As we pointed out earlier, too little nitrogen can make for small, inferior heads. But the other extreme, too much, also will cause problems. An excess of nitrogen will encourage rapid growth of the inner head leaves, which will grow faster than the outer ones, resulting in a split head. Most gardens with plenty of organic matter in the soil will provide the correct amount of nitrogen. Just be careful not to tip the balance by adding a massive infusion of nitrogen in the form of large amounts of fresh poultry or rabbit manure right before planting your cabbage. Also don't overlook the importance of potassium. An ample supply of this nutrient will encourage rigid, well-folded, and dense heads to form, but too much potassium can cause splitting.

Early-maturing varieties do well in lighter soils than do later ones, which prefer heavier soils. Light-textured soils warm up more quickly than heavy ones, providing the conditions for rapid growth under cool spring conditions. You can even grow a successful crop in soil that is on the salty side, especially if you plant green varieties rather than red ones. Since saline soil tends to hinder the root growth of transplanted seedlings, plan to start your crop by direct seeding. (For more on salty soil, see the box "The Lowdown on Salty Soil" in chapter 5.)

One of the keys to successful cabbage growing is maintaining the proper moisture content. Cabbage grown under water stress will have a strong, unpleasant flavor, and crops produced in soil that is always on the dry side will be significantly smaller than those grown in moist soil. Although cabbage roots need moisture to function efficiently, sopping-wet soil is just as bad as dry soil. Not only will a fully saturated soil discourage deep root growth (there's no need to probe down deep for water), but it also will limit nutrient uptake. In addition, soggy soil encourages bacterial and fungal diseases. And if your soil is saturated with water, the heads will be slightly smaller, and they will be late in maturing. The goal is to keep the soil moist but not wet.

Cabbage Varieties

Don't let the cabbages you usually see in the supermarket fool you into thinking that this vegetable comes in only two types: round and red or round and green. Once you start studying the seed catalogs, you'll discover that there are any number of colors, leaf types, shapes, sizes, and times to maturity. Best of all, many of the varieties available to home gardeners are much better tasting than those in the store. The reason is that thin-leafed cabbages have a better taste than those with the thick leaves required for commercial handling and shipping.

In terms of color, red varieties can range anywhere from dark purple ('Autoro') to ruby red ('Ruby Perfection'). Green cabbages come in shades of blue-green to deep green and almost white. There are two leaf types—smooth (either red or green) and savoyed, or crinkly (green only). The crinkly leaves of savoy cabbages have a distinctive puckered appearance because the veins grow much more slowly than the rest of the leaf. You can even select among various head shapes—round, flat, or pointed. In general, the round and flat varieties tend to be bigger and denser, while the pointed varieties are on the small side. There's actually quite a range of sizes available; for example, in the category of round green cabbages, you can grow anything from the 2- to 3-pound 'Quickstep' to the 20-pound 'Hybrid O-S Cross.'

Time to maturity is another factor you should consider in your selection. Cabbages are classified as being early, mid-season, or late. Early varieties mature in roughly 60 to 80 days, midseason in 80 to 90 days, and late in 90 to 110 days. (All these dates to maturity are figured from the time seedlings are set out in the garden.) In general, early varieties such as 'Early Jersey Wakefield,' 'Golden Acre,' and 'Quickstep' have small heads with thin leaves and a sweet flavor. The later, larger varieties have thicker leaves, which help them maintain the moisture needed for long-term storage.

Environment and climate also play a role in flavor development, and these should to be considered when you are selecting cabbage varieties. To develop a full, sweet flavor, cabbages need to mature during cool weather. When heads grow in the cooler but sunny weather of fall, the lower temperatures slow respiration, allowing the plant to accumulate sugars and other flavor compounds. This means that spring-planted early varieties that mature during the summer often do not develop the best flavor. For the best-tasting heads, grow early varieties so that they mature in your cool season.

If you have only limited space, the early varieties of cabbage can be planted close together, making them a good choice for raised beds. However, these varieties often crack or split shortly after reaching maturity and so do not stand well in the garden. If you plan to leave your cabbages in the garden rather than bring them in as soon as the heads are firm, choose early varieties that have good split resistance. Their inner leaves are less likely to put enough pressure on the outer ones to crack the head. Even so, most early varieties with good split resistance won't stand much more than two weeks.

If you'd like longer-standing cabbages, choose mid-season varieties. These can stand four or more weeks and have little space between the leaves. Their heads are firmer than those of the early varieties and are easier to cut up for coleslaw or sauerkraut. If you plan to use your cabbages for sauerkraut, grow them for a fall harvest so that they are high in sugars. The sugars are converted to lactic acid during the fermentation process, giving the sauerkraut its characteristic sharpness. If you like a crisp kraut, use mid-season to later-maturing fall varieties with thicker leaves.

Red cabbage varieties generally take longer to mature and so often fall in the mid-season category. Their leaves are generally thicker than those of green varieties, which is why red cabbage is often used for braising or pickling: it keeps more of its texture. Look for varieties that have a mild taste, or you might end up with an overly spicy crop. Diane has found that the flavor of red cabbage, more than that of any other type, reflects its growing conditions. When she unintentionally grew 'Ruby Ball' in soil that needed more organic material and was too dry, the heads were much hotter in flavor than those grown in better soil that held more moisture.

Savoy cabbage leaves are very tender, mild tasting, and flexible, making them the ideal choice for cabbage rolls. Most savoy cabbage varieties mature at mid-season, except 'Spivoy Hybrid,' which is ready in fifty days. This variety is smaller (15 to 18 inches) than most savoy cabbage varieties, which can be 3 to 4 feet across. Diane has enjoyed both the flavor and beauty of 'Savoy Ace' and 'Savoy King.' These varieties produce unusually attractive, crinkled frame leaves that are darker than the light-colored head leaves. Their large rosettes also provide a landscaping focal point.

If you plan on storing your cabbage harvest, it pays to check each variety's reputation in storage. Most smooth green cabbages store better than savoy or red cabbages. Storage varieties of green cabbage can be kept for months under the proper conditions. Red varieties such as 'Autoro' and 'Red Perfection' will keep for a couple of months.

If you live in the South, early green varieties, especially pointed-head types, are your best choice for winter cropping. But if you want a larger, round head, try 'Bravo.' When choosing new varieties, look for frost resistance, as overwintering varieties must be able to take light frosts.

The hardiness of cabbages depends a great deal on the variety. If you want to store your cabbages, choose a frost-hardy variety such as 'Green Jewel Hybrid' or 'Lariat' so that you don't have to pick the crop too early to store. Diane has found that 'Quick-Green Storage' and 'Survivor' easily survive 20°F before storing.

One final tip for choosing cabbages: look for a variety with a short core, or stem. Many varieties have a stem that extends most of the length of the head and must be removed, wasting much of the head. A short core allows you to use more of the head. This feature is particularly important if you are using a cabbage cutter for sauerkraut. Long-core heads need to be cut into smaller pieces, which requires more time and effort. Also, long-core cabbages have a greater tendency to split because the large core can push through the tight leaves.

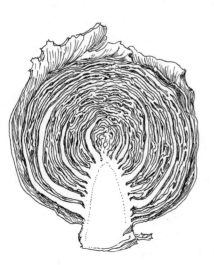

Cabbage Cores: Cabbage varieties with short cores (left) are preferable to those with long cores (right). Long-core varieties are more likely to split and need to be cut to remove the core.

Starting and Caring for Cabbage

Get your cabbage off to a good start by planting the seeds only ¼ to ½ inch deep. They will germinate over the surprisingly wide range of 40°F to 95°F, but germination takes a long time at the lower end of the range. At 50°F germination takes around fourteen days, while at 68°F it takes only a week. Diane has had cabbage seeds emerge in four days at about 80°F in a very warm cold frame. Of course, she didn't keep the seedlings at that temperature once they were up. As soon as they germinated, she moved them to a cooler spot so that a strong root system would develop and the tops would grow sturdy, not spindly. If you're trying to start a fall crop and are direct-seeding in temperatures above 86°F, use lawn clippings, peat moss, or some other moisture-holding mulch to cover the seeds rather than soil. This will encourage better germination, as the soil will dry out too fast at high temperatures. Cabbage seedlings can be damaged by 25°F, so wait until two weeks before the last spring frost date to transplant them or use row covers to protect them at night.

When you transplant your seedlings, space them carefully. The closer together you place them, the smaller the heads will be. The small-headed varieties can be as close as 12 inches apart, but larger types require 20 to 30 inches. Cabbages planted too closely together will have a stronger flavor than those that are spaced properly.

Remember to keep your cabbage patch weeded or well mulched. The most important weeding time is when the plants are small, around three to four weeks after germination. If you keep weeds down then, the plants can hold their own later. Since cabbage prefers cool, moist soil, mulching around the plants is the best way to meet their needs and to keep weeds down at the same time.

Winter Cabbage Cropping

If you live in the South or in a mild coastal area, you may be able to grow cabbage both as a fall/winter crop (seeding in August or later depending on the variety) and an early spring crop (seeding in January). Cabbages grown in the fall often have a slightly conical head, whereas those grown in the spring are rounder. Some varieties produce slightly larger spring than fall heads, perhaps because early spring growing temperatures are a little cooler than late fall temperatures.

In some areas, cabbage can be grown only during the winter because it is too hot during the rest of the year. To do this successfully, you'll need to know how to prevent your cabbage plants from flowering. The cabbage is a biennial plant, taking two years to mature. The trigger for flowering is cold temperatures, generally below 40°F. But cabbages need to have reached a certain size before they will respond to cold temperatures; this is why they can be grown in the winter in some parts of the country. Cabbages whose stems are thicker than a pencil when exposed to low temperatures for two to four weeks will bolt once the temperature warms up. So your cabbages can't be too large when the cold weather hits. They also can't be too small because they won't be able to take the cold. Young cabbage plants can take a light frost, but they are much more tolerant when they are half-grown and the temperature drops gradually. As we mentioned in our discussion of cabbage varieties earlier in this chapter, some varieties are more sensitive to cold than others.

Taking all these factors into consideration, you must select a variety for winter growing that will stand up well to cooler temperatures and then plant it at the right time. Here are some tips on how certain varieties respond to fall planting. Pointed-headed varieties generally bolt less readily than round-headed types. Late varieties such as 'Copenhagen Market' are likely to bolt if planted in the fall, while 'Jersey Wakefield' will produce a good crop as long as it is planted at just the right time. For example, in California 'Jersey Wakefield' planted between mid-August and mid-September is likely to be too big when winter comes and will bolt in the spring. But if you plant it in October, it is not likely to respond to winter weather by flowering, and you will get a nice crop of cabbage in the spring.

Since each area has its own conditions, you should contact your county extension agent to find out what cabbage varieties can be planted in the fall in your area and when to plant them. In any area, the best months to grow cabbage are those in which the average temperature ranges from 59°F to 68°F.

Bringing in the Cabbage Harvest

Cabbages can be harvested anytime after they have headed. You can test the heads by pushing on them lightly to see if they are solid. A cabbage can look like a head from the outside but still be quite loose inside. If the head doesn't give when you push on it, it's ready for harvest. If you leave your mature heads in the garden, check them frequently for signs of cracking. If a head does break open, cut it and bring it inside right away. It should be eaten or made into sauerkraut as soon as possible, for it won't keep well, even in the refrigerator.

Sometimes your efforts to control cabbage worms fail, and the outside of your cabbages look pretty unappetizing. Don't assume that the entire head is a loss, however. If you cut off the head and keep cutting the outer leaves away, you are likely to end up with a tight central head that the caterpillars haven't penetrated.

If you're harvesting late in the season and are removing garden debris as you go, pull up the entire cabbage plant, cut off the head, and then add the roots and outer frame leaves to the compost pile. If you're harvesting an early spring-planted variety, you can grow a second crop of little cabbages before the fall frost arrives. To do this, simply cut off the heads without pulling up the plants and leave two or three large outer leaves attached to the stump. The axillary buds of those leaves will grow, forming several small sprouts. Cut off all but one of these and watch it develop a small second head. You must maintain a fertile, balanced soil to coax a second crop to appear.

Storing Cabbages

For the longest-lasting cabbages that retain their color and firm texture, store them in a place that is as close as possible to the ideal conditions of 32°F and 90 to 95 percent humidity. Under these conditions, late cabbages can keep for as long as three to four months. Early varieties will last only three to six weeks. If you have only a few heads, you can clean and trim them, then store them in plastic bags in the refrigerator. If you have a root cellar, you can wrap the individual heads in newspaper and store them there. Be aware, however, that cabbages have a strong odor that can easily taint your other foods.

Problems with Cabbages

Have you ever cut into a nice firm head of cabbage and found some brown leaves near the center? This is called internal tip burn and is due to insufficient calcium. The lack of calcium may not be due to your soil but may result from the peculiar way a cabbage head grows.

While many nutrients are stored in the outer leaves, not all the nutrients the cabbage needs can be kept there. As we discussed in chapter 2, minerals from the soil are transferred from the roots to the leaves by way of the xylem. Water evaporating from the leaves produces a negative pressure that pulls the sap from the roots and into the rest of the plant. But in a cabbage head, the internal leaves are protected by the outer leaves. Water cannot evaporate from their surface, so they don't always get their share of minerals from the roots. If the cabbage is growing in moist soil where the humidity is high, the roots themselves produce enough pressure to force water and nutrients up into the head. If, however, the soil is dry or the humidity, especially at night, is low, the root pressure is not strong enough to move the minerals into the head, setting the stage for internal tip burn. Soil that is very high in nitrogen also will encourage tip burn.

There is a very simple way to prevent internal tip burn or stop it if it's already started. Just place a paper bag over the cabbage head at night to maintain the humidity. Make sure to remove the bag during daylight hours. This paper bag trick, combined with an application of bone meal to correct any calcium deficiency in the soil, should solve your problem.

Growing Cabbage Seeds

You can grow your own cabbage seeds if your winters are not too harsh. Plant your spring or summer crop a little later than you would for fresh use or plant your winter crop earlier. Then let the plants overwinter in cool but not killing temperatures (lower than 40°F but above 11°F is okay). Cabbages that are forming small heads at the time winter hits will be the most likely candidates to bolt the next spring. Half-grown plants with loose heads are much hardier than either

Above: *Humans aren't the only ones who can enjoy a well-tended garden.*

Left: *The home gardener today can grow a much greater variety of lettuce than can be found in any grocery store.*

Opposite, top: 'Melody Hybrid' spinach is a very popular, semi-savoyed variety that resists bolting in hot weather.

Opposite, bottom: The beautiful heads of savoy cabbage are attractive for landscaping as well as delicious to eat.

Left: Broccoli is a nutritious and easy-to-grow garden crop that produces abundantly for the attentive gardener.

Right: Carrots have an extended taproot that goes beyond the part we eat.

Below: Besides the familiar red beets, white and yellow varieties, which don't bleed when cooked, are also available.

Opposite: Radishes come in an appealing variety of sizes, shapes, and colors.

Opposite: 'Nebraska' is an especially hardy leek variety.

Left: When their basic needs are met, it is easy to grow all kinds of onions—mild or spicy, red or white, large or small.

Below: Rich soil helps onions grow into big, satisfying globes that store well like these, almost ready for harvest.

Above: Home gardeners can grow
potatoes with a variety of flavors
and textures as well as colors.

Right: 'Kennebec' is a very popular
potato for home gardens; you can
see here how the potato grows
from the end of the stolon.

young or old plants and can stand temperatures close to 0°F, especially if they are mulched or covered with snow. If the climate provides you with several freeze-thaw cycles during the winter, or if your plants are exposed to freezing temperatures without snow cover, be sure to mulch your seed cabbages well after the ground has frozen. Otherwise, their apical tips may be killed by the cold. If this happens, they won't be able to bloom when spring arrives. In addition, alternate freezing and thawing of the ground can damage the roots and even kill your plants if they're not protected with a layer of mulch.

If you notice that the heads are tight in the spring, you might want to borrow a trick from commercial growers, who cut a cross about 2 inches deep in the top of the head to help the flower stalk emerge. Remember that you will need at least two flowering plants and that other cole crops should not be flowering at the same time nearby. As with all cole crops, harvest the seeds while the pods are still yellow but the seeds are brown and fairly dry. Another good indication that the seeds are ready to be harvested is that they will not split when rubbed between your fingers. If the pods are getting brittle, hold a paper bag under them as you break them off to catch any seeds from pods that pop.

Cabbage Frontiers

Producing a better cabbage is a frustrating business because a desirable trait often is linked to one that is less desirable. This linkage of the good and the bad occurs to a greater extent in cabbage than in other crops. For example, size is linked to lateness; it is hard to get a cabbage that will grow quickly to a large size. Increasing the yield of storage cabbages also is difficult because varieties that produce heavily in a small area do not store well. A dark red color can't be produced in a very early cabbage, and firm heads of savoy cabbage can't be bred because the firmer the head is, the smoother the leaves are.

Even so, breeders continue to develop earlier varieties, as well as cabbages with very solid heads and types that are resistant to cracking. Resistance to club root has been bred into some varieties of green and savoy cabbages, and resistance to fungal diseases such as downy mildew also is being developed. Breeders have found that some cabbage varieties that are resistant to tip burn also have less zinc in their leaves. They hope to use this as a genetic marker for breeding varieties that will be very resistant to tip burn.

KALE AND COLLARDS

Kale has become popular among landscape-conscious vegetable gardeners who are interested in adding color as well as attractive leaf forms to their gardens. Many of these gardeners may not realize that the beautiful flowering varieties are just as tasty as ordinary kale grown in the vegetable plot. Collards, unfortunately, have been stereotyped as a southern crop, fit for making a good "mess of greens." Kale, on the other hand, is often looked upon as a northern crop. But both kale and collards thrive under a variety of growing conditions, and deserve to be grown more widely throughout the country. They provide hefty amounts of calcium, iron, and vitamins A and C, and they even supply some protein.

Kale and collards are so closely related that they are botanically the same variety; the difference in appearance comes from the way they grow. While collards have fairly flat leaves, the leaf margins of kale grow faster than the rest of the leaf, giving the leaves a distinctive ruffle-edged look. Collards start out looking like young cabbage plants, but instead of heading up, they continue to produce more leaves as the stem elongates, rather like leaf lettuce. A collard plant can grow to 4 feet tall during a long growing season if the lower leaves are harvested as the plant grows. Because these crops are so closely related, their growth requirements and other traits are essentially the same. They also share a similar flavor, though there's just enough difference to tell them apart. The flavor of kale, especially after a frost, is tangier than that of collards.

Kale and Collard Varieties

There are quite a few varieties of kale and almost as many opinions about which ones have the best flavor. Because there is so much disagreement, we suspect that the taste of kale may depend quite a bit on the type of soil in which it is grown. We'll avoid stepping into the fray by simply describing the growth habits of several popular varieties.

Diane really enjoys 'Red Russian,' which has purple veins early in the season and redder leaves later in the fall, making this delicious variety a landscaping plus for the vegetable garden. Its leaves also are tenderer than those of many other kale varieties. 'Siberian' kale grows 12 to 16 inches tall but can spread 36 inches, has very large blue-frilled leaves, and is very hardy. The ornamental flowering kale varieties come in many different colors with white, blue, red, or purple centers. They are called flowering kale because their compact leaf clusters look like giant flowers. The newest form of ornamental kale is 'Peacock Red,' which has finely serrated, or notched, leaves. The outer leaves are dark red and the center leaves a brighter, lighter red.

In contrast to kale, the selection of collard varieties is limited. 'Vates' is especially tasty, vigorous, and hardy. It grows to about 3 feet tall. 'Champion' is a newer 'Vates'-type collard that is shorter, hardier, and more bolt resistant. 'Georgia' has attractive blue-green leaves with white veins and can tolerate poor soil and extreme heat. 'Hicrop Hybrid' has a mild, sweet flavor and is very slow to bolt. Although 'Blue Max' (also a hybrid) is not commonly available, it does well under a variety of growing conditions.

Kale is often thought of as a cool-weather crop, but it does well in any season. Since there are so many other crops that can be grown only in the summer, most gardeners restrict their kale growing to fall and early spring. Collards, too, can tolerate a wide range of temperatures. In Texas collards can be planted in early spring along with turnips and again at the beginning of August for a fall crop. If kept well picked, the spring-planted collards will still be producing in the fall.

Both of these cole crops can be grown in lighter soils than winter cabbage and will deliver a harvest even when grown in poor, nutrient-deficient soil that would be the ruin of many plants. Too meager a soil, however, will result in poor taste. For the best-quality crop you should promote quick, succulent growth. This calls for fertile soil, so you should work in plenty of well-rotted manure or compost before planting. Kale and collards are slightly more drought resistant than cabbage, but they have the same inefficient, fibrous root system.

You can sow kale and collard seeds directly in the garden anytime from early spring to early fall. The tender young thinnings are very tasty sautéed or raw, so sow your spring planting thickly and enjoy an early treat. Thick seeding also will help foil the hungry leaf-eating insects that hunt for greens early in the spring. Diane has found that a first thinning to 12 inches apart allows young plants room to grow. She does a second and sometimes a third thinning to open more space for the spreading kale varieties, which often need 2½ to 3 feet per plant. The ornamental kale varieties need only 1 foot between plants. Collards should be spaced 18 inches apart. If you aren't interested in eating thinnings, plant your seeds in clumps of three or four at intervals that correspond with the final spacing. Once the seedlings have emerged, thin each clump, leaving the sturdiest plant standing.

Cultivate very lightly around your kale and collard plants, no deeper than an inch or two. Keep your patch of greens weed-free so there's no chance that the weeds will gain the upper hand.

Growing Kale and Collards

While tender spring thinnings of kale and collards are delicious and the fine greens are always welcome no matter what the season, the best-tasting harvest comes from plants that have been touched by frost. This accounts for their popularity as fall crops. As the growing season draws to a close, you can ignore these plants while you are busy harvesting your peppers, tomatoes, and other frost-sensitive crops. When these less hardy vegetables have been processed or stored, you can turn to your fresh kale and collards.

You have several options for harvesting these crops. First, you can harvest the whole plants, clearing your garden for the winter. If you store both crops just above freezing, they'll last for a few weeks. Second, you can leave the kale

Harvesting and Overwintering Kale and Collards

and collards in the garden, picking the leaves as you want them and effectively stretching the harvest out over a longer period. Both crops can withstand temperatures as low as 0°F. Just be sure to apply a mulch after the ground freezes as insurance against any freeze-thaw cycles. The mulch will keep the soil temperature from fluctuating wildly, thereby protecting the roots from damage. If the temperature in your area goes much below 0°F, bury the plants completely with loose leaves or hay to insulate them from the frigid air. When you want some fresh greens, even in the dead of winter, brush aside the protective covering and harvest what you want. Even if the greens are frozen solid and stiff as a board, gather them anyway and let them thaw out at room temperature before cooking.

Gardeners in the North can try overwintering a patch of relatively young plants for an extra-early harvest in the spring. To give them enough time to reach a winter-hardy stage, plant kale or collards at least six weeks before the first hard frost is expected. Cover the young plants with a thick layer of mulch or with row covers as soon as the ground freezes, just to be sure they'll survive the winter. 'Dwarf Blue Curled Scotch' grows only 15 inches tall but will spread to more than 2 feet, making it an easy variety to mulch. When springtime temperatures start thawing the ground, uncover the greens so that they can resume growing. Like cabbage, kale and collards will bolt if exposed to temperatures below 40°F. Before they flower, however, they will produce a much-appreciated harvest of fresh greens far ahead of any spring-planted crop.

Gardeners in the Deep South should plant collards and kale in their coolest season, but just as with cabbage, the plants need to be the right size so that they won't bolt before producing a tasty harvest. Plant them at least a month before the coldest part of the year. If you have problems with bolting, try other varieties and keep notes about what works and what the temperature was when they bolted.

BRUSSELS SPROUTS

Young Brussels sprouts plants look a lot like young cabbage plants, mainly because their first leaves have long petioles. As both plants grow, the new leaves develop with shorter and shorter petioles, but Brussels sprouts never get around to heading up. Instead, the internodes get a bit shorter, and the axillary buds swell, forming the tasty "little cabbages." Like the axillary buds on other plants, those on Brussels sprouts are under the hormonal control of the apical bud at the top of the plant. The sprouts won't form until the top of the stem has stopped growing or has grown far enough away to have less hormonal control over the developing buds. How you can use this to your advantage will be discussed later in the section "To Top or Not to Top?" Like cabbage, Brussels sprouts are a biennial crop sensitive to cold temperatures. After making it through a cold winter, the plant will blossom, with the main flower stalk emerging from the top of the stem.

W e are fortunate to have a better selection of Brussels sprouts varieties today than ever before because seed houses now import some of the wonderful European varieties. For many years 'Jade Cross' was the only variety offered in many catalogs. Still, most catalogs carry at most three varieties, a very small sample of what has been developed by European breeders. For a wider selection, look through catalogs from Thompson and Morgan, The Cook's Garden, William Dam Seeds Ltd., and Stokes Seeds.

The European varieties have been developed for different growing conditions in Western Europe. They tend to be taller than American varieties and require a long, cool growing season, making them best suited to mild coastal regions. Some of the European strains have been developed for growing in a specific type of soil, so be careful that the variety you buy is adapted to your garden conditions. A variety developed for light soil will produce a short stem in heavy soil, while a variety intended for heavy soil will grow too fast in light soil, producing loose sprouts. If your catalog doesn't indicate the soil type, ask the supplier what the variety requires.

You might think that a tall plant would produce more sprouts than a short one, but this is not always true. The shorter varieties often have shorter internodes, so the sprouts are packed tightly on the stem. This can lead to difficulties in harvesting, especially if you want to pick your sprouts bit by bit from the bottom up. Dorothy had particular trouble with one variety, 'Early Dwarf Danish.' The sprouts were wedged so close together that they were flat rather than round. Once she got them off the plants, though, they were delicious. The original 'Jade Cross' strain also produced sprouts that were close together. Breeders developed a new version, 'Jade Cross E,' with longer internodes, making the sprouts easier to harvest.

If you live in a short-season area, you are better off growing one of the shorter varieties, as the tall ones take longer to mature. But if you live in a mild climate and want to harvest gradually over a long period, the taller varieties are better for you. When you look at the days to harvest, remember that the sprouts must mature in frosty weather to develop their best flavor. For instance, if your growing season is generally only 90 days long, you don't need a 90-day variety but a 100- or 120-day variety so that the sprouts are forming when the first light frosts occur.

If you want to harvest your sprouts throughout the winter, choose varieties that are hardy and will hold tight sprouts over the winter months. These varieties include 'Achilles,' 'Citadel F1 Hybrid,' and 'Widgeon.'

Brussels Sprouts Varieties

Growing and Harvesting Brussels Sprouts

The most important thing to remember about Brussels sprouts is that they grow best when the weather is cool. If your summer daytime temperatures average 65°F or less, you should be able to grow an outstanding crop. Gardeners in Florida, along the Gulf coast, and throughout much of the Midwest are out of luck; these areas get too hot for Brussels sprouts to do well. Northern gardeners can harvest Brussels sprouts well into the cold, dark days of winter.

Culture for this crop is much like that for cabbage, since Brussels sprouts have the same sort of root system. One thing you must watch out for is very rich or peaty soil. Under these conditions the plants may grow too quickly, forming loose bunches of leaves rather than tight sprouts. Also, plants grown with too much nitrogen are likely to be bitter.

Your best bet is to start Brussels sprouts indoors as you would cabbage, since seedlings in the garden face the usual problems with flea beetles. When you set out your plants, place them about 2 feet apart in rows 2 to 3 feet apart. If you leave more space than is necessary between the plants, they will grow too fast and the sprouts will be too loose. Planting only 10 inches apart in rows spaced 24 inches apart will encourage small, tight sprouts that are spaced farther apart along the stem. If you live in a humid climate, close spacing can cause problems with fungal or bacterial diseases. If you want to harvest all your sprouts at once, plant them a little closer together (18 inches apart). This will delay lower sprout growth so that all the sprouts mature at the same time and you can harvest them in one session.

When you plant your Brussels sprouts depends on the fall and winter conditions in your area. Once the tiny sprouts are visible in the leaf axils, it will be about three weeks before they begin to swell into edible buds. The best-quality sprouts mature during cool fall weather, and a touch of frost enhances their sweetness. Sprouts that mature during warm weather are likely to be loose and less sweet. One year Diane eagerly set out seedlings of an early-maturing variety in mid-April and had sprouts forming by mid-August. Unfortunately, August that year was exceptionally warm, and the loose sprouts were invaded by a discouraging assortment of insect pests that burrowed all the way inside, making the crop a total loss. She learned her lesson the hard way and now transplants her early-maturing varieties in late May or early June so that the sprouts form no sooner than late September or early October.

Brussels sprouts are said to be hardy down to 10°F. Our experience has shown that 'Early Dwarf Danish,' 'Jade Cross E Hybrid,' and 'Oliver' will survive even colder temperatures. Instead of harvesting our sprouts in the late fall, we mulch the plants with about a foot of leaves after the ground has frozen. The tops of the 'Jade Cross E Hybrid' protrude above the mulch, but it doesn't seem to matter. One year, when winter temperatures in Montana stayed above −15°F most of the time, Dorothy harvested overwintered Brussels sprouts for Easter dinner! Other years her family has eaten them fresh from the garden on Christmas Day.

The only time winter weather ruined her winter sprouts crop was when it dropped down to a very chilly −30°F. The plants were still green, but the sprouts were flabby once they thawed out, and they had an off flavor.

If you don't trust your weather or don't like to blaze your way through the snow and cold to pick your Brussels sprouts, you can dig up the plants and transfer them (with plenty of soil around their roots) to a box in an unheated garage or deep cold frame. Water them lightly to keep the roots from drying out, and the sprouts will continue to mature.

In areas with a mild winter, where frost arrives in late December or January if at all, you can plant Brussels sprouts in the early fall. With this timing there will be sprouts forming when the frosts begin. Brussels sprouts, like cabbages, will bolt after 40°F temperatures, so you can't expect them to form sprouts in the spring.

When you harvest your sprouts will dramatically affect their vitamin C content. If temperatures hover around freezing (31°F to 33°F) right before harvesting, the vitamin C level will be at its peak. If temperatures have been below 31°F for two or three weeks prior to harvesting, the vitamin C content will be lower. Temperatures above 33°F also can decrease vitamin C content.

To Top or Not to Top?

Many garden books recommend cutting off the top rosette of leaves to encourage sprout formation. Others tell you only to remove the yellowing leaves between the lower sprouts. As we pointed out in chapter 2, the apical tip of a plant produces a hormone that inhibits growth of the axillary buds found at the leaf bases. Brussels sprouts are no exception. The hormone, however, has its greatest effect closest to where it is produced. That is why the first sprouts to form are near the bottom of the plant, farthest from the apical tip. Plants that are not topped (the apical tip is left intact) will produce a crop of sprouts gradually, starting at the bottom and working their way up the stem. These plants need picking several times as the sprouts mature. (If the lower sprouts are not picked, they can become overmature and loosen.) So if you want to harvest your sprouts gradually over a long period of time, don't top your plants.

If, however, you want to pick all your sprouts at once, cut off the top rosette, including the apical tip, four to eight weeks before you want to harvest. This will stop hormone production, allowing all the axillary buds to grow into sprouts at the same rate. Topped plants that are left outside and not picked for a while will hold their crop better than untopped ones. Northern gardeners who leave their sprouts outside should top their plants. In regions with an early frost, topping will increase the yield by allowing the top sprouts to fill out when they otherwise might not mature.

Topping can be done too early or too late, with bad results in either case. If you top too early, you will decrease your final yield because the plants won't

Topping Brussels Sprouts:
Topping your Brussels sprouts plants will allow you to harvest the crop all at one time. Cut off the top rosette four to eight weeks before you want to pick the sprouts. The middle leaves of the plant shown here have been removed to expose the maturing sprouts.

have enough leaves to feed the developing crop through photosynthesis. Topping too late can cause the lower sprouts to grow too big. The best time to top is right after the lower sprouts have begun to swell.

On both topped and untopped plants, feel free to remove the older yellowed leaves from the lower parts of the plants. This will give the sprouts more room to grow and will make it easier to pick them when the time comes.

KOHLRABI

Kohlrabi certainly doesn't rank among the ten most popular home garden crops, and many gardeners aren't even quite sure what it looks like. This is a shame, for kohlrabi is ideal for gardens too small for cabbage. It is a very versatile vegetable that can be used as a substitute for expensive water chestnuts in Chinese dishes, as a crunchy salad addition, or as a steamed or sautéed side dish. The flavor of kohlrabi is milder than that of cabbage, so even if you are not a cabbage fan, you may become a kohlrabi lover.

Kohlrabi: Kohlrabi is a strange-looking vegetable, but it is delicious and versatile.

The mature kohlrabi plant looks rather strange. The crop consists of the swollen bulblike stems, which have a few rather spindly leaves radiating out from them. For all its homeliness, kohlrabi is a delicious, easy-to-grow crop that deserves a bigger fan club.

Kohlrabi Varieties

Only in the last few years has the selection of kohlrabi varieties given the gardener much choice. Some rediscovered heirloom and new varieties take much less time to mature, and others are still tender and sweet when very large. 'Kolpak' is a very tender, easy-to-grow white variety. 'Express Forcer' is a fast-maturing variety, and 'Grand Duke' is a fine variety offered by many seed houses. If you'd like to grow very large kohlrabi that stays tender and sweet, try 'Gigante,' an heirloom variety from Czechoslovakia. Two other large varieties are 'Giant Purple' and 'Giant White Super Schmelz.' In Europe gardeners have a wider selection of varieties, some of which produce small, early bulbs and others that form larger, later-maturing ones.

Growing and Harvesting Kohlrabi

Kohlrabi seeds should not be planted outdoors if there's a chance that temperatures will dip below 40°F; otherwise, the seeds may be vernalized, giving you little flowering plants instead of fat bulbing ones. You are better off planting indoors at room temperature or waiting until nighttime temperatures outside are above 40°F. Diane has had great success planting in the first two weeks of July, when the summer nights are warm.

Direct seeding of kohlrabi generally works better than transplanting, as the secret to its success is steady, rapid growth. Transplanting can be a shock to the plant's system that will result in a small, tough bulb. If you do start seeds indoors, follow these guidelines to lessen the shock:

• Make sure that you use good potting soil with no nutritional deficiencies.
• Give each plant its own little pot or compartment.
• Do not let the seedlings become root bound before transplanting.
• Begin hardening off as early as possible and set out the plants in the garden while they are still small.

Whether you're sowing seeds or transplanting, space your kohlrabi 4 inches apart in rows 15 to 18 inches apart. Never plant kohlrabi in a shady spot because shade-grown plants produce long, narrow bulbs instead of plump ones. Also, their flesh will not be as crisp as that of sun-grown plants.

Early and late varieties of kohlrabi have different reactions to cold temperatures. Some early varieties will bolt whenever they are grown at low temperatures (even when they are young seedlings), never forming a bulb at all. These plants usually will not bolt if the cold nights are offset by warm days. Late kohlrabi is very similar to cabbage—only older plants are affected by cold temperatures (below 40°F). If late varieties are grown at low temperatures in the early stages of development, they won't bolt. With late kohlrabi, plants ready to go to seed will have tough, oval bulbs instead of round ones.

As you can see, when you plant your kohlrabi depends on whether it is a late or an early variety. But most American seed catalogs do not provide this important information. Ask the companies for this information or ask other gardeners nearby which varieties they have grown successfully in which season. If you try one variety of kohlrabi and it doesn't work for you, don't give up. Another type might be just fine for your area.

If only one or two varieties are available to you and they bolt when planted in early spring, try planting them a bit later when nighttime temperatures are warmer. Although kohlrabi is less heat sensitive than some cole crops, it grows best when average daytime temperatures are no higher than 70°F. If the temperature soars above the 70-degree mark for a few hours each day, don't worry. But if the weather is consistently hot, be prepared for woody kohlrabi. Remember, the part you eat is the stem. The hotter the temperature, the more water the stem must transport to the leaves from the roots to keep them from wilting. During consistently high heat, the plant will develop more xylem to transport water, and these transport tissues form the woody part of the plant. Placing a 2-inch layer of mulch around the base of each plant will help keep it moist and tender if you have an unexpected heat wave.

To avoid woody bulbs, harvest your kohlrabi while it is still young and tender, about 1½ to 2 inches in diameter for most small varieties. Some of the best newer varieties, such as 'Kolpak' and 'Express Forcer,' stay tender at a larger size and can be picked at the 4-inch stage. The larger varieties can be harvested when they are up to 10 inches across.

Fortunately, kohlrabi stores well, so you don't have to worry about it perishing before you can eat it all. The bulbs will keep for several weeks in a plastic bag in the refrigerator, or you can keep them alongside the cabbages in your root cellar. If you live where winters are cold, you can bury kohlrabi bulbs in the ground and cover them with a thick layer of mulch to keep the ground from freezing. The coolness and moisture of the soil will keep them in good condition well into the winter.

CAULIFLOWER

Cauliflower is the prima donna of the cabbage family. This crop is so sensitive to temperature, both hot and cold, that you can do everything right and still end up with little or no harvest. But if you are a persevering gardener who loves a challenge, the lure of those fat, tight, creamy-white heads is worth the risk of frustration and disappointment.

Cauliflower grows like cabbage, with the first leaves having long petioles. As the plant gets older, the leaves form shorter and shorter petioles until they attach directly to the thickening stem. When this happens, the plant is ready to form a head. The head is actually a giant cluster of fleshy flower buds. These are quite different from flowers as we think of them on other plants, and most will not develop into "real" flowers if the head goes to seed. Often only the blossoms on the edge of the head will bloom.

Cauliflower Varieties

Seed companies are getting better about indicating which cauliflower varieties are sensitive to heat and about giving cultural tips on cauliflower growing, but there's still a lot of room for improvement. Whatever catalog you use, one trait to look for is abundant wrapper leaves that help keep the head creamy white.

Our current favorite for detailed cultural and varietal information is the Stokes catalog, which tells you what you need to know about choosing the best varieties for your growing conditions. The Stokes catalog also includes a listing of the causes of common problems with cauliflower. Without such detailed information, it is very hard to pick a variety of cauliflower that will succeed in your area.

Some varieties are very sensitive to hot weather and won't produce a head at all in the heat. Others react to cold weather with buttoning—premature heading resulting in a tiny head the size of a button. Still others are very susceptible to riceyness, a condition in which the curds appear fuzzy and separated. The cause of riceyness is uneven growth of the tiny flowers in the head. A whole gamut of environmental conditions can bring on riceyness, but again, different varieties rice under different conditions. If the catalog from which you order does not provide the information you need to make an informed choice, write or call the seed company and encourage them to put the information in the catalog.

When choosing varieties to match your climate, look for information such as "Use for a fall crop," which translates as "Do not use for an early spring crop because the variety cannot take the uneven temperatures of spring growing." Fall varieties also generally head better in cooler weather than varieties that are billed as being tolerant of the heat. In Diane's experience cauliflower varieties that are listed for spring or fall without the words "heat tolerant" generally are not heat tolerant. They must be able to be harvested before temperatures reach the 90°F range or be planted late for a fall harvest. Early varieties listed as cold and heat tolerant often are able to withstand a little more temperature fluctuation. Early varieties not listed as cold tolerant should be planted only when you expect the weather to be mild; a cold start will make them button. These varieties produce fewer leaves before heading, and a cold spell will slow growth so that the plants flower before they have enough stored nutrients to produce a nice-size head.

Ask your county extension agent and other gardeners in your area about their experiences with cauliflower. Also keep your own records of what happens to the cauliflower you plant. Try to figure out why a particular type didn't work. Was the temperature high (or low) when the cauliflower was ready to head? Did you have some cold nights while the plants were young? Were you too slow in setting out the transplants? Some of the conditions you note may be normal for your area, but others may be unusual. (We live in a place where there has not been a "normal" year for at least the past ten, which makes picking cauliflower varieties quite interesting and challenging.) If your area has an unpredictable climate, try the shotgun approach to cauliflower selection: plant three or more varieties with different growing requirements so that at least one will make it to harvest. You also might try a commercial grower's technique: plant on every third day over a two-week period so that at least one of the sowings will have the right growing conditions.

Besides the traditional white cauliflower, you can choose varieties that are really crosses between cauliflower and broccoli and have yellow-green, green, or purple heads. These varieties include 'Alverda' (yellow-green) and 'Green Broccoli Type Cauliflower.' 'Burgundy Queen' and 'Violet Queen' (both dark purple) must be grown in cooler temperatures to develop a deep purple color. The colored varieties have an advantage over the white ones because they do not have to be blanched.

Growing Cauliflower

Germination of cauliflower is a bit touchy. If you plant outside in soil that is 50°F, you may have to wait twenty days before the seedlings appear. If, however, you plant at 68°F, little green nubbins should pop up in only six days. Seeding while the weather is still cold also can lead to another problem called *blindness*. Temperatures just above freezing can destroy the apical tip of some varieties, effectively stopping any further growth of the plant. Once a young plant has more than seven leaves, it is resistant to blindness.

If you have a short spring with frequent frosts, you can avoid problems with germination or blindness by starting your cauliflower indoors or in a protected cold frame. Time your indoor seed sowing so that the seedlings can be planted in the garden at four to six weeks old when there is little chance of frost and when growing conditions are likely to get slowly but steadily warmer. Planting or transplanting outside too early will encourage buttoning. Use row covers to increase the heat in an unusually cool season or when trying for very early harvests, but be sure to remove them if the weather gets hot.

Plant mid-season or late varieties when the weather is mild and frost-free.

If your area has a long, fairly frost-free spring and your soil doesn't develop a heavy crust, you can safely direct-seed your cauliflower. In the South, where cauliflower is planted in the fall, it is important to start seeds early enough that the plants will be past the seven-leaf stage by the time a frost may strike.

Like kohlrabi, cauliflower is very susceptible to checks in growth. Transplants must be grown very carefully, or you can shock the plant's system to the point where a full white head will never develop. For this reason, indoor-grown plants should be given their own compartments and be tended carefully. Keep them in a cool room or on an unheated sun porch. If they're exposed to warm indoor temperatures, they'll grow quickly; then when they're greeted by cool outdoor temperatures after transplanting, they're likely to button. You can avoid the buttoning response by growing your cauliflower seedlings at 57°F to 68°F.

If you are buying plants at a nursery, pick ones with long petioles. Plants with thick stems and short petioles are likely to button when transplanted in your garden. They have probably been grown under cold temperatures (below 57°F) or crowded conditions. They may have gotten too little nitrogen, or they may be too old. Also beware of cauliflower plants grown in a flat rather than in individual depressions. When the soil is cut to separate these plants, their roots will be damaged. Any such setback can shock your plants into buttoning.

Space your transplants 1½ feet apart in rows 2 to 3 feet apart. Less space will result in much smaller heads unless the variety you are growing is one that will head up under such conditions. In Minnesota, scientists studied the spacing of 'Snow Crown' cauliflower, using rows 3 feet apart. They found that fruits from plants spaced about 6 inches apart in rows averaged less than ¼ pound. Those from plants spaced about 12 inches apart averaged slightly more than ½ pound, while those from plants about 18 inches apart averaged over a pound. At the smaller spacings more than half of the heads were culls, less than 6 inches in diameter.

The early ('Garant') and late ('Predominant') mini-cauliflower varieties will produce a head when the plants are set in 6- by 6-inch spacings. The heads are small, but these varieties can be direct-seeded and provide enough cauliflower for a small family or for mixed salads.

If you decide to seed your cauliflower directly in the garden, plant two to four seeds about ¼ inch deep in clusters 1½ feet apart (or 6 inches apart for the small varieties). When the seedlings are up and growing, thin each cluster, leaving the sturdiest plant. You should thin by the time the seedlings have their fourth true leaves so that the roots of the plants you leave aren't disturbed by the thinning.

Because cauliflower must grow evenly and rapidly for successful heading, plant it only after the weather has settled down (when there's little chance of frosts, heavy rain, or cold, cloudy weather) and nights are warm. Rapid, even growth also depends on rich organic soil with abundant nitrogen. Cauliflower grown in soil with too little nitrogen will button. An overdose of nitrogen also can be a problem, as it can cause the plants to grow too fast and develop heads too slowly. These heads often have loose curds that fall apart when cooked, and leaves may develop inside the head.

Cauliflower also is susceptible to soil deficiencies in the micronutrient molybdenum. Without enough molybdenum, the leaves will be unnaturally narrow at the base, and there won't be enough leaf area to cover the developing head adequately. Plants with these symptoms also are likely to produce small heads. Ground limestone will add the necessary molybdenum and will correct an overly acid soil at the same time.

Young cauliflower is very sensitive to salty soil, so make sure that the potting soil you use to start your seeds, as well as the soil in the garden, doesn't have an excess of salt. Avoid using high-salt manures such as poultry and steer manure in your potting soil mix, and don't work them into the garden right before you plant. Since manure teas also can be high in salt, use another fertilizer, such as fish emulsion, to avoid any problems. (For more information on salty soil, see the box "The Lowdown on Salty Soil" in chapter 5.) Young cauliflower also has an aversion to acidic soil (pH lower than 6.5). Steer clear of using peat moss in your potting soil mix and as a soil enhancer in the garden, since it may create an unfavorably low pH level.

Your garden soil should be on the heavy side for the best cauliflower head. A light soil can dry out too easily, leading to buttoning. Cauliflower grown in light soil also may form a loose head after a sudden rise in temperature, something that doesn't happen as often in heavier soil.

The time to check for excess salt, low pH, and too heavy a soil is *before* you plant. Once you expose your cauliflower to these conditions, you are less likely to have a successful crop.

Temperature and Heading

Cauliflower heads best when daily temperatures average 57°F to 68°F. Some varieties will head above 77°F, but most do not. (If you are lucky, your catalog may list the characteristic "Heads well in warm weather.") Once heading has started, a streak of hot weather can inhibit the heading process, causing leaves to grow up between the curds. High temperatures also can cause the curds to loosen. If the weather is consistently hot, you may end up with no heads at all.

The climate will determine whether spring or fall is better for growing cauliflower. If you live in the South and want to grow cauliflower during the fall or early winter, bear in mind that the temperature must be at least 42°F to 44°F for the head to form. Most cauliflower can tolerate an occasional dip down to 28°F, but it won't head after a 25°F night. One variety, 'Snow Crown,' will head after the temperature dips to 25°F but only if it warms up during the day. Plants that have grown very quickly will not survive the cold as well as those that have grown more slowly.

Direct sunlight is a developing cauliflower head's worst enemy. If it's not protected from the sun, the sensitive head will turn brown and develop a strong flavor. Even varieties that are supposed to be self-blanching often must be covered, though not as carefully as other varieties.

There are several ways to protect your developing heads from the sun. As soon as the curds are walnut size, pull up the leaves around the head and tie a string around them or hold them together with a clothespin. You also can break the petioles of some of the larger leaves, bending them over the top of the head to protect it.

Check the head every few days at first and then every day as it approaches maturity. As long as the head is small and very compact, leave it be. But once the curds begin to loosen, pick it no matter how big (or small) it is, as they will only get looser. Ideally, you should harvest heads when they are 6 to 8 inches across the top and still fairly compact. Unless you're going to carry the head directly into the kitchen, cut some wrapper leaves along with it to protect the curds.

Storing Cauliflower

You can hold your harvested cauliflower heads in good condition for two to four weeks, as long as you keep them at 32°F and 95 percent humidity. A root cellar is the best storage spot. If you leave the heads in a plastic bag in the refrigerator, they will last only two weeks, and there's a good chance that the curds may turn brown. If this happens, don't throw the head away. Just scrape off the brown part. After scraping the head, cook it right away, or it will turn brown again.

How to Harvest Snowy-White Heads

WHAT WENT WRONG?

This checklist will help you figure out why the giant white cauliflower heads of your dreams failed to materialize in your garden.

Buttoning: A premature flowering of the plant. Buttoned plants have fewer and smaller leaves than normal and form heads that soon flower. The following conditions can cause buttoning:

- Temperature is too cold (generally below 40°F)
- Soil is poor or low in nitrogen
- Soil has excessive salt, which slows growth
- Strong weed competition, which slows growth
- Drought

Riceyness: The result of uneven flower growth. The curds look fuzzy and may separate. The following conditions promote riceyness:

- Temperature is too high
- Soil has too much nitrogen
- Humidity is too high

Green leaves in the curds can be caused by the following conditions:

- Temperature is too high
- Drought

A lack of curds may result from the following condition:

- Temperature is too high

Growing Cauliflower Seeds

Growing cauliflower seeds is a tricky business. Many of the buds never develop flowers, and the flowers that do form often are infertile. Firm heads, the kind from which you would want to save seeds, bolt much more slowly than the undesirable loose heads. To get the best seed set, you need warm, dry weather. If the head bolts unevenly and some of the unflowering curds start to rot, cut out the rotting part. Because cauliflower is subject to uneven flower development, the seeds that are formed on one plant often do not ripen at the same time, so you must collect them a few at a time, as you would cabbage seeds.

Cauliflower Frontiers

As you can see, there is a lot of room for improvement with cauliflower. Breeders are trying to develop varieties that are not so sensitive to temperature fluctuations, and work is under way to perfect self-blanching heads by increasing the number of wrapper leaves. Only a few of the self-blanching varieties now available have enough leaves to cover the head completely and keep it from turning brown, and they must head in cool weather for adequate coverage.

BROCCOLI

Broccoli is the second most popular cole crop in the United States after cabbage, and its popularity is well deserved. It is the most nutritious of all the cole crops, and only cabbage can compete with it in terms of ease of culture and amount of edible material per plant. Broccoli stems and leaves as well as heads make tasty eating, and you can harvest up to five leaves per plant without reducing your total yield of spears. The spears we eat are the undeveloped flower heads. After you cut the main head, broccoli will continue to provide a harvest of smaller but equally delicious side shoots. And when your plants are finished at the end of the season, you can eat the remaining leaves.

Broccoli Varieties

Broccoli varieties vary in how they head and in how long they will hold the head before flowering. Some types form very large initial heads followed by small side shoots. Others form a small head and then larger side shoots. It is up to you to decide whether you want large amounts in your initial yield and less later on or a steadier harvest of smaller pickings for sustained use in the kitchen. We like to plant enough of a large-heading type, such as 'Premium Crop,' so we can harvest the large heads for freezing and then use the side shoots for fresh eating during the rest of the season.

Broccoli does have a premature heading stage similar to buttoning in cauliflower, so you must choose your variety carefully if the weather will be cool. Diane had this problem recently when she was growing 'Early Emerald Hybrid.' That year the month of May was unseasonably wet and cold, with high temperatures in the 40°F to 50°F range—a chilly start for young broccoli plants. By the first part of July the plants had all formed 2-inch heads. When she cut off these tiny heads, the side shoots that later formed were even smaller. She found out that this variety is a poor choice for a cold spring, but it will do fine if daily temperatures are above 50°F. Fortunately, Diane also planted 'Premium Crop,' which isn't as sensitive to cold temperatures, so she still harvested plenty of broccoli.

Buttoning will occur in susceptible varieties ('Early Emerald Hybrid,' 'Packman,' 'Waltham 29,' and 'Spartan Early') when young broccoli plants are grown at cold temperatures (below 40°F for two or more weeks) or when transplanting older plants (more than 14 inches tall) when temperatures are in the 50°F range. For those of you who like to push the growing season, 'Green Valiant' is one variety that can take the cold, and you might find other varieties listed as cold resistant in seed catalogs.

When choosing a variety, you must consider the weather at heading time. A sudden heat wave can make broccoli heads form on some stalks that are much taller than others, resulting in an uneven head with some buds tight and others already open to flower. These heads do not keep well in storage. 'Citation,' 'Green Hornet,' 'Green Valiant,' 'Premium Crop,' and 'Saga' are good choices if you think you might get a heat wave during broccoli heading. If your broccoli heads unevenly without excessive heat, it might be suffering from downy mildew or bacterial soft rot. With the latter, the flower buds on the heads will die and turn brown. Use a resistant variety such as 'Citation,' 'Emperor,' or 'Green Dwarf #36.'

Another consideration when choosing broccoli is the spacing between plants. If you want to leave only 6 to 12 inches between plants, choose a variety that the catalogs say will make a sizable head at close spacings. 'Emperor,' 'Eureka,' 'Green Dwarf #36,' and 'Green Valiant' are all possibilities.

For a change of pace, you might want to consider growing some of the different-colored or different-shaped varieties. Romanesco varieties, such as one by the same name, 'Bronzino,' and 'Minaret,' have a very interesting shape. The spears are a light white or cream color, with each tip forming a spiral dome, making the entire head look like a collection of shells. White, green, and purple forms of sprouting broccoli produce a long succession of side shoots without a central head. Purple broccoli that forms a large head tends to be both hardier and more heat tolerant than the standard green type. For a hardy fall variety, try 'Rosalind.' Many gardeners contend that purple broccoli is easier to grow because it attracts fewer pests than green broccoli. While the color is different, the flavor is unmistakably that of broccoli. When you cook the purple heads or stalks, the color changes to emerald-green.

Growing and Harvesting Broccoli

Like other cole crops, broccoli will germinate over a wide range of temperatures but comes up most quickly when the temperature is 75°F to 80°F. If the climate in your area isn't extremely hot and there is little variation between daytime and nighttime temperatures, you may be able to get both a spring and a fall broccoli crop. Start your spring crop in the house or greenhouse so the young plants aren't exposed to temperatures below 40°F. You can seed the fall crop directly in the garden in late spring. Set out your spring plants when the weather has warmed up and frosts are not likely to occur. The seedlings should be four to six weeks old when transplanted, and temperatures should stay above 40°F for the most part. If you've transplanted your young plants to the garden and suddenly have a cold spell, protect them with row covers if you have varieties that might button.

Broccoli should be spaced about 2 feet apart in rows 2½ to 3 feet apart for standard or large-head varieties or as close as 6 inches apart in rows 3 feet apart for varieties adapted to close spacing. The closer you space your plants, the smaller the heads will be. For example, in one study done by scientists in Minnesota, 'Southern Comet' produced a small, ¼-pound head with 6-inch spacing and heads about twice as large with 18-inch spacing. The yield will be higher with close spacing because, even though each head is small, there will be more heads per foot of row. If you like large heads and many good-size side shoots, give your broccoli plenty of room. But if you want smaller heads all produced at the same time for freezing, use more plants spaced more closely together. You should be aware, however, that if you crowd broccoli varieties that need more space, the stem may be hollow and the crop will mature later.

Broccoli needs rich soil but not as rich as cauliflower. Unlike cauliflower, broccoli can be grown in salty soil, such as that in the Southwest. Soil that is extremely high in nitrogen will result in broccoli with hollow stems. For the tenderest, most succulent spears, be sure your broccoli gets an even and adequate supply of water, as water stress produces fibrous spears.

Broccoli heads best in cool weather, around 68°F. If the weather is very hot, the flower buds will open prematurely, creating a loose head. Once that happens, the head will be tougher and stronger in flavor than a tight one. When you see a head begin to form in the middle of the plant, check it every day or two so that you can harvest it at its peak. If the head begins to look loose, cut it right away, even if it is small.

A common complaint heard from beginning gardeners is that their broccoli plants never formed a head but flowered instead. Don't expect your broccoli heads to look like those you see in the supermarket. With many garden varieties, the heads will be much smaller and will have shorter stems than supermarket varieties. Even if you harvest a small central head from your plant, don't be discouraged. You will still get many side shoots as a secondary crop. If some flowers do develop, cut them off right away so that more shoots will form later. If you let the flowers go to seed, your plants will be finished, but if you keep broccoli picked, it will

Harvesting Broccoli: When you cut the central heads of your broccoli plants, you will probably notice the beginnings of smaller side shoots, which can be harvested throughout the season.

continue to produce well into the fall after other crops have been killed by frost. Several varieties of broccoli are quite hardy. 'Green Valiant,' 'Premium Crop,' and 'Waltham 29' can take temperatures as low as 15°F, and 'Italian Sprouting' can survive dips down to 10°F.

Unfortunately, broccoli has a short storage life. Even under the best conditions (just above freezing at 90 to 95 percent humidity) it will keep only about two weeks. It isn't likely to last more than a week in the refrigerator.

If you're interested in saving seeds and you've never done it before, broccoli is a good crop to start with. Since it's an annual, it will flower at the end of one season and needs no special treatment. Just let some side shoots go to seed after you have harvested enough broccoli for the table and collect the seeds as you would cabbage seeds.

The unfortunate trend in broccoli breeding is toward varieties that form a single central head without side shoots so that commercial growers can get the most out of a single harvest. We hope that varieties with a more modest head followed by a good secondary crop will continue to be available to home gardeners. Breeders also are trying to develop varieties that will not bolt prematurely and that hold a head for a longer time. 'Northwest Waltham' was developed from 'Waltham 29' in an effort to reduce premature bolting. Scientists also are working on getting sprouting types of broccoli to produce a larger number of uniform sprouts.

Broccoli Frontiers

Chapter 7

Onions and Their Allies

VITAL STATISTICS

Family: Amaryllidaceae

Species: *Allium cepa* (and other species)

Soil: Rich organic soil that retains moisture well

pH: 6.0 to 6.8

Soil temperature for germination: 50°F to 85°F; 75°F optimum

Air temperature for best growth: 70°F to 80°F

Seed viability: 2 years under best conditions

Seed germination: 4 to 13 days

Seed planting depth: ¼ to ½ inch

Onions and their allies have been among our most valuable crops for more than five thousand years. Not only have they provided nourishment, but two, garlic and onions, were once worn around people's necks to ward off evil spirits. In the American colonies onions were used to treat a variety of diseases, including diabetes and pneumonia. Onion juice was served as an antiseptic and was considered so essential that General Ulysses S. Grant refused to move his troops without a generous supply of onions. Even today many people swear by the medicinal properties of some onion family members.

Onions are among the less expensive vegetables in the supermarket, and they also are one of the easiest and most fun crops to grow. There is something very satisfying about seeing those slim stalks fatten up almost as you watch! Some people, however, have trouble growing onions, and their difficulties almost always can be traced to a lack of understanding of how this environmentally sensitive plant functions. What causes onions to bulb, why they sometimes rebel and send up a flower stalk instead of bulbing, and how proper curing and storing can extend your supply well into the winter all relate to onion biology.

The onion family includes more than four hundred species worldwide, most of which have the familiar onion odor and flavor. An impressive variety of these plants has been molded to the needs of the home garden. Most of these crops, all called alliums after their scientific name, originated in the Orient. As people moved into areas with a different climate, they took their onions with them, select-

ing types that would thrive in their new environments. This centuries-long process resulted in a wealth of onion variations. Today's gardeners are sure to find onions that meet their needs no matter what sort of growing conditions they have.

To grow these garden staples successfully, it is important to understand how different onions respond to various environmental conditions. This chapter provides all the basics you need to grow a successful crop of bulbing onions. It also introduces some of the less familiar alliums, which are equally delightful to grow and use. These offbeat alliums include Egyptian onions, potato onions, ever-ready onions, shallots, garlic, elephant garlic, leeks, Japanese bunching onions, and regular and garlic chives.

How Onions Get Their Flavor

All alliums derive their special flavor from organic sulfur compounds within their cells. The tiny onion seedling already possesses these distinctive flavor components when its first leaf unfurls. These chemicals are released only when the cells are damaged, as when the onion is chopped up by a cook. Enzymes within the onion tissues are responsible for releasing the sulfur compounds. If you cook onions before cutting them, the heat destroys most of the enzymes, and the onion flavor is greatly reduced. For this reason onions for drying should not be blanched, or the resulting product will have little flavor.

The same sulfur compounds are responsible for your crying as you cut up onions. Set free by the knife, they drift through the air, coming into contact with the fluid in your eyes. There they dissolve to produce a weak, eye-irritating sulfuric acid solution, stimulating the release of tears to wash the acid away. You can minimize this problem by using a very sharp knife, which will disturb fewer onion cells than would a dull one. You also can peel and begin to cut up the onions under cold running water. When the onion is cold, less of the irritating chemicals are released, and the water carries much of the irritant away. A variation on this technique is to put the onions in the refrigerator long enough before you plan to use them that they become thoroughly chilled.

These sulfur compounds act as antibacterial and fungicidal agents. Strong onions, which have more sulfur compounds than mild ones, keep longer partially because they can fend off decay better.

BULB ONIONS

Onions come in a wonderful variety of flavors and colors. There are red, white, and yellow onions which are sweet, spicy, pungent, or downright hot. Some onions keep for months in storage, but others must be used within a few weeks of harvesting lest they sprout or rot.

The pigments in the "skin" (properly called the scale) that give red and yellow onions their attractive colors also help lengthen storage life, as they can prevent some of the fungal diseases common to onions. Smudge and neck rot disease occur mainly in white onions because their skin lacks the protective pigments.

Onions are the third most popular vegetable in the American diet after lettuce and tomatoes. It's a good thing, then, that onions are nutritious. When you add diced, sautéed onions to your omelets or blend them into your favorite meat loaf, you are incorporating a reliable source of iron, calcium, potassium, and vitamin A into your diet. When you use bulbing onions in their immature form as green onions, you're providing your family with almost twice as much iron, close to sixteen times more calcium, and one-third more potassium than an equal portion of corn supplies.

What Makes Onions Form Bulbs

Depending on light and temperature, the onions in your garden can do one of three things—bulb up, remain bulbless and produce nothing but scallions, or bolt and burst into bloom. Most of the time you will want them to bulb up, so it is important to understand how light and temperature affect the plants. Day length influences onion bulb formation, while temperature chiefly affects flowering.

Each onion variety will bulb up only after being exposed to days of a particular length. Some onions need short days for bulbing, and others require long ones. If you live in the Deep South and plant a long-day variety such as 'Autumn Spice,' chances are your onions will never bulb up, for such varieties, developed for northern growing, may require sixteen-hour days for bulbing. Southern days are never that long. In fact, the longest day a gardener in, say, South Carolina, could expect would be less than fifteen hours. (Refer to the day-length map in chapter 2 to find out the maximum day length in your area.) In contrast, a northern gardener would end up with tiny onions if he or she tried to grow a short-day variety such as 'Red Creole,' as the plants would still be very small when they were triggered to bulb by the day-length signal. 'Red Creole' can even bulb up after producing only two tiny leaves if the day length is long enough. Thus southern gardeners should plant varieties that require twelve- to fourteen-hour days for bulbing, while northerners should choose the longest-day varieties.

Temperature also plays a minor role in bulbing. If it is especially cool, bulb formation may be delayed, even after the proper day length is reached. For this reason, high-altitude gardeners and those living in cool northern regions may find that they can grow short-day varieties after all. Because cool temperatures delay bulbing, the plants can reach adequate size to produce good-size onions before actually bulbing up. Such gardeners might have problems with long-day varieties, as bulbing could be delayed too long for mature onions to develop before a heavy frost sets in.

Scientists working in Ithaca, New York, have experimented with growing onions at different temperatures. They grew the same variety in three different temperature ranges: 70°F to 80°F, 60°F to 70°F, and 50°F to 60°F. The onions grown at the warmest temperatures had mature bulbs with dead tops at the end of the growing season, while those raised under the coolest temperatures had no mature bulbs at all. The plants grown at the intermediate temperatures had mature bulbs, but their tops were still green at the end of the season, which can lead to problems in storage. Be forewarned: if your summer is unusually cool, you may be eating a lot of fresh onions in the fall.

A few other factors also affect bulbing. Larger plants bulb up faster than smaller ones, which is why large sets will produce an earlier crop than small ones. In general, also for this reason, plants grown from sets mature first, those grown from transplants second, and those grown from seeds last. Spacing also affects bulbing, as onions planted close together will mature earlier than those planted farther apart. The onions of the closer plants also will be smaller.

While onion varieties vary greatly in their tendency to bolt, once an onion plant has reached a critical size, temperatures of 40°F to 50°F will cause it to send up a flower stalk instead of bulbing. This has important consequences for gardeners, both northern and southern. If you live in the North, you will want to plant your onions as early as possible so that the plants will be large when they reach the critical day length for bulbing. You don't want to plant too early, however, or a late spring cold snap could turn your onion patch into a flower garden! One year Dorothy confidently planted a northern variety, 'Autumn Spice,' looking forward to fat storage onions in only ninety-eight days. But instead of bulbing up nicely, almost all her plants went to seed. She suspects that this variety is especially sensitive to cold temperatures and is not suitable for growing in Montana, where cold springs are common. Southern gardeners who overwinter their onions must plant late enough in the fall that the plants do not get bigger than about ¼ inch in diameter before the onset of cool winter temperatures, or their crop will bolt come spring.

Bulb Onion Varieties

Unfortunately, few seed catalogs give the information you need to choose the right onion varieties for your region. If you buy from a small regional supplier you can be confident that the varieties you choose are adapted to your area. But if you buy from a national supplier, you may need more information than the catalog provides. Much of the information provided is useless. For example, one catalog says that a particular variety is "slow to bolt in unfavorable weather." What does "unfavorable" mean? One might guess that it means too cold, but that would be just a guess. Catalogs from Parks and Burpee's identify onions as either long-day or short-day varieties.

See the box "A Sampling of Bulb Onion Varieties" to find some varieties that are suitable for your climate. If you need more information, try writing to your favorite seed company requesting information as to day-length requirements for bulbing, bolting temperatures, and days to maturity for the varieties in which you are interested. If enough customers ask for this information, maybe more seed companies will include it in their catalogs.

As with so many other crops, your own records can be your best guide to choosing onion varieties. If you plant a variety that never gets around to forming bulbs, you will know that either the climate is too cool for it or the day length isn't long enough to trigger bulbing. A variety that bolts when planted from seeds is probably too sensitive to cold springs to be grown in your area—unless you planted especially early or had an abnormally cold spring. If your plants bulb up too soon and you end up with small onions that are suitable only for stew, you will know that you must either discard that variety or plant it earlier so that the plants are larger before bulbing.

Also consider storage life when choosing onion varieties. While the sweet Spanish types are wonderful, they generally do not keep very well, so you will want to plant some better keepers along with them to get you through the winter. Storage onions generally have firmer, drier bulbs with more protective skin around them than do milder, shorter-lasting types. Catalogs are better about describing eating and keeping qualities than they are about day-length and temperature requirements, so that should make your choices somewhat easier.

Plant breeders made a welcome breakthrough with onions only a few years ago. They developed 'Sweet Sandwich,' a variety that gets sweeter in storage. After three months in storage, 'Sweet Sandwich' onions taste at least as mild as 'Sweet Spanish.' Not only does this special onion provide a welcome flavor in the middle of the winter, but it also outproduces older varieties such as 'Sentinel' and 'Sweet Spartan.' 'Sweet Sandwich' can be planted at low densities without delaying maturity, so you can get nice, big onions for storage if you want.

We have a couple of favorite onion varieties. Diane enjoys 'Redman,' an attractive red onion that stores well, unlike other reds. Dorothy is enthusiastic about 'Italian Blood Red Bottle.' These onions have a deep, rich, mild flavor to go along with their unusual torpedo shape. The only problem is that they do not keep long in storage.

A new type of onion has recently become available in North America—the Japanese winter onion. Popular in Europe and Asia, seeds of this type of onion are planted in mid-August and mulched during the winter for harvest the following June. Japanese winter onions fill the gap between crops of standard bulbing onions and keep well for several weeks in storage. Only a few companies offer them. An especially good variety of Japanese winter onion is 'Keepwell F-1 Hybrid', which has a rounder shape than other Japanese winter onions and is therefore better for slicing.

A SAMPLING OF BULB ONION VARIETIES

Variety Name	Average Days to Maturity	Characteristics
Northern (long-day) Onions		
'Buffalo'	88	Can be overwintered; large yellow bulb; short-term storage only.
'Early Yellow Globe'	100	Popular in the Northeast; nice kitchen medium-size onion with strong flavor; stores well.
'Ebenezer'	105	Widely grown for sets; strong-flavored onion that stores well; white and yellow varieties available.
'Italian Blood Red Bottle'	120	Very sweet and mild bottle-shaped red onion.
'Redman'	105	Mild, sweet red onion; one of the best-keeping red onions.
'Southport Red Globe'	105	Round bulbs with purple-red skin and pinkish flesh; pungent flavor; stores well.
'Southport Yellow Globe'	115	Medium-size bulbs with excellent flavor.
'Sweet Sandwich'	110	Pungent at first but mellows to a mild, sweet taste in storage; one of the best storing onions.
'Sweet Spanish' (also known as 'Yellow Utah')	120	Mild, sweet onion with large bulbs; good for fresh eating; does not store well.
'Walla Walla Sweet'	110	Matures much later if planted in the fall and overwintered; one of the sweetest onions and very large; short storage.
Southern (short-day) Onions		
'Creole C-5'	110	Large red onion that performs well under hot, humid conditions; excellent keeping qualities.
'Crystal Wax'	95	Mild-flavored onion that seldom bolts; does not store well; used for pickling when closely planted.
'Excel 986'	180	Sweet, mild-tasting Bermuda type; excellent keeper.

Variety Name	Average Days to Maturity	Characteristics
Southern (short-day) Onions, *continued*		
'Granex'	162	Popular in Deep South; large, round, juicy onion with mild, sweet flavor; stores well if hung to dry in an area with good air circulation.
'Red Bermuda'	93	Crisp texture with mild flavor; large, flat bulbs with red skins; makes good table onion.
'Red Creole'	170	Small- to medium-size onion; pungent bulbs; resistant to thrips; susceptible to bolting; moderately good for storage.
'Texas Early Grano 502'	168	Excellent for fall planting; exhibits some resistance to thrips; mild flavored but doesn't store well; not susceptible to bolting.
Japanese Winter Onions		
'Express Yellow F-1'	300	Firm, medium-size bulbs with mild flavor and brown skin; flattened bulbs keep well in storage.
'Keep Well F-1 Hybrid'	250	Almost globe shaped with thick bronze-colored skin; keeps well.
'Top Keeper F-1'	300	Deep yellow medium-size globes with mild flavor; keeps well.

How an Onion Grows

Whether you grow your onions from sets, transplants, or seeds, it is important to understand something about how onions grow and mature. When onions germinate, they look very different from plants such as cabbage, peppers, and tomatoes. That's because onions are monocots and have only one cotyledon and the others are dicots, with two cotyledons. When the onion root pushes out of the seed coat, the cotyledon starts to grow up toward the soil's surface. It forms a loop that onion growers call a *knee.* The knee breaks through the soil, so the first sign of your onions is a row of tiny green loops. The loops continue to grow until they are 2 to 3 inches tall. By then the old seed coat, which is still attached to the tip of the cotyledon, has been pulled out of the ground. Growth between the seed coat and the knee has stopped, but the area from the knee to the stem continues to grow. At this stage the loop begins to straighten out so that the little plant looks like a flag. During the flag stage you can see the first true leaf growing alongside the cotyledon.

The onion plant is very different from a dicot. While most familiar garden crops have a recognizable stem that supports the plant and holds the leaves up into the sunlight, the onion plant has hardly any stem at all. It is actually the thick woody area just above the roots that you cut out when you are chopping or slicing an onion in the kitchen. Even in a full-grown onion, the stem is no more than ¾ inch wide and ½ inch tall.

The onion leaves grow straight up out of this stem. Onion leaves also have a peculiar shape. Each leaf is like a hollow tube at its base; the new leaves grow up through the tube formed by the bases of the older leaves. Only one side of each leaf actually grows upward to form the hollow green spike we recognize as a leaf. The rest of the leaf stays put, firmly encircling the emerging newer leaves inside its hollow core. As the plant grows, these leaf bases become longer and longer, creating a structure that looks like a stem but is properly called the *neck* of the plant. The neck is not a stem at all but merely a conglomerate of all the leaf bases and growing leaves inside them.

The process of bulb formation gets under way when some of the leaf bases start to thicken. Bulbing is a time of great metabolic activity. In the four to six weeks of bulbing, onion plants triple or quadruple their weight. As the leaf bases thicken, the flavor precursors move from the blades of the leaves to the bases. The first thickened bases send up green leaves, but soon the thickening leaves put all their energy into becoming part of the bulb and do not send up any more leaves. These thick, tubular bases become the rings of the mature onion. The onion bulb is not a tuber or a root but a collection of fattened leaves.

If you cut a stored onion in half down the middle from top to root, you can see that the rings are really short, thick leaves growing up from the small stem. The dry scales covering the outside of the onion are the oldest three or four leaf bases that never thickened and dried into a protective covering for the bulb. The next three to five leaves have thick bases and leaf blades that form the neck of the onion. The interior leaves consist only of thickened bases. At the very center are the youngest and smallest leaves, which can sprout and grow through the top of the bulb during storage.

When an onion is mature, the inner leaves are not producing blades. The resulting hollow center in the neck weakens it, and the top begins to bend over, signaling that the onion is reaching maturity. When an onion bolts and forms a flower stalk, the stem grows right up through the neck, forming a tough, fibrous tube in the center of the bulb. The plant puts all its energy into this flower stalk. The bulb does not increase in size, since no more fleshy leaf bases are being formed. It may actually decrease in size, for the stored food in the bulb may be used to build the flower stalk. If you don't want to save the seeds, you can still use such onions in the kitchen. They are not very big, and the tough stalk must be cut out of the center, but onions suffer no loss of flavor when they bolt.

Occasionally onions form double bulbs. The center of the bulb may have been damaged in some way, forming two lateral buds instead of one central stem. For some reason, double bulbs often result from larger onion sets. Dorothy once inadvertently raised a crop of double bulbs when she planted some red onion sets. As a further twist in their curious development, one of the buds in each pair produced a flower stalk, while the other rounded up into a small red onion.

Onions can be started from sets, transplants, or seeds. All these methods work well, but each has some advantages and disadvantages.

Planting the Onion Crop

Onions from Sets

Onion sets are miniature onions that were grown under crowded conditions so that they formed bulbs while the plants were still small. Growing your onions from sets will give you quicker results than growing them from seeds, and sets are a lot easier to plant and care for than seeds. You can place them in the ground at their final growing distance if you like, or you can plant them closer together and use the thinnings as scallions.

Unfortunately, there is one serious problem with growing onions from sets. If the sets are larger than ½ inch in diameter and have been stored at temperatures of 40°F to 50°F, most of the plants will bolt instead of producing big bulbs. Some years we've gotten beautiful onions from sets, and others we've ended up with nothing but flowers. Diane especially remembers the time she carefully picked out all the biggest sets from the bins at the gardening store, congratulating herself on how big her onions would be since they started out as such large sets. What a disappointment it was when almost the whole crop bolted!

Onion sets should be stored at temperatures just above freezing (33°F) or above 65°F but never in between. The higher temperatures can result in excessive loss of sets from drying out. There is no way of knowing whether the sets you buy have been stored properly. All you can do is buy from a reputable dealer and store the sets correctly once you have them. If you don't know how the sets were stored, choose small ones. If you are certain that the sets were stored properly, select large ones to produce the fattest, fastest-maturing bulbs.

Onion sets often are sold as white, yellow, or red onions with no mention of the variety, much less of day-length requirements or bolting temperatures. Sets generally result in good storage onions; after all, the sets themselves had to survive the winter without rotting or sprouting. Most onion sets in this country are grown in the Chicago area and, therefore, are long-day varieties. Those of you in the South could have trouble getting harvestable bulbs from these plants. You will have better luck with sets grown in your own area.

As you can see, growing onions from sets is the easiest route, but you must be mindful of their problems. Until you can find a reliable source of sets, don't count on them for providing your entire onion crop. Once you know which varieties will grow well in your area, you can grow your own sets and store them properly to guarantee an abundant harvest.

There is no trick to growing sets. Some varieties ('Ebenezer White,' 'Ebenezer Yellow,' and 'Stuttgarter,' for example) are especially well adapted for growing sets. You might want to try one of these the first time around. You can sow the seeds at the same time you plant the rest of your onions. Plant them in a small area, spaced ¼ inch apart, so the resulting bulbs will be small. Make sure they get plenty of water, for crowded plants use up water faster than more widely spaced ones. Your sets will probably bulb up before your other varieties (crowding induces onions to bulb two to five weeks early). Once they have bulbed and the tops start to fall down, push the remaining tops down.

When the greens have withered, dig up the tiny bulbs and let them dry outside in a warm, shady spot. If you have a spare window screen handy, elevate it on a couple of bricks to make a handy rack for drying sets. Let the sets dry until their skins are crackly and the roots have completely dried and withered. Then gather them up and store them either above 65°F with some humidity (not over 65 percent) or just above 32°F. Check on your sets just as you do your stored onions and remember that sets stored at higher temperatures will suffer some losses from drying out.

When planting time rolls around, take care to orient the sets with the root end down and the top up, positioning them so that the top is close to the surface of the soil (½ to 1 inch deep depending on the size of each set). Firm the soil gently around your sets to anchor them; otherwise a spring downpour may knock them out of the ground or turn them sideways before their roots have grown.

Onions from Transplants

Onion seedlings for transplanting are available through the mail and sometimes in gardening stores. They are generally quite expensive and often are not identified by variety. Thus, as with sets, you won't know whether you are buying onions that have the proper day-length requirements for your area. Dorothy once bought plants through the mail called 'Texas Sweeties,' which would seem to indicate a short-day variety. Apparently, the appellation 'Texas' meant only that the plants were grown in that state, for they flourished and bulbed just fine in Montana. If a gardener living farther south had bought the same plants, they may never have bulbed up!

There are other drawbacks to buying transplants. The plants will have been out of the light and soil for several days by the time you get them, and you won't know under what sort of conditions they were grown. For these reasons such plants are bound to be handicapped no matter how carefully you plant them.

There's no need to rely on commercial sources of transplants, since growing your own is easy. And when you plant them yourself, you can be sure the variety is appropriate and you are familiar with their growing conditions.

Start your onions about six weeks before you plan to plant them outside. Sow the seeds thickly in rows or clumps, or scatter them all over the flat or other planting container. We have found that a milk carton placed on its side and cut lengthwise to make a planter provides plenty of room for a sizable crop of transplants. Plant the seeds ¼ to ½ inch deep. Be sure to keep the soil damp until the seedlings emerge, which should take five to ten days at room temperature. At 75°F germination can occur in only four days.

Once the seeds have sprouted, grow the plants outside in a cold frame or on an unheated sun porch if possible. Onions can withstand some frost even when tiny, and if they are grown outside, they will need no hardening off beyond the usual decrease in watering. Also, they will grow slowly into sturdy plants that are well equipped for life outdoors. Onions raised inside at higher temperatures will grow more quickly, resulting in skinny, weak plants that will need a long period of hardening off to adjust to the cooler outside temperatures. If you have no choice but to grow onion seedlings indoors, be sure they get a lot of light. If you have no sunny south-facing windows, supplement the sunlight they receive with a fluorescent light. Remember to turn off the fluorescent fixture when the sun goes down. If you give your baby onion plants too many hours of light, they may be triggered to bulb up even though they are very tiny. Once an onion begins to bulb up, it stops producing new leaves, the number of roots declines, and you are stuck with baby onions in June.

Many gardening books recommend trimming the roots or tops of onion plants when they are transplanted. This may be necessary with purchased transplants, for the ends of the roots often have been damaged and the tops must be cut back to compensate for the lack of adequate roots. With homegrown plants it is better to separate them carefully, place them 4 to 6 inches apart in shallow furrows about 2 inches deep, quickly push dirt around their roots, and water them immediately. This will minimize transplant shock. Don't forget that because onions run on an inner clock that responds to day length, you want them to grow as fast as possible so you can harvest the largest bulbs.

Onions from Seeds

Onion seeds are especially perishable. If they are kept in a warm, moist environment, they can lose their ability to germinate in less than a year. For this reason most authorities recommend that you not save onion seeds from year to year. But if you take the special precautions for storing seeds described in chapter 1, you may be able to keep onion seeds viable for two years or more. Scientists have kept onion seeds viable under very dry conditions (around 6 percent humidity) for as long as nine years. As with any seeds you store, you should run a germination test before planting. Be aware that by using old seeds, you run the risk of planting seeds whose food reserves are less than adequate, resulting in weakened plants that produce small bulbs.

Since onion seeds are so small, you should plant them no deeper than ½ inch. Keep the soil moist so the seeds won't dry out and the surface won't crust over, making it hard for the delicate seedlings to break through. This may require some ingenuity and special care if you live in an area where the wind dries out the soil. To counteract the effects of the wind, prepare a seedbed that is depressed about 1 inch from the surface of the surrounding soil. Sprinkle the seeds on top and cover them with ¼ inch of fine-textured mulch, such as grass clippings, premoistened peat moss, or some of your own compost pressed through a sieve. The final spacing of your plants should be 4 to 6 inches apart, but you may want to seed more thickly to provide yourself with fresh green onions during the growing season.

Row covers can give your onions a head start in cool weather and can help provide you with fat green onions earlier than if you grew them out in the cold. Do not use slitted polyethylene covers however, because the plants won't put enough pressure on the plastic to open the slits, and it will be too hot for them inside.

Onion seeds will germinate at a wide temperature range, from 50°F to 85°F, with best results at 75°F. If your soil is cool, it may take as long as two weeks for the seeds to germinate. Remember to keep the soil uniformly moist until those tiny plants appear.

Planting Onions for Overwintering

Some onion varieties are adapted for planting in mid-August and harvesting in late spring or early summer. 'Walla Walla Sweet,' famous in the West, is one such variety. People living in the Pacific Northwest feel that summer has really arrived when the first 'Walla Walla Sweet' onions appear in the stores, even if the weather is still cool and damp. This variety can be grown from spring planting, but the yield is never as big or as sweet as that from overwintered plants. 'Walla Walla Sweet' onions can be sown in late August where temperatures stay above −10°F and harvested three hundred days later. As mentioned earlier, several Japanese varieties are designed for overwintering, as is the winter-hardy 'White Lisbon.'

You always take a risk with overwintered onions, as a prolonged cold spell could ruin your crop. But since there are no other demands on your garden space at that time of year, you might as well experiment with winter onions. The key to success with these varieties is to mulch them generously before the ground freezes. Frost heaving is the main cause of crop loss. The onion's sparsely branched root system provides little resistance to the upheaval. In addition, organic soils, with their loose structure, suffer more from this problem than do hard soils low in organic matter. When the temperature warms up in the spring, pull the mulch away from the plants so they can soak up the sun and begin to grow again.

Onion Roots and the Soil

You'll get the best crop of onions if you understand how onion roots grow and do your best to meet their needs in your garden. The onion seedling produces only one primary root; all the other roots are secondary ones that grow directly from the stem. Each secondary root has a short life span, and new ones are constantly growing to replace dying ones. For the new roots to form, the soil must be moist. Onion roots do not branch very much and are generally limited to a 6-inch area around the bulb. They rarely descend more than 10 inches into the soil, so keeping the ground moist enough for onions can be a challenge in hot, dry weather. Onions grown under water stress are generally stronger in flavor and smaller in size than those that have received enough water, so it's important to be sure your onions get enough moisture.

Onions do best in a good organic soil. A heavy clay soil that becomes waterlogged is not healthy, and a sandy soil will require such frequent watering that you may leach out the nutrients necessary for the fast, even growth that leads to large bulbs. The roots of onions can afford to be on the skimpy side, for they cooperate with mycorrhizal fungi that allow them to extract phosphorus and sulfur more efficiently from the soil (see chapter 2). Gardeners who use chemical fertilizers on their onions risk killing these beneficial fungi and thus inhibiting the growth of their crop. Since sulfur compounds are important to the flavor of onions, chemical fertilizers could result in an inferior crop in more ways than one.

To provide the moist, rich soil your onions need, dig some compost or well-rotted manure right into the rows where you will be planting. It's important for your onions to get enough nitrogen. If they are undernourished while growing, they may be triggered into bolting when a cold spell hits, and you'll never get a crop. Since onion roots do not extend very far down, this localized treatment will be very effective. Onions do poorly in salty soil, so avoid using large quantities of poultry manure. Onions grow best in soils that are not too acid (a pH of 6.0 to 6.8 is the ideal range). If you need to sweeten your soil, add wood ashes, which also will contribute valuable potassium. Sprinkle some of the ashes around the bases of your onion plants to discourage the onion maggot fly from laying its eggs there.

Although onions need rich soil, too much nitrogen can delay bulbing. If you plan to enrich your soil with fresh manure, do it in the fall if you plant your onions in the spring or vice versa. Be sure your soil has adequate phosphorus; a defi-

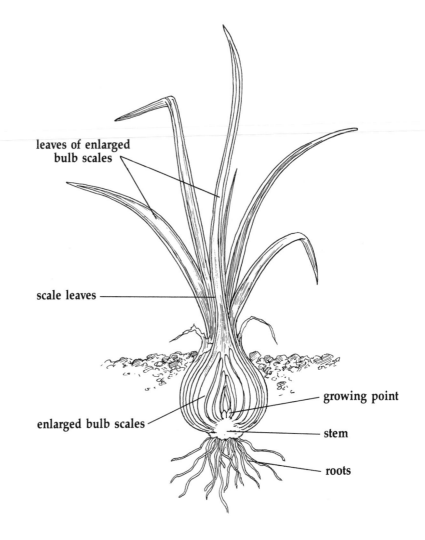

leaves of enlarged
bulb scales

scale leaves

growing point

enlarged bulb scales

stem

roots

ciency in this mineral can result in onions that have thick necks and don't store well. Sometimes a potassium deficiency also produces thick necks. If the oldest leaves are yellowing and their tips are turning brown, dig in some wood ashes around your onions to give them more potassium.

Beware of Weed Competition

You have to watch out for weeds in the onion patch. Your tiny onion plants are in very rich soil but grow slowly at first. Because their leaves grow straight up, they produce practically no weed-inhibiting shade. For these reasons, weeds can quickly overwhelm young onion plants. You must keep them well weeded, especially when they are tiny. Seedlings at the flag stage are especially susceptible to weed competition, for it is at this time that the first true leaf is unfolding. If weeds run rampant and crowd your onion seedlings, their growth will be slowed, and you will end up with small bulbs. Weeds also cut your onion yield about 4 percent per day.

An experiment at the University of the Philippines graphically showed the effects of neglecting weeding. A scientist there let the weeds in an onion patch grow for the first seven and a half weeks of seedling growth. All he got was very tiny bulblets. Not only did the weeds crowd and shade the onions, but they also took so many of the nutrients from the soil that the weak onion roots were nutrient stressed. This experiment showed that if you want big onion bulbs, you should keep your patch weeded for at least the first two months of growth.

The best plan of attack is to pay frequent visits to the garden—at least once a week—so that you can get to the weeds before their roots have spread very far. If you wait too long, you will disturb the shallow onion roots when you pull up the competition. Weeding only when the soil is moist also helps minimize disturbance to the onion seedlings. A trick Dorothy uses when weeds are growing close to her small onion plants is to use a screwdriver to take out the weeds. She gently inserts the screwdriver into the soil next to the weed on the side farthest from any onion plants, then carefully pulls out the weed. Mulching onions also helps to keep down weeds, but you need to wait until the soil is warm before mulching. Keep thinning the onions and using the fresh green scallions in your kitchen, too; an overcrowded onion patch will have the same problems as a weedy one.

Harvesting Bulb Onions

When the tops of your onions begin to fall over, you know they have finished growing and are into the last stages of bulbing up. At this time you should stop watering them so that the bulbs can dry out. Moist conditions also encourage disease organisms to infect the onions and either ruin them entirely or limit their storage life.

When at least one-quarter of the tops have fallen over, you can hurry things along by pushing over the rest. After the tops fall, nutrients from the leaves move into the bulb and increase its weight. This process stops when the leaves die and turn brown. If you push down the tops too early, while the leaves are still growing, you will be interfering with the natural sequence of events leading to the dormant dry bulb, and your onions will sprout sooner than properly matured ones. Onions that haven't matured properly will have thick, moist necks instead of narrow, dry ones. The damp necks are a perfect breeding ground for fungi and bacteria, and the onions are very likely to rot in storage.

Do not let your onions sit in the field too long, as they can overmature. The bulbs also can become sunburned and lose their protective outer scales, making them more susceptible to disease and early sprouting. You have probably seen sunburned onions; they have shriveled-up circular areas on the outermost thickened leaf bases. One season Diane was so busy harvesting other crops that she left her white onions in the ground too long. By the time she got to them, they were already sunburned, and they began to spoil soon after harvesting.

Once the onions have started to dry out and their tops have withered, you can lift the bulbs out of the ground. If the weather is warm and dry, you may be able to dig them up just a few days after knocking down the tops. If it's wet and cool, the tops will take longer to become limp. Be sure to dig up the bulbs before the tops start to rot.

The next step is to cure your onions. Curing is simply the process of drying the onions evenly so that they have no moist areas susceptible to decay. The longest-lasting storage onions are those with hard, dry bulbs completely surrounded by scales. Be sure to cure your onions out of direct sunlight so that they don't get sunburned. If you leave them in the sun, their skins will bleach and soften, providing an easy route for disease organisms to enter and spoil the bulb. It may seem strange, but moderately high humidity (60 to 70 percent) provides the best conditions for curing onions. When they're dried at a lower humidity, most of the scales often are lost. If the humidity is above 80 percent, however, the bulbs are more likely to rot and will be very slow to cure.

You can cure your onions in the garden if you lay them out so that the leaves lie on top of the bulbs and shade them. Lay the onions down in bunches, with the leaves of one bunch lying over the bulbs of the previous one. This open-air method is practical only in areas that have warm, sunny weather at curing time. Curing onions can't be left out in the rain, and cool temperatures will inhibit proper curing. Onions can cure in a week when the weather is sunny and hot. In cool, cloudy weather, it may take them as long as two weeks.

Dorothy knows all about the effects of cool temperatures on onions. Several years ago a very cool summer kept her onions from bulbing up quite as fast as they should have. When fall came, their tops began to topple over as they were supposed to. But cool fall weather arrived ahead of schedule, and the tops refused to turn completely brown and dry. Dorothy dug up the crop anyway, but even then the tops never turned brown and the onions just wouldn't cure properly.

During damp or extremely hot weather bring your onions into a shed, carport, attic, or garage for curing. The curing process takes at least two weeks (longer in cool weather). During this time it is very important to make sure that the air circulates freely around your onions. If you are curing them inside, spread them out in a single layer.

Once the curing is done, cut or break off any of the tops that are left within an inch of the neck. Leave the protective scales on. Don't remove the top when the neck is still wet, or you will create a site where fungi and bacteria can enter.

Diane learned this lesson the hard way. One year she planted 'Sweet Spanish' (also known as 'Yellow Utah') onions, which aren't meant for long storage. She stubbornly ignored this fact and tried to cure the bulbs anyway. After three weeks of patient curing, the necks were still thick and hadn't dried out. After two more weeks she gave up and realized that the reason this variety wasn't recommended for storage was because the onions had such thick necks. She decided to cut off the tops, and her family began an onion-eating marathon. They ate onions at every opportunity, but they couldn't finish them off before they began to spoil, only four weeks after she'd cut off the tops. Most of the spoilage occurred at the necks. She probably would have been better off leaving those green leaves on instead of cutting them and opening the bulbs up to infection. If you have similar problems, you can chop your onions and freeze or dehydrate them rather than let them spoil.

Storing to Avoid Sprouting

For best results store your onions as close to 32°F as possible without freezing them and at 60 to 70 percent humidity. Under these conditions there will be little if any sprout growth, and good-keeping onions should remain usable for six to eight months. Even poor keepers such as 'Sweet Granex' will keep well for six months when kept this cold. Be forewarned, however, that once sweet onions are brought back to room temperature after cold storage, they will sprout or decay very rapidly. Also, sweet onions lose their sweetness over time in storage at cold temperatures, and their flavor becomes more pungent.

Sprouting generally indicates overly warm storage temperatures, improper curing, or premature harvesting. An old refrigerator set at a low temperature with a pan of water in it to keep up the humidity is an excellent place to store onions. An unheated basement or storeroom that doesn't go below freezing or a corner of a garage against the house also is a good place to stash your onions. Be sure to allow plenty of air circulation by storing them in mesh bags or setting them in boxes raised off the floor on bricks. Diane has had good luck storing onions in plastic laundry baskets set against an outside basement wall. The wall provides both humidity and cold. Once a month she rummages through each basket and ferrets out any rotting or sprouting onions. Like onion sets, onion bulbs will remain dormant if stored at high temperatures (from 77°F to 86°F). However, high temperatures result in significant losses from rotting and drying out.

Growing Onions for Seeds

You may want to try your hand at growing your own onion seeds. If so, choose an open-pollinated variety rather than a hybrid (see chapter 1 for a discussion of hybrids). Onions grown for seeds must be encouraged to bolt; this is easily done by storing them at 40°F to 50°F for at least two weeks. For most gardeners, this will mean picking out the nicest bulbs from the crop you've grown for eating and storing them for the winter before replanting them in the spring. After this cool rest period most of the replanted bulbs should flower.

Onion flowers take a long time to mature into dry seed heads, but you must be patient and wait until the seeds are thoroughly dry before harvesting them. This drying process can take up to two weeks; you'll know the seeds are ready when you can rub them easily from the flower heads. There are anywhere from 6 to 120 seeds per flower head, and they tend to ripen at an uneven rate, so some will be ready before others. Visit your onion flowers regularly to harvest the seeds as they dry. Remember, it's especially important to store onion seeds in a cool, very dry place.

Onion breeders who grow hybrid seeds for sale have found that flies pollinate onion flowers better than bees. However, many areas do not have enough flies to pollinate onions adequately. For example, in Idaho fields are pollinated by bees brought in to make up for the natural insect population destroyed by insecticides.

Problems with Onions

Few diseases bother the onion, which has built-in defense mechanisms. However, root maggots can be a problem. See the section "Secrets of Radish Success" in chapter 8 for suggestions on dealing with this pest.

Onion thrips: These minute insects (about 1/25 inch long) are serious threats to both bulbing onions and others. Thrips cause damage in the adult and larva stage by piercing plant cells and sucking out the contents. If you see small whitish patches on your plants that may run together and form silvery areas, you probably have thrips. You can control these bothersome insects by keeping the area around the onion patch free of weeds, which can shelter the thrips during the winter. If thrips are a serious problem, try growing sweet Spanish onions, which often are quite resistant.

Onion Frontiers

Breeders keep trying to develop new onion varieties that will keep well but have a mild taste. This is difficult, but there are a few mild varieties that keep moderately well, including 'Fiesta 61' and 'Granex Yellow F-1.' The relatively new variety 'Sweet Sandwich,' described under the section "Onion Varieties," is a result of this persistent work of onion breeders.

Another goal is to find ways to stop plants from bolting by using natural plant hormones. Much recent breeding work has been aimed at developing plants that produce no functional male flowers. Such varieties are useful in producing hybrids because the male flowers need not be removed from the flower clusters by hand to avoid self-pollination. As with just about any crop, onion breeders are always on the lookout for disease-resistant strains. New gene-splicing techniques may turn out to be useful with onions, as many other allium species are resistant to diseases that bother bulb onions. If the genes for such resistance could be isolated and spliced onto garden onion cells, growing onions would become even easier than it is now.

OTHER TYPES OF ONIONS

Besides the familiar and widely grown bulbing garden onion, the genus *Allium* includes many other cultivated crops, all of which contain similar organic sulfur compounds giving them that distinctive oniony or garlicky flavor. Even though they all taste different, the resemblance is noticeable.

Confusion exists as to the identity of many plants and animals because common names often are unrelated to scientific ones. For example, the name *robin* in Britain, North America, and Australia refers to three completely different, basically unrelated birds. With alliums, not only is there confusion about common names, but there also is disagreement among scientists about scientific names. There are six species of commonly cultivated alliums. Two of these are further divided into groups. An assortment of names has been suggested for these groups, but scientists cannot agree on which names to use. In this chapter we try to avoid the controversy by using only common names that are widely accepted.

Unfortunately, in using common names we run into the same sort of problem as with robins: the same name may be used in various regions to describe dif-

ONIONS: MANY KINDS, MANY NAMES

To help you keep track of the various alliums, we've organized a family tree of sorts to introduce you to some of the less familiar members and show you which ones are related to which.

Allium cepa
  Common Onion Group:
  Bulb onion
  Aggregatum Group:
    Potato onion (also multiplier
    onion, potato hill onion,
    underground onion; rarely,
    Egyptian onion)
    Ever-ready onion
    Shallot (Spanish garlic)
  Proliferum Group:
    Egyptian onion (also top, tree,
    nest, evergreen, or winter onion)
Allium sativum
    Garlic
    Rocambole (a form of *Allium
    sativum;* also called sand leek,

Allium sativum (continued)
    serpent garlic, Spanish garlic,
    Spanish shallot)
Allium ampeloprasum
  Great-headed Garlic Group:
    Elephant garlic
  Leek Group:
    Leek
Allium fistulosum
    Japanese bunching onion
    (also Welsh onion, evergreen
    onion, ciboules)
Alium schoenoprasum
    Chives
Allium tuberosum
    Garlic chives (also Chinese or
    Oriental chives)

ferent species. For example, the name *multiplier onion* may refer to Egyptian onions, potato onions, or the perennial Japanese bunching onion. Also, different names may be used for the same crop in different areas. The box "Onions: Many Kinds, Many Names" lists the names most widely used for all the commonly cultivated onions. In all cases the first name in the list is the one we use here when discussing each type of onion.

The most confusing part of scientific onion classification is how to divide up members of the species *Allium cepa*. Three groups are generally accepted, with the division made on the basis of how the plants grow. The Common Onion group includes all varieties of the garden bulbing onion, which form a single large bulb in the ground. The Proliferum group contains just the Egyptian onion, which forms a cluster of tiny bulblets at the top of the plant. The Aggregatum group might be confusing, as it includes three different types: the potato onion; the ever-ready onion, which is cultivated in England but is rare in North America; and the garden shallot, which has several varieties of its own. All of the onions in the Aggregatum group produce a cluster of bulbs at the base of the plant. Let's take a closer look at the various types of onions.

The Egyptian Onion

The Egyptian onion is very popular with home gardeners and with good reason. It is very hardy and sends up its welcome green shoots very early in the spring, providing the gardener with the knowledge that his or her garden is revived and giving fresh green onions before any other perennial crops have awakened. This interesting plant, with its crown of aerial bulblets, seems to be trouble-free as well, a welcome relief from plants that must be carefully monitored for invading pests and diseases.

You can start growing Egyptian onions in your garden from clump divisions or bulblets. As the plants grow, they send up several shoots, developing a tight cluster. Each cluster can be carefully broken apart and each shoot planted separately to start a new bed. As summer progresses, each plant sends up a tough hollow green stem, at the top of which a bunch of bulblets develops. The bulblets look like miniature bulbs, even having a papery brown outer covering. If you leave the bulblet cluster alone, the stalk bends down as the maturing cluster gets heavier. Each bulblet, which has already started to sprout while the stalk is erect, roots itself when it touches the ground.

You can control where the bulblets root by gathering them before they begin to sprout and planting them about an inch deep. Space them closely if you want to harvest them as green onions. The final spacing to allow full-size plants to mature is 4 inches apart in rows 15 inches apart.

If you don't want to plant the bulblets, you can cure them in the shade until they are hard, then store them in a cool place. During the winter the bulblets can

Onion Relatives: *Egyptian onions (left) and shallots (right) are easy-to-grow members of the onion family.*

be peeled and added to meat and vegetable dishes.

Since Egyptian onions are perennial, you can harvest indefinitely from the same plants. Although they are very hardy, Egyptian onions do best if mulched with loose material such as straw before the ground freezes. This will protect them from freezing and thawing and help them awaken as early as possible come spring. Cover the plants about a foot deep, and in February or March you will see lovely green leaves poking their way up through the mulch, just asking to be eaten.

The Potato Onion

This onion with the curious name has been a subject of much conjecture among gardeners, although not much is known about it. Some people say it is called the potato onion because of the brown color of its papery scales. Others insist that the proper name for this crop is the potato hill onion. These folks say that it was brought west by the pioneers who planted it as a companion to their potatoes. During the westward journey, these onions may have been the pioneers' only fresh vegetable and may have protected them from scurvy. Potato onions are hard to come by without a cooperative neighbor to give you a start.

Potato onions should be planted in midwinter in mild climates and in early spring in colder areas. Culture is the same as for bulb onion sets, except the bulblets should be planted 10 inches apart. Potato onions come up quite early in the spring. As the bulb cluster forms, brush the surrounding soil gently away so that the bulbs are exposed to the sun to assist their ripening. The entire bulb cluster is surrounded by a protective covering of papery scales. The tops of potato onions die down in midsummer. Don't leave them in the ground, or they will sprout again in late summer and not be of much use for cooking. Potato onions have a mild flavor and can be used to help tide you over between crops of bulbing onions.

The Ever-Ready Onion

Little is known about this interesting multiplier onion except that it helped sustain the British during World War II, when commercial bulb onions were in short supply. The ever-ready onion forms a cluster of ten to twelve bulbs with reddish brown coats. The bulbs are narrower than those of potato onions, and the leaves are especially narrow. The sets are planted in March, and the bulbs are harvested in the fall. The name *ever-ready* apparently refers to the fact that the tops of these plants do not die down after the bulbs have formed.

Shallots

Shallots are considered the gourmet member of the onion family, for their delicate flavor can enhance and enrich any meal. Stores demand a gourmet price for shallots, which is ridiculous considering how easy they are to grow. In fact, the only regular tending shallots need is conscientious weeding. They grow better in poor, dry soils than do bulbing onions, and their midsummer harvest coincides conveniently with the planting time for fall and overwintering crops. This early harvest, combined with the fact that shallots take up little space in the garden, makes them a fine crop for gardeners with limited space.

Shallot Varieties

There are several varieties of shallots. The most familiar is the 'French' shallot, which has a pinkish brown skin and somewhat tear-shaped bulbs. Another variety is called the 'Frog-legged' shallot. Its bulbs are longer and thinner than those of the 'French' shallot. Many cooks say that 'Frog-legged' shallots have the best flavor, but the bulbs do not store well. Any bulbs that are not used in early winter shrivel up in storage. 'Frog-legged' shallots also are not very prolific, and gardeners who want to have plenty for both future planting and eating will have trouble producing enough bulbs to meet their needs. 'Dutch' shallots, with their yellow skin, are the largest and most strongly flavored shallot variety.

Growing Shallots

If you choose the rather temperamental 'Frog-legged' shallots, try planting them in the fall and mulching heavily before the ground freezes. Other shallots also can be grown this way, but they don't seem to produce any earlier or more abundantly than when planted in the spring, and you run the risk of losing them to the weather. It's best to wait until the ground is no longer frozen before planting.

Dorothy always plants her shallots in a bed rather than in rows, placing each starter bulb 6 inches from its neighbors and staggering them to keep the maximum distance between bulbs. Using this method, she harvests an abundant crop for a family of four from only about 9 square feet of ground. Remember when you plant your shallots to plan for enough extra bulbs for planting the next year.

One season Diane and Dorothy both discovered the importance of keeping shallots weeded. Dorothy planted her shallots near the edge of the garden and was too busy to keep up with the weeds. Diane gave her shallots a prominent place in the garden where they wouldn't be forgotten and worked some wood ashes around them at planting time. What a difference there was in the crops! Diane's conscientious care was rewarded by a huge harvest of big fat bulbs, while Dorothy's neglect resulted in meager clumps of tiny bulbs.

As shallots grow, the bulbs first send up clumps of healthy green leaves. You can cut a few leaves for early summer seasoning if you like. As more bulbs form, the plants work their way through the soil until the clusters are almost completely above ground. When the tops die down, it's time to harvest. Gently dig up each cluster of bulbs and cure them in the garden for a few days, bringing them in if rain threatens. Keep the bulbs in clusters for storage, breaking them off as needed. 'French' and 'Dutch' shallots store very well in a cool, dark part of the house in a paper or net bag. Shallots are more likely to dry out than to sprout in storage.

Garlic

People have been acquainted with this special allium at least since the time of the pharaohs. Six garlic bulbs were found in King Tut's tomb, left there to serve him in the afterworld 3,340 years ago. Garlic worn around the neck was believed to protect people from evil in a variety of cultures; in others it was considered an aphrodisiac or a cure for headaches. The assignment of magical properties to this special allium are probably due to its genuine antibacterial and antifungal activity.

Garlic has been put forth as a treatment for everything from tumors to high blood pressure. Interest has recently revived in garlic's possible use in controlling hardening of the arteries (atherosclerosis) because garlic is one of a very few edible plants containing certain polyunsaturated fatty acids that seem to help control this disorder. In addition, garlic has been shown to lower cholesterol levels in

Garlic Types: Elephant garlic (left) is an increasingly popular, mild alternative to conventional garlic (right).

chickens. Whether or not garlic ever finds a niche in modern medicine, its place in the kitchen as a unique and flavorful ingredient is undisputed.

Garlic is as useful in the garden as in the kitchen. Garlic planted among cole crops helps keep down cabbage worms, and garlic sprays made by mixing minced garlic with water in a blender repel a variety of sucking and chewing bugs. Proof of the germicidal activity of garlic is clear in the effectiveness of garlic sprays against a variety of plant diseases, including angular leaf spot, cucumber scab, and downy mildew in cucumbers; bean anthracnose and a bacterial disease in beans; and brown rot disease in almonds, apricots, and peaches.

The chemical that works these wonders is called allicin. Allicin also gives garlic its special flavor and is formed by enzymes in the garlic bulb from the odorless, water-soluble amino acid alliin when garlic is injured or chopped up. Because allicin is produced only upon trauma to the bulb, recipes calling for garlic instruct the cook to chop or mash the cloves before adding them to a dish. As in onions, the enzymes that perform the flavor-inducing conversion are inactivated by heat or freezing, resulting in very little garlic flavor.

A French recipe for mashed potatoes is based on this principle. Two entire heads of garlic are used for only 2½ pounds of potatoes! The cloves are peeled but not mashed or chopped, then simmered in butter before being added to the potatoes. The resulting dish has a wonderful, rich flavor that diners often don't ascribe to garlic. Some people enjoy eating whole roasted garlic heads for the same reason. After roasting the heads for an hour at 325°F, these garlic lovers peel the cloves and squeeze the soft, buttery contents onto crackers, vegetables, or meat.

Once allicin is formed, it is quite unstable and will break down into other, less pleasing chemicals. That is why salads and other dishes using uncooked chopped garlic should be eaten the first day after mixing; otherwise they develop a strong, disagreeable flavor.

The garlic head is formed in quite a different fashion than is the onion bulb. Each garlic clove is a swollen axillary bud, the papery covering of which is the remains of the leaf that gave rise to the bud. Because the garlic clove is not made up of individual swollen leaf bases, as is an onion, it lacks rings. As in an onion, the true garlic stem is a small area inside the bulb; thus the stem of a garlic plant is a collection of leaf bases, just as in an onion.

While long days help induce garlic to form bulbs, temperature is much more important. Garlic sets must be exposed to temperatures below 41°F during the winter, or they will not form compound bulbs when the growing season arrives, even with long days. Although onion sets should be stored in a warm place, garlic sets should be stored where it is cool. Extended periods (two months) of temperatures below 50°F, however, can harm your garlic sets. The central cloves will form higher on the false stem than normal, giving the head a rough appearance.

Garlic Varieties

Garlic is one of those rare crops that do not produce flowers. All reproduction is vegetative—that is, the cloves that form the bulb can produce new plants, but seeds are never made. Because there is no sexual reproduction, the genetic make-up of each new garlic plant is just like that of its parent. This makes breeding for improved garlic impossible, as two strains cannot be crossed to get a new type of garlic. Each garlic variety is referred to as a clone, meaning that all individuals are genetically identical (just as each strawberry plant that develops from a runner is genetically identical to the parent plant). Some garlic clones do tend to bolt, but instead of forming flowers they produce clusters of tiny bulblets. The bulblets can be planted to yield compound bulbs, but they are likely to be small.

The mysterious thing about garlic is that, even though it cannot reproduce sexually, it has many clones, which differ greatly from each other. More than three hundred clones of garlic, each with its own flavor, color, and degree of pungency, have been identified. Did all the clones develop long ago, at a time when garlic could reproduce sexually? If that were so, all the clones would have had to lose the ability to reproduce sexually independently, a very unlikely event. But it is also difficult to imagine that the variability of garlic results from mutations in cells that are not involved in sexual reproduction, for such vegetative mutations are generally quite rare. This variability of garlic may be a mystery, but it is fortunate for the home gardener, for it allows each of us to try different types of garlic and find clones that will produce reliably in our gardens. Be sure to save clones that do well in your garden for planting every year, for you may have trouble finding them again.

One type of garlic is different enough from the others that it often has been mistakenly thought of as a different species. This is rocambole, a mild garlic grown commonly in Europe. Rocambole, also called serpent garlic, regularly produces a central stalk topped by a head of tiny bulblets. For this reason some gardeners confuse it with the Egyptian onion. But rocambole is definitely a type of garlic in both flavor and aroma, though gentler than the standard varieties. The cloves of rocambole are easy to separate and peel because the dry covering is very loose.

Growing Garlic

In the North garlic planted in October will establish its roots before winter sets in and will really take off in the spring to form big healthy bulbs. Some northerners plant their garlic in July, right after harvesting that year's crop, but fall planting results in just as good a harvest and doesn't use up valuable garden space during the summer. Whenever you choose to plant your garlic, mulch the bed after cold weather sets in. Southern gardeners can plant garlic in the late fall or early winter (late November or December) if they know that the soil temperature will drop below 68°F during the winter. Wherever you live, don't wait until spring to plant your garlic. Garlic responds to long days by bulbing, so spring-planted garlic won't have time to grow large enough to form big bulbs. Remember not to plant garlic where other onion family plants grew the year before because they share pests such as thrips. Garlic will thrive in rich soil but also can produce well in poorer soils. Just make sure that your garlic plot is well drained. A bed 3 feet by 6 feet will provide enough garlic for a full year's supply for a family of four.

Garlic bulbs should not be broken up into individual cloves until just before planting, since the cloves don't keep well once they've been separated. Don't peel the cloves. Some gardeners feel that only the outer cloves should be used for planting, since they're usually the larger ones. Larger cloves will produce larger bulbs because the extra stored nutrients will result in a faster-growing young plant. Garlic cloves should be spaced about 5 inches apart, either in rows 15 to 18 inches apart or in a bed, as described for shallots. Plant them about 2 inches deep. Overwintered garlic will begin to peek out over your mulch quite early in the spring. Leave the mulch in place to discourage the weeds and treat your garlic patch as you would your bulb onions.

Garlic is ready to harvest when the tops turn yellow, usually early enough in the summer to allow the bed to be used for a late planting of a fall crop. Cure garlic as you would onions. Garlic for kitchen use should be stored at 32°F and 65 percent humidity. Garlic sprouts most quickly at 40°F, so avoid this temperature for a long-lasting storage crop.

Garlic Problems

Although garlic is usually a trouble-free crop, it can become infested with the stem and bulb nematode. This tiny worm is too small to see easily with the naked eye, but you will know your garlic is infected if the bottom of the plant is swollen and spongy and the skin has lengthwise splits. Sometimes nematode-infested plants have twisted leaves and stems as well. If you pull up your garlic and find that the roots and stem stay in the ground, you may have nematodes. Infected cloves are the usual cause of nematode infestation. It takes many years for the worms to die out completely, and you should not plant host crops such as celery, garlic, onions, parsley, peas, or salsify in the area for four years. To help eliminate this pest, clean up your garden debris and place it in the garbage rather than the compost pile. Do not use any garlic from an infected patch for planting.

Scientists in Great Britain have discovered that garlic grown there commercially is universally infected with viruses. Garlic grown in North America probably is similarly afflicted. When the viruses are eliminated by special growing techniques, most garlic varieties produce significantly larger bulbs. Perhaps in the future virus-free garlic sets will be available to home gardeners, allowing us to grow bigger crops in the same garden area.

Elephant Garlic

Elephant garlic is graphically named for the size of its heads—just one clove weighs an ounce and will give you two or three tablespoons of chopped garlic. The flavor of elephant garlic, however, is much milder than that of the real thing. So if you find regular garlic too strong, you might try its milder cousin.

Elephant garlic is more closely related to leeks than to regular garlic. While garlic and elephant garlic cloves resemble one another superficially, they are really very different. The elephant garlic clove is a single thick storage leaf, quite a different thing from the enlarged axillary bud that is the garlic clove. Tiny bulblets are produced around the outside of the elephant garlic head; these can be saved and planted in the spring for a fall harvest of small bulbs. Although these bulbs aren't large enough to be of use in the kitchen, you should store them carefully and plant them the next spring to yield harvestable compound bulbs.

Space the starter bulbs or cloves 10 inches apart to allow plenty of room for the large, vigorous plants to grow. They resemble giant garlic and should be treated in a similar way. If you garden in an area where cool, damp summers make growing a good crop of regular garlic an iffy proposition, give elephant garlic a try, since it tolerates cool, damp conditions well.

As it matures, elephant garlic produces a cluster of several cloves and a gigantic, impressive flower stalk. The flowers, however, rarely produce seeds. For the best bulb production remove the stalk before it develops into the flowering head so that the plant's energy is directed to bulb development. Sometimes elephant garlic doesn't flower. When that happens, it also doesn't make a clove cluster but instead forms one single, massive clove referred to as a round. Rounds taste just like the mild cloves and can be used in the kitchen or saved for planting the following spring.

Leeks

Like shallots, leeks are considered a gourmet member of the onion family. Their mild, sweet flavor and creamy texture when cooked are delightful, and when leeks are combined with potatoes, they make one of the most delicious simple soups imaginable. It is strange to think of leeks being more closely related to elephant garlic than to Japanese bunching onions, which resemble them superficially. But if you have ever left some leeks in the ground long enough for them to flower and then pulled them up, you have seen the tiny bulblets that form around the base of the plant like miniature versions of elephant garlic cloves. Leeks are quite an easy crop to grow because you don't need to worry about providing the proper conditions for bulbing; leeks never bulb up. The elongated leaf bases of the plant, which look rather like giant scallions, make tasty eating at any stage of growth, but most gardeners wait until they are about an inch in diameter before harvesting them.

Leek Varieties

Fortunately for gardeners everywhere, there are many varieties of leeks adapted to different growing conditions. Leeks are generally planted very early in the spring outdoors in mild-season areas or indoors for later transplanting in the North. Most varieties require a long growing season. Many varieties are very hardy and can be left in the garden, covered with mulch, well into the winter, even in northern areas. If you want leeks that can withstand the cold, choose a variety such as 'Nebraska,' which has dark blue-green leaves. As in other crops such as kale, the blue-green color appears to be related to hardiness. If you live in a cold-season area and do not want to start your leeks indoors, try one of the quick-growing summer leeks, such as 'King Richard.' This variety is ready in only seventy-five days and produces a pleasing, long white stem. Be forewarned that summer leeks do not keep well in storage, nor do they overwinter in the garden, so you should dig them up before heavy frost hits and use them in short order.

Growing Leeks

Leek seeds keep better than onion seeds. Under favorable conditions two-year-old seeds will produce a vigorous crop. Leek seeds appear to be very sensitive to high humidity, however, so if you live in a damp area, you should buy fresh seeds each year.

Leeks are usually the first crop northern gardeners get started in anticipation of spring, for the earlier the seeds are planted, the fatter the final stalks will be. Leeks require high levels of accumulated solar radiation to produce a good crop. February is not too early to get those seeds started, germinating them at room temperature and using the same methods as for onions. In frost-free areas, leeks are grown as a winter crop and are planted in late summer, when maximum daytime temperatures no longer exceed 80°F.

When planting time comes, place the leek seeds or transplants in a trench

Leeks and Scallions: *Leeks (left) and scallions (right) are mildly flavored alliums. Scallions are simply the immature plants of bulb onions.*

6 inches deep and 6 inches across. Cover the seeds with ⅛ inch of soil or place transplants a little deeper than they were growing before. A friend of ours claims that the secret to growing fine leeks is to clip both the tops of the leaves and the bottom half or so of the roots before transplanting; this treatment may reduce transplant shock. The final spacing for leeks should be 4 to 8 inches apart, depending on how fat you want the final stalks to be. As the leeks grow, gradually fill in the trench so that the thickening stems are covered. Be careful never to bury the point where the leaves branch off, however. When the stalks grow in darkness, they won't turn green, and your harvested leeks will be gleaming white and tender.

If you plant leeks from seeds, you can enjoy the thinnings in your kitchen, unless you want to transplant them to increase your final crop. Young leeks can be substituted for green onions in any dish, although they impart a different but equally delicious flavor.

The familiar pearl onion that is used in cocktails belongs to the same species as elephant garlic and leeks. These plants are cultivated in Italy and Germany, and surprisingly little is known about them. The tiny bulbs are single storage leaves, like the cloves of elephant garlic, and thus are very different from the small pickling onions we often grow in our gardens.

Japanese Bunching Onions

These plants are most commonly called Japanese bunching onions, but they are also referred to as Welsh onions. The name has nothing to do with Wales, however, for these onions have never been grown commonly there. The label seems to be a corruption of the German word *welsche,* meaning "foreign," which was probably used to describe the plant when it was introduced in Germany near the end of the Middle Ages. The confusion over the name matches the confusion over the plants, only some of which we can clear up.

Japanese bunching onions are used extensively in Asian cuisine. When Asian recipes are adapted for American cooks, Japanese bunching onions usually are translated as "scallions." Our scallions are almost always just immature plants of bulb onions, usually of a white variety. But the flavor of the Japanese bunching onion is not the same as that of our scallions, so if you are a fan of Asian cuisine, you should grow the real thing in your garden.

Japanese Bunching Onion Varieties

There seem to be two different classes of Japanese bunching onions. Some varieties, such as 'He-Shi-Ko,' 'Kujo Green Multistalk,' and 'Sakata's Evergreen White Bunching Onion,' definitely can be grown as perennials. The tops may die down in a harsh winter, but in spring a cluster of shoots will form where each original plant grew. For a continuous harvest break off a few shoots from the cluster as you need them. The clumps also can be divided to propagate the crop, and the young, first-year plants can be harvested for kitchen use as well.

Other Japanese onions, such as 'Ishikura Long,' are described as single-stalk plants, which implies that they never form a cluster. You can stretch out the harvest with some of these varieties by overwintering them under a protective mulch.

To confuse the issue even further, hybrids have been made between Japanese bunching onions and other species. 'Beltsville Bunching' is a hybrid with bulbing onions and produces scallions with a slightly swollen bulb. 'Delta Giant' and 'Louisiana Evergreen' are hybrids with shallots and produce a shallotlike crop.

Growing Japanese Bunching Onions

Japanese onions are grown like other alliums. In the North, you can plant them in the fall to get a head start and mulch them well before the ground freezes. If you prefer, however, you can put them in when spring arrives. In the South, plant these onions in the fall for a continuous crop over the coming year. For a change of pace you can blanch bunching onions like leeks to produce long white stalks.

Chives

Chives are an elegant addition to the herb garden and can be cultivated quite easily from seeds or clump divisions. Chives are not widely grown commercially, and thus little is known about their biology. They do die down in the winter, and it takes a long cold season to break their dormancy. However, that isn't the only way to awaken them from their seasonal slumber. One scientist discovered that if dormant plants are heated to 110°F for thirty-six to forty-eight hours, dormancy is broken and the plants grow vigorously when potted. The home gardener who wishes to grow chives indoors during the winter might try this trick to get them going.

Chives will flower in the spring. If you don't pick the flowers, the plants may die down and go dormant during the summer. You still may end up with some chive plants, however, because the seeds from the flowers can sprout and produce a crop.

The easiest way to grow chives is to get a clump from a friend or buy one in a garden store. If you start them from seeds, you'll have to wait two to three months before cutting any for the kitchen. Chives will grow well in any good garden soil, but rich, loose soil results in the fastest growth. Plant chives as you would onions. Place the seeds or clumps in small areas (about 2 inches square) about a foot apart; the chives will soon fill in to make a solid row.

To harvest chives, cut the leaves with sharp scissors ½ to 1 inch above the soil. When the plants start to flower, cut the clump as usual but throw out the flowering stalks, as they are tough and have a strong flavor.

In cold areas chives should be mulched in the winter. They are quite hardy, but extreme cold can kill them, and frost heaving may damage the clumps. The only time Diane lost her chives was the year she didn't mulch them and temperatures got down to −10°F with little snow cover.

Garlic Chives

Garlic chives are another Oriental specialty that is gaining popularity in North America. It's easy to understand why after you've savored their mild, garlicky flavor. Overall, they resemble ordinary chives except that their leaves are triangular in cross section instead of round and hollow. Garlic chives are not quite as hardy as ordinary ones and require a rich soil for good growth. Other than that, you can grow them just as you would regular chives.

Chapter 8

Radishes, Beets, Swiss Chard, and Carrots: Colorful Root Crops and Greens

There is something almost magical about pulling on a cluster of leaves and watching a colorful, fat root come up from its hiding place in the soil. Radishes, beets, and carrots provide the gardener with a symphony of colors from cherry red and gleaming white through deep violet-red and sunny orange. While these popular garden vegetables belong to unrelated plant families and produce their succulent roots in different ways, there are many similarities in their growth patterns and in their reactions to the conditions under which they grow, so it makes sense to discuss them all together.

Radishes, as members of the mustard family (Cruciferae), are related to cabbage, horseradish, turnips, and watercress. Like other family members, radishes contain pungent chemicals called glycosides that impart the characteristically sharp flavor. Beets are in the goosefoot family (Chenopodiaceae) along with spinach and that invasive weed shepherd's-purse. You may be surprised to learn that beets and Swiss chard are the same species. The critical difference between them is that beets put their energy into producing sweet, succulent roots and Swiss chard concentrates on abundant, tasty leaves. Since its growing requirements are identical to those of beets, we've included Swiss chard in this chapter even though it isn't a root crop. Carrots belong to the parsley family (Umbelliferae), which gives the gardener and cook so many wonderful herbs and spices—anise, caraway, coriander,

---

VITAL STATISTICS

Family:
Cruciferae—radishes
Chenopodiaceae—beets and Swiss chard
Umbelliferae—carrots

Species: *Raphanus sativus*—radishes
Beta vulgaris (Crassa group)—beets
Beta vulgaris (Cicla group)—Swiss chard
Daucus carota—carrots

Soil: Loose, well-drained sandy loam

pH: Radishes—6 to 6.5
Beets and Swiss chard—6.5 to 8
Carrots—6 to 6.5

Soil temperature for germination:
Radishes—45°F to 95°F; 85°F optimum
Beets and Swiss chard—50°F to 85°F; 85°F optimum
Carrots—45°F to 85°F; 80°F optimum

Air temperature for best growth: 45°F to 75°F; 60°F to 65°F optimum

Seed viability:
Radishes—5 years
Beets and Swiss chard—4 years
Carrots—3 years

Seed germination:
Radishes—3 to 10 days
Beets and Swiss chard—1 to 2 weeks
Carrots—1 to 2 weeks

Seed planting depth:
Radishes—½ to 1½ inches
Beets and Swiss chard—½ to 1 inch
Carrots—¼ inch

dill, fennel, and parsley. Unfortunately for seed-saving country gardeners, the wildflower Queen Anne's lace also is in this family, a variation of the same species as the cultivated carrot, meaning that these two plants can interbreed.

Radishes have been cultivated for thousands of years, as evidenced by writings found in Egyptian pyramids dating from 2000 B.C. Speculation has it that these roots probably originated in the same area. Beets were originally grown for their tasty leaves, but by the time of the ancient Greeks, the roots also were being enjoyed. In contrast to the venerable heritage of garden beets, sugar beets, a commercial crop from which sugar is refined, were not developed until the late 1700s.

Few details about the early stages of radish and beet cultivation are known, but we do know quite a bit about the long and interesting history of carrots. The first carrots were not orange but purple or violet and were grown in the remote mountainous country of Afghanistan in the tenth and eleventh centuries. Like beets, these old-time carrots leaked their purple pigments into the cooking water and were used to color sauces a rich brownish purple. Such "black-rooted" carrots are still grown commercially in India and the Middle East. Yellow carrots started to appear later; these had lost the genes directing the manufacture of the purple pigments (anthocyanins).

The cultivated carrot spread from Afghanistan to other countries, and around 1600 plant breeders in the Netherlands carefully worked with the yellow carrots to produce an orange one. Only four major varieties resulted – 'Early Half Long,' 'Early Scarlet Horn,' 'Late Half Long,' and 'Long Orange.' Up until the 1980s every carrot variety in cultivation was descended from one of these original types. Thus present-day carrots, despite their ostensible diversity, were quite similar genetically until very recently.

Nutritional Profiles

When compared to the nutritional merits of beets and carrots, radishes seem to make a poor showing. But before you write them off completely, you should note that they will add to your daily requirement of vitamin C. Many people do not realize that radishes make delicious fresh pickles and are delightful when cooked, adding a nice crunchy texture to stir-fried dishes. Young radish leaves often are overlooked as tasty greens, but they also are good to eat, especially when steamed or sautéed with an equal amount of spinach. We like to add some sautéed shallots and stir in some yogurt for a delicious creamed-vegetable dish.

Beets are an especially versatile crop, for it's a tossup whether the leaves or the roots are better tasting. Nutritionally speaking, beet greens and Swiss chard are hard to beat. They're rich in vitamin A and will contribute to meeting your daily requirement of iron and riboflavin. The naturally sweet roots also contribute to good nutrition: a cup will supply about one-fifth of your daily vitamin C requirement.

You can almost *see* the abundant vitamin content of carrots. The orange color is due to the pigment carotene, which the body converts to vitamin A. It's good to eat carrots regularly because they are such a rich source of this important vitamin. Carrots also are a good source of riboflavin and thiamine. When you eat carrots, just wash and scrub them. Do not remove the peel, as many of the nutrients are concentrated in and immediately under the skin. Although store-bought carrots often have a tough skin, probably from being stored for so long and shipped long distances, you'll find that the skin on your homegrown carrots is very tender.

Loose soil is vital for producing fat, tender roots; this rule applies to all root crops. If you ignore this rule and grow your root crops in heavy clay or rocky soil, any roots that develop will be forked or otherwise abnormally shaped. Carrots grown in compacted ground or heavy clay often will be short and stubby, even if the variety you planted was supposed to be long and slender. Long beets such as 'Cylindra' can have the same problem. Scientists have found that carrots grown in loose soil can be twice as large as those grown in compacted soil. Even though the common round red radishes are usually small and grow near the surface, the tiny young radish taproots can have trouble working their way through heavy or compacted soil. If you get any radishes at all from such a plot, they will be misshapen and tough.

Dorothy's first venture into gardening included putting in a modest row of radishes. Since her house was rented, she didn't dare disturb the flower beds too

The Importance of Proper Soil for Good Roots

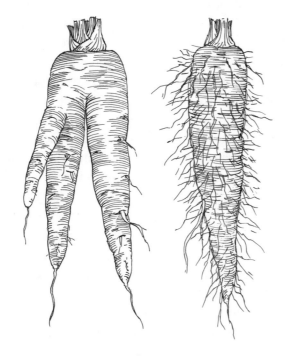

Forked and Hairy Carrots: *Heavy, compacted soils cause carrot roots to fork and become abnormally shaped (left). Excessive nitrogen in the soil from green manure crops or the application of fresh manure can lead to an abundance of feeder roots that result in hairy, undesirable carrots (right).*

much, so she chose a spot where little was growing (her first mistake). She had heard that radishes were easy to grow, so she planted them and waited. When the rain came, it pooled up in the radish bed because the soil there was compacted clay (her second mistake). At least she didn't have to water them! She waited in vain for nice round radishes; not one plant formed a plump root, and eventually all she had was a bunch of puny flower stalks.

If your soil is at all heavy, taking the time to lighten it before putting in any root crops will be well worth the effort. Work the soil deeply, loosen it well, and then leave it alone. Never step on the part of the garden where your root crops will grow, or you'll undo all your hard work. A rototiller is ideal for loosening the bed. If you don't have one, loosen it with a spade or shovel to a depth of 8 to 10 inches, breaking up any clods and removing any sizable stones you unearth.

When you're faced with a heavy clay soil, you can lighten it along the intended rows by digging a trench 3 to 4 inches wide and 8 inches deep. Fill the trench with any of the following mixtures, using the proportions of 2 parts to 1 part to 1 part: soil, well-rotted manure, and sand; peat moss, wood ashes, and sand; shredded leaves, wood ashes, and sand. Check the pH of your mixture; it should be 6 to 6.5 for radishes and carrots and 6.5 to 8 for beets. If the pH needs adjusting, add peat moss to make it more acid or wood ashes to increase its alkalinity.

After you've planted the crops, water them gently with a fine spray from a soaker hose rather than with an overhead sprinkler that will beat and compact the earth with large droplets of water. Do not flood-irrigate these crops until they are two to three weeks old, and then only if you have no choice.

Although root crops like a rich soil, that soil should not be too high in nitrogen. Never use large amounts of fresh manure in the carrot bed because too much nitrogen will encourage the growth of feeder roots, resulting in unappealing hairy carrots. Fresh manure also can cause the carrot roots to fork and become misshapen. (Scientists still aren't sure why this happens.) If you grow soybeans or other legumes as a nitrogen-rich green manure crop, don't plant carrots in the same area right after the green manure crop has been tilled in; wait at least six months. Scientists who compared carrots grown in soybean stubble with those grown in rye stubble (grass, as opposed to a nitrogen-fixing legume) found that the rye-stubble carrots were fine but the soybean-stubble ones had more top growth and small, very hairy roots. Beets and radishes can be grown in more nitrogen-rich soil than is ideal for carrots, but it is wise to avoid fresh manure for them as well.

All three crops are more likely to be limited by a potassium or phosphorus deficiency than by inadequate nitrogen. Enrich your soil with wood ashes and bone meal to provide plenty of these two key minerals; work them thoroughly into the row before you plant your seeds. (It's very important to disperse wood ashes throughout the soil, since a concentration of ashes will harm the seeds.)

Carrots and beets are susceptible to a deficiency of the trace element boron.

HOW FOOD IS STORED IN ROOTS

Although radishes, carrots, and beets all store food in their roots, they grow in different ways. All roots have xylem to bring water and minerals up from the soil to the rest of the plant and phloem to carry nutrients into the roots (see chapter 1). The tissue from which the xylem and phloem develop is called the cambium. The cambium produces xylem cells toward the inside of the root and phloem cells toward the outside. In addition to the transport cells, xylem and phloem tissue may have an abundance of storage cells, which contain nutrients.

The core of a carrot is the xylem, which contains some storage cells, while the outer portion of the carrot is the phloem, which contains more nutrient-storing cells than the xylem. That explains why the core is the smallest portion of the carrot root. The core separates easily from the outer portion because the cambium separates easily between the xylem and phloem.

The radish root, however, has many more storage cells mixed in its xylem. The cambium, which doesn't separate easily, is near the outside of the root, and the outermost part of the radish root is a thin layer of phloem, with only a few storage cells mixed in. Radishes also differ from carrots in that the swollen, crisp part we eat is more than just the root. The top part of the radish is actually the embryonic stem, which develops storage cells right along with the root.

Beets differ from both carrots and radishes in that the cambia form rings. Each cambium ring produces xylem toward the inside and phloem toward the outside, with storage cells mixed in with both. The rings we see in a sliced beet are those produced by the cambia.

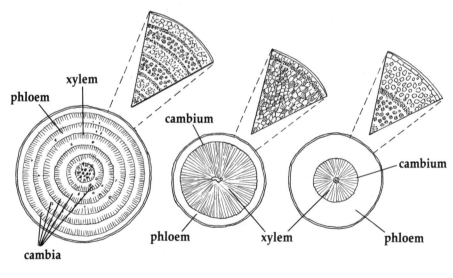

Cross Sections of Root Crops: The cambium in the beet (left) produces secondary rings, with each ring producing xylem to the inside and phloem to the outside. The xylem and phloem have the same number of storage cells. The radish root (center) has most of the storage cells mixed in with the xylem, and there is only a thin layer of phloem on the outside. In carrots (right) the phloem contains most of the storage cells, and there is only a small core of xylem.

If you have been adding compost or other organic matter to your soil, it's unlikely that you will have this problem. If, however, you start finding black cores in your carrots or corky black tissue inside your beet roots, your soil may have a boron deficiency. If you have any doubts about your soil's boron content, call your county extension agent and ask if soils in your area tend to be boron deficient. Granite dust or compost rich in sweet clover or vetch will provide adequate boron for your garden.

Why Storage Roots Are a Luxury for Plants

When we grow radishes, beets, and carrots, we want to harvest good-size, tender roots. But to reap a satisfying harvest, we must first realize that growing such roots is a luxury for the plants. Plants need leaves to carry out photosynthesis and grow. They have to produce flowers and seeds to continue as a species. If environmental factors are in any way unfavorable, a carrot plant can survive and probably even reproduce—but without forming the big storage root that we treasure. Under adverse conditions such as insufficient light, inadequate nutrients, limited water, or too much weed competition, these plants will devote whatever energy they have to meeting their basic survival needs and will not produce the plump, succulent roots we want.

Scientists studying sugar beets have found that if the soil is limited in nutrients, sugar beets will devote their energies first to respiration to stay alive and then to top growth to increase photosynthetic area. Only after these two requirements are met will the plant develop storage roots and accumulate sucrose in those roots.

The same has been found to be true for radishes. If radishes are grown under low light intensities and short day lengths, such as the levels present in a greenhouse during winter, the familiar swollen roots never develop. The low level of sunlight limits the amount of food that the plant's leaves can produce, so there is not enough food for the radish to channel into a storage root. In fact, there is nothing to store! Dorothy found this out the hard way one spring when she tried to grow radishes very early in the season in her small greenhouse. She wasted valuable space on them and ended up with plants that looked like those ill-fated radishes she grew in the wet clay: puny plants with a few small flowers and no sign of swollen roots. Carrots are no different from beets and radishes: under nutrient stress enlarged roots just won't develop.

So remember, big fat storage roots aren't the number one priority as far as your plants are concerned. You must encourage them in that direction by providing close to ideal conditions so the plants can turn their energy away from merely surviving to building up a store of carbohydrates in a swollen root.

The Best Growing Conditions for These Crops

These crops need to grow rapidly and evenly to produce a good-size, tender crop. While they are still young, they send down a long, slender taproot. This deep root is able to draw water up from the deeper soil, but you can't let your plants depend on that for all their moisture. It's essential to provide them with abundant water. If you don't, they will become tough, as extra xylem cells will develop to help bring more water up from the deep soil layers. These extra cells are visible as white rings in beets grown under water stress. If you are growing your root crops in a concentrated block or otherwise closely spaced, be extra careful to water them generously, since many roots will be competing for the water.

A layer of mulch will help hold in moisture around your crops, as well as keep down weeds. Mulching also will protect the tops of the enlarged roots to prevent rough shoulders on beets and green shoulders on carrots. Exposure to dry air makes beet shoulders rough and can crack the roots as well. When the top of a carrot is exposed to light, it forms green chlorophyll along with other, bitter-tasting chemicals that make the top of the root inedible.

Your root crops won't grow well if they have to compete with weeds or with one another. Since carrot and radish seeds are small and beet seeds are actually fruits containing several seeds, all these crops must be thinned while the plants are small. Weeding also is vital. If you give the weeds a chance to establish themselves, the competition for nutrients will leave your crops with no extra energy to put into storage roots. Taking that extra time to thin and weed will really pay off come harvest time. The size of the roots harvested from a diligently weeded plot can be more than double that of those from an unweeded plot, and the roots will be tender instead of tough.

Keep radishes, beets, and carrots well weeded until they are about half-grown; from then on they should be able to outcompete any weeds that might spring up. When weeding, be careful not to disturb the plants. Their tiny feeder roots will be damaged if you chop the soil with a hoe, so carefully pull by hand the weeds that are growing within a foot of the plants. Do your weeding when the soil is moist and get those weeds out before they get too big. If you disturb the roots of these crops, you can end up with stunted plants or misshapen roots.

In 1973 scientists were able to show just how much weeding can help beets. In experimental plots where beets had to compete with weeds, they formed fewer, smaller leaves with less chlorophyll than did plants grown in weed-free plots. When the beet bed was allowed to get really weedy (from 15 to 240 weeds per square yard), the beet roots were reduced in size by 45 to 98 percent. The researchers also found that once the beets were well under way—two to four weeks after coming up—they could outgrow any weeds that tried to invade their territory.

Why Root Crops Bolt

Radishes, beets, and carrots are all sensitive to day length but not in exactly the same way. Carrots, beets, and Swiss chard are biennial crops and usually do not bolt until their second year. Since we eat them the first year of growth, most gardeners never see these plants flower. But some conditions can bring on flowering the first year, much to the gardener's frustration. And once carrots or beets have bolted, the roots turn bitter, tough, and inedible.

Any time beets or carrots are grown in temperatures below 45°F and are then exposed to long days, there is a chance that they will bolt. Some varieties are more susceptible to early bolting than others. For instance, 'Scarlet Nantes' carrots bolt more readily than 'Danvers Half Long' and 'Royal Chantenay.' That's why most gardening books tell you to plant these crops around the last expected frost date or only a couple of weeks earlier, despite the fact that they are quite hardy. The larger the plants are when exposed to the cold, the greater the chance that they will bolt when days get long.

Diane has always planted her 'Royal Chantenay' carrots early, about six weeks before the last expected frost date. But one year she was especially conscientious. She enriched the soil with bone meal and wood ashes before planting her seeds, and she weeded and thinned the carrots just when she was supposed to. The carrots responded to this treatment and grew quickly, and by June she was harvesting young carrots. In July, however, she got a nasty surprise: some of the carrots bolted. This variety had never bolted in her garden before, but she also had never had such big carrots so early in the season. The carrots had grown so fast that they responded to the combination of cold spring days and long June days by bolting. Even so, she only lost about fifty carrots out of two 50-foot rows—not too high a price to pay for learning a valuable gardening lesson.

Beets are more susceptible to early bolting than carrots, and in areas that experience the twin forces of cold spring temperatures and long June days, beets shouldn't be planted any earlier than three weeks before the last expected frost date. To be on the safe side, gardeners in those areas may wish to grow the slow-to-bolt varieties 'Red Ace' and 'Vermilion.' In general, Swiss chard is more bolt resistant than beets.

Spring radishes—the kind most gardeners grow—are annuals and will bolt when days get long, regardless of the temperatures to which they've been exposed. Growing radishes at a high density will speed bolting under long-day conditions. But the less familiar winter radishes are biennials and react to temperature and day length in much the same way as carrots and beets.

If you want to save seeds from any of the biennials (beets, Swiss chard, carrots, or winter radishes), you must step in at the end of the first growing season and see to it that these plants get a cool (below 45°F) rest period over the winter. Start by picking a few of the plumpest, healthiest, most vigorous roots from the garden. If you live in a mild-winter area, your best bet is to place the roots in a plastic bag and set them in the refrigerator. If you garden in an area with cold winter temperatures, you can leave the chosen roots in well-mulched ground so they won't freeze. When spring rolls around, replant the refrigerated roots in the garden or pull back the mulch from the roots left in the ground. Either way the plants should bolt and produce elongated flower stems from which you can harvest seeds. Carrots produce a stalk with a cluster of flowers called an umbel. The first umbel that is produced will be the first to provide seeds, so be prepared to harvest seeds in stages as they dry.

RADISHES

Most gardeners find that radishes make a very satisfying crop because they grow quickly into pretty, tasty globes. One of the joys of springtime is a tender salad of lettuce thinnings and tiny radish slices served with a light dressing of lemon juice and oil. If you are a real radish fan, you can grow mid- to late-season varieties to accompany the more familiar early-season ones. That way you can eat these crunchy roots throughout most of the growing season instead of facing a springtime feast followed by a summer famine.

Radish Varieties

The most familiar radishes are the very early round red ones. Some of these varieties are ready to eat in twenty days or less ('Saxa' is ready in only eighteen days), while others take as long as thirty-five days. But spring radishes don't have to be round and red. There are round white, pink, or purple radishes and long, taper-rooted white or red ones. Our favorites are the white-tipped red varieties, such as 'Sparkler,' and the long white ones, such as 'Icicle.' You can use these to make crispy pickles, add them to stir-fried dishes, or simply savor them raw. If you want a variety of colors without planting more than one kind, choose 'Easter Egg,' which will provide you with red, pink, purple, and white globes. Some varieties, such as 'Crimson Giant,' 'Easter Egg,' 'Parat' (sometimes called 'German Giant'), 'Plum Purple,' and 'White Icicle,' have a longer harvesting season because they remain crisp even when they grow large. Others become pithy and should be picked quickly as soon as they are mature. If you grow radishes when the weather might become hot, choose a variety such as 'Comet' that can stand the heat, or your crop will provide you with hot, spongy roots rather than crisp, refreshing ones.

If you are adventuresome and have loose, sandy soil, you may want to try growing large Japanese daikon radishes. The popular interest in Asian cuisine has prompted many seed catalogs to increase their varieties of this specialty radish. Daikon radishes can be especially mild and flavorful, and one root—which can be a foot or more long—can feed the entire family. They also stay crunchy and mild in hot weather. Different varieties are suited to spring, early summer, and late summer sowing and mature in forty-five to seventy days. Daikon radishes can bolt in long day lengths, so be careful to plant varieties in the proper season, or you will have flowers and no roots come harvest time. For instance, you should plant 'Miyashiga,' a white storage type of daikon, no earlier than the end of July, or it will bolt. If you want to grow daikons in the early spring, try 'April Cross Hybrid' or 'Mino Spring Cross.' Any roots harvested in the fall can be stored the same way you'd store winter radishes or carrots.

Biennial winter radishes, such as 'Black Spanish' and 'China Rose,' have creamy-white flesh and deep rose or black skins. They take from fifty-five to sixty days to mature and can be stored all winter in barely moist sand or in plastic bags in the refrigerator. 'Black Spanish' is heat resistant and can be planted in mid-July, while 'China Rose' likes cool weather and should be planted in late summer. Winter radishes need to mature in a cool season.

Secrets of Radish Success

While radishes are easy to grow, they can be disappointing. That's because they are picky about growing conditions. If it is too cool (below 60°F), they will grow slowly and have a hot, biting flavor. If the temperature is too high (above 70°F), radishes will grow too fast and become hot and pithy. Pithy radishes have grown so fast that the cell walls have separated from one another. They are fit only for the compost pile.

The ideal conditions for radish success are temperatures between 60°F and 70°F and a fairly rich soil with an abundant, even supply of water. Uneven watering, where dry spells alternate with wet spells, will check the roots' growth, making them hot, pithy, and tough. Rapid, even growth is the secret to crisp, pleasantly piquant radishes. Prompt harvesting is important, too, for most radishes do not hold their quality long in the garden. Many times we've pulled just enough for a tasty salad one day and come back only a couple of days later to find that the rest of our radishes were already past their prime. If you want radishes over a long season, sow small amounts every five days.

You can grow radishes in the spring or fall depending on local conditions, as long as the weather is cool. If your summers are hot, plant your radishes as soon as the air and soil temperatures average 45°F in the spring. Don't worry if a late frost strikes; radishes can tolerate some frost. For the earliest harvests, use row covers as soon as the seeds are planted. Remove the covers when temperatures get above 70°F. Radishes for fall eating should go in after the heat of summer is past.

Plant your radish seeds ½ to 1½ inches deep. If you save your own seeds, use the largest ones to get the biggest radishes. Radish seeds that you buy will look pretty much the same size because commercial seed companies discard all the smaller seeds.

In 1962 the *Proceedings of the American Society for Horticultural Science* reported the work done by scientists studying 'Cherry Belle' and 'Comet' radishes. These researchers found that deeper planting led to larger radishes. If you like large radishes, plant the seeds 1½ inches deep and space them 1½ inches apart in the rows. Rows can be as close together as 2 inches. If you prefer average-size radishes, plant the seeds ½ inch deep and space them 1 inch apart.

The researchers also found that radishes grew best when the temperature was between 60°F and 65°F, although they also did fairly well between 50°F and 55°F.

Temperatures in the 70°F to 75°F range resulted in pithy roots. The study also revealed that the best day length for these two varieties was twelve hours; many plants bolted under sixteen-hour days. 'Comet' bolted after only thirty days, while 'Cherry Belle' held for forty-five days. Since 'Cherry Belle' is ready to eat in twenty-two days, bolting should be no problem, making this variety a good choice for northern areas. 'Cherry Belle' also develops a larger radish when grown in longer spring day lengths than in the shorter days of fall and early winter.

Radishes will germinate in three to ten days when soil temperatures range from 45°F to 95°F. They will come up most quickly when the soil is 85°F. This doesn't help the gardener, however, since hot soil results from days that are much too warm for good radish development. As soon as the radishes are up, thin them to stand 1 to 2 inches apart depending on the variety and how big you want them to be. Daikon and winter radishes should be sown 2 to 3 inches apart and thinned to 6 to 8 inches, with rows spaced at 18 inches apart.

A good way to enjoy radishes without devoting any extra garden space to them is to plant them with other crops that germinate slowly, such as carrots. Some gardeners plant radish seeds right in the carrot row with good results. Dorothy worries that pulling the radishes may hurt the delicate carrot seedlings, so she plants the radishes in their own row just an inch to the side of the carrots. Either way you interplant, when the radishes are ready to pull, the carrots are ready to thin, so you might as well do both jobs at once; it will help you remember to do that tedious but important task of thinning the carrots. If you plant the radishes right with the carrots, be sure to cover any exposed carrot roots when you pull the radishes.

In general, radishes are untouched by pests and diseases. Only flea beetles and root maggots are likely to bother them. To prevent both these problems, cover your crop with row covers, burying the edges in the soil. Since radishes are so sensitive to high temperatures, be sure to use one of the more porous types of row covers. If the temperature still gets too hot under the covers, you can use other prevention methods. For serious flea beetle infestations, dust with diatomaceous earth or rotenone. If your garden has a history of root maggot problems, the best preventive measure is to dig hardwood ashes into the soil and spread them on top after planting to repel the flies that lay the maggot-producing eggs.

Like potatoes, radishes can be affected by scab, so they should not be planted in areas where scab-infested potatoes grew. If you have problems with this disease, keep your radishes evenly moist for the first two weeks after planting to prevent scab from occurring.

Do not plant radishes in areas where cole crops have suffered from club root, as radishes can be affected by this disease. High soil moisture and warm temperatures increase the chances that club root will develop. Crop rotation, good soil drainage, and planting in cool rather than wet weather will help prevent this problem.

Harvesting and Storing Radishes

It takes a little practice to learn when radishes are ready to pull. Some varieties send up only a few short leaves before the root swells. It's amazing that those few leaves can produce enough extra food for the radish to form. If the seeds were not planted deep, the radishes may begin to peek out of the ground as they round up. If you aren't sure whether your radishes are ready to pull, probe gently around the base of the leaves with your index finger, and you will be able to tell if the root has swelled. And remember that all the radishes of one variety will mature over a period of just a few days; don't expect them to hold for long in the garden.

If you have more radishes than you can eat, remove the tops and store the roots in a plastic bag in the refrigerator. If you leave the tops on, they will rot after a week or two, turning the contents of the bag into a slimy, unpleasant mess. But if you remove the tops, you can store the roots as long as four weeks.

Radish Frontiers

Plant breeders are working on developing more radish varieties that grow well in the heat and are slow to bolt. They also are working on decreasing pithiness and pungency. Most radish research is being done in Europe and Japan because there's a greater consumer demand for radishes there.

Because radishes grow so quickly, scientists use them to study the effects of pollutants such as acid rain, heavy metals, and ozone on crops. This research can help home gardeners who are looking for varieties that are especially resistant to particular pollutants.

BEETS AND SWISS CHARD

Many gardeners do not realize how delicious beet greens are. One year when Dorothy bought some beets from a truck gardener, all the leaves had been removed. When she asked about the greens, he said she could have the big pile he had accumulated for free. That year her family ended up with a freezer full of wonderful greens for the winter. If you don't care for the roots but love the leaves, plant Swiss chard and grow it in the same way that you do beets.

Beets get their lovely rich color from pigments called anthocyanins. The particular anthocyanin of beets is beta cyanine. This pigment is water soluble and is not destroyed by heat, so when beets are cooked, the beta cyanine leaks into the water and stains it red. Beta cyanine can be used to dye Easter eggs, and as any beet lover knows, it should be wiped up immediately from kitchen counters, or it will stain them red. Golden beets lack beta cyanine, so another pigment present in all beets—beta xanthine—shines through to give the roots a beautiful golden color. Beta xanthine breaks down when heated, so yellow beets do not stain the cooking water the way red ones do.

To the uninitiated a beet is a beet is a beet, but to gardeners in the know different beet varieties are suited to different purposes. If you're new to beet growing, study the seed catalogs carefully to make your selection. If you want to store your beets fresh to have them on hand for winter use, try 'Detroit Dark Red,' 'Long Season,' 'Lutz' (also called 'Lutz Green Leaf'), or 'Winter Keeper.' If you'd rather can your beets, small varieties such as 'Baby Canning,' 'Dwergina,' and 'Little Mini Ball' are a good choice. One of the sweetest beets is 'Albine Veredura,' which is pure white, so it won't bleed or stain. Several varieties have especially delicious greens as well as fine roots. Dorothy's personal favorite for greens is 'Golden Beet,' but Diane loves 'Chiogga.' Other varieties that have abundant, tasty greens are 'Early Wonder,' 'Formanova,' 'Lutz,' and 'Red Ace.' 'Formanova' and 'Cylindra' are good for small gardens and for slicing because of their long, slender cylindrical shape.

Different beet varieties often have very different flavors, so you should try several to find your favorite. Diane loves the sweet taste of 'Red Ace,' a hybrid whose sweetness comes from its sugar beet parentage. 'Chiogga' is another sweet-tasting beet with white and pink rings. When you pull this beet out of the ground, the skin is cherry red, much like a large flattened radish. Diane also has found that 'Chiogga' doesn't get tough when left in the ground, so it can provide tender beets throughout the summer. Other varieties that provide a longer harvest period include 'Dwergina,' 'Long Season', and 'Lutz.'

Swiss chard varieties come in an amazing range of colors—solid green, green and white, green and red, and bright red—making it a wonderful landscaping

Beet and Swiss Chard Varieties

Swiss Chard: While beets put most of their energy into fat roots, Swiss chard develops abundant tasty greens.

addition to your garden. Some chard varieties, such as 'Swiss Chard of Geneva,' have wonderful thick stems that can be cut out separately and used like celery, while others have hardly any stalk at all. Diane's favorite small-stemmed variety, 'Perpetual' (also called 'Perpetual Spinach'), is so mild that she can pass it off as spinach and her children will ask for seconds, even though they won't eat any other variety of Swiss chard. Swiss chard is a great substitute for spinach because it continues to grow all summer long, while spinach will bolt during hot weather or long days.

Growing and Harvesting Beets and Swiss Chard

Beet and chard "seeds" are actually fruits containing several seeds. When you plant these little star-shaped fruits, several seedlings will come up where each was planted, and you must thin this tight clump. If you don't, the more vigorous seedlings will take over, and the roots will be uneven in size. Some newer beets such as 'Mobile' have only one seed per fruit and do not need to be thinned if planted far enough apart. If the single seeds germinate unevenly, however, you might have to replant to fill in the row.

Sow the seeds ½ to 1 inch deep, 2 inches apart, in rows 1 to 2 feet away from each other. If you prefer wide rows, space seeds about 2 inches apart in all directions in a 3-foot-wide row. Use row covers to increase the temperature during early spring plantings. Diane has found that row covers result in faster, more even germination from direct-seeding in cool spring soil. Beets and Swiss chard will germinate in soil temperatures from 50°F to 85°F, but optimal germination occurs at 85°F. They take one to three weeks to come up depending on the temperature (the warmer it is, the faster they'll come up).

When the plants are 2 to 4 inches tall, thin them to stand 2 to 4 inches apart depending on whether you want large beets or small ones for pickling. To prolong your harvest, space the beets just 2 to 3 inches apart at the first thinning, then thin a second time when the beets start to crowd one another, leaving 4 to 6 inches between the plants. For a special springtime treat take beet thinnings to the kitchen and steam them lightly, both leaves and roots. Chard should be thinned to a final spacing of 6 to 8 inches; the thinnings are just as delicious as those of beets.

If you want to start beets indoors, use a variety specially developed for transplanting, such as 'Little Egypt' or 'Replata.' Plant one seed cluster in each individual pot of a plastic six-pack. Transplant to a prepared garden bed as soon as the seedlings come up, being very careful not to disturb the roots. Space the seedling clusters 8 inches apart in a wide bed under row covers. These varieties don't need to be thinned; they are designed to be harvested when only 1 to 2 inches in diameter by pulling the whole clump.

Aphids, leaf miners, nematodes, and webworms may visit your beet or chard patch from time to time, but they usually don't pose a serious threat. Check the undersides of the leaves for the small white egg clusters left by the leaf miner and just pinch off any infested leaves. Ladybugs will keep any advancing aphids at bay, and if you see any webworms, just pick them off by hand. Crop rotation is a must for controlling nematodes. If you have a nematode problem in the soil, try not to plant beets or any other susceptible crops for four or five years to give the worms a chance to die off.

There's no hard and fast rule about when you should harvest your beets. Let your own preference as to size be the judge of when it's time to pull them up. Just remember that many varieties are tenderer when they're on the small side; large beets can be tough and woody. You can scrape the soil away from around the stem and feel to find out how big the roots are.

After you pull up beets, cut off most of the greens, leaving about a 2-inch stubble attached to the root. This will help the beets keep longer in good condition. If you leave the greens on, they will quickly start to deteriorate and serve as a source of infection for the roots. Besides, when you trim away the greens and use them, you're getting a double harvest from the same plant. Just be sure to eat or process your beet greens as soon as possible; they will keep in the refrigerator for a maximum of two weeks. The roots will keep much longer depending on the variety. Those bred for long storage can be kept as long as five months, providing the temperature is close to 32°F at 95 percent relative humidity. Diane covers her beets with leaves, just as she does her carrots, for fresh winter eating (see the section "Harvesting and Storing Carrots" later in this chapter).

Swiss chard leaves can be harvested singly as soon as the plant is about 4 inches tall. Keep picking individual leaves as the plants grow to encourage new, succulent growth. Once the leaves become large, they will be tougher. Use these larger leaves as wrappers around spicy vegetable or meat mixtures just as you would cabbage leaves. To prolong the harvest into the fall, cover the plants with a plastic sheet or row covers held up by wire hoops.

Beet Frontiers

The great commercial importance of sugar beets has had some pleasant repercussions for home gardeners. The new monogerm (single-seed) beets originally were developed for commercial growers of sugar beets who wanted easy, even spacing of their crops. (It's not very efficient to have to go back over a huge field to thin the clusters.) After being developed for sugar beets, the monogerm trait was bred into table beets as well. Plant breeders also are working on pest and disease resistance for sugar beets, which should trickle down and influence varieties bred for home gardeners. The problem with relying on sugar beet developments for table beet improvements is that sugar beet growers are concerned only with the roots, not the more nutritious tops.

Commercial growers of table beets aren't concerned with the tops either, for beet greens are not an especially popular commercial crop. What large-scale growers and home gardeners look for in a crop often are at opposite ends of the spectrum. Commercial growers want uniform small beets that can be harvested all at once. The home gardener isn't in such a rush to harvest and usually favors a longer harvest rather than a glut. Commercial growers don't care about the ability of the roots to hold in the garden and to stay tender, for they get more money for small canning beets than for large ones. In the eyes of a home gardener, a longer-standing beet that stays tender means that good-quality fresh produce can be harvested as needed over an extended period. Only when plant breeders start to consider the needs of the home gardener will we see more rapid advances in beet varieties.

Like many other crops home gardeners enjoy, Swiss chard is not important commercially, so research on its biology and development of new varieties is just about nonexistent.

CARROTS

If you're looking for an especially high-yielding crop that stores well in its fresh state to carry you through the winter, look no further than carrots. Their contained growth habit allows you to space them close together, increasing the yield per square foot of garden space. Under the proper storage conditions carrots are edible for up to six months, providing your family with the welcome taste of a homegrown fresh vegetable during the winter. The lovely, sunny carrot color comes from the pigment carotene, which is converted to vitamin A in the human body. The darker the orange color, the more nutritious the carrot is for you. If you are looking for the most nutritious carrots to grow, try the newest varieties that are high in carotene, such as 'A+' and 'Ingot.'

Carrot Varieties

Despite the limited genetic base of most of the older varieties of carrots (which we discussed at the beginning of this chapter), several types are suitable to different uses and garden conditions. If an early harvest is what you're after, try one of the small, sweet kinds such as 'Gregory' (fifty-five days), 'Little Finger' (sixty-five days), or 'Minicor' (fifty-five days).

When selecting main-crop carrots, you must take your soil into consideration. Not everyone can grow those long, straight 8-inch beauties that the supermarket carries. Long carrots such as 'A+' and 'Imperator' will grow well only in loose, sandy, rockless soil. If your soil is heavy or rocky, try a shorter (about 6 inches long) stump-rooted variety such as 'Danvers Half Long,' 'Royal Chantenay,' or

'Scarlet Nantes.' Even in very difficult soil you can have a successful crop of carrots when you grow a short, fat variety such as 'Oxheart' or 'Parmex.' For winter storage in the garden 'Oxheart' or 'Royal Chantenay' is good, or you can try any variety described as holding well in the garden.

Besides choosing carrots for a shape that will grow in your soil, varieties vary greatly in sweetness and the amount of objectionable piny flavor. The piny flavor comes from chemicals called terpenes that develop early in the carrot root. The sugars and other desirable flavor components are manufactured after the carrot has enlarged. Commercial growers often harvest their carrots as soon as they are large enough to sell, before they have had time to develop the delightfully sweet mature-carrot flavor. Terpenes compose the main flavor component of such disappointing supermarket carrots. Home gardeners have a real advantage over commercial growers because they have time to let the natural flavor develop fully. This principle also explains why many so-called baby carrots don't have a great taste: they haven't had time to mature properly.

When you are trying new varieties, don't harvest the entire crop before conducting a taste test. If you find that harsh flavor, wait and let the carrots get a little more mature before passing final judgment on them. Diane's favorites include 'Ingot,' 'Lindoro Hybrid,' and 'Royal Chantenay.' Early summer and fall harvests come from 'Ingot' and 'Lindoro,' which mature in fewer than seventy days; 'Royal Chantenay' can be left in the ground for fresh winter eating.

◥◤

Tips on Growing Carrots

For a good crop of carrots you should lavish attention on them before they even come up. The early stages of a carrot's life are the most critical, and this is the time it demands the most regular attention. Because the seeds are very small and slow to germinate, carrots are sometimes tricky to get started, particularly if the weather is especially sunny or windy after planting.

Conventional gardening practice is to plant carrots in single rows, but we've found that we get better results when we plant in blocks. Block planting gives us a much higher yield for our garden area, and the slightly depressed planting area creates a moist haven for germinating seeds that tends to counteract the drying effects of the sun and wind. We've also found that it's easier to space the seeds evenly in a block than in a narrow row. If we drop a cluster of seeds in one spot (which is easy to do with tiny carrot seeds), we just brush them out over the wide area of the block. Another advantage to this method is that when you set aside a block of soil for carrots, the area in which they grow won't be stepped on and compacted. The conventional arrangement of narrow rows with paths running between them leads to compacted soil perilously close to where the carrot roots are growing. Despite all these advantages, there is one disadvantage to block planting: early weeding and thinning can be a bit trickier than in single rows.

If you'd like to try block planting, here are a few guidelines. To make a narrow block (4 to 6 inches wide), drag the flat surface of a garden hoe along the ground. For a wider block (12 to 14 inches wide), use the head (teeth side up) of a garden rake. Don't make the block too wide, though, for all the plants inside should be within comfortable reach so that you can weed and thin easily. The act of pulling the tool across the ground will displace some soil and, in addition to marking the boundaries of the planting area, create a slight depression. This sunken planting area (which should be no deeper than 1 inch) will collect and hold water around the germinating seeds and shelter them from drying winds. This technique is ideal for raised beds, which have been shown to increase the sweetness of carrots.

Once you've marked off the block, scatter the seeds as thinly as possible (mixing them with sand can help). You might want to try seed moisturization, as described in chapter 1. Cover carrot seeds with ¼ to ½ inch of dampened peat moss, fine soil, or sieved compost. Water them thoroughly with a gentle mist.

Carrots germinate under a wide temperature range (45°F to 85°F) and come up fastest at 80°F. They should be up in a week or two, but if the soil is especially cool (below 50°F), they may take three weeks to show their feathery heads. While you are waiting for them to emerge, be sure you keep the seedbed moist. If you let it dry out, you'll be waiting in vain for carrots to emerge. If the sun is hot or the wind is blowing pretty steadily, you may have to mist your carrot patch faithfully every day until the seedlings poke through the soil. Diane has found that row covers provide not only additional warmth but also more even moisture for early spring carrot germination.

The first three weeks of growth are critical in the life of a carrot. During this time the young carrot produces a long, thin taproot that ultimately will swell to produce the storage root we harvest. Any damage to the young root can affect the size and shape of the carrot. If the soil is flooded during this early period, you are likely to harvest forked roots. If the soil becomes compressed, either through foot traffic or heavy flooding, the pointed varieties of carrots will be blunt or forked. Soil compression also leads to shorter roots. Soil temperature can influence the length of the carrot as well. Warm (82°F or higher) soil will shorten the root, while cool (68°F to 75°F) soil will encourage longer roots to form. Cooler growing temperatures also will increase carotene levels.

When the plants are 3 to 4 inches tall, thin them to stand 2 to 3 inches apart. It's always hard to pull up so many promising young plants, but it's necessary for a good crop. Thinning thick clumps of young seedlings can be a little touchy because you don't want to disturb the roots of the seedlings you leave behind. We find that patience and a steady hand are two of the best tools you can bring to the garden. Just zero in on the one seedling in a cluster you want to leave in place and gingerly pull out the others in that area, one by one. If the seedlings are almost on top of one another, be sure to grasp them close to the soil line; that way you'll get only one at a time and won't disturb the remaining seedlings too much.

As the carrots grow, thin them again so that their final spacing is about 3 to 4 inches apart. This second thinning can be done as the roots are getting fat and turning orange. Just how much space you leave between plants depends on how wide the carrots are. If you are growing a slim variety such as 'A+' or 'Imperator,' you can leave them 2 to 3 inches apart, but fat varieties such as 'Oxheart' and 'Royal Chantenay' need about a 4-inch spacing.

Well-drained soil is a must for carrots. If the soil surrounding the roots retains water, they will absorb too much and split. Underwatering is no better, as it encourages the carrots to develop more xylem, making them tough, and many feeder roots to soak up what moisture is available, making your carrots hairy. To avoid either extreme, water only when the top 2 inches of soil have dried out, and then water thoroughly.

There aren't many pest and disease problems when growing carrots. Root maggots are the most common pest, but they can be lured away from your carrots by a trap crop of radishes. Once the maggots have infested the radishes, pull them up and discard them, leaving your carrots to grow unmolested. Or cover the crop with row covers, burying the edges. Bacterial soft rot, carrot-rust flies, carrot weevils, and nematodes can be controlled with a simple three-year rotation pattern alternating carrots, lettuce, and peas. If wireworms become a nuisance, sprinkle wood ashes along the carrot rows. If leaf blight is a recurring problem, control it by soaking the seeds for ten minutes in 126°F water before planting.

Harvesting and Storing Carrots

Many people are surprised to discover just how sweet and crispy a homegrown carrot can be. Once you've tasted one, supermarket carrots will pale in comparison. The sweetness of your carrots will depend in part on their genetic composition, so pay particular attention to varieties noted for their fine flavor. The growing environment also influences how sweet your carrots will be. Cooler soil temperatures help develop more flavor and sweetness in carrots. When carrots are allowed to remain in the soil through the cool fall and into the winter, they become much sweeter. Diane enjoys serving freshly dug carrots to guests during the winter months because they are always surprised that carrots can be so sweet.

You can harvest your carrots anytime after they've reached a usable size. When you want to pull them up, water them first so that the roots will slide out of the ground easily. Some varieties, such as 'Little Finger,' have weak tops that break off as you pull on them. To avoid this, loosen the soil next to the row or block with a garden fork and then pull gently on the leaves at the top of the root. If you have problems harvesting your carrots, try planting 'Royal Chantenay,' which has strong tops.

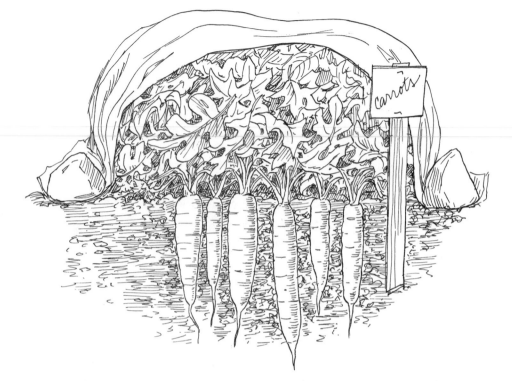

Storing Carrots in the Garden:
An easy way to overwinter carrots
is to pile on a loose mulch such as
dry, unshredded leaves and cover
the leaves with black plastic. During
the winter you can dig your way
down the row until the last sweet,
crisp carrot is gone.

Once you've unearthed your carrots, trim off their greenery right away, leaving about an inch of stubble at the top of the root. Otherwise the top growth will draw moisture out of the roots, leaving them flabby instead of crunchy. Carrots store very well in plastic bags in the refrigerator, layered in moist sand in a container placed in a cool spot, or anywhere with a temperature of 32°F and a relative humidity of 95 percent.

Our favorite way to store carrots is right in the garden. If you leave your carrots in the ground after they have grown, the cool autumn temperatures will encourage them to build up their sugar content. Just be sure that carrots you intend to store in the garden are planted in well-drained soil. If not, fall and winter moisture will waterlog the soil, and the carrots will rot. Also be sure to leave a buffer zone of bare soil around the storage area to discourage rodents from settling in for a long winter's nap. One year Dorothy's in-ground carrot cache was right next to a stand of weeds, and when she went to dig carrots for Christmas dinner, they were all gone. The only thing that the satisfied tunneling rodent had left behind was a few orange crumbs.

If the winters in your area get cold enough so that the ground freezes, bury your carrots under a thick mulch, such as a foot of unshredded leaves. Lay down the mulch while the ground is moist but before it freezes. Cover it with a sheet of heavy plastic and anchor the sheet around the edges with heavy rocks or a few shovelfuls of soil. Extend the mulch at least 6 inches around the row or block in all directions to make sure the carrots are well insulated from the cold.

When you need carrots, lift up the plastic at one end and carefully dig up a portion of the row or block, loosening the carrots and then pulling them out. Remove all the carrots that have become loosened from the soil; if there are more than you need right away, they will keep just fine in the refrigerator. Dorothy likes to dig enough at one time for about a week's use, which is 2 pounds for her family of four. As it gets closer to spring, be sure to eat up the last of the carrots because any that are left in the warm soil will bolt and turn bitter and woody.

An exciting field of carrot breeding is the reintroduction of genetic material from wild Eastern carrots into the cultivated Western varieties. These wild species, descendants of the first carrots grown in Afghanistan, will help in the development of disease resistance and broaden the genetic base of carrots. Another bright spot for home gardeners in carrot breeding is the work of Philipp Simon at the University of Wisconsin. Simon is breeding carrots with higher carotene content ('A+' and other newly released carrot varieties were a product of this breeding program) and, most refreshingly, is concerned with breeding sweeter and better-tasting carrots. These characteristics can be incorporated without creating difficulties for commercial growers, but breeding for carrot tenderness and succulence is a problem for them. That's because commercial growers need tough carrots that can stand up to rough handling. We hope that commercial harvesting methods change so that tenderer, more succulent varieties will be bred.

Carrot Frontiers

Chapter 9

Potatoes:
Those Tasty Tubers

VITAL STATISTICS

Family: Solanaceae

Species: *Solanum tuberosum*

Soil: Sandy loam; good drainage and looseness important

pH: 5.0 to 8.0; 5.5 or lower if scab is a problem

Soil temperature for sprouting of sets: 50°F to 70°F; 64°F optimum

Air temperature for best vine growth: 60°F to 80°F daytime; 45°F to 60°F nighttime; lower than 30°F kills vines

Soil temperature for tuber formation: 59°F to 68°F

Seed potato viability: 6 to 7 months

Seed potato planting depth: 8 inches

Growing potatoes in your garden can be very rewarding, as the yield from even a small area can be surprisingly high. And besides, nothing you buy tastes as good as the tiny, creamy new potatoes dug straight from your own garden. Once under way, potatoes require little attention except watering because their foliage is so vigorous. But cultivating these fine tubers also can be frustrating. You may end up with a bunch of tiny potatoes that are too small for baking, or your crop may be scabby, requiring extensive peeling before use and curtailing its storage life. Storing potatoes through the winter also is rather tricky. But a little lesson in potato biology will give you the edge you need to grow them successfully and store them properly.

Potatoes belong to the same botanical family as eggplants, peppers, and tomatoes. Some seed catalogs even sell *pomatoes*, which consist of potato rootstock grafted onto a tomato top. This plant will produce a small crop of both potatoes and tomatoes. Potato breeders sometimes do the reverse combination—tomato roots with potato tops—so the potato part will be able to invest all its energy into making seeds instead of tubers.

Potatoes have an especially colorful history. They are native to the Andes Mountains of Peru and Bolivia and are still grown there in greater variety than anywhere else in the world. Andean potatoes come with blue, brown, purple, or red skins. Different types tolerate a wide range of climatic conditions, and some can even produce a crop at an elevation of 14,000 feet.

The conquistadors introduced potatoes to Spain in the early 1500s. One explorer's journal describes this new vegetable as "a kind of earth-nut, which, after it has been boiled, is as tender as a cooked chestnut, but it has no more skin than a truffle, and it grows under the earth in the same way." The conquistadors recognized the high nutritive value of potatoes and included them in their sea-going larders to ward off the scurvy that plagued many early sailors.

Potatoes were quickly accepted in Spain, for the people were already growing and enjoying sweet potatoes. The superficial similarity between the two (sweet potatoes are in an entirely different plant family and are actually tuberous roots, whereas potato tubers are modified underground stems) led to the name for the new vegetable. Sweet potato is *batata* in Spanish, and potato soon became *patata*. Both translated into English as "potato," so in the old days, *potato* referred to both vegetables.

Potatoes quickly became popular throughout Europe, and in the mid-1700s, royal edicts in Sweden and Germany required the people to grow this crop. In Germany, failure to comply could lead to having your nose and ears cut off! Potatoes became one of the staple foods in many European countries. The Irish, unfortunately, were forced by economics to rely too heavily on them, which led to tragic consequences when the late blight disease hit and caused one of the worst famines in history in the mid-1800s. More than a million people died, and another million emigrated to the Americas.

Potato Nutrition

Before the potato famine, many Irish people lived on a diet of boiled potatoes and milk; a working man would consume 10 pounds of potatoes each day. This might sound like a pretty boring diet, but surprisingly 7 pounds of potatoes plus 1 pint of milk will meet all your nutritional needs for a day. Potatoes are one of the most nutritious foods we have, but their association with the junk-food industry has given them the undeserved reputation of being an all-starch, no-nutrition food.

Despite the fact that most people eat potatoes as a source of starch, potatoes are high in protein. Many commonly grown varieties contain 6 to 8 percent usable protein on a dry weight basis (some varieties are 10 percent protein). In terms of amount of protein produced per acre, potatoes rank second only to soybeans, though the quality of this protein is higher than that of soybeans. Protein quality is quantified as net protein utilization (NPU). The NPU of several important foods follows: eggs, 100 (an ideal protein); beef, 80; potatoes, 71; soy flour, 56; wheat flour, 52; and peas, 44. If you ate nothing but potatoes, you would satisfy your protein needs before fulfilling your caloric requirements. The high NPU of potatoes means that they can satisfy the protein requirement of more people per acre than any other major crop.

Potatoes also are high in vitamin C. The average amount of potatoes consumed each year per person in the United States (about 120 pounds) provides enough vitamin C to meet the recommended daily allowance. The humble potato contains substantial amounts of copper, folic acid, iron, vitamin B_6, and vitamin B_{12}. And when you consume a baked potato, skin and all, you are getting considerable amounts of fiber. Just about all that potatoes lack nutritionally are fats and fat-soluble nutrients.

Most people think that the potato's nutritious materials are concentrated in and just under the peel, but this is a misconception. Scientists at Cornell University carefully analyzed potatoes chemically and found more vitamin C in the central part of the tuber than in the outer portion; the opposite is true for protein. However, since only 2 percent of the total protein in the tuber is in the peel, peeling your potatoes will not decrease the protein significantly. Whenever the skin of the potatoes has a greenish cast, you should be sure to peel them. Exposure to light stimulates potatoes to manufacture not only chlorophyll but also chemicals that can make you sick.

Potato Varieties

In light of the nutritional bonanza potatoes offer, it is hard to understand why they are one of the least popular homegrown vegetables. While potatoes are being grown commercially throughout North America and are planted or harvested during every month of the year, they rank among the ten *least* favorite home garden crops. Many gardeners don't bother with potatoes because they take up quite a bit of room and are readily available in the supermarket at a relatively low price. And if you grow supermarket varieties, they may be no tastier than what you can buy. But stores don't normally carry delicious high-quality bakers such as 'Butte' or special salad potatoes such as 'German Fingerling.' If you don't grow your own, you miss out on these treats.

When you do decide to devote a corner of the garden to potatoes, you may have trouble finding a good selection from which to choose. While hundreds of potato varieties exist, relatively few are readily available to home gardeners. Seed potatoes often are sold by local stores simply as red or white, with no indication of which type of red or white is in the bag. Many major mail-order suppliers don't even offer potatoes. And when they are offered, usually only a few varieties are listed. Considering the vast differences among varieties, how satisfied you are with the results of your gardening efforts will depend heavily on which varieties you grow. Perhaps the best choice if you're serious about raising potatoes is to order from a specialist such as Roninger's Seed Potatoes, which offers more than one hundred varieties.

Potatoes come in three basic growing types based on their time to maturity—early, intermediate, and late. Early varieties have nonvining, compact plants, while intermediate to late varieties have indeterminate, semivining foliage. If you want to store your potatoes into the winter, you should choose a late variety. Early varieties sprout in storage earlier because they have been out of the ground longer. But early types will give you new potatoes sooner than late varieties.

Here is a run-down of the characteristics of some of the common varieties:

- **'Russet Burbank'** is probably the most commonly grown potato variety in the United States. It is late maturing and stores better for a longer period of time than most other varieties. You can keep 'Russet Burbank' with little sprouting for five months at 45°F. Primarily a baking potato, it also is wonderful for frying.
- **'Butte'** was introduced in 1977 as a new baking variety from Idaho. Its excellent all-around quality makes it equally useful for frying. 'Butte' has 25 percent more protein and 50 percent more vitamin C than 'Russet Burbank.' Although it is late maturing, it will sprout after only three months of storage at 45°F. Butte also needs more water to grow well than does 'Russet Burbank.'
- **'Centennial Russet'** potatoes are well suited as spring or early summer crops in California. They do not do well in short-season areas. They mature medium-late and are good for baking. This variety keeps in storage for five months but tends to accumulate sugar, which can produce an unpleasant flavor.
- **'Kennebec'** is another medium-late variety used for baking, boiling, or frying. 'Kennebec' is a cook's delight because it doesn't get watery or soggy. It doesn't store very long, however, and will accumulate sugar in storage. 'Kennebec' also tends to set tubers close to the soil's surface, where they can push out of the ground and turn green. This popular variety does best covered with a mulch that can be hilled up as the potatoes mature.
- **'Nooksack,'** developed by the Washington State University–USDA Cooperative Potato Breeding program in 1973, is a late variety that produces especially large bakers (up to 1½ pounds each). 'Nooksack' stores so well that it may be slow in sprouting when planted.
- **'Norgold Russet'** is a good all-purpose early variety that is resistant to scab. It has a short storage life and accumulates sugar at a rapid rate.
- **'Norland'** is a very early, high-yield red boiling potato not suitable for long-term storage. It is moderately scab resistant.
- **'Red Pontiac'** is a medium-late boiling variety especially good for mashed potatoes. It yields better than 'Norland' but is very susceptible to scab.

Besides these traditional varieties, potatoes in rainbow hues are now available to home gardeners: purple ones from Peru, such as 'Purple Peruvian' fingerlings; yellow ones from Europe, such as the firm-fleshed 'Yellow Finn'; and red-fleshed ones such as 'Levitt's Pink.' All these and more are available from Roninger's Seed Potatoes, which grows all its potatoes organically.

In general, small, waxy new potatoes and fingerling varieties are recommended for boiling and use in salads because they hold their shape when cooked. Most white potatoes, when mature, are best used for baking, mashing, or frying to take advantage of their dry, mealy texture. Mature red potatoes, however, are excellent for boiling and steaming.

We also should mention that the terms *Idaho* and *Maine* refer to the geographic region where the potatoes were grown and not to distinct varieties. Many varieties are grown in these two famous potato states, and the basic differences between them seem to be mineral content and texture. Idaho potatoes contain more calcium than Maine potatoes because western soils have more of this mineral, and their texture is mealier than that of their Maine counterparts.

What is a Potato?

We already mentioned that a potato is an underground stem. But what does that really mean? If you have ever disturbed your potato plants to rummage for new potatoes, you probably have noticed that the tuber forms as a small swelling on the end of a long white stolon, which grows from the underground portion of the potato stem. If you look closely at a stolon, you will see that it is a modified

Potato Plant: *Each potato develops from a small swelling at the end of a modified underground stem called a stolon.*

stem. It has small purple or dark brown bracts along its length; these are rudimentary leaves. The tuber that you ultimately harvest is merely the enlarged end of this underground stem.

Let's look at a potato more carefully. One end has a cluster of eyes that are close together, and the other end has a scar where the stolon that connected it to the plant was broken off. If you stand the potato on end, with the stolon scar against the table, you can see it as a swollen stem. You may recall from our discussion of plant structure in chapter 2 that all stems have a series of nodes and leaves, with internodes stretching between them. The potato is no exception. Each potato eye has what you might call an eyebrow, except that it is below the eye instead of above it. These eyebrows are actually the traces of what would have been leaves on an aboveground stem.

You also may remember that all stems have axillary buds above the leaves that can grow into stem branches. On the potato tuber the eyes are the axillary buds, and they are right where they should be, just above the leaf scar on the swollen stem, the tuber. The top end of the tuber, with its cluster of eyes, represents the old apical tip. If you plant an entire potato, the first sprouts will come from that end because in the potato tuber, just as in the aboveground stem, the apical tip inhibits growth of the axillary buds. When you cut up a seed potato, however, the apical dominance is broken, and all the eyes can sprout.

Choosing and Preparing Seed Potatoes

What you use for seed is very important with potatoes. Many people are content to take a chance and plant sprouting store-bought potatoes or homegrown ones. This may work in many cases, but caution is advised. More than a hundred diseases can affect potatoes, and they don't always manifest themselves in the seed potatoes. Yours may look perfectly fine and still carry one of these diseases. Some potato varieties are more susceptible than others to certain viruses. Unfortunately, a resistant variety can act as a carrier, showing no signs of disease but infecting other varieties. Once your soil has been contaminated with a potato disease, that part of the garden can't be used for potatoes for at least three or four years without risk of reinfection. However, if your crop is free of disease and your garden isn't plagued by the sucking insects that spread it, you may want to use your own seed potatoes; just be alert for any problems.

You also may be tempted by the prospect of saving a little money by cutting up store-bought potatoes and planting them. In addition to carrying the hidden risk of disease, store-bought potatoes often are chemically treated to prevent sprouting and may not sprout readily, if at all, in your garden. Two types of chemical sprays are used—maleic hydrozide and chloropropham (which is very volatile). A friend who works at a potato research station planted some potato tubers for seed that he knew had not been treated with chloropropham. He was

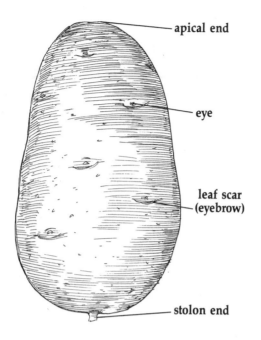

apical end

eye

leaf scar
(eyebrow)

stolon end

*Potato Tuber: If you stand a
potato on end, you can see that it is
just a swollen stem. Each eye,
actually an axillary bud, has an
"eyebrow" below it, which is a trace
of where a leaf would be on a stem.
At the top is the apical tip, where
the first sprouts will grow if the
whole tuber is planted.*

confident that they would sprout when he planted them, but he was disappointed when the tubers didn't start to sprout until July, and even then, only a few finally came to life. The mystery was solved when he found that another person had stored a sack of chloropropham-treated potatoes in the same room with his seed potatoes. Apparently enough of the chemical had gotten into the air to affect all the potatoes in the room.

Certified disease-free seed potatoes generally are grown in northern areas where plants affected by viral diseases show detectable symptoms and aphids are not too big a problem in spreading disease. Planting them is the safest route to a trouble-free potato harvest.

If you have your heart set on growing a particular potato variety, you may have no choice but to order sets from a mail-order catalog. But if you do have a choice, buy seed potatoes by weight at a local nursery or order whole seed potatoes by mail. Potato sets are tiny pieces that are cut out of potatoes and that contain one or two eyes each. The cut surfaces are treated with chemicals to kill any fungus that might damage them. Sets have several drawbacks. For one thing, mail-order companies often mail their sets too early for safe planting, and the sets do not store well in the refrigerator for more than a few days. Second, some of them may shrivel up and die because the single eye was damaged during processing or shipping. And third, commercial potato sets are much smaller than the optimum size for vigorous early growth of potato plants.

The size of the potato set is a critical factor in the eventual development of the plant and its tuber production. The sprouting potato stems gain all their early nourishment from the starch stored in the potato tuber. They must grow up through several inches of soil before they can reach the sun and begin to make their own food. Researchers have spent a great deal of time determining the optimum size for a potato set. A set weighing 3 to 4 ounces and having two or three eyes will give the best results. Sets weighing 1½ ounces or less, such as those purchased by mail order, will result in a weaker plant that yields much less than one from a larger set.

One final guideline to keep in mind is that you're better off not buying sets that have already begun to sprout. Sometimes, however, sprouted sets may be all that are available. If so, you must be very careful not to break off any of the sprouted stems. In addition to being fragile, such sets will contain less stored food because the leaves that have been forming in the dark have not been able to photosynthesize any food for the growing stems. Instead, they have been draining the reserves of starch in the tuber that are needed to fuel vigorous growth in the garden. When you finally put these sets in the ground, they probably will get off to a lackluster start.

Preparing Seed Potatoes for Planting

If your seed potatoes begin to sprout before you're ready to plant them, you can keep the sprouts short (thus less likely to break off) by putting them under a low-wattage light bulb. The sprouts will develop as small green nubbins and will not elongate until the seed piece is put back in the dark or planted in the ground. The Europeans routinely presprout their seed potatoes under diffuse light; they call this process chitting. Do not expose your eating potatoes to light, or they will turn green and develop a bitter taste. It doesn't do any harm for the seed potatoes to turn green, however.

If you've been lucky enough to buy whole seed potatoes, you're in a good position for a bumper potato crop. But first you must cut the potatoes into sets. When you cut your tubers, leave a good amount of starchy food for each piece. Make sure each set has at least two but not more than four eyes. A plant that develops two or three stems will produce the best number of tubers. More than four eyes will result in too many stems and tubers, and the competition among them will lead to smaller potatoes. If you have really small seed potatoes (less than 2 to 3 inches in diameter), leave them whole. Because of the apical dominance of the end eyes, only one or two stems will form from each seed tuber. Whether small uncut sets or cut sets from larger potatoes produce a better yield is a source of controversy in the potato business. Both methods appear to be fine for home gardeners.

Once you've cut your sets, you've removed their protective armor of skin and exposed the flesh. If you plant them right away, you'll risk invasion by fungi and bacteria. To avoid this problem, place the cut sets out in the open air five to ten days before planting. Whole sets can be planted at any time.

To dry cut sets, put them in a place with diffuse light and a temperature range of 55°F to 65°F with about 85 percent humidity. Indoors is best, as the wind outside can dry out the cut surfaces too much, and a cold spring night could freeze the sets and ruin them. It doesn't matter what type of container you use to dry your sets. We use cardboard boxes because they're convenient, but any dry surface will do.

Soon your sets will start to sprout, they will turn green, and the cut surfaces will heal over. The new leaves will begin to produce food for the developing plant, and poisons called alkaloids will form in the sets and shoots. Exposure to the light encourages the formation of these alkaloids. Maturing potatoes that stick out of the ground and are exposed to light also will develop alkaloids. You should never eat green potatoes because the alkaloids can make you sick. The alkaloids do, however, protect the sets from insects and some fungal diseases.

When the sprouts on your sets are 1 to 2 inches long and the cut surfaces have developed a corky layer, you know it's time to plant.

There are many good ways to plant potatoes, and the method that works best for you depends on the climate in your area. If you have warm days and nights in the spring, you can plant your sets 6 to 8 inches deep right from the start. But if your soil is cold and your spring tends to be cool, you will be better off planting them only an inch or two deep and mounding up the soil around the sprouts as they grow until they are buried 6 to 8 inches deep.

Since the stolons form on the underground stem portions, the more of the stem that is underground, the more stolons you are likely to end up with and, hence, the more potatoes. Also, by having the sets deep in the soil, all of your potatoes will develop under the surface, and you will not have to discard any because they turned green. An easy way to accomplish this gradual burying is to plant your sets in trenches. You can fill up the trenches as the plants grow, ending up with rows at ground level.

Potato plants need plenty of space if they are to produce many big tubers. To give them sufficient room, place them at least 9 inches apart (12 inches is even better) in rows 30 inches apart. The closer you plant the sets, the smaller your tubers will be because the plants will compete with one another for nutrients and available sunlight. For years we planted our potatoes 6 inches apart in rows 24 inches apart and ended up with disappointing yields of small potatoes. Now we plant at the proper spacing and have much better crops.

If you have heavy clay soil, try Diane's grandmother's method. She digs individual holes for her sets and then lightens the soil in the holes by mixing in peat moss. She plants the sets 4 to 6 inches deep and, as the potatoes sprout, hills them up with more peat moss–soil mixture. Besides lightening up hopelessly heavy soil, the acidic peat moss helps inhibit scab formation. (Pine needles also

The Deep-Planting Method

are acidic and have the same propensity for discouraging scab.)

If you are a new-potato fan, you can't help disturbing your deeply planted or hilled-up potatoes as you poke around looking for those lovely little gems. When we've planted deep, we've noticed that the disturbed plants wilt after we dig around them. Luckily, they recover when watered and go on to produce more new potatoes. By rummaging around among their roots, we interfere with the plants' ability to provide a good yield of large storage tubers. But neither of us can resist the temptation of new potatoes. To resolve this dilemma, we plant some sets just for new potatoes and other sets for winter potatoes. If you don't have room for two potato plantings, harvest your new potatoes in the evening, when the soil is damp, to minimize the disturbance.

The Surface-Planting Method

If you live in a humid climate, you can plant your potatoes right on the surface of the ground and cover them with a deep layer of fluffy organic material. This method often doesn't work in hot, dry areas because the loose mulch dries out too quickly. For surface planting to work, the soil under the potatoes must be loose so that the roots can grow down into it.

If you use this technique, place a layer of leaves about a foot deep on the ground in the fall in the area where you plan to plant your potatoes the following spring. Cover the leaves with a sheet of plastic. By planting time the leaves will have compacted and composted into a soft, rich layer through which the potato roots can grow. Place your sets in rows (following the spacing given earlier) and cover them with a foot or more of hay, pine needles, or straw. If you have a good supply of well-aged sawdust or peat moss, you can use a 6- to 8-inch layer of this instead.

Potatoes planted on the surface require a bit more attention than those planted deep, but when harvest time comes, you will have less work to do. As the season progresses, you'll probably have to add more mulch to make sure the layer is deep enough to keep green potatoes from forming. You also should add an extra few inches of mulch when the plants start to flower. One year when Dorothy planted her crop on the surface, she ran out of straw before the plants flowered. Her potatoes were easy to get at, but most of them were green. In addition, they were numerous and small and appeared on branched stolons. This is a problem with surface planting. The stolons respond to resistance provided by the soil by stopping growth and forming tubers. If there isn't enough resistance, the stolons may continue to grow and branch, eventually forming a number of small potatoes instead of fewer larger ones.

If you care for your surface-planted patch properly, all you need to do to harvest new potatoes is lift the mulch gently and pick them carefully off the stolons without disturbing the plant's roots. The mulching method has yet another advantage in

hot, humid areas: it helps keep the soil cool. Potatoes grow better in cool (60°F) than in warm (80°F) soil. Warm soil also can encourage growth of a rough, scaly skin on your tubers.

Those of you who garden in the cool North and have lots of clay in your soil should make sure that the ground is warm enough (at least 50°F) before covering your sets with mulch. Otherwise the mulch will keep the soil *too* cool, and your plants won't grow well. A friend of ours here in Montana lays her sets on top of the ground and doesn't cover them until the stems are 6 to 8 inches long. By that time the soil has warmed up enough to support vigorous growth.

Hay mulch has one serious disadvantage: it leaves lots of weed seeds behind. The year the potatoes are growing in it, the mulch inhibits the growth of weeds. But the next year, when you plant a different crop in that spot, you are likely to be plagued by a veritable carpet of grass seedlings.

Potato Planting Methods:
Potatoes can be planted in the conventional way and hilled up (left), or placed on the soil surface and layered with mulch as the plant grows (right).

Potato plants start to form tubers before they bloom, so the old saying that you can dig for new potatoes when the plants are flowering usually is correct. Oddly enough, potatoes can form tubers without blooming at all. However, the conditions that favor one also favor the other, so they generally occur at about the same time. 'Russet Burbank' potatoes start to develop small tubers when the plant is only 8 to 10 inches high and small flower buds begin to show at the top of the plant. By the time the plant is 50 percent in bloom, there may be many small tubers and even a few sizable ones weighing 4 to 5 ounces.

Blooming and Tuber Formation

Wild potato species living in Central and South America are sensitive to day length and won't produce tubers when days are long. Some researchers believe that late-maturing cultivated varieties may be at least somewhat sensitive to day length. But any natural response to the hours of daylight has been bred out of most cultivated potatoes, and they can be grown successfully in any part of the country.

Effects of Basic Nutrients on Potato Growth

It's very important that you pay attention to the amount of nitrogen available to your potato plants. This nutrient is a critical element in both plant growth and tuber development, and either too much or too little of it will adversely affect your harvest. Too much nitrogen will encourage lush foliage growth at the expense of tuber production. If the soil where you plan to grow your potatoes lacks nitrogen, it is best to apply any fresh manure or other high-nitrogen fertilizer (such as cottonseed meal or dried blood) in the fall rather than in the spring. During this interval between fertilizing and planting, some of the nitrogen will leach out of the soil. Fresh manure also can encourage scab, another reason to avoid using it in the spring. If your soil lacks nitrogen but you didn't do anything about it in the fall, go ahead and plant. When your plants are about a foot high, give them a shot of compost or manure tea. Keep feeding them through the blooming period. Be aware that too much nitrogen can delay the formation of tubers by a week to ten days, especially in late-season indeterminate varieties.

Don't wait too long to give your potato plants the nitrogen they need. If they are in the throes of a nitrogen deficiency, they will respond by forming tubers prematurely. Once this process has begun, nothing will reverse it. You can pour on nitrogen to your heart's content and still end up with a poor yield of puny tubers. These measly little potatoes also are likely to sprout in storage much earlier than healthy potatoes. The correct amount of nitrogen is so important to potatoes that commercial growers snip off bits of their plants and send them to laboratories to have them tested for nitrogen content.

Like other plants, potatoes need more than nitrogen. They need potassium and phosphorus as well. These nutrients have interesting effects on potato yields. Experiments in India demonstrated that increasing nitrogen and potassium led to larger tubers, while increasing phosphorus resulted in smaller potatoes. All three nutrients, however, increased the total weight of the crop. Potatoes grown with too little potassium also may become soggy when cooked, while those grown with too much can be mealy.

Picturing your potatoes growing under the ground can help you understand why a loose, well-drained soil is so important for this crop. The stolons that form the tubers push out through the soil away from the base of the plant. Once the tubers begin to swell on the ends of the stolons, they grow rapidly. To accommodate this expansion, you need to give them loose soil. If the tubers are expanding in heavy soil that is hard to push aside, they will be misshapen and will have deformed eyes. As the tuber forms, it needs oxygen for its rapid metabolism. In a soggy or dense soil that is low in oxygen, the pores through which air enters the developing potato will become very large, resulting in a rough skin.

Like other plant parts, the potato tuber increases in cell number first, then expands rapidly as the cells enlarge. At first the number of cells is multiplied by about five hundred. Then each cell increases its volume to ten times the original by filling with starch and water. While the tubers are growing, they command nearly all the plant's resources. In the first two weeks of their development alone, the tubers claim almost all the nitrogen, phosphorus, and potassium that the plant is absorbing. To give you an even more graphic idea of just how much the tubers draw from the plant, scientists have determined that plant sap can flow into them at a rate of 20 inches per hour!

You can understand why potatoes need plenty of water during this period, considering how much fluid it takes to fill out the tubers. If potatoes do not get enough water while the tubers are growing, they will grow slowly. Then, when enough water is provided, the normal growth rate will resume, resulting in knobby, misshapen potatoes. Because irregular watering disrupts the normal growth process, it also can cause hollow heart (a cavity in the middle of the potato) and growth cracks. Regular watering should extend from the time the tubers begin to form (about the same time the flower buds appear) until just before the foliage dies. During this period the soil should be kept consistently moist.

The upper part of the potato plant also reacts to water stress, with important consequences for tuber growth. If the plant isn't getting enough water, it will wilt and the stomata will close, slowing photosynthesis. Even if you water right away, the stomata will reopen very slowly. Since the leaves are sending 75 to 85 percent of the food they produce to the tubers, such a slowdown will ultimately decrease your harvest.

Wilting and a decrease in tuber production also will occur at prolonged high temperatures (above 90°F), even if you conscientiously keep the soil moist. Hot weather also slows the beginning of tuber growth and the process of tuber development. Mulches that cool the soil can help. Because potatoes have such an aversion to extended heat waves, if your area has regular periods of prolonged high temperatures, try to plant your crop in a cooler part of the season. If summer is the only time you can garden, try a variety such as 'Norchip,' which will form tubers even when the days are long and hot.

Potatoes need to be weeded, but if you time it right, you can get away with

Soil, Watering, and Weeding

a minimal amount of that tedious chore. If quack grass or crabgrass is the principal culprit, keep your potato plot weeded for the first two weeks after the shoots appear above ground. If other weeds are the problem, you can get away with weeding your potatoes once about four weeks after planting the tubers. In one study in India a weed-free potato patch produced 71.5 percent more potatoes than one that was left unweeded. But a single weeding session at four weeks or six weeks after planting resulted in almost as big a crop. By eight weeks after planting, the weeds will already have done their damage in suppressing the vegetative growth of the potato plants. Without adequate foliage to nourish the tubers, your crop will be a disappointment.

Digging and Storing Potatoes

Steamed new potatoes tossed with butter and parsley are a special home garden treat; so are peas with new potatoes. Not only do new potatoes have their own special flavor and texture, but they also offer some nutritional bonuses. New potatoes have more protein than mature ones. This accounts for their firmer texture. In addition, the combination of new potatoes and peas is a perfect food: the amino acids in one combine with the amino acids in the other to make complete protein that is just as nourishing as that found in meat. While we usually eat peas and potatoes as a side dish, this nutritious combination can serve as a main dish.

New potatoes can be dug at any time, but the storage crop should be left in the ground for at least two weeks after the tops have died down. If you don't let them age in the ground, they won't develop the tougher skin necessary for long-term storage. Someone told a friend of ours to wash his newly dug tubers, which had not been properly hardened, before storing them. He turned the hose on them, and their fragile skins promptly peeled right off! The underground rest period also allows the potatoes to convert sugars into starches, making them better for baking and frying.

Many commercial potato growers have machines called vine beaters that literally thrash or roll the vines to death. Then they spray the vines with a chemical to make sure all of them die off at the same time. After the tubers have aged in the ground, they can all be harvested at the same time. If you want to harvest your crop all at once, you can simply cut the vines off at ground level. If you live in the North, an early frost may do the work for you. In any case be sure to leave your tubers in the ground for two weeks after the vines have died, no matter how they meet their end. Another gardening friend grew a mid-season variety that was late in producing. To ensure that she could harvest mature potatoes before the ground froze, she cut off her vines before they died and was able to dig her properly matured potatoes before a hard frost hit.

A garden fork is the best potato-digging tool. Push the fork into the soil about 10 to 12 inches away from the dead plant and lift up. This should give you the least number of speared potatoes. Eat any potatoes that are impaled as soon as possible. The tines can carry disease organisms into the vulnerable insides of the tubers, so these wounded potatoes won't last in storage.

Leave the tubers you've unearthed outdoors for several hours to dry in a spot shielded from direct sun. Let them dry until any remaining dirt crumbles off. You can wash them if you wish, but you must be careful not to break the skins in the process, and you should be sure that they are dry when you put them into storage.

Keep in mind that potatoes that were stressed by lack of water, high temperatures, or rough handling in harvesting and those that were attacked by a disease may sprout earlier than those grown under better conditions. Make sure that air can circulate throughout your stored potatoes. Air movement keeps condensation from building up and encouraging spoilage.

Unfortunately, most home gardeners cannot provide ideal storage conditions for potatoes, which demand high humidity (95 percent) and cool temperatures (40°F to 50°F) to keep for the longest time. They also must be stored out of the light to prevent greening and sprouting. The storage area doesn't have to be dark, but the potatoes must be well covered to shield them from the light. The best storage location is a cool, moist environment that is unlikely to experience freezing temperatures. The basement is the best bet for most people. One friend stores his potatoes in well-covered wooden boxes on the cement floor of his cool basement, wetting the floor in the storage area to increase the humidity before he puts the boxes down.

You will want your own potatoes to last as long as possible in storage so you can avoid buying commercially grown and treated tubers. Keep the temperature as close to 40°F as possible without letting it get any colder. Lower temperatures encourage the starches in the potatoes to turn to sugars, which can give the tubers an off taste. Avoid storing your potatoes in the refrigerator, where the temperature is likely to be too cold. Have you ever made French fries from homegrown potatoes and noticed that the fries were unusually dark? This is a visible clue that the potatoes were kept too cool and the starches were turning to sugars; the heat of the frying oil actually caramelized the sugars! Be sure never to let your potatoes freeze in storage, or you will ruin your crop.

If you are experimenting with saving potatoes for seed, they can be stored at 38°F to keep them from sprouting early, as a buildup of sugar won't harm them.

Potatoes, like all plants, are susceptible to their share of diseases and pests. But fortunately for the home gardener, most of these will not devastate your crop. By following the advice given in this chapter, you can avoid many of the common problems, such as knobby and undersized tubers.

Problems with Potatoes

Colorado potato beetle: This is the most common insect pest that plagues potatoes. Surprisingly, this native insect was not originally a potato eater. Its host was a wild relative of potatoes. But when Americans began growing potatoes in the late 1860s, this enterprising beetle switched over to the new crop.

Overall, potatoes have few insect pests because of the poisons in their leaves. But the Colorado potato beetle zeros in on the same chemicals that protect the plant from other pests and are attracted by their telltale aroma. Because they feed on the poisonous leaves, the beetles also are poisonous. They have bright black and yellow stripes to discourage birds and other predators. This also makes them easy for you to find.

If you see just a few beetles on your plants, you may be able to pick them off by hand. Turn the leaves over and look for small clusters of bright orange eggs on the undersides. Both the adult beetles and the larvae (which have plump reddish orange bodies and dark heads) feed on potato leaves, and it doesn't take them long to eat their way through your plants. If there are too many beetles or larvae to pick off by hand, sprinkle powdered rotenone on your plants, and the beetles will disappear. One rotenone treatment should do the trick, but keep an eye out in case some beetles escape and reproduce.

Colorado Potato Beetle: This pest can devastate your potatoes. Fortunately the beetles are easy to see and remove by hand. Larger infestations succumb readily to rotenone.

Brown center or hollow heart: As we already mentioned, a hollow center in a potato tuber can be caused by irregular watering. Actually, either a hollow heart or brown center can result from any stress that kills cells in the central pith area of the tuber. 'Russet Burbank' is especially susceptible to these problems. Adding nitrogen just after the tubers have begun to form but before they begin growing also can encourage them.

Internal black spot bruises: At some time you may have cut open a potato and found a black bruise inside. Sometimes when potatoes are handled roughly during harvesting, the injury to the outside stimulates cells inside to produce a black pigment, even though the outside looks perfectly normal. To avoid this problem, gently set, not drop, your potatoes into containers or onto the ground when you're harvesting them.

Early dying, or verticillium wilt: This unpleasant potato affliction is caused by a fungus. If the leaves of some of your plants begin to turn yellow and die earlier than they should (beginning with the lower leaves and working up), you should pull the vines and dig out the tubers right away. Although your crop will be small and you'll have to eat the potatoes quickly, you may be able to prevent the fungus from spreading. Keeping the soil moist also will help delay the spread of the fungus. To avoid contaminating the rest of your garden, destroy the vines instead of adding them to the compost pile.

Spores of early-dying fungus may persist for seven years after an infection, successfully overwintering in the soil and feeding off dead organic material. Once your soil has been infected, you must wait at least three or four years before you can safely plant any susceptible crops in the contaminated spot. This limitation can be a serious problem, since a variety of crops, including eggplants, mint, muskmelons, peppers, strawberries, tomatoes, and watermelons, can contract this nasty disease. Using certified seed potatoes will reduce the possibility that verticillium wilt will develop in your garden.

Common scab: Scab is one of the most common potato diseases. A soil-borne bacterium begins the infection, which weakens the tuber. Other organisms often join in. Scab is favored by dry soil, especially early in the plant's life, as well as by high calcium levels, neutral pH (around 7.0), and the use of uncomposted manure. Scab also afflicts beets, radishes, rutabagas, and turnips, so if this disease attacks your garden, you will have to avoid growing all these crops in the infected area for at least three years.

Scab begins to form as small rough spots on growing tubers. If you see any signs of it developing when you are harvesting new potatoes, be sure to keep your soil moist; this may be enough to control a light scab infestation. By moist we mean keeping the soil wet through the top 9 inches, which can call for watering every five days for five to seven hours at a stretch.

If scab is a continuing problem, try growing resistant varieties such as 'Early Gem,' 'Norgold Russet,' and 'Targhee.' Avoid susceptible varieties such as 'Bliss

Triumph,' 'Kennebec,' 'Norchip,' 'Red Pontiac,' and 'Russet Burbank.' Crop rotation also can solve a recurrent scab problem. Rye and soybeans are both good rotation crops to help reduce the severity of scab. Both increase the acidity of the soil, and some scientists believe that they also may encourage the growth of beneficial microorganisms that produce antibiotics inhibiting scab.

If you have severe, persistent problems with soil-borne diseases, you should solarize your soil (see chapter 4). This method has been successful in university trials in both California and Idaho, where significantly better potato yields were measured even two and three years later. You may lose one growing season for that plot of ground, but the benefits can last several years.

Potato Frontiers

Scientists are trying to breed new and better potato varieties, but they must overcome several obstacles. To produce new types, the flowers of one variety must be pollinated with pollen from those of another. With potatoes this isn't easy. The potato flower often is sterile and cannot be fertilized. Even when the flower is pollinated, it can fall off before fertilization occurs. Potato plants channel most of their energy into tuber formation, but breeders have found clever ways to prevent this process. They often graft the top of a potato plant onto tomato roots so that the potato can devote most of its energy to producing flowers. Another method is to plant the seed in sand-covered bricks. The plants are fed with a hydroponic solution, and their roots become anchored in the pores of the bricks. The sand can be washed away and the tubers removed as they begin to form.

Scientists are trying to breed in traits such as disease resistance, more dry matter and less sugar, less discoloration of raw potato flesh, higher yields, and increased protein and vitamin content. In the past breeders (who gear most of their work toward the needs of commercial growers) didn't spend time working on resistance to the Colorado potato beetle because commercial growers sprayed to eliminate this pest. But this infamous insect has been developing a resistance to pesticides in the eastern part of the country, and farmers are worried. Modern genetic engineering may come to the rescue. Scientists are trying to incorporate the gene for the natural toxin produced by the bacterium *Bacillus thuringiensis*, which kills potato beetles, into the genes of the potato. If they succeed and potato plants make the toxin themselves, spraying with pesticides will be unnecessary. Breeding virus-resistant strains also has been difficult, but modern genetics has helped here. Monsanto has managed to insert genes into 'Russet Burbank' potatoes that make them resistant to two different viruses.

Fortunately, biological control methods for potato problems are receiving some attention. Fungi may be able to provide natural control of diseases such as verticillium wilt. It will take time, however, to figure out how to apply such techniques in a practical way.

Because potatoes are an exceptionally nutritious food crop that produces abundantly, the range over which they are grown is increasing. Potatoes grow best in cool, humid climates but are important crops in most areas of the world, from the tropics to subpolar regions. Therefore, breeding for varieties that can survive under stressful conditions is important. Unfortunately, experiments indicate that two traits of potatoes that make them undesirable for growing in hot climates — lack of tolerance of hot soil and high air temperatures — are probably under separate genetic control. This will make breeding heat-tolerant varieties more difficult.

The nutritional benefits of potatoes also put them in line as possible space food, so scientists are hard at work studying the effects of variables such as carbon dioxide, light, temperature, and water on different potato varieties. Some varieties are injured by continuous light, so they would not be suitable for the kind of intense growing that space crops must undergo. Others grow well when the lights are left on.

Breeders also are looking outside the genetic pool of cultivated potatoes to wild species. Some of these untamed relatives have very sticky hairs that can trap aphids. This trait would be helpful in organic pest management of gardens. Unfortunately, breeders so far have been unable to introduce this highly desirable trait into domesticated potatoes.

Chapter 10

Beans and Peas: The Generous Legumes

I f you've never tasted tiny peas shelled, cooked, and served fresh from the vine, you're missing one of the great culinary delights. Peas and green beans are among those peerless homegrown crops whose quality can never be equaled by any supermarket produce. What the supermarket bills as "fresh" are peas and beans that were harvested weeks before they reached the produce counter, and they are usually overmature even before they leave the farm. During the long interval between farm and table, the natural sugars in the food start turning to starch, the crispy texture turns flaccid and tough, and the nutrient content begins to decline. What you end up with are too-old vegetables that are bland and stringy instead of sweet and crunchy. But when you grow your own, you can pick them when they're still young, fresh, and delicious.

Raw beans and peas are just about the tastiest and most nutritious snacks around. The only problem is that once your kids get hooked on these vegetables, they can be the worst pests in your pea patch. Our kids love to take a colander full of fresh-picked peas into the TV room to shell and eat while watching their favorite shows. Children aren't the only ones to go for raw legumes; many adults are turning to snap peas and young green beans as healthy substitutes for potato chips served with low- or no-fat yogurt-based dips.

Beans and peas are fun for kids not only to eat but also to plant. The seeds are large and easy to work with, and a beanpole tepee makes a great summer hideout, complete with built-in snacks.

Where Beans and Peas Come From

People's affinity for legumes is nothing new. They have been eating peas in particular for a long time. Archaeologists have uncovered carbonized pea seeds in Middle Eastern and European neolithic settlements that are at least nine thousand years old. Now modern genetic techniques can map special enzyme patterns that mark varieties with a common ancestry. These methods are being used to determine where varieties originated and how they were dispersed along trading routes through time. They point to the Near East as the area where peas were originally domesticated.

Knowing where varieties of any crop come from is important, as such knowledge can provide clues to their adaptations to special climates, pests, and soil conditions. This information is invaluable to plant breeders, who often use native varieties, with their greater genetic variation, to develop specially adapted garden varieties.

Dry, lima, and green beans originated in Middle and South America. Dry beans are the oldest; they've been cultivated for more than seventy-five hundred years. Limas and beans have been grown for around forty-five hundred years. Although green beans have been grown for a long time, stringless green beans are relatively recent. Researchers have found only a few such varieties in the Andean areas of South America where green beans originated. They speculate that the genetic factor(s) preventing the pod from forming strings came from a recent mutation or, alternatively, that plants with stringless pods don't survive or reproduce easily in the wild. The mutation might be common, but the stringless pods so desired by gardeners would be a disadvantage under natural competitive conditions.

If you've had a few plants produce flat, stringy beans when you planted stringless varieties, you are already acquainted with the stringless bean's high rate of reversion to its original form. Stringless pods frequently don't open to release the seeds. In nature the pod, along with its seeds, would likely rot before the seeds germinated. Even if the pods do open, releasing the seeds, they might not produce seed-bearing plants, as stringless bean seeds often do not germinate as well as the stringed varieties. Only under garden conditions where they are coddled by appreciative humans do stringless beans thrive.

Three major areas of domestication led to the variety of beans we see today. Small-seeded dry beans such as the navy or pea bean, 'Great Northern' bean, and pinto bean were developed in Middle America (Mexico and Guatemala). Beans were cultivated in two areas of South America—the southern Andes region of Peru, Chile, and Argentina and the northern Andes region of Colombia. Bean varieties from the southern Andes and Middle America were mixed in Colombia, resulting in a great variety of seed sizes and plant forms.

Lima beans evolved to thrive in the lower, more tropical regions, while common beans were adapted to cooler, higher areas. Their different origins help explain their different cultural requirements. Although some varieties of lima beans such as 'Carolina' and 'King of the Garden' can tolerate cool weather, most require warmer weather than common beans. Among the snap and dry beans, the growth habit seems to be related to climate. Upright bush beans thrive at warmer, lower altitudes, while climbing beans do best in cool, wet highlands with long growing seasons. Beans with an intermediate growth habit frequently are found in drier regions at medium to high altitudes.

The large-seeded dry bean types of the northeastern American Indians included cranberry, eye, horticultural, red kidney, and trout beans. Some of these may have come directly from the southern Andes where they originated, but others, such as 'Swedish Brown' and German trout beans, probably were brought to the area by European settlers. These bean varieties may have been taken back to Europe by early explorers of South America, developed in Europe, and then returned to America by early settlers. They grow well in western Europe and the northeastern part of the United States because they were originally developed to flourish in cool, short summers.

*   *   *

The Nutritional Profile of Legumes

Besides tasting delicious, peas and beans pack a nutritional wallop that's hard to beat. A cup of fresh shelled peas contains about 9 grams of protein, 5.4 grams of fiber, and 122 calories. That same cupful will supply you with 70 percent of the vitamin C, 45 percent of the thiamine, 40 percent of the niacin, and 20 percent of the vitamin A you should receive each day. Chinese snow peas have less protein and fewer calories but also are high in vitamins. Snap peas, which have edible pods with developed seeds, are probably comparable in nutritional content to regular peas.

Green snap beans have only 2 grams of protein, 3.2 grams of fiber, and 35 calories per cup, but this same cupful supplies 60 percent of the vitamin C and a portion of the vitamin A you need each day. Yellow snap beans contain less vitamin C than green ones. Cooked dry beans are a more concentrated food, with as many as 300 calories per cup. Along with their stick-to-the-ribs heartiness, they supply large amounts of niacin, riboflavin, and thiamine, plus some calcium and iron. They're high in potassium but low in sodium—good news for people on a low-salt diet. For those of you battling high cholesterol, dried peas, lima beans, and cooked dry beans can benefit your diet in two ways. First, they are a great source of soluble fiber, which helps lower cholesterol levels. For instance, a ½-cup serving of cooked kidney beans contains 7.3 grams of soluble fiber. Second, you can take advantage of the high protein content of legumes to cut down on meats containing saturated fat. This in turn will help decrease your cholesterol level.

Although peas, lima beans, and cooked dry beans contain a hefty dose of protein, that protein is not complete. It is deficient in three essential amino acids: cysteine, methionine, and tryptophan. Peas growing in a soil with adequate sulfur have more of the first two amino acids, so they have more available protein. Of the different kinds of dry beans, pinto beans come closest to being a complete protein source. Red kidney beans are the least complete but still provide two-thirds of the protein of most pinto beans.

Beans can be eaten with other protein sources, such as grains and dairy products, to provide complete protein. Dishes such as succotash and bean enchiladas provide protein that is comparable to that available in meat, as corn makes up for the amino acids that beans lack.

Beans and Peas Are Unique

Besides being tasty and easy to grow, beans and peas are good for your garden. As members of the very large legume family, they have the ability to form special associations with bacteria in the soil, enabling them to fix nitrogen—that is, to take nitrogen from the air trapped in soil pores and convert it chemically into a form that they can use. To understand just how significant this is, you need to understand how soil nitrogen and plants interact.

Nitrogen is only available to plants when it exists in compounds such as ammonia, nitrates, or urea. In these forms the nitrogen is considered to be "fixed." Fixed nitrogen in the soil comes from a variety of sources besides the activities of legumes. Lightning, photo-oxidation, and volcanic activity produce fixed nitrogen that is washed from the atmosphere into the soil by rain. Fixed nitrogen also can become available by the application of chemical fertilizers, the breakdown of organic matter into its component parts (such as occurs in compost piles), and the activities of certain free-living bacteria and blue-green algae in the soil.

Since nitrogen is usually the limiting factor in soil productivity, the ability to use the limitless supply of atmospheric nitrogen enables legumes to thrive where other plants can barely grow. There are thirteen thousand species of legumes in the world, living in every environment from tropical forests to arctic tundra. These plants account for about 40 percent of the fixed nitrogen worldwide, making them extremely important to the ecological balance on Earth. Many legumes, such as alfalfa, beans, clover, and lupine, are small plants. Some legumes are bushes; others, such as acacias, are small trees; still others are large forest trees such as the Kentucky coffee tree and the honey locust.

The bacteria that live in legume roots are called rhizobia, from their genus name, *Rhizobium.* Each legume species has its own special *Rhizobium* species living in lumps on the roots called nodules. The nodules create a special environment for the bacteria so that they can fix nitrogen efficiently. The enzyme nitrogenase, which enables the bacteria to perform their task, is ineffective when oxygen is present. Another chemical found in the nodules, called leghemoglobin, binds any free oxygen so the nitrogenase can do its work. Leghemoglobin is very similar to the hemoglobin in your red blood cells and performs the indispensable

HOW RHIZOBIA ENTER LEGUME ROOTS

Just how do these nitrogen-fixing bacteria get inside bean and pea roots? As the young root grows, it secretes a chemical into the soil that attracts the proper species of rhizobium to the roots. (The bacteria have tiny flagella that enable them to move through the water held in the soil pores.) When the bacteria reach a small root hair and touch it, they stick to it because a protein on the surface of the root hair bonds chemically with a sugar molecule on the surface of the bacteria. Each legume-rhizobium pair has its own specific protein-sugar combination, so only the correct species of rhizobium will bind to the root hair of a particular legume.

In at least one species of rhizobium (associated with a type of clover) the next step is especially interesting. The clover root releases the amino acid tryptophan into the soil, and the bacteria respond by converting the tryptophan into a plant-growth hormone. The hormone makes the root hair curl around and through the mass of attracted bacteria, increasing the chances of further bacteria–root hair contact.

The bacteria gain entry into the root hair through an infection thread, a tunnel-like in-growth of the root hair. (Imagine the root hair as a long balloon; if you pushed your finger into the balloon, you would produce a cavity similar to the infection thread.) The infection thread, filled with multiplying bacteria, continues growing farther into the root hair. Eventually it grows all the way back to the base of the hair and enters the main part of the root. Then its tip ruptures, and bacteria spew forth into the main root cells. The cells containing the multiplying bacteria enlarge to the point where they form a root nodule.

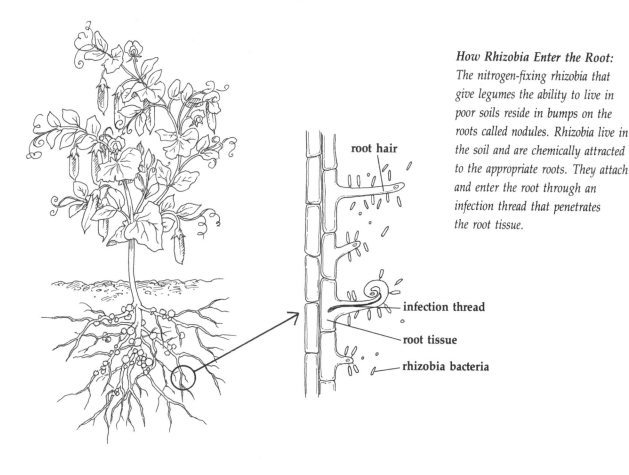

root hair

infection thread

root tissue

rhizobia bacteria

How Rhizobia Enter the Root:
The nitrogen-fixing rhizobia that give legumes the ability to live in poor soils reside in bumps on the roots called nodules. Rhizobia live in the soil and are chemically attracted to the appropriate roots. They attach and enter the root through an infection thread that penetrates the root tissue.

task of latching onto oxygen molecules so they don't come in contact with the rhizobia. If you pull up a healthy clover plant and examine the nodules on its roots, you will notice that they are pink; the color comes from the leghemoglobin.

The bacteria that live in the root nodules of peas, snap beans, and lima beans are all different. Although you may have grown beans in a particular part of your garden, you can't count on that population of bacteria to help out a new crop of peas. You need to inoculate the pea seeds with a dried preparation of bacteria before planting them in the former bean patch. The reverse also is true. Inoculant powders are readily available through seed catalogs and usually contain the various bacteria appropriate for peas, snap beans, and lima beans. These preparations do not contain the bacteria that infect clover, cowpeas, scarlet runner beans, or soybeans, so you will have to buy a separate inoculant.

Once nodulated beans or peas have grown in a particular spot in the garden, the soil in that area will contain the proper bacteria, and they will be capable of inoculating plants for several years. But if you have any doubts, buy some inoculant, as it can increase your yield dramatically. Trials conducted by Herbst Brothers Seedsmen revealed that inoculated bean plants produced 65 percent more beans than uninoculated plants, while inoculated pea plants yielded 77 percent more peas than uninoculated plants.

The results are so impressive and the inoculant so easy to apply that there's no reason for any of your beans or peas to go uninoculated. The "shake and plant" technique is a simple and effective way to apply the bacterial powder to your seeds. Dampen the seeds, pour them into a paper bag, and sprinkle them with the powder. Close the bag, shake them up, and plant them right away before they dry. The bacteria are activated once the inoculant powder has been moistened. If you allow the powder to dry, you will kill off the microorganisms.

We have noticed that beans need more nitrogen than peas. Despite the fact that both plants fix nitrogen, they use the first fixed nitrogen coming from the nodule in different ways. Peas export the nitrogen to the shoots as soon as the nodule begins to form, fueling seedling growth. Beans use the nitrogen for the further growth of the nodule, leaving a young bean seedling that's growing in nitrogen-deficient soil with too little nitrogen. For this reason make sure that your bean plot has enough nitrogen at the beginning of the season. In addition, pea nodules continue to grow and produce fixed nitrogen throughout the life of the plant, while bean nodules stop growing after a certain length of time. This is another reason why extra nitrogen is necessary for good bean growth.

To encourage nodulation in your legumes, make sure that your soil pH is above 5.5. The soil should be loose rather than compacted so plenty of air gets in. If you have high soil temperatures (95°F) when germinating bean seeds, cover the soil with mulch to cool it, or few nodules will form. Seeds that have been stored under hot, humid conditions also will produce plants with fewer nodules. Keep your plants adequately watered to encourage abundant nodulation.

Peas, lima beans, and snap beans all come in bush and pole varieties. Bush variety seeds produce a short, bushy plant. The vines can be determinate or indeterminate—that is, with or without tendrils that allow it to climb onto its neighbor or a trellis. Pole variety seeds produce a single vine with weak stems that must be supported. In general, bush types will yield an earlier crop, and the harvest will be concentrated over a shorter period. The short internodes that make these plants bushy also account for the accelerated maturation. The rate of growth is the same for pole and bush types, but since the bush varieties spend less time growing stems between nodes, they mature faster and their flowers are produced more quickly. Bush beans, lima beans, and short-vined, or dwarf, peas (the pea version of bush beans) are best if you want an early harvest concentrated in a few pickings. Pole beans and tall peas are best if you want a sustained harvest and are willing to wait a few more days before the crop comes in. Although bush beans have the shortest time to maturity, pole beans and tall peas mature early enough for northern gardeners to reap a generous harvest. Pole lima beans take too long to mature to be very reliable in the North, so gardeners in short-season areas should plant only bush lima beans.

Bush beans do not require supports to grow. Although short-vined peas often are billed as not needing supports, they grow better if they have something to hold them up off the ground. They yield better, too: supported dwarf peas may yield 17 percent more than unsupported ones. Tall peas and all varieties of pole beans need supports to cling to as they grow.

Peas and beans climb in different ways and need different supporting surfaces. Peas have thin tendrils, which are highly specialized leaves that twine around a trellis or other nearby object and help hold up the vine. A tendril rotates slowly through the air as it grows until it touches something. As soon as the tendril makes contact with a support, it begins to wrap around it. These slender green appendages grow quickly: a tendril can encircle a string or wire with one turn in less than an hour, and you can see the beginning of the curling within two minutes of contact. The colder it is, the slower the coiling goes, and if it dips much below 50°F, the tendrils won't coil at all. If one of your pea vines isn't making good contact with its support, gently push the vine up against the fence or strings, and it will grab hold quickly. Don't expect your peas to grow well on poles; their tendrils are too small to surround the pole and won't be able to cling securely.

Pole beans, including lima beans, have no tendrils; instead, their stems react to contact with support. If the stem is growing without the aid of a pole or trellis, it grows in wide circles along the ground, spiraling around other stems it may meet. But if your beans have the proper support, as soon as the stem touches a pole, it will begin to grow along the surface. When it comes to an edge, it will turn along the edge, always maintaining contact with the surface as it climbs upward in a spiral. This serpentine growth means that beans can be trained along strings, poles, or chicken wire supports. The vines will make smaller spirals around

The Long and Short of Growing Legumes

SURE-FIRE SUPPORTS FOR BEANS AND PEAS

One of the best ways to grow climbing vines is on a chicken wire fence, as both pea tendrils and bean vines can cling to it. While it takes some work to put a tall fence together, once it is made, you can take it down at the end of the season and reuse it year after year. For tall pea varieties such as 'Alderman' and 'Sugar Snap' and for all pole beans and pole lima beans, begin with stout, 8-foot-long poles. Two-by-fours cut lengthwise to make two-by-twos work well. Lay your poles down on the ground parallel to each other, about 5 feet apart. Make 10-foot-long sections of fencing, placing one pole at each end and one in the middle. You can make as long a row as you like with these sections, tying or wiring the end poles of two adjoining sections together to give the fence stability.

Leaving the bottom 18 inches of the poles free for burying in the ground, use heavy staples or U-shaped nails to attach chicken wire to the poles. Catch every wire that crosses the poles with a nail or staple. Since chicken wire is generally only 6 feet tall, you will have to secure narrower widths of wire along the top to fill the space between the poles. If you prefer, you can string twine along the top.

When your fence is finished, take it to the garden and set it up. Carrying and setting up the fence takes two people. With one person supporting the fence, the other one can stand on a chair or ladder and use a sledgehammer (carefully) to pound the poles into the ground. If your soil is very rocky, dig holes instead, making sure to compact the soil around the posts by pressing it with your foot. Put the fence in place before planting your seeds so that you don't disturb them. As the season progresses, you may have to use wires tied to nearby trees or anchored in the ground with pegs to help support any sagging fence sections.

Most pea varieties do not grow taller than 3 feet, and supporting them is much easier than supporting beans. Cut 6-foot-tall chicken wire in half to make 3-foot-tall lengths if you can't find the shorter fencing. Cut a length of wire to the length of your pea row and take it to the garden along with some sturdy, pointed 4-foot-long stakes. Weave the stakes through the wire at about 3-foot intervals, and pound them into the ground, keeping the wire taut between the stakes, until their tops are at the top of the wire. This makes a stable support for peas that is easy to dismantle and store for use the following year.

The simplest way to support dwarf peas is to buy 18-inch-tall folding border fencing at a hardware store, anchor it in the ground, and plant your peas along both sides. Some dwarf peas will grow a bit taller than the fencing, but it will support them sufficiently until the end of the harvest. If you don't want to build your own supports, you can find trellises of various sizes in mail-order catalogs. Such trellises provide strong support and are generally light weight and very easy for one person to put up.

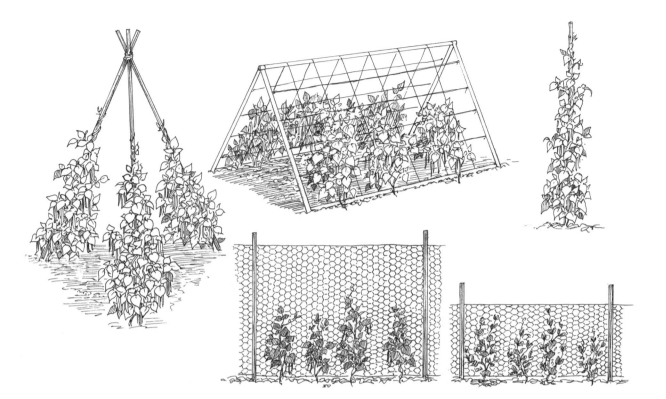

a string than up a pole, but either type of support will work.

Providing support for long vines is important for several reasons. Aside from saving garden space, climbing takes the leaves up into the sunlight and gives each leaf its share of sun for more effective photosynthesis. Also, if vines are allowed to trail on the ground, air can't circulate freely around them, and the damp vines can become infected with diseases. The beans or pea pods themselves can be splattered with mud if the vines are on the ground and can develop rust or rot from lying on damp soil.

Peas and beans also are very sensitive to abrasive sand or dust particles carried in the wind. The yield from these crops can be significantly reduced in a windy area. If you have strong prevailing winds, plant a row of sunflowers on the windward side of your peas and beans to protect them.

Bean and Pea Supports: There are many ways to trellis beans and peas—homemade tepees (left), purchased trellises (upper middle), individual poles (upper right), and homemade chicken wire trellises (bottom).

The structure of a legume flower is very different from that of other plant flowers. The distinctive appearance of the flowers of acacias, beans, lupines, peas, and vetch makes these very dissimilar-looking plants instantly recognizable as legumes. Even the puffy flower heads of clover on close inspection reveal clusters of tiny, typical legume flowers. The characteristic form of legume flowers is easy to see in a pea blossom. The graceful pea flower resembles a delicate white butter-

Legume Flowers and How They Grow

fly with outspread wings. It has one large petal that stands up vertically, two side petals that form wings, and a pair of bottom petals that are fused together in the shape of an upside-down V with extensions on each side. You cannot see any pistil or stamens, for these are hidden inside the flower.

Peas and beans are largely self-pollinating. In some varieties, such as 'Blue Lake Bush' beans, the stamens pollinate the pistil before the flower even opens, so cross-pollination is virtually impossible. Lima beans do, however, achieve up to 18 percent cross-pollination with the help of bees.

After the flower is pollinated, the pod begins to grow. If you look closely, you'll see the miniature pod appear just as the petals are withering. You may never have thought of them this way before, but pea and bean pods are actually modified leaves. A little investigative work in the pea patch bears this out. If you open a pea pod carefully, you can see that half of the peas are attached to one edge of the pod seam and the other half to the other edge. These two edges represent the margins of a leaf that have fused together to form a closed pod. The opposite seam on the pod (along the flatter edge) is equivalent to the vascular midrib of a leaf. When you string a bean or pea, you're removing the tough midrib vein of xylem and phloem.

To develop stringless beans or peas, breeders look for plants whose vascular tissue contains few tough fibers. It is impossible, however, to breed a completely stringless bean or pea, for such a plant would have no xylem or phloem to transport nourishment to the pod and developing seeds. Once you realize that the pod is actually a modified leaf, it should come as no surprise to learn that as much as 66 percent of the food needed by developing peas during their peak growth period inside the pod is supplied by photosynthesis of the pod itself. This insight into how peas grow should help you see why it's important to grow your peas on supports: that way, the pods can be out in the sun making food.

Legumes and the Soil

Beans and peas have shallow, fibrous roots, so you must be careful when weeding around the plant bases. Your best bet is to hand-pull any weeds within a 1-foot radius of the legumes. Keep the pea and bean rows thoroughly weeded until the plants are about half-grown; from then on they can outcompete the weeds.

These crops are very sensitive to overwatering and will languish in waterlogged ground, so make sure they are planted in light, well-drained soil. Gardeners growing peas during a cool, damp time of year must be especially on guard against overly wet soil. If you don't garden in raised beds, you can mix in sand to help with drainage or build up a ridge of soil and plant your peas on top of it to make sure excess water can drain off.

Legume roots extend only about 1½ feet down, so they also are susceptible

Well-filled, ripe ears of corn are a goal for many a home gardener.

Above: Green beans are really at their best when picked early, while the pods are smooth and slender.

Right: 'Royal Burgundy' beans are widely adapted and easy to find amidst the foliage because of their purple color.

Opposite: 'Green Arrow' is a tasty pea variety that produces up to ten peas per pod.

Opposite: Gardeners today can choose from a rainbow of bell pepper varieties.

Above: Tomatoes grown in the home garden are far superior to anything from the supermarket.

Left: Cooks who garden can indulge themselves in a wide selection of hot pepper varieties.

Opposite: A good crop of fresh, crunchy cucumbers can be savored twice: when you first harvest them; and later, after you've pickled them.

Left: Summer squash is one of the easiest garden crops to grow and comes in a wonderful variety of shapes. When the fruits are picked at the baby stage, the flowers can be eaten as well.

Below: Properly stored, winter squash will keep for three to eight months, depending on the variety.

Above: Melons can now be grown
in most of the country thanks to
new, early varieties.

Right: Early small-fruited varieties
like 'Sugar Baby' make growing
watermelons practical for
the home gardener.

to drought. Flowering is a critical time for both peas and beans, so make sure they have adequate moisture at that time, or your yields will be low. Water-stressed snap beans often develop fewer, smaller pods that can be quite fibrous even if they are a stringless variety. Unfortunately, low soil moisture can decrease the yields of these plants even if they aren't visibly water stressed, making it difficult to judge how much water is needed. During hot, sunny weather, Diane waters as soon as the top ½ inch of soil is dry. For peas, which grow better at cooler temperatures, she puts a light 2-inch mulch of grass clippings around the base of the plants as soon as they germinate to help hold in the moisture. She does the same for beans but only after the soil temperature warms up in July. In regions where the soil temperature is already 70°F or higher at planting, use a light mulch as soon as your beans have germinated. Just remember that legumes need evenly moist soil that is neither too dry nor too wet. A large amount of organic material will help hold the water in the top soil layer and keep the soil loose to aid in nodulation.

Because beans and peas fix their own nitrogen, your soil doesn't need to be especially rich for them to grow well. As a matter of fact, if there is a lot of nitrogen in the soil, the rhizobia will shut down, and your garden won't benefit from the presence of legumes. All the plants need is enough nitrogen to support their early growth, before the rhizobia get down to business. If you plan to work in a little manure to fuel their early growth, use cow or steer manure that isn't too salty, as peas and snap beans are sensitive to salt. Add salty manure, such as poultry manure, the fall prior to spring planting so that rain and melting snow can leach excess salt from the soil by planting time.

Phosphorus and potassium are important nutrients for legumes because they assist in blooming and pod formation. Don't skimp on these nutrients; work generous amounts of bone meal and wood ashes into the ground before you plant your beans and peas. Just remember that wood ashes can raise the soil pH, so you may have to add pine needles or peat moss to bring it back down to a suitable level. Peas and beans can tolerate acid soils better than many garden crops, but if the pH falls below 5.2, manganese in the soil can become toxic to the plants.

SNAP AND DRY BEANS

Snap beans are one of the most rewarding crops you can grow. The plants are vigorous, thrive over a wide temperature range, and provide an abundant harvest of tender, tasty pods in a relatively short time. Dry, or shell, beans take longer to grow but are equally rewarding, whether you harvest the buttery-tasting seed before it's hardened or wait until the pods are crisp and full of colorful, rich-tasting seeds.

Numerous names are used to refer to the different types of garden beans classified in the species *Phaseolus vulgaris*. The terms *green bean, snap bean,* and *string bean* all refer to any one of the popular varieties of green beans grown for their crisp pods, even though most modern varieties do not require stringing. *French beans* are somewhat more finicky (they don't do well in cool, wet weather) and are harvested when the pods are very slim and sweet. *Wax beans* are the yellow snap beans that generally have a milder flavor than the green ones. Most wax bean pods start out green but turn yellow as they lengthen and mature. *Dry beans*, such as kidney, navy, and pinto beans, are varieties grown for their mature-green or long-storing seeds rather than their green pods. You can eat the pods of dry beans, but they will be very fibrous.

Bean Varieties

When you're flipping through the glossy pages of a seed catalog or perusing a rack of seed packets, you can use several criteria to narrow down your choices from the dizzying array of varieties. The first thing you must decide is whether to grow pole beans or bush beans. As we pointed out earlier, pole beans take more work (you must provide them with support) but less space and give you a somewhat later but more prolonged harvest. Bush beans don't require support and give you an earlier, concentrated harvest. Some gardeners insist that pole beans have a better flavor than bush beans and always grow the climbers.

Certain varieties of pole beans are classics. 'Kentucky Wonder' is the standard by which all others are judged. If you want to gain notoriety among your gardening acquaintances, grow 'Oregon Giant,' which climbs up to 10 feet tall and produces long, flat, speckled pods. 'Romano Pole' is popular with bean lovers, as the flat pods of this Italian variety have a distinctive flavor that some bean connoisseurs say is unmatched by any other, even 'Bush Romano' (also known as 'Roma').

The number of green bush bean varieties is seemingly endless, so it is difficult to recommend particular ones. A quick glance at any seed catalog will reveal that bush beans come in a number of pod shapes and lengths. Some have flat pods and others round ones; some have lanky 8-inch pods and others short 2-inch ones. Flavor also varies, so your best bet is to try several kinds to see which you prefer. To our mind, 'Blue Lake Bush' beans have an especially fine flavor, but their short pods make them more work to prepare for freezing or canning than longer-pod varieties. Diane likes 'Oregon Trail,' which is more productive than 'Blue Lake Bush' but has the same great flavor.

Some bush beans produce more heavily than others. Several especially prolific varieties are 'Greencrop,' 'Tendercrop,' and 'Topcrop Stringless.' In general, the more branched the plant, the more beans it will set because a branching plant has more nodes, and flower clusters are produced at the nodes. Another factor that affects plant size and yield is the degree to which the plant's growth pattern is determinate. Certain varieties, such as 'Daisy' and 'Remus,' are advertised as being superior because all the beans are set high on the plant. As you might guess, such varieties were developed with the commercial grower in mind, since plants with all the beans at the top are easier to harvest. These determinate types set their crop all at once, as the plant grows to a certain size and then blooms.

In marked contrast to determinate-type bush beans are varieties that keep growing after the first flowers have set and provide a more continuous harvest. If you live in an area where the climate is unpredictable and heat waves can hit the garden at the same time beans are likely to be flowering, you're better off growing varieties that bloom over a longer period. Constant temperatures above 88°F can cause the blossoms of a heat-sensitive variety such as 'Blue Lake' to fall off. The reason the blossoms drop is that the pollen is damaged by the heat and can't fertilize the flowers. If you get a heat wave when a sensitive determinate bean is blooming, you'll lose your whole harvest. For unpredictably hot climates choose a heat-tolerant variety such as 'Contender,' 'Gator Green,' 'Hystyle,' or 'Legacy.'

There is another way to hedge your bets if your area is prone to early hot spells. Some bean varieties, such as 'Contender,' set flowers twice. If heat ruins the first crop, the second one still has a chance. And if you are spared from the heat, you'll get two bountiful harvests from the same crop.

'Commodore,' 'Bush Kentucky Wonder,' and 'Provider' are very sensitive to acid rain and can have the yield decrease from one-third to one-half when sub-

Types of Beans: *Regular bush beans (left) produce beans all over the plant, sometimes making the beans hard to find. Pole beans (middle) grow upward, making the beans easier to find. Some newer varieties of bush beans (right) produce the entire crop at the tops of the plants, making harvesting simple.*

jected to acid rain of pH 3.5 – a common rainwater pH on the East Coast. Varieties that yield well under acid precipitation include 'Blue Lake Bush,' 'Blue Lake Stringless' pole, 'Contender' bush, 'Tendergreen' bush, and 'Topcrop' bush.

Wax beans can be incredibly prolific. Our own personal favorite is 'Beurre de Rocquencourt,' which begins to produce long, delicate pods within forty-eight days of planting and goes on and on, providing pods continuously for a couple of weeks. Another cold-tolerant variety is 'Rocdor,' which has slender, 6-inch-long pods. Both these varieties are recommended for areas like Montana, where nights are cool. 'Sunglow' is a popular heat-tolerant wax bean with fat pods that hold longer before the seeds develop. 'Cherokee Wax' is a widely known wax bean with oval pods, while 'Top Notch Golden Wax' has distinctive flat pods. Wax beans make wonderful pickled beans, but we have found that they usually do not freeze as well as green beans.

Purple-podded beans are a colorful addition to the garden and have a delicious, mild flavor to boot. The foliage is a darker green than that of most beans, and the stems as well as the pods are purple. The pale purple flowers look as though they belong in a watercolor painting, making the plants something to behold when they're in full bloom. Since purple vegetables in general seem to be less bothered by insect pests than green ones, you might want to try these if your bean plants keep getting chewed up by the local wildlife.

'Royalty' was the first purple bush bean and is still offered by many catalogs. However, 'Royalty' has short, weak plants that let the long pods droop onto the ground, where they tend to curl and get splattered with mud. The newer 'Royal Burgundy' variety has sturdy, upright growth that holds the long, straight pods well off the ground. Both of these purple bush beans tolerate cool, wet soil better than green varieties and thus can be planted earlier in the spring. In the kitchen these obliging beans signal the chef when they're cooked to perfection: the purple pods turn green when just crisp but ready to eat.

More and more varieties of dry beans are being offered by seed companies. This expanding selection comes at a time when people are becoming more concerned about their health and the global environment as the tropical rain forests are being leveled to raise cattle. Gardeners who want to cut down on meat consumption and are interested in being as self-sufficient as possible will find the jars of plump, pretty dry beans on their pantry shelves reassuring.

Which varieties you choose depends on your personal taste (flavors and cooking characteristics vary a great deal from one variety to the next) and on the length of your growing season. In short-season areas your choices are rather limited, but you can grow several tasty kinds. 'Jacob's Cattle' (also called 'Trout') beans are about the earliest type, producing within eighty-eight days of planting. These are one of the prettiest beans, with deep red speckles covering the white seeds. They can be used in recipes where you'd normally use red kidney beans and white beans. 'Maine Yellow Eye' is popular for baked beans and is ready in ninety-two days. Diane has used 'Squaw Yellow' beans for baked beans because they mature in only seventy-five days, making them more prolific for her short growing season. Other varieties adapted to short seasons include 'Midnight Black Turtle' beans and the strain of 'Red Kidney' beans from Garden City Seeds. Those of you who have the luxury of a long season can choose from a wide variety of dry beans, including 'Navy' beans, standard 'Red Kidney' beans, and 'Black Turtle Soup' beans. If you are concerned about space, choose a dry pole bean variety.

A good all-purpose bean is 'Dwarf Horticultural.' When the red-streaked pods are small (3 to 4 inches long), they can be cooked and eaten like green beans to savor their nutty flavor. Within sixty-five days of planting you can harvest green dry beans and use them like lima beans (this is especially important if you live in areas where lima beans don't do well). These beans can also be dried for winter use in your favorite bean recipes. Another all-purpose bean is 'Limelight,' which you can use in the same fashion as 'Dwarf Horticultural.'

Tips on Planting and Raising Beans

For a good bean crop plant when both the soil and air have warmed up. The reason for this goes back to their place of origin, which had mild, rather constant temperatures. Planting early during cold weather won't give you an early harvest. The phloem of bean plants clogs up in the cold, and carbohydrates and nutrients can't be transported throughout the plant. You can sow bean seeds a week or two before the last expected frost if the weather and soil are warm enough; purple-podded beans can go in even if the soil is still on the wet side.

Beans will germinate when the soil temperature is between 60°F and 85°F. At 68°F germination will take about eleven days, while at warmer temperatures your beans may poke through the soil in just six days. Beans planted when the soil is 50°F or colder often do not germinate because the cold causes cracks to form in the cotyledons as they take up water. These cracks are perfect sites for fungi to enter and often are the cause of seed rot. The cracks can be so numerous that no food is transported to the embryo, so it dies before germinating. Even if such beans do germinate, they aren't likely to grow into productive plants. If your beans were subjected to cold germinating conditions and are growing very slowly or look stunted, replant them if it's not too late to raise another crop.

If you can't resist planting your beans early, cover the bean plot with clear plastic at least one week ahead of planting to warm up the soil. The night before planting start germinating the seeds indoors between moist paper towels. (Don't leave them any longer than twenty-four hours in the towels.) Then remove the clear plastic and plant the seeds 2 to 4 inches apart and 2 inches deep. It is best to do this in the afternoon when the soil is warmest. Use floating row covers to keep the soil warm, then remove them once the daytime highs reach 80°F. If you do choose to plant your seeds early directly in the soil, use cold-tolerant varieties such as 'Provider' and 'Venture.'

Space-conscious gardeners can plant bush beans in a solid block instead of in rows to make better use of available space. The plants don't seem to interfere with one another the way corn, onions, and some other crops do. Block planting is especially good for shell beans that you intend to dry, since they need no care other than watering and a light weeding once the plants are up. The beans' abundant foliage shades out weeds very effectively when planted this way. We also block-plant purple-podded and wax beans, mainly because the pods are easy to see. The pods of block-planted green beans can be missed, since the pods and foliage blend into a mini-jungle.

To block-plant, excavate the bean bed to a depth of 2½ inches. If you'll be harvesting the crop as snap beans, make the bed no more than 2 feet wide so that all the pods are easy to reach from one side or the other. After you've dug out the 2½ inches of soil, scatter the bean seeds at random over the bed, trying to keep them about 4 inches away from their neighbors in all directions. Gently step on the seeds to press them into the ground, then replace most of the soil, leaving the final smoothed surface of the bed about ½ inch below the surrounding ground. This slight depression ensures that the seeds will get plenty of water.

If you'd rather plant rows, try saving space by spacing rows 6 to 12 inches apart. One problem with close spacing is that it can encourage leaf diseases. If you have had disease problems with beans, plant two rows spaced 6 inches apart and then leave 18 inches between each double-row set. This will give you adequate picking room and better air circulation to prevent disease.

Plant pole beans on one or both sides of their supports, spacing seeds 2 to 4 inches apart. Keep the rows 36 to 48 inches apart depending on how tall the beans will grow. If they will climb higher than 5 feet, use the wider spacing.

Your beans will really take off when temperatures are between 60°F and 70°F. The lowest temperature that most varieties can tolerate is 50°F. Alternatively, if it is too hot, the blossoms will drop off. Dry beans also can develop seedless pods when the temperature soars. If your summers tend to be scorchers, plant your beans as early as possible so that they will mature before the temperature really starts to rise. If it's hot while your plants are flowering, you may be able to save your crop by spraying the plants with cold water during the afternoon. Be careful not to disturb the plants or work around them when they are wet, as this can spread disease. Also remember to keep your plants well watered once the blossoms appear and the pods start forming, as water stress will lead to tough, stringy pods.

Bringing in the Bean Harvest

Snap bean pods are ready for harvest a week or two after flowering, which translates to roughly six to eight weeks after planting. Once the harvest begins, pick your beans every two or three days. Keep them picked because if even a few overmature pods are left on the plant, it will stop producing, putting all its reserves into making the seeds in those pods. If you get tired of picking them green, let the pods fatten and develop seeds. Although the beans aren't as pretty to look at as those varieties developed specifically for drying, they make delicious winter eating.

We think snap beans are best when the pods are thin, before the seeds get very big, but many people prefer them when the seeds have begun to swell. Experiment with picking at different stages to see which size you prefer. Fresh snap beans can be stored at 40°F to 45°F with a relative humidity of 90 to 95 percent for a week or slightly longer.

If your beans are curled or shorter than expected, low nighttime temperatures could be the culprit. Temperatures below 50°F prevent the ovules at the end of the pods from developing, so the pods don't lengthen and often curl at the tip. Use row covers to ensure the longest, straightest pods. Uncover the plants in the daytime if temperatures rise above 80°F.

You might have some pods that are knobby or pinched at regular intervals. This is called inch marking and is the result of conditions being too good: the pods literally grow to pieces, tearing a hole between the developing seeds. To prevent this problem, plant resistant varieties such as 'Blue Lake' pole or 'Hystyle' and add less nitrogen-containing manure or compost to your soil before planting. Overwatering also will encourage inch marking.

If you want mature green beans, wait until the beans are mature but not yet dry. Pick the pods and shell the beans. For dry beans the usual procedure is to let the pods stay on the plants until the beans are large and hard and the pods are dry and papery. If you have a spell of wet weather after the beans have filled the pods but are not yet dry, pull the plants and set them in a protected place such as the garage. Place them in single layers in cardboard boxes so that no beans will be lost if the pods shatter. Don't let these drying beans freeze.

When the pods are dry and crackly, you can shell them. An easy way to do this is to place the pods in an old pillowcase and tie it shut with a string or plastic garbage bag tie. Put the pillowcase in the dryer, turn it on low, and dry the beans for about half an hour. The dry heat and bouncing action should be enough to break open the pods and release the beans. When you pour the contents out of the pillowcase, the heavy beans will be easy to separate from the lighter pod material, especially if you do it outside in front of a small fan. The fan will blow away the light, papery debris, and the heavy beans will fall straight down into a waiting bowl. The dryer method ensures that the beans are thoroughly and evenly dried, so they can be stored immediately. If you don't use this method, your beans may not be dry enough to store when they're shelled. Leave them in a single layer in a warm, airy place until they're hard enough that you can't dent them with a fingernail.

If you live in an area where bean weevils are a problem, spread the shelled beans in a single layer on a baking sheet and pasteurize them for fifteen minutes in a 175°F oven. This heat treatment will kill any weevil eggs that may be inside the beans.

Saving Bean Seeds

To save bean seeds, let them dry on the plants just as for dry beans. (If you need to dry them in a garage as described previously, the beans probably will have good germination rates if the seeds were full size when you pulled the plants.) Don't let them get too dry before you pick them, or the pods may split and drop their cargo onto the ground. And don't use the dryer technique or the oven method of pasteurization on seeds intended for planting, as the heat can kill them. One year Dorothy planted some 'Jacob's Cattle' beans that never came up. She had forgotten to label which seeds had been pasteurized and must have picked up the wrong jar. To make sure the seeds are evenly dry, put them in an open container, a single layer deep, for a couple of weeks and stir them up with your hand every few days. Then store them in an airtight container in a cool, dry place.

Problems with Beans

If you save your own bean seeds, watch for seed-borne diseases and pests. Because there is so much stored food in beans, they are a favorite target for many unwelcome invaders. If you have a lot of trouble with insect pests, try planting purple beans instead of green and yellow ones. No one knows for sure why insects seem less likely to attack purple vegetables, but there are several theories. One is that insects adapted to zeroing in on green plants aren't attracted by the purple color. Another is that the purple pigments are distasteful to insects.

Anthracnose: This fungus is especially devastating to beans and is carried in the seeds. Infected plants develop dark brown, sunken spots on the pods and seeds. In humid weather the spots may have pink centers. Moist, cool weather favors anthracnose, which is most common in the northeastern and northwestern parts of North America. If your beans suffer from this disease, check your seed source. If you have been saving seeds, you may have to give up this practice and buy fresh ones every year. If you bought the seeds, try to find out where they were grown. Most bean seeds come from the dry western states where anthracnose is not a problem, and it is unlikely that western-grown seeds will carry the disease.

Anthracnose is the reason that gardening books caution you not to work among your beans when the foliage is wet. It can spread like wildfire from plant to plant under those conditions. Fortunately, you can buy resistant varieties, so if anthracnose is a recurrent problem in your garden, check for these varieties in seed catalogs.

Rust: This can be a bothersome disease for many gardeners, especially throughout the East and on the Pacific Coast. The fungus causes many rust-colored lesions to form, usually on the undersides of leaves, although they also may appear on petioles, stems, or pods. The leaves will turn yellowish and drop off in the advanced stages of the disease. If you live in an area with a reputation for rust, your best defense is to grow resistant varieties such as 'Golden Wax' and 'Pencil Pod Black Wax.' Keeping the garden clean and disposing of any diseased plants help discourage the rust-causing fungus and many other diseases.

Mexican bean beetle: This spotted brown beetle attacks the leaves of young plants, leaving them with a skeletonized appearance, before moving on to the pods and stems. Try to plant as early as possible to avoid these voracious beetles, which tend to prefer late-season crops. If you spot any of them on your plants, remove them by hand and be sure to check the undersides of leaves for tiny yellow egg clusters. Try interplanting potato plants as a catch crop between every two rows of beans, or alternate rows of garlic and nasturtium with the beans to help repel these pests. Introducing praying mantises into the garden also may help reduce the beetle population. Some bush varieties, such as 'Goldcrop Wax,' exhibit a certain degree of resistance to bean beetles and are worth trying if all else fails.

Nematodes: These tiny, eel-like worms form knots on plant roots, preventing the transfer of nutrients to the aboveground parts. Malformed blossoms, leaves, and stems; poorly developed plants; and yellow foliage are signs that nematodes are sabotaging the roots of your plants. Don't plant beans or any other susceptible crop such as lettuce, peppers, squash, or tomatoes in the same spot more than once every five years, since it takes at least that long for the soil to become free of nematodes.

Potato leafhopper: Gardeners in the East and South may have a few bouts with this wedge-shaped, spotted green insect. If your bean leaves turn white and curl up, you can be almost sure that the culprit is the leafhopper. 'Tendercrop' and 'Tenderette' are good snap bean varieties to grow if you've had problems with this pest.

Bean Frontiers

Home gardeners can look forward to many bean improvements in the near future, as bean breeding and research continue at a rapid pace. Breeders are trying to develop higher-yielding beans, but there is some disagreement about how to go about this. Some breeders want to select for high yields in specific environments, while others think it is better to look for types that have wide adaptability and increased yield. When a variety does well only in a limited environment, there is always the risk of crop failure during an off year. Widely adapted plants may not produce as much every year, but they are more reliable.

Breeders also are developing more varieties with pods at the top of the plants, which are better for mechanical harvesting. Fortunately, some of these varieties (such as 'Remus') still retain that nutty, fresh bean flavor and are equally suitable for home gardeners who don't want to stoop and hunt among the leaves for their beans.

Another way that home gardeners will benefit from commercial research is the special breeding efforts to find snap bean varieties that retain their color and crispness when frozen. For those of you who can beans, researchers have identified the enzymes responsible for keeping the pods crisp in canning and can identify varieties with this trait.

Breeders also are working on increasing not only the total protein but also the protein quality of dry beans. Unfortunately, the higher-yielding varieties of dry beans often have the lowest-quality protein. Using new gene-cloning techniques, researchers may be able to insert the genes responsible for producing the amino acids missing or present in low quantities, thus making beans a source of complete protein.

Breeders have enlisted the aid of biochemists and nutritionists in a coordinated effort to reduce the levels of problem chemicals in beans, but progress has been slow. Although beans are a nutritious food, they contain some chemicals that can interfere with good nutrition. One chemical inhibits the important digestive enzyme trypsin. Another can cause red blood cells to clump together. And as we all know, cooked dry beans can cause intestinal gas, the work of two different chemicals.

LIMA BEANS

Because of their tropical origins, lima beans need warmer conditions than common beans. And since the gardener has to wait until the beans have developed in the pod before picking them, lima beans take longer to mature to an edible crop. For both these reasons, lima beans are a reliable crop only in the warmer, longer-season areas of the continent. But their delicious flavor and excellent nutritional properties make them worth trying wherever there is hope of getting a crop.

Lima Bean Varieties

Lima beans come in bush or pole varieties. Since the pole varieties can reach up to 8 feet tall, they need a sturdy support, such as the one described earlier in the box "Sure-fire Supports for Beans and Peas." In addition to the two sizes of vines, there are two sizes of beans from which to choose. Baby lima beans (also known as butter beans) have small seeds, while regular lima beans have large ones. The ancestors of baby lima beans were first domesticated in Mexico, Guatemala, and Colombia, and the progenitors of large-seed lima beans came from Colombia and Peru. Other edible beans also belong to this species—including Java beans, red Rangoon beans, and white Rangoon, or Burma, beans—but these generally aren't grown in North America. All contain at least a trace of the poison hydrogen cyanide, so they must be cooked before eating to drive off the hydrogen cyanide as a gas. While the lima bean varieties in this country are low in hydrogen cyanide, other varieties in the Caribbean can be highly toxic and dangerous to eat raw.

Lima beans traditionally are eaten when the beans are green mature. The seeds at this stage are green to pale white. They are excellent cooked with a few herbs or in soups. If you let the pods dry, the beans will turn different colors depending on the variety. The dried beans can be used just as you would pinto or kidney beans.

If you have a long enough season to grow pole lima beans, 'King of the Garden' is an especially popular large, white-seed variety. 'Christmas' lima beans are a fine, large-seed pole bean with a delicious buttery flavor. Although catalogs say 'Christmas' lima beans take eighty-five days to mature, they will produce a harvestable crop for us in Montana, so they must be more tolerant of cool weather than some other varieties. Some pole baby lima beans you might want to try include the prolific 'Carolina' (also called 'Sieva') and 'Florida (Speckled) Butter,' which grows well under hot, dry conditions, making it a good choice for southern regions.

More and more bush lima bean varieties are becoming available, and many of the newer varieties are especially adapted to colder growing conditions. 'Geneva' bush lima beans will germinate in colder soil than most varieties, giving them the head start they need to mature in the North. Diane found that 'Geneva' needed row covers to speed growth, but she loved this variety's great-tasting baby beans. Bush baby lima beans that grow quickly include 'Henderson Bush Lima' (sixty-five days) and 'Thorogreen' (sixty-seven days). 'Eastland' (sixty-eight days) and 'Fordhook 242' (seventy-five days) are early bush varieties with larger white seeds.

Tips on Growing and Harvesting Lima Beans

Plant your heat-loving lima beans only after the soil has warmed up to at least 70°F, the minimum temperature they need to germinate. The exception is 'Geneva,' which will germinate in 60°F soil. Many varieties will rot in the ground even at 68°F. If you'd like to give your lima beans a head start, sprout them on moistened paper towels in a warm (70°F) place about two weeks before you expect the last spring frost. When the first root emerges, plant them in a biodegradable pot for later transplanting in the garden when there's no chance of frost. (Be sure to use peat pots or other containers that you can peel away easily without disturbing the roots. See chapter 4 for a discussion of suitable containers.) Use row covers to speed early growth. Uncover pole lima beans as soon as they outgrow their covers. If you want to try direct sowing early, follow the guidelines given in the section "Tips on Planting and Raising Beans" but germinate the seeds under warmer conditions.

Plant lima beans 3 to 6 inches apart, using the greater distance for large-seed varieties. Use the same guidelines for between-row spacing as for regular beans. Plant each seed with its "eye" down. (The eye is the small, colored, indented portion of the seed where it was attached to the pod.) The root emerges from the eye, and because lima bean seeds are so large, it may be difficult for the embryonic stem (hypocotyl) to push the cotyledons up through the soil if the seed is upside-down. If you are growing large-seed lima beans, be sure to plant them in loose soil so that the massive seed can push its way up without a struggle. Lima beans need well-drained soil for the best growth, but unlike peas, they don't do well when planted in ridges.

Although lima beans like warm weather, very hot weather can be bad for them. Temperatures above 90°F can inhibit seed setting and those above 97°F can turn the seeds within the pod white even if they are supposed to be green. Even a prolonged spell of 70°F weather early in the season can affect your harvest. These warm temperatures will trigger the plants to flower before they have reached full size. Although you'll get an earlier harvest, it won't be as abundant as one from full-size plants. But temperatures in the 80°F to 90°F range seven to fourteen days before harvest will increase the sugar content of the seeds and make them tastier.

Harvest your lima beans while they are still green or before they are completely white if you have been having high temperatures. If you let them linger on the vines too long after they've turned white, you'll end up with a starchy, unpalatable batch of beans. When Diane is lucky enough to get a crop of lima beans in her cool mountain valley, she candles the pods against the setting sun before picking to see how large the beans are. That way she knows for sure when the beans are plump and ready for harvest. If you're growing your lima beans for drying, follow the guidelines given for shell beans in the section "Bringing in the Bean Harvest."

If you store your lima bean pods in a very cold place (close to freezing), they will keep well for about ten days. In a cool basement they will keep for only a couple of days. When you shell the beans, use a pair of old scissors to cut open the pods rather than struggling to shell them by hand.

Problems with Lima Beans

Luckily, you are likely to encounter only a couple of problems with your crop of lima beans.

Downy mildew: Lima beans and peas are bothered by this disease. If your lima bean patch constantly falls victim to it, try growing 'Eastland,' a variety that is resistant to downy mildew.

Lima bean pod borer: This inch-long caterpillar is especially active in southern gardens. It does its dirty work by burrowing into the pod and eating the seeds inside. While it may consume many seeds in a baby lima bean pod before its appetite is satisfied, one bean may be all it needs from a large-seed variety. You can hand-pick these pests, but be prepared for the fact that they crawl quite rapidly. Plant early so that the crop is in before the pests become abundant.

Rust: Lima beans are susceptible to rust. See the discussion of this fungal disease in the section "Problems with Beans."

Breeders are working on developing more cold-tolerant and heat-tolerant varieties for both the North and the South. Most of these varieties are bush beans that can be picked commercially. Another important breeding goal is lima beans that hold their sweet flavor as the seed matures.

Lima Bean Frontiers

PEAS

Even a small garden has room for a few peas. A row of dwarf peas with their delicate tendrils and soft white flowers also makes an interesting addition to a flower bed. The trick to growing a good pea crop is to be sure to plant them so that they will mature during cool weather. If the temperature gets above 80°F while the peas are blooming, the flowers will not be properly pollinated, reducing or eliminating your harvest. An extended warm spell while the vines are developing will hasten flowering, causing the plants to bloom when they're still small and not ready to support a heavy crop. During a warm spring you might find that a plant that was supposed to grow 3 feet tall ends up at only 2 feet. This effect can be dramatic. In the cool winter growing season around San Diego, California, the prolific vines of 'Sugar Snap' can reach 14 feet. But in the hotter, drier conditions of Twin Falls, Idaho, 'Sugar Snap' reaches only 6 feet.

At the other end of the thermometer peas can take a lot of cold before they keel over and die. The vines can survive 20°F while growing and 28°F during flowering. The pods themselves can tolerate temperatures as low as 24°F and still deliver undamaged peas. Even here in Montana we can plant a late pea crop in August and harvest some pods after the first frosts in September.

In areas with a milder climate peas can be grown as a winter crop, and in many parts of the United States and Canada the spring planting can be done as early as January or February. Wherever you garden peas should be the first crop you get into the ground, as soon as the soil is dry enough to work.

Pea Varieties

The names given to the three basic types of peas sometimes can be confusing. The terms *English pea* and *garden pea* refer to the familiar shelling varieties of which you eat only the seeds. The terms *Chinese pea, snow pea,* and *sugar pea* are used interchangeably to refer to the Asian edible-pod varieties. These peas produce earlier than garden peas. You harvest them as soon as the pods reach their full size but before the peas themselves have developed fully. The third type of pea, the *snap pea,* is also the newest. It has a thick, crisp edible pod filled with sweet, fat peas.

Garden Peas

Garden peas come in a great array of heights, from rambling 5-foot vines to the more petite dwarf vines that usually measure less than 2 feet. For the best yields, look for varieties that bear two pods at each flowering stem.

Early double-podded varieties that grow only 2 feet tall include 'Maestro,' 'Daybreak,' and 'Knight.' We really enjoy the sweet taste of 'Maestro' and, partly because it is resistant to powdery mildew, have had good luck growing this variety as an early spring and a fall crop. Diane likes the flavor of 'Daybreak,' a new early variety that bears in only fifty-two days. 'Knight' is another good early variety with a high percentage of double pods.

Many gardeners claim that 'Lincoln' peas have the best flavor of all, but we prefer 'Green Arrow,' a vigorous variety with long pods, each containing ten or eleven peas, with a wonderful, rich flavor. Shelling peas can be a real chore, and it takes less time to shell pods with many peas than those with only five or six. If your climate is unpredictable and subject to hot spells in the spring, grow 'Wando,' another delicious variety that is more heat resistant than others.

'Novella' is an almost leafless pea. This rather eccentric growth habit is the result of genes that direct tendrils to form instead of leaves. While you might think that these strange-looking plants would not be able to collect enough sunlight to develop sweet-tasting peas, the tendrils and petioles seem to do the job just fine. 'Novella' was developed for commercial growers, who want varieties that can be block-planted and can grow upright without support. The open structure of the plant allows good air circulation, which discourages diseases that commonly afflict plants with dense, leafy growth under moist conditions. Another attractive feature of this variety, especially for gardeners who want to process the harvest, is that the peas mature almost simultaneously and freeze well. Unfortunately, neither of us cares for the flavor of 'Novella'; it isn't as sweet as standard types. Perhaps better-tasting leafless pea varieties will soon be available. These would be a great asset to home gardeners who block-plant their peas or live in areas where damp weather prevails.

If you are really in a hurry for peas, try planting 'Alaska.' As you're planting, you'll notice that this variety has round, full seeds instead of the wrinkled seeds common to many other peas. That's because it contains more starch than sugar, so the seeds hold their shape when dried. 'Alaska' is hardier than regular peas and is ready to harvest in as few as fifty-six days. Although the peas aren't as sweet as those with wrinkled seeds, 'Alaska' peas are better than the average fare you can buy at the supermarket. If you allow 'Alaska' peas to dry on the vine, they are a delicious substitute for split peas.

Snow Peas

Snow peas come in quite a few varieties. Some, such as 'Mammoth Melting Sugar,' are tall and produce very large, flat pods. These must be grown on fences at least 4 feet tall. Others have dwarf vines that grow only 16 to 24 inches tall. Several of these small varieties, such as 'Dwarf Gray Sugar,' have lovely two-tone purple flowers that add a delicate touch of color to the garden. Diane's favorite early variety, 'Snowbird,' bears double and triple pods on small 16- to 18-inch vines. Snow peas are best eaten raw or slightly cooked (overcooking renders them limp and a drab shade of green) and are especially suited to Chinese stir-fried dishes. You usually have to remove the strings from the pods before cooking or eating.

Snap Peas

The development of the snap pea involved a combination of curiosity, persistence, and intelligence. Calvin Lamborn started work at the Gallatin Valley Seed Company in Twin Falls, Idaho, in 1969. As M.C. Parker, the research director, showed Lamborn around, he explained his frustrations in trying to develop a snow pea with fewer strings and a tenderer pod lining. Parker had just about given up on the project, for every time he came up with a tenderer pod, it was misshapen and therefore less desirable. Parker also showed Lamborn a mutant shell pea that had appeared in the fields. This mutant was called a tight pod because the pod hugged the seeds closely. Upon closer examination, Lamborn found that the pod walls of this mutant were very thick, which explained why they clung so tightly to the seeds. Something clicked, and he realized that if he could incorporate the thick walls of the tight pod into the snow pea, maybe he could get a tender pod that wasn't distorted. Lamborn never produced a tenderer snow pea but ended up instead with the wonderful snap pea.

Lamborn used a good shell pea called 'Dark Seeded Perfection' and a good edible pod pea called 'Mammoth Melting Sugar' as parents in the crosses with the tight pod mutant. That's why snap peas have such great flavor. From then on it was a question of breeding and selecting until he had a reliable variety that bred true with predictable traits. In 1980, after ten years of development, snap peas were introduced to home gardeners with rave reviews.

While most of us think of snap peas (also called sugar snaps) as a new class of peas, the gene that makes the flesh thick and tight occurs naturally. Throughout the past sixty-five years various seed companies have offered snap-type peas, but they never caught on. Before Lamborn's snap pea was introduced, a friend of

Dorothy's kept pestering her to find an edible podded pea she remembered from her father's garden. The friend insisted that it existed, but Dorothy never could find it in any catalog.

The first variety of snap peas to be introduced was 'Sugar Snap.' This variety's vines grow very tall—at least 7 feet—so they must be grown on a tall fence. Both the peas and the pods of 'Sugar Snap' stay sweet and tender for a long time on the vine. They are so delicious that many gardeners have trouble harvesting any for use in the kitchen; adults and children alike tend to sneak into the garden, pick a handful of the peas, and eat them on the spot. Aside from stringing, 'Sugar Snap' peas need no preparation prior to eating. If you insist on cooking these tasty vegetables, do not cook the pods longer than three minutes, or they will turn mushy.

In 1982 a full line of short-vine snap peas became available to home gardeners under the names 'Sugar Bon,' 'Sugar Mel,' and 'Sugar Rae.' These compact plants, named after Lamborn's wife and two daughters, grow to about 2 feet, making them easy to manage. The early-maturing 'Sugar Bon' and the late-maturing 'Sugar Rae' help spread out the harvest. 'Sugar Bon' and 'Sugar Mel' are resistant to powdery mildew.

Six years before 'Sugar Snap' was released, Lamborn was beginning his breeding program for a stringless snap pea. It took 110 crosses to get an acceptable stringless pea variety because the stringless trait was found only in a variety that seemed to have lost a portion of a chromosome. To get an acceptable variety, much of the lost portion of the chromosome had to be bred back. Lamborn succeeded, producing 'Sugar Daddy,' the first stringless pea. (A thin string may develop when the average daily temperature falls below 70°F.) Lamborn also is developing new leafless varieties of stringless snap peas that will make block planting a cinch. Diane had a chance to sample some of the experimental varieties and can't wait for them to be released.

Tips on Growing and Harvesting Peas

Peas can germinate at temperatures as low as 40°F, but it takes them almost thirty-six days to do so. At 68°F the peas will be up in only eight days. Even though they can take quite a bit of cold, putting your peas in very early may result in their rotting in the ground. For earlier harvests use row covers to warm the soil and speed germination and growth. Take the covers off as soon as daytime temperatures are above 60°F.

When planting time comes, remember to give your peas something on which they can climb, even if they are dwarf plants. Put your support in place first, then plant your peas 2 to 3 inches deep on either side, spacing the seeds 2 to 3 inches apart. Keep a space of at least 3 feet between double rows; if you can spare the room, a 4-foot space makes it easier for you to pick from the vines.

How do you know it's time to harvest those plump green pods? Garden peas usually are fat enough for picking anywhere from twenty to thirty days after blooming. As the peas swell the pod, check them often to make sure they don't overmature, a condition signaled by the loss of the bright green pod color. Timing the harvest is critical: if you wait too long, that sweet, fresh garden-grown pea flavor is gone. Young garden peas are sweet because they are full of sucrose transported from the leaves or pod to the seeds. As the seeds mature, the sucrose is changed into starch, the storage form of carbohydrate. The seed, as a natural part of its life cycle, is getting ready to nourish a young plant during germination and early growth.

Pod size can be a deceptive indicator of the size of the peas within. Some varieties have a lot of space between the walls of the pod and the peas, so the pod can be very fat but the peas very tiny. Other varieties, such as 'Green Arrow' and 'Maestro,' have pods that hug the peas tightly and are ready to pick at a smaller pod size. You will learn from experience which varieties fit into which category.

Pick snow pea pods just as they reach full size but before they begin to swell with developing seeds. Ideally, the seeds should be the size of a BB when you harvest the pods. If you overlook the pods and they fatten up to full-blown maturity, be sure to pick and discard them; otherwise the vines will stop producing. When snow peas have gone past their prime, the pods become tough and stringy and the peas bitter.

Snap peas can be harvested anytime after the pods have developed. Young pods are delightfully sweet, but older pods with fully mature peas also are sweet and crisp. Do pick the pods before they lose their rich green color, which signals a change to a starchier flavor.

If you haven't kept up with the harvest and are faced with a glut of overmature garden or snap peas, don't just throw them away. You can make pea soup with them without bothering to go through the process of drying and splitting them. Many people think that fresh pea soup tastes better than the kind made with dried peas.

If you are growing smooth-seed peas for drying, let the pods dry on the vine until most of them have turned brown. Pull the vines and stack them in a warm, airy, sheltered place for a final drying session. When the pods are crackly, shell the peas and store them in airtight containers.

Once you've harvested your peas, if you can't shell and eat or freeze them right away, place the pods in a plastic bag and put it in the refrigerator. Although peas are at their tastiest when fresh, even those you keep in the refrigerator for up to two weeks will be better than any you buy in the supermarket. Do not shell your peas before storing them, as shelled peas convert sucrose into starch more rapidly than unshelled ones.

The pods of regular peas are good to eat, too, but they have a tough, waxy inner layer that helps prevent the pod from losing moisture. You can carefully peel off this layer and eat the pods if they aren't too old and tough (the pod walls also develop fibers as they age). Because snap pea pods and snow peas lack this protective layer, they do not keep as well in storage as garden peas. The pods quickly lose their crispness even when stored in plastic bags, and the pods of snap peas can develop an off taste after a week or so in the refrigerator. If this happens, you can still shell them and eat the peas.

Saving Pea Seeds

If you want to save your pea seeds for next year's garden, let the pods dry on the vine until you can hear the seeds rattle inside. Watch them carefully and pick them just as they are approaching dryness. If you ignore them, you run the risk of having the pods break open and dump their seeds on the ground. If rainy weather descends while the plants are drying in the garden, pull up the vines and stack them in a dry, airy, sheltered place. On the average it will take one to two weeks for these uprooted vines and pods to dry. When the pods are papery and brown, shell or hand-crack them to release the seeds. Make sure the seeds are completely dry before you store them in an airtight container in a cool, dry place.

Problems with Peas

In general, peas are bothered less than most garden crops by pests and disease. Perhaps this is true because they grow and mature during cool weather, before most pests have had a chance to proliferate.

One peculiar pest does bother peas, though: a tiny worm that burrows into the root nodules, where it feeds on the rhizobia, preventing them from fixing nitrogen for the plant. Peas that are infested by these worms can develop severe symptoms of nitrogen deficiency. If you have this problem, plant your peas in another part of the garden next year.

Powdery mildew also can be a problem with peas because it thrives during the cool, wet weather that peas also enjoy. When it strikes, the leaves become covered with grayish patches that also can cover the pods. In Montana mildew doesn't usually strike spring-planted peas until the main harvest is just about over, so it is not a serious problem. But when we plant in August for a fall harvest, we are careful to choose a mildew-resistant variety such as 'Maestro.'

Pea Frontiers

Breeders are continuing to work with leafless varieties of peas and to increase the yield of peas by developing more varieties that carry two or more pods at each node. Not only do such varieties produce a larger yield, but more of the peas are produced at one time, facilitating mechanical harvesting and making life easier for the home gardener who wants to process the harvest in only a few pickings.

Because peas are self-pollinating, each variety is quite inbred. Many people are becoming concerned about the narrow genetic base of modern peas. Unfortunately, until recently no one systematically saved old varieties, so much of the genetic variability of peas has been lost forever. If you're concerned about the loss of heirloom pea varieties, contact Seed Savers Exchange for more information on how you can help preserve these heirlooms.

As the price of grain increases, some people have begun exploring the possibility of using peas for livestock feed. Varieties with a higher amino acid content would be needed, which also might increase the protein quality of peas grown for human consumption. Unfortunately, the narrow genetic base of peas makes the search for peas with high-quality protein difficult.

Chapter 11

Corn: The Oddball Crop

VITAL STATISTICS

Family: Gramineae

Species: *Zea mays*
Zea mays rugosa — sweet corn
Zea mays praecox — popcorn

Soil: Any good, rich soil

pH: 5.5 to 6.8

Soil temperature for germination: 60°F to 95°F; 95°F optimum

Air temperature for best growth: 60°F minimum; 75°F to 90°F optimum; 95°F maximum

Seed viability: 1 to 2 years

Seed germination: 3 to 12 days

Seed planting depth: 2 to 3 inches; 1 to 1½ inches for super sweet varieties

It may be hard to believe, but corn is actually a huge grass that would make a lawn fit for a giant. Imagine what would happen to the family corn plot if all the towns that have laws about mowing your grass to a certain height strictly enforced their rules! Despite the fact that it takes up so much space, corn is one of the most popular home garden crops, for no corn you can buy in the store can come close to the tender sweetness of a homegrown crop. Since corn begins to lose sweetness the second it is picked, it does not keep its quality when mass-produced and shipped. Some dedicated corn lovers, such as Diane's children, can't even wait for the corn to be cooked. They pull the ears right off the plants, peel back the husks, and munch away. Growing corn is fun, too, as adults and children alike enjoy watching the tall stalks shoot up quickly from small, shriveled seeds.

Corn has been cultivated by people for so long that its origins are uncertain. For years scientists have carried on a lively debate about where corn originated. Archaeologists shed some light on this unsolved mystery in 1960 when they found tiny corncobs in Tehuacán, Mexico, that date back to 5000 B.C. Much of the controversy about corn's origins hinges on whether these cobs represent an ancient wild corn that the Indians gathered or an early variety of domesticated corn. A key trait of cultivated corn is that the husks enclose the kernels tightly and do not open, so the kernels can't fall from the ear as do the seeds of wild grasses. Unfortunately, no one has been able to determine for certain whether the ancient corn found in Mexico could shed its seeds.

Today there are no clearly identifiable species of wild corn to be found. But there is a grass called teosinte that is related to corn closely enough to crossbreed readily with it. As a matter of fact, teosinte grows frequently in Mexican corn fields, where the farmers encourage interbreeding of corn and teosinte because they believe it improves their crop. Corn expert George W. Beadle believes that teosinte is the true ancestor of corn because when you crossbreed the two for several generations, the resulting ears look like a slightly larger version of the ancient cobs and have many of the same botanical differences from modern corn. Teosinte would have been an attractive crop for early humans to cultivate, for its kernels will pop like popcorn and it can be ground into a coarse flour.

Another prominent corn scientist, Paul C. Mangelsdorf, believes that the wild ancestors of corn have died out and that teosinte is a hybrid between those ancestors and an ancient type of popcorn called pod corn. The controversy is a variation on the age-old question: "Which came first, the chicken (corn) or the egg (teosinte)?"

The fact that we can't know for sure how corn came into being emphasizes just how ancient a crop it is. A key difference between wild corn and cultivated corn is the development of kernels that stick to the cob. Wild plants must be able to scatter their seeds so that the next generation can survive. If a cultivated corn-cob fell to the ground and the seeds germinated, they would be too close together to grow to maturity. But kernels that stay in place are a lot easier for people to gather than those that fall off. So once cultivated corn was developed, the only way it could survive was in a continuing partnership with people. Instead of having its seeds scattered at random by a natural process, corn became dependent on human intervention to separate the kernels and plant them season after season.

The great Indian cultures of Mexico and Central and South America, such as the Aztecs, Mayas, and Incas, based their civilizations on corn. One could say that these ancient peoples "built" corn by propagating and selecting the best types over the centuries. All the different forms of corn—dent, flint, popcorn, and sweet corn—had already been cultivated by the time Columbus came to America. We owe the great variety of corn types to the ingenuity and imagination of these peoples, for they provided us with a diverse collection of genetic material for the development of even more varieties of corn.

Here in North America we see only a fraction of the existing types of corn. Paul C. Mangelsdorf, who has devoted his life to studying the origins and evolution corn, describes the seemingly endless variety of corn plants grown around the world:

> There are early maturing varieties, such as the Gaspe flint from
> the Gaspe Peninsula in Canada or Cinquantino from the Pyrenees
> Mountains of Spain which mature in sixty to seventy days, and
> very late varieties in the American tropics that require ten or eleven

months to reach maturity. The number of leaves varies from eight to forty-eight, the height of stalk from less than two feet to more than twenty, the number of stalks produced by a single seed ranges from one to fifteen. The size of the ear varies from the tiny ears of some of the popcorn varieties which are no larger than a man's thumb to the gigantic corn grown in the Jala Valley of Mexico, which produces ears up to two feet in length borne on stalks so tall that the ears may be conveniently harvested from horseback and so stiff and strong that they are sometimes used for pickets in enclosures for domestic animals. *

Little-Known Corn Facts

When most of us talk about corn, we are referring to the sweet corn that we eat as a table vegetable. This type of corn is not the original type, for the starch in corn seeds is an important source of nourishment to the corn seedling. From a biological point of view, a seed that stores sugar instead of starch is inferior. Sweet corn originates through a defect in its genes that inhibits the conversion of sucrose from the leaves into starch. The gene for this defect is called *shrunken 1*, as the lack of starch in the kernels causes them to shrivel when dried. Field corn leaves produce sucrose that is transported to the developing kernels. Once the sucrose is inside the endosperm (food storage area) of the seed, enzymes convert it to dextrin and then to starch. In sweet corn the shrunken 1 gene slows down the conversion of sucrose and dextrin, so the kernels accumulate sucrose and some dextrin rather than starch, making the corn taste sweet.

Because there is little starch to nourish the seedling, sweet corn seeds do not germinate as easily or store as well as starchy types. This calls for special care by the gardener and an attention to detail that other, starchier types of corn don't require. Sweet corn is, not surprisingly, more susceptible to disease than field corn.

Corn is one of the most efficient of all cereal grains in using energy from the sun. Most plants can use sunlight only up to a certain point, regardless of how brightly the sun is shining. At high light intensities, the level of carbon dioxide in the plant leaf drops because the plant is using it up so fast. This low level of carbon dioxide limits the ability of the plants to photosynthesize. Corn, however, can adapt to low carbon dioxide levels and can increase its rate of photosynthesis very quickly. This special ability is the reason some people say that you can hear the corn grow, an acknowledgment of the fact that corn grows faster than other crops. Crabgrass, a plant unfortunately familiar to every gardener, is able to exploit light the same way corn does. You aren't just imagining that crabgrass grows faster than most of your crops; it really does!

* Paul C. Mangelsdorf, *Corn: Its Origin, Evolution, and Development* (Cambridge, MA: Harvard University Press, 1974), 2. Reprinted by permission.

Corn's Nutritional Profile

The diet of early Mexican and South American Indians was based on corn, beans, and squash. This is an especially nutritious trio because these vegetables complement one another to create a well-balanced blend of the proteins, vitamins, and minerals essential to good health. Corn provides carbohydrates, small amounts of protein, and fat. Beans supply protein and supplement the two essential amino acids (tryptophan and lysine) that most corn varieties lack. They also provide vitamin B_2 and another B vitamin, nicotinic acid. Squash supplements the carbohydrates, providing large amounts of vitamin A and supplying some fat by way of its seeds.

How does corn measure up by itself? Compared with broccoli, the most nutritious vegetable of all, corn provides significantly less nutrient value for the calories it contains. While corn has more protein than broccoli, it has fewer vitamins, only one-fifth as much iron, and three times as many calories. But an average ear of corn, which provides so much pleasure, contains only 70 calories. Like potatoes, corn is fattening only because of all the butter we insist on putting on it!

Corn Varieties

There are so many different varieties of corn (a typical seed catalog will list twenty to forty varieties) that it is impossible to recommend specific ones. We can, however, give you some ideas about how to choose the best variety for your garden.

As with most crops, corn is available in open-pollinated and hybrid forms. It grows best when it has a varied genetic make-up, as inbreeding leads to a significant loss of vigor. For this reason hybrid varieties of corn are almost always superior to standard types. While the genetic variability necessary to keep standard varieties vigorous leads to unevenness in the quality of the crop, each plant of a hybrid variety, as explained in chapter 1, is genetically just about identical to others of the same variety. But each hybrid plant has many different genes, leading to increased vigor. Thus hybrid corn grows faster, is more uniform, and yields more than standard varieties.

If you live in the Corn Belt, you might be able to grow open-pollinated varieties. But if you live in an area that is in any way marginal for corn, you're better off sticking with hybrids. As you might guess, Montana is not exactly prime corn country, and the one year Diane planted two varieties of nonhybrid corn, she was very disappointed. She was barely able to harvest an average of one ear per stalk, while the minimum that she usually gets with hybrids is two ears per stalk. Some ears from the standard varieties were nice and big, but others were very small. In addition, a high percentage of the stalks produced male and female flowers intermixed. While these may have been interesting to look at, no ears resulted, or ever will result, from such flowers.

With many crops, such as tomatoes, you can save seeds each year from the plants that grew best, thus continuously improving the yield by selecting for strains best adapted to your growing conditions. But if you try the same thing with open-pollinated corn, instead of steadily improving the crop, you will slowly decrease its genetic variability. Corn that is inbred too long yields poorly and grows weakly. But when inbred corn is crossed with another type, it becomes vigorous in its growth and yield. Thus your ability to improve your own corn is limited, for you must introduce new types every few years to maintain the genetic diversity of your seeds.

In recent years corn breeders have had a heyday breeding wonderful new types of corn that are far sweeter than your grandfather ever imagined possible. Because new varieties have appeared so rapidly, the terminology surrounding them can be quite confusing. We've summarized the important points about these wonderful new garden treats in the box "Sweet Corn Basics."

There are three basic types of especially sweet corn—super sweet (also called

SWEET CORN BASICS

TYPE	GENE	VARIETIES	SWEETNESS	SEED VIGOR	ISOLATION	SOWING	COMMENTS
Normal	su	Most varieties	Varies, but declines rapidly after harvest	Good	No	2-3" deep no earlier than 14 days before last frost date	Most reliable in marginal corn areas
Sugar Enhanced	se (EH)	Crusader, Kandy Korn	Varies, but sweeter than normal type; declines more slowly after harvest	Moderate	No	7-10 days later than extra early normal type	Tender kernels; adapts poorly to stress
Sugar Enhanced	se (SE)	Miracle, Precocious, Sugar Buns, Tuxedo	Varies, but sweeter than normal type; declines more slowly after harvest	Moderate	No	7-10 days later than extra early normal type	Tender kernels; adapts poorly to stress
Super Sweet or Xtra Sweet	Sh2	How Sweet It Is, Northern Xtra Sweet, Sweet Desire, Sweet Dreams	Sweetest flavor, sweetness lasts longer than SE, se, or normal	Poor	Yes	Untreated seed in moist 75°F soil; 1-1½" deep 7 days after last frost	Crisp kernels; tip cover problems under stress
Sweetie (Super Sweet)	Sh2 cross	Sweetie 70, Sweetie 73, Sweetie 76, Sweetie 82	Sweetest flavor, sweetness lasts longer than SE, se, or normal	Fair	Yes	7-10 days later than extra early normal type	Ears almost silkless; fill well to tip of ear
All Sweet	su + +	Earlivee, Earlivee #II, Norgold, Silver Queen	As sweet as SE types	Good	No	Same as normals	Survive stress better than SE

Xtra sweet), sugar enhanced, and all sweet. Each has a different genetic basis, but the principle behind them is the same. We've already discussed the gene called *shrunken 1* that inhibits the conversion of sucrose into starch, which distinguishes sweet corn from the normal starchy field corn. These new corn types have additional "defects" in their genetic make-up that further limit the transformation of sugar into starch in the kernels. Most of them taste much sweeter than normal garden corn and lose their sweetness much more slowly after harvest.

The super sweet varieties are the sweetest of all. A gene called *shrunken 2* accounts for their sugary flavor. *Shrunken 2* almost stops the conversion of sucrose to dextrin, so the kernels have even more sucrose in them and are even more shrunken than regular sweet corn when dried. This lack of dextrin causes some varieties of super sweet corn to have a rather watery texture. In ordinary sweet corn, the dextrin confers a creamy texture.

Super sweet varieties may be delicious, but they have their problems. First, they must be isolated from other varieties in the garden (see the section "Growing Corn") to guarantee their sweetness. Another problem is the low vigor of these varieties, which have even less food available for the growing seedlings than sweet corn, since there is less starch. This means that garden conditions must be close to ideal for these rather finicky varieties to grow well.

Corn breeders trying to avoid the defects of the super sweet varieties developed yet another type of very sweet corn. These varieties are designated as sugar enhanced and come in two types, EH and SE. Sugar enhanced varieties are not as sugary as super sweets, but they germinate well and don't have to be isolated. Their sweetness varies with the variety, but they all hold their sweetness much longer than regular varieties. These varieties are ideal for gardeners who want to sell their corn. They also last longer on the stalk and do not get overripe as quickly as other types. This is an advantage for small families and those who want to freeze or can in small batches instead of all at once.

All sweets are like normal sweet corn in that they lose their sweetness quickly upon harvesting. But they are much sweeter than regular types and are not sensitive to less than ideal garden conditions. In fact, some of the best short-season varieties, such as 'Earlivee' and 'Earlivee II,' are all sweet varieties.

When choosing corn varieties, it is important to pick those that will grow well in your area. More than any other crop corn fails in the home garden because growers choose the wrong varieties. Here in Montana many people grow delicious, abundant corn, but just as many complain that their corn freezes before it bears any ripe ears. Seed racks in stores tend to sell standard varieties that thrive in the Corn Belt but can't make it in marginal areas. A key to success with corn is to underestimate the number of days in the growing season. Where we live, for example, there are usually ninety frost-free days during the summer. But to get a decent crop of corn, we have to grow varieties that are rated as requiring only sixty-eight days to mature. The optimum growing temperature for corn is 75°F.

If the temperature doesn't average that, day and night, the corn will mature more slowly than stated in the catalog or on the packet. Because we live in the mountains, our nights are cool, and that slows corn growth considerably. If you live in the mountains or in a cool area, be sure to choose corn varieties conservatively. Check with your county extension agent and other local gardeners to find out which varieties can be counted on to give you a crop.

Corn's Unique Problem

There is one more thing to keep in mind when planning your garden and choosing which corn to grow. You may wish to grow popcorn along with sweet corn, but unless you have a very large garden (or a long enough season to stagger the plantings so the two crops won't tassel at the same time), you'll have to give up that idea. Many other corn varieties must be separated to produce a quality product. Super sweet varieties, white corn, and flint corn (the Indian corn that is ground into flour) also require isolation from one another and from other types of sweet corn.

Knowing a little about how corn develops will help you understand why this is so. With crops such as cabbage and tomatoes we eat the fruit or part of the mother plant. But with corn the crop is the seeds themselves. The flavor and texture of the kernels are affected by the pollen that lands on the stigmas, as well as by the mother plant. In all our garden crops, including corn, a double fertilization takes place once the pollen tube breaks through to the egg cell. The pollen grain carries two sperm cells. One of these fuses with the egg nucleus to form the embryo, and the other unites with the nucleus of the central cell to form the endosperm.

Remember that most of the corn kernel is endosperm, and it is the endosperm that gives the corn its flavor and texture. Whatever the source of sperm fertilizing the endosperm, the genes of that sperm will influence the characteristics of the endosperm. If the sperm comes from field corn, the genes from it will cause the conversion of sucrose to dextrin and then to starch, making a starchy kernel instead of the sweet one you'd expect. If popcorn pollen fertilizes sweet corn, the endosperm will be starchy and the outer skin of the kernel tough.

To avoid any unpleasant surprises when you peel back the husks, you should realize that if two different types of corn are growing side by side and shed their pollen at the same time, many of the kernels on each cob of one variety will end up containing genes from the other variety. If you are growing two kinds of super sweet corn or two varieties of regular sweet corn, this cross-fertilization will make no difference. But if one variety is a type requiring isolation, you're in for trouble.

Since corn is pollinated by the wind, the pollen can be carried long distances. If you plant varieties 100 feet apart, the ears may contain some kernels that are not true to type but probably not enough to notice when you take a juicy bite. A purist who wants no contamination whatsoever might plant his or her varieties

700 feet apart, thinking that that distance will ensure complete isolation. However, much depends on wind conditions in your area. You also may need to take your neighbors' gardens into consideration. Paul S. Mangelsdorf tells the story of a professor who found one blue kernel on an ear of his corn and wanted to know where the pollen came from. He searched the neighborhood until he found the culprit corn—5 miles away!

If you have a small garden but a long season, you can get around this problem by planting varieties with at least a ten-day difference in their time of maturity; then they won't be shedding pollen at the same time. Or you can time your planting to provide the differential. You also can use the wind to your advantage. If the prevailing wind blows in one direction, you might be able to plant some pollination-sensitive varieties closer than would otherwise be possible. For example, you might get away with planting a super sweet variety less than 100 feet upwind of a regular sweet corn variety. The super sweet corn won't hurt the regular corn, and by planting the super sweet variety upwind, you decrease the chances of regular corn pollen getting to it. Popcorn and flint corn, however, will harm any sweet corn variety and should be planted conservatively. You don't want to make enemies of your neighbors if you live in a subdivision with small lots but many corn lovers!

How Do the Ears Form?

The means by which corn produces ears is a fascinating testimony to the simple yet complex ways of nature. Becoming familiar with this process will help you to understand why various cultural practices such as block planting and careful watering are important and how they work with, rather than against, the natural processes of your plants.

Remember that the tassels contain the male corn flowers. When your plants are only 3 to 4 feet tall, you can see the tassels starting to emerge from the top leaves if you peek down into the plants. How many leaves the plants have and how long they take to make tassels are significantly influenced by temperature and day length. Hot or short days will lessen the time to tasseling, while cold or long days will increase it. (Perhaps our long northern days are another reason why our corn matures slowly here in Montana.)

Once the tassel emerges, all the leaves of the plant have been formed and all remaining growth occurs through lengthening of the internodes. Imagine the cornstalk as one of those telescoping fishing poles popular with hikers. When all the sections are pushed in, the pole is short, just like a cornstalk with the nodes close together. When you pull the rod out, the joints are farther apart, just like the nodes on a corn plant after it has grown. When the internodes expand, they carry the developing leaves up into positions where they do not shade one another, and each leaf can photosynthesize freely, maximizing use of the sun's energy.

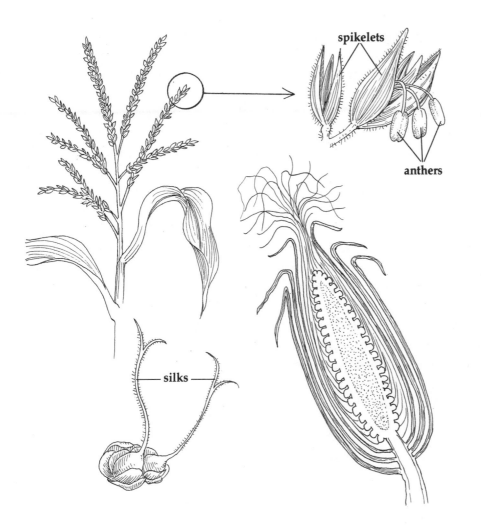

spikelets

anthers

silks

Corn Flowers: The tassel (upper left) contains the male corn flowers (enlarged at upper right). The female flowers (lower left) are born on the cob (lower right). The silks are actually the elongated styles of the female flowers. Both male and female flowers occur in pairs on tiny spikelets. Wind carries the pollen to the silks, where the pollen tubes grow all the way down through the slender silks to pollinate the flowers.

During this period of rapid growth your corn needs plenty of water and abundant nutrients. If your plants look at all yellow during the early stages of growth, feed them right away with fish emulsion and mulch them with compost. Otherwise they will use up the limited soil nutrients during this critical growth spurt, leaving nothing behind to nourish the later stages of development.

The tassel is a cluster of male flowers. In grasses such as corn the flowers are borne in tiny spikelets. Corn spikelets are paired: one spikelet in each pair has a tiny stalk, and the other is stalkless. Each spikelet has two flowers, and each flower has three anthers. Thus there are six anthers per spikelet. The anthers form the pollen grains, just as in other flowers, and as the wind rustles the tassels, these grains sprinkle downward toward the silks or are carried aloft to pollinate the female flowers of other plants.

Corn enhances its own chances of successful pollination by producing a large amount of pollen. Each anther is estimated to carry 2,500 pollen grains, and since there are roughly 7,000 anthers on each plant, about 18 million grains are produced by a single plant! One scientist estimated that 42,500 pollen grains were produced for each square inch of a Nebraska corn field. Pollen grains are very small—$1/250$ inch in diameter—making them easily transportable by the wind. If the pollen gets wet, either through careless watering or an untimely rainfall, the water will carry the pollen to the ground, and it won't get a chance to pollinate the silks.

Corn plants fill the air with pollen for about a week. Bees take advantage of this bonanza, and our fields really get to buzzing while the corn is shedding its pollen. Even though the bees don't actively pollinate corn by carrying pollen to the silks, they can aid in the process by shaking pollen down onto the silks.

Many people mistakenly assume that the silks alone comprise the female flowers. But the silks are only one part of the flowers, with the rest hidden on the immature cob inside the husks. The base of the cob is actually a compressed stem. Despite its shortness it has just as many nodes as the stalk that holds up the tassels, but the internodes haven't grown. Instead, the cob stays like the unexpanded fishing pole. Because the leaves on this squat stalk are borne on such short internodes, they overlap, forming the husks that wrap around the ear.

The female flowers, like the male ones, are carried on paired spikelets that cover the tiny cob. Each female spikelet has two flowers, but only one of these (the upper one) develops completely in most types of corn. After the flowers are pollinated and the ear has developed, the kernels are arranged in pairs, because the spikelets were paired; that's why an ear of corn has an even number of rows of kernels. The variety 'Country Gentleman' is an exception to this rule, as its lower flower also develops and eventually becomes a kernel. This overabundance of kernels so crowds the ear that there is no orderly arrangement of kernels. Instead, they look as if they've been stuck on at random.

Since the husks enclose the flowers, the styles have to be long enough to extend to the outside, where they can be pollinated. The familiar corn silks, which can be several inches long, are actually the styles of the female flowers. Each silk is covered with fine hairs and looks feathery when examined under a microscope. These hairs increase the surface area of the silks and thus increase the chances of pollen grains being captured as they drift through the air. Each immature kernel, which is a potential seed, is attached to its own silk, which must be pollinated for the kernel to develop. Since there may be a thousand kernels on an ear, there are also up to a thousand silks. Because a kernel's silk must be pollinated for it to develop, poorly pollinated corn results in partially filled ears. A poor rate of pollination usually occurs under wet, rainy conditions, but hot, dry winds or temperatures above 98°F also wreak havoc with the corn crop, for pollen dies if it dries out. High temperatures have another effect as well: they interfere with the synchronization of the silks and the pollen, and the emergence of silks may be delayed until after most of the pollen is already shed, reducing the chances of getting full ears.

When the pollen grain lands on the silk, it produces a very long pollen tube that grows all the way down through the silk to the female flower. As we mentioned earlier, when the tube reaches the flower, one of the sperm nuclei unites with the egg to form the embryo, and the other combines with the central nucleus to form the endosperm, the food storage part of the kernel. The kernels require a lot of energy from the plant as they develop. As with other plants, sucrose is manufactured in the leaves by photosynthesis and is transported through the phloem to the developing kernels. There it is either retained as sugar (in super sweet and sugar enhanced varieties), partially retained (in standard sweet corn), or converted to starch (in field corn and popcorn).

Getting Started from Seeds

You can save corn seeds for up to two years, but some varieties do not store well, so it is best to buy fresh seeds each year. If you do have leftover seeds, store them in a very cool, dry place and do a germination test before planting.

You must plant corn seeds in fairly warm, loose soil, or they will rot. Corn takes as long as twelve days to germinate in 59°F soil and only three days in 95°F soil. Cover the ground with clear plastic as soon as the snow has melted and you anticipate some sunny spring days, and leave it there until you're ready to plant your corn. Use a soil thermometer to check the soil temperature at the seed planting depth.

You can speed germination by moisturizing the seeds (see chapter 1). This will hasten germination and increase the number of seedlings that come up. Plant your corn seeds 3 inches apart and 2 to 3 inches deep to ensure proper growth. The super sweet varieties are the exception to this rule. Because they grow so weakly at first, they should be planted 1 to 1½ inches deep and kept moist until they push up out of the soil. Another way to baby your corn is to plant it only ½ inch deep at the bottom of 3-inch-deep trenches. Cover the trenches with clear plastic so that the sun can warm the soil. If you use this technique, you must monitor the soil temperature, especially if the weather turns warm and sunny. You don't want to cook the corn seeds! After the corn has germinated, remove the plastic and cover the seedlings gently with soil. You can keep the corn warm by using row covers supported by hoops. Don't just lay the row covers over the seedlings, as their growing tips are too sensitive to tolerate pushing up against even a light-weight cover.

Knowing how corn seeds germinate and grow before peeking out of the soil will help you understand why it's a mistake to plant corn less than 1 inch or more than 4 inches deep. As with other seeds, the first part of the corn to break through the seed is the root, followed by the young stem, or stalk. The growing stalk is surrounded by a protective sheath that keeps it from getting damaged. The area between the old seed and the bottom joint of the cornstalk, called the mesocotyl, is especially important to the plant. The elongation of the stem, which brings the shoot to the soil's surface, occurs only at the mesocotyl. The mesocotyl stops growing when exposed to light, so once the shoot reaches the surface, the mesocotyl stays where it is and the stalk keeps growing upward.

The permanent root system grows from the buried mesocotyl, so if you were to plant your corn only ½ inch deep, the root system could develop from only a small part of the stem. The result would be a poor root system that wouldn't be able to meet the nutrient and water demands of the plant or to anchor it firmly in the soil. Planting too deep also is a problem. Since the mesocotyl can't grow any longer than 4 inches, if you plant deeper than that, your corn will never reach the soil's surface. Some varieties of corn grown in the Southwest have a mesocotyl that can grow 12 to 14 inches and so take advantage of the moisture that lies deep in the desert soil. These varieties are highly drought resistant during germination, since they are planted so deep, and throughout the growing season, since their well-developed permanent root systems can gather more moisture than shallower, less extensive ones.

Starting Corn Indoors

Most people do not know that it is possible to start corn early indoors if you give it special care. If you'd like to try getting your corn crop off to a head start, follow Dorothy's example. One year Dorothy wanted to try a super sweet variety, and she knew her only chance was to start it early. Dorothy placed the seeds between damp paper towels until they started to germinate. When the roots just began to show, she carefully planted the seeds in the deepest peat pots she could find, two seeds to a pot. When the shoots began peeking out, she placed the pots in full sun in her attached greenhouse. (A south-facing window with no obstructions between it and the sun also would work, but if you can't give the seedlings full sun, forget about starting them early.) She then planted the seedlings, peat pots and all, in her garden so as not to disturb the roots. A rule of thumb is to start your corn indoors no more than two weeks before it can be planted outdoors.

Corn and Temperature

We've been careful to emphasize how sensitive corn is to the cold, but sometimes corn behaves like a hardy crop. One year Dorothy planted her corn before leaving on a June vacation and made arrangements for a friend to keep an eye on it while she was away. As Dorothy and her family drove home through the potato-growing country of Idaho at the end of June, they wondered why the tops of all the potato plants were brown. They found out why soon after getting home. A frost had hit the entire mountainous region of the Northwest on June 26. Her friend was sorry to report that her corn had disappeared. But when Dorothy went to check on it the next day, new shoots were already sprouting through the soil. Luckily, she had planted the corn deep enough so that the growing tips were not killed by the frost. If she had been home, she probably would have dug up the corn patch in disgust and planted a late crop of beans or carrots there. She was glad she didn't have that chance, for she harvested some good corn despite the setback.

Corn does need heat to thrive. If the temperature drops to around 54°F, the plants can't photosynthesize. A prolonged cold snap can even inhibit photosynthesis to the point where the leaves turn yellow. But when warm weather (say 82°F) returns, the corn recovers, turns dark green, and resumes growing.

If you're a real corn fanatic living in a cool climate, here's a way to warm up your corn and increase the usable light so that you get the most from your corn patch. Reflective surfaces placed between the rows will reflect light onto the lower leaves, which often are shaded by those higher up on the plant. You can glue aluminum foil to 4- by 8-foot plywood sheets and support them 6 inches above the ground angled 60 degrees from the horizontal, keeping them about 2 feet from the plants. The sheets should be situated on the north and south sides of the middle row of corn. Of course, this method will work only if you have a big garden to give you the space you need.

Arranging Corn Rows Strategically

Because corn is pollinated by the wind, you should design your corn patch to help bring about the greatest possible transfer of pollen. Too many gardeners learn this the hard way, as did one enthusiastic but inexperienced gardener who shared this tale. He went out to the garden and, with the help of his young daughter, planted a nice long row of corn. Visions of a sweet, juicy harvest nourished them as they conscientiously took care of the corn through the summer. But when harvest time came, they were crushed when all they got was a few skimpy, poorly filled-out ears. As this well-intentioned gardener learned, if you plant corn in a single long row, the wind just picks up the pollen and carries most of it away from the corn, resulting in very poor pollination. But if you plant several rows close together, the wind will carry the pollen from one plant to another as it blows, ensuring good pollination. If you are planting only a small amount of corn, arrange it in several short rows to form a block rather than in a few longer rows. If you plant in hills, plant six seeds per hill, sowing the seeds a couple of inches apart and thinning to three plants per hill. Space the hills 2 feet apart in all directions. If all you have room for is three or four hills, place them at the corners of a triangle or square.

The final spacing of corn plants in a row depends in part on the variety. Taller, more vigorous kinds need more space than small, early types. Veteran gardener and author Richard V. Clemence studied corn spacing and found that planting his Xtra sweet hybrid corn 2 feet apart in all directions gave him the highest yield—

up to four ears per stalk. When he planted in 1- by 2-foot blocks, only two ears developed per stalk; in 1- by 1-foot blocks only one large and one much smaller ear developed per plant. Diane spaces her small-eared varieties 8 to 12 inches apart in rows 36 inches apart. With this generous spacing most of her corn produces one large ear, with a smaller one maturing four to eight days later.

Thin your plants to their final spacing well before the silks emerge. Experiments with field corn in Illinois showed that thinning two and a half weeks before the silks peeked out increased the yield by 41 percent per plant compared to unthinned plots. Thinning three weeks after silking, however, increased the yield by only 11 percent.

Interplanting with Corn

Corn takes up so much space that many gardeners grow beans, melons, or pumpkins alongside their corn. If you live in a warm, long-season area, you can try this method. But if corn is a marginal or problem crop in your area, don't expect it to share its resources with demanding crops like these, or you could end up with little or no corn. But you still can make some use of the three-foot space between corn rows by planting lettuce there. The corn will shade the lettuce plants when days get warm, and the lettuce will be finished by the time the corn completely takes over.

In areas where corn thrives you can plant beans in with your corn. Select a tall corn variety, such as 'Country Gentleman' or 'Iochief,' that will grow 6 to 7 feet tall and provide sturdy supports for your bean vines. Plant the corn a couple of weeks before the beans to give it a head start. Otherwise the rapidly growing beans will overwhelm the corn, and you won't be harvesting any sweet, juicy ears. Sow just one bean seed about an inch from each young corn plant, and locate the beans only along the south side of the corn patch. Beans planted in the middle of the patch or on the north side will be shaded by the cornstalks and will not get enough sunlight to produce much of a crop.

Corn's Relationship to the Soil

Before the permanent root system forms from the mesocotyl, the tiny corn plant must depend on small secondary roots that branch off the primary root. Most of these are in the top of the soil, and it is not until the plant starts to shed pollen that the roots penetrate deep into the ground. They can extend 3 feet or more down and 3 to 4 feet laterally. That is why corn does best when widely spaced, so the roots of the plants don't compete with one another. But before this extensive root growth can occur, the young plants must have plenty of water and good, rich soil so they can grow fast and become well established.

Corn requires abundant nitrogen (remember, it is a grass) and phosphorus. The lower leaves are the first to show signs of nutrient deficiencies, so keep an eye on them. If they start to yellow, the plants need nitrogen fast. Give them a good dose of compost tea, fish emulsion, or manure tea right away and work rich compost or well-rotted manure into the soil. If corn doesn't have enough nitrogen while the ears are forming, it will extract so much from the leaves that they will die. This means decreased photosynthesis, which in turn means less vital sugar for producing succulent ears.

Corn also is sensitive to soil deficiencies in trace elements such as boron, iron, magnesium, and zinc. At least corn lets you know quickly when it is suffering. Because it reveals these deficiencies with spots or discolorations of its leaves under relatively low stress, scientists often use corn to study the effects of nutrient deficiencies on plants in general. Working barnyard manure into the corn patch will provide trace elements and increase the nitrogen and phosphorus content of the soil.

Corn provides some dramatic examples of the effects of manure on soil fertility. In a long-term study scientists monitored nitrogen levels in a Nebraska corn field from 1912 to 1972. For the first ten years no fertilizer was applied, and the yield declined rapidly from year to year. From 1941 to 1972 the field was manured every year, and by 1972 the nitrogen level was back up to 90 percent of its initial 1912 level, even though a crop of field corn grew there each year. The enriched soil also increased the corn yield. Don't be tempted, however, to plant your corn in the same spot every year. Because corn takes so much from the soil, it should be rotated, although this example offers excellent testimony to the virtues of manure!

Some manures require judicious use. In another study reported by scientists at the University of Delaware, large amounts of poultry manure (56, 90, 168, and 224 metric tons per hectare) were applied to various plots, resulting in a decline in the corn yield because there was too much salt in the soil. All fresh manures are best dug into the corn patch in the fall before spring planting. Winter rain and melting snow will leach some of the salt out of the soil, and soil organisms will get a head start on breaking down the manure to release some of the nutrients so they'll be available to your plants come spring.

Corn grows relatively slowly for the first four to six weeks, and during this period it is very important to keep it weed-free. As with other crops, you can mulch corn plants once the soil warms up to discourage weed growth and retain soil moisture.

Corn requires a total of 12 to 24 inches of water during the season to produce well, so you must be generous with your watering. When the leaves roll up lengthwise, the plants are water stressed. Never let your corn get to that point. If water stress occurs while the plants are shedding pollen, the pollen may not

Important Facts about Weeds and Waterings

be viable and may not be able to pollinate the female flowers. Greenhouse studies in Illinois showed that ears from plants that were water stressed a week after the silks appeared had more than 50 percent fewer kernels than ears from plants given enough water. Water also was vital more than five days later, as the grains were filling. Stress at that time halved the weight of kernels on water-stressed ears compared to normal ears.

At the same time you don't want to water heavily from overhead during pollination, or you will wash the pollen down to the ground, keeping it from reaching the silks. The best way to water corn is by drip or trickle irrigation. If this is impossible for you, water during pollination by flooding or by turning a soaker hose upside-down so the tassels don't get wet.

If you're willing to experiment, try sprinkling your pollinating corn at night. Diane's husband, Dave, is a botanist who uses corn pollen for some of his plant research. He has found that he can't collect any pollen in the morning until the corn has been in direct sunlight for at least an hour. Perhaps the pore through which the pollen is released closes at night. Whatever the reason it appears that corn pollen is not shed during the night, so watering then ought to be safe.

What to Do about Suckers

Many corn varieties produce small side shoots called suckers. Since suckers generally do not produce ears, many home gardeners believe that by cutting them off, they will prevent an energy drain on the plant. A number of scientific studies have shown, however, that it is better to leave the suckers on the plant. Most of these investigations indicated that there was no difference in yield between plants with suckers and those without them. But a few showed that cutting off the suckers was actually harmful to the corn plant. Scientists recently showed that the extra photosynthesis of the suckers can be important in providing nourishment for the plants. Using radioactively labeled phosphorus, they found that suckers send large quantities of phosphorus into the main plant. Chances are that other nutrients get transported from the sucker along with the phosphorus. In addition, it's possible to damage the main stalk or disturb the roots while removing suckers.

Harvesting the Best Corn

You can't just eyeball your corn to see if it's at its sweetest and most succulent. You must feel the ears along their length to see if the kernels are plump and full. The color of the silks also gives a clue to ripeness, as they are brown to blackish when the ears are ripe. If you think an ear is ready, carefully slit a part of the husks with a sharp knife and peek at the kernels to make sure they are filled out. Press your fingernail into a kernel; a ripe one will burst with milky fluid.

Depending on the weather it can take anywhere from fifteen to thirty days for the ears to mature from the time the silks first appear. Once you have developed a feel for ripe ears, you can harvest them without checking each one individually. With some varieties all the ears ripen at once, but others provide a gradual harvest, with the top ears ripening first and the lower ears later. If it is hot while you are harvesting, with temperatures in the 80s or 90s, corn can become overmature almost overnight, so check the ears carefully every day.

When you pick an ear, hold the main stalk with one hand and grab the ear with the other, twisting it gently but firmly downward. The ear should separate without damaging the rest of the plant. Do not husk the ears until just before cooking, as husking speeds up the conversion of sugar to starch. Because a normal sweet corn ear will convert its sucrose to starch after being picked, you should harvest at the last possible minute before eating. Every minute between picking and cooking means starchier corn. Don't allow more than an hour between picking and eating with standard sweet varieties.

When you are harvesting corn for freezing or canning, pick it in the morning or evening, when it is at its sweetest. Then rush like mad to can or freeze it. If you are growing super sweet or sugar enhanced varieties, you don't need to be in such a hurry, but even those types taste better when they are fresh.

Storing Corn and Saving Seeds

The best advice about storing corn used to be *don't!* That was before the new varieties, which don't lose their sweetness as fast as the older ones, were developed. That advice, however, still holds true for normal sweet corn and for the all sweet varieties. No matter how you store it, corn will decrease in quality very quickly. But if you cannot eat it right away and have to store it for a while, keep it as close to 32°F and 90 to 95 percent humidity as possible. Remember to leave the husks on. Super sweet and sugar enhanced varieties are preferable if you know you will have to store your corn in the fresh state, since they deteriorate more slowly than ordinary sweet corn. Do your best to plan ahead so that you will be able to freeze, can, or dry your harvest when it is at its sweetest.

If you're growing popcorn, you need to follow a few steps before storing it. Leave the ears on the plants until the stalks turn brown. Then twist the ears off the stalks and peel away the dry, papery husks. Pile the ears in a basket and set them in a dry, dark place. During this curing period the outer shell of the kernel will become dry and hard to seal out the air, while the inner portion will retain the moisture that causes the kernel to explode when heated.

The curing process usually takes three to four weeks. Test-pop a few kernels to see how they do. If they don't pop well, they may not be dry enough. Conversely, they may be too dry. To test whether they're too dry, put a few kernels in a jar, sprinkle some water on them, and let them sit for half an hour. If the kernels are too dry, this water treatment should revive them, and they should pop just fine. If they still don't pop, they haven't dried enough. After another week or so test a few kernels to see how they pop. When the kernels reach the stage where they pop satisfactorily, strip them from the ears and store them in an airtight container. If they lose their popping vigor over time, just give them the water treatment or put half a cut apple in their tin for a couple of days. Either method should restore any moisture they might have lost in storage. If you want to save your own corn seeds, grow only varieties advertised as open pollinated. Let the corn stay on the plants until the stalks turn brown. Then pick the ears, peel back the husks, and let them cure until the kernels are very dry. Remove the seeds from the cobs, place them in an airtight container, and store the container in a cool, dry place.

Problems with Corn

Although corn is plagued by relatively few diseases, it is susceptible to a great variety of insect pests. If you garden organically, you have a fighting chance against most of them, for their natural predators will help keep them in check. You may have to donate some of your crop to the pests, but there should be enough corn for you and your family.

In general, remember that when you plant can help you avoid corn pests. If earworms are a problem, early planting is best, especially in the North. But avoid early planting if the European corn borer is a problem in your area, for early plantings are more susceptible to this pest. In addition, you can use *Bacillus thuringiensis* to kill many corn pests. Check with your county extension agent if you have serious problems with pests, since the types of pests and the best control methods (such as the timing of planting) vary from region to region.

Corn earworms: Corn earworms attack sweet ears of corn—first the silks, sometimes inhibiting pollination, and then the ears themselves, leaving behind messy piles of frass on top of the chewed-up kernels. Controlling earworms organically requires a lot of hand labor. You can systematically patrol the corn patch, cutting out any earworms you find near the tips of the stalks. Or you can apply a dab of mineral oil to the tip of each ear after the silks have withered and begun to turn brown. The mineral oil will suffocate the worms. Some corn varieties are resistant to this pest by virtue of their especially tight, long husks, which protect the ears from the worms.

European corn borer: This imported pest attacks many crops besides corn. Fortunately, some varieties are resistant to these pests, which also can be kept under control through good garden management. Since the borers overwinter in corn stubble, plow under your corn patch in the fall or early spring before the adult moths emerge. As with the earworm, corn borers can be hand-picked. You can see the sawdustlike castings outside their entrance holes. Use your penknife to cut the stalk just below the hole and pluck out the worm.

Armyworms: Armyworms are likely to attack your corn during the night or on cool, cloudy days. These brown or green caterpillars are favorite fare for a number of predators, such as toads and birds. But sometimes they get out of hand. A ditch dug around the corn patch can trap them, and interplanting with rows of sunflowers also can help keep them under control.

Smog: One special problem that faces the urban corn grower is corn's great susceptibility to smog damage. Smog causes dark spots to form on the leaves; when these spots die, the leaves have a scorched look. 'Bonanza' and 'Merit' are two smog-tolerant varieties. If you live in a smoggy area, consult your county extension agent and other gardeners about which varieties grow well in your region.

Corn Frontiers

As you may suspect, breeders are concentrating their attention on producing new and improved super sweet and sugar enhanced varieties and on developing varieties that produce high-quality corn in a short growing season. They also are trying to produce varieties that are resistant to various diseases. Because commercial growers rely on pesticides, pest-resistant varieties have a low priority with corn breeders.

Because of the importance of field corn to the North American economy, scientists are studying the effects of increased carbon dioxide in the atmosphere, which is predicted to become a big problem in the future. They also are experimenting with using fly ash—the residue from coal-burning electric generators—as a fertilizer for corn and other major crops such as soybeans.

Bio-priming is an exciting new technique for getting the most out of corn. Under development at Montana State University, bio-priming combines seed moisturizing and a preplanting treatment with bacteria to protect the seeds against damping off. After the seeds are treated, they can be dried for later planting without losing the benefit of the premoistening treatment. This technique holds promise as an organic control for some corn diseases and perhaps for diseases that affect other crops as well.

Chapter 12

Tomatoes:
America's Garden Favorite

VITAL STATISTICS

Family: Solanaceae

Species: *Lycopersicon esculentum*

Soil: Sandy loam; good drainage important

pH: 6.0 to 6.8

Soil temperature for germination: 60°F to 75°F

Air temperature for best growth: 70°F to 75°F daytime; 50°F to 55°F nighttime; lower than 32°F kills the plant

Seed viability: 5 to 7 years

Seed germination: 5 to 14 days

Seed planting depth: ½ inch

Every summer gardeners across the country wait eagerly for the first ripe tomato of the season. Somehow this juicy delicacy symbolizes the satisfaction of home gardening, perhaps because the homegrown tomato so far surpasses anything you could hope to buy in a store. If you take the time to become familiar with some tomato facts of life, you can hasten the day you pick that first tomato, increase the harvest from your vines, and get the best flavor from the late fruits that you may be forced to ripen indoors at the end of the season.

It's hard to believe that something as nutritious and tasty as a tomato could belong to the dangerous and deadly nightshade family (the informal name for Solanaceae). One wild member of this family is actually known as deadly nightshade, as its unripe berries are poisonous enough to kill people and livestock. While many solanaceous plants are very dangerous, the rest of the family is benign. Many plants that are important to us—including eggplant, garden peppers, potatoes, flowering nicotiana, and petunias—also belong to this family.

Actually, all members of the nightshade family do contain powerful poisons called alkaloids. All parts of the tomato plant except the tomatoes themselves are supposed to be toxic if eaten, but deer in Montana don't seem to know that! Even those succulent fruits carry within them a small amount of the tomato's own alkaloid, called tomatine, as they develop. Luckily for us, however, the fruits are completely safe to eat, even when green. If you look closely at tomato leaves, you can see that they are covered with many tiny hairs. The chemicals in the hairs may inflict an annoying skin rash on the sensitive gardener, but they also aid him or her indirectly, as they help defend the plant from some of its insect enemies.

It took a long time for the juicy red tomato to shed its poisonous reputation in Europe and the United States. In fact, tomatoes weren't cultivated as a food crop in these areas until well into the nineteenth century. Prior to that they were grown strictly as ornamental plants, and no one dared to eat them. This long period of avoidance was certainly unfortunate, for people were forsaking a significant source of vitamin C, as well as a generous amount of vitamin A.

The ancestral wild tomato still thrives in the Andes Mountains of South America. With its scraggly vines and clusters of hard, marble-size fruits, it is a far cry from its domesticated cousin. Some modern tomato varieties, such as 'Early Cascade Hybrid' and 'Sweet 100,' recall their humble ancestor with their long trusses and viny growth. But the satisfying juiciness and sweetness of their fruits put them in a completely different class from the original tomato.

The tomato grows year-round in its native habitat, but gardeners treat it as an annual, letting it grow and produce an abundant harvest, then adding its remains to the compost pile. Because it is a perennial, the tomato could live for several years in regions free from heavy frosts. Dorothy has a friend with a hydroponic greenhouse who takes advantage of this perennial tendency and lets the vines grow until they are 20 feet long and amble from one end of the greenhouse to the other, studded with juicy red fruits along their length.

Tomato Varieties

As befits this most popular home garden vegetable, there is an almost limitless number of tomato varieties. As you flip through seed catalogs, it's easy to be overwhelmed and opt for the variety with the prettiest photograph. To help you narrow down the field and make informed choices, here are a few criteria to keep in mind.

First, how do you intend to use your harvest? Some tomatoes hold up well under canning; others are best when used fresh; and still others, the paste types, have a low juice to meat ratio, which makes them ideal for sauces and ketchup.

Second, how long is your growing season? If you're a northern gardener, your selection is limited to early varieties (those that ripen within fifty-five to seventy days). Gardeners with a longer season can indulge in mid-season (seventy to eighty-five days) and late-season (eighty-five to one hundred days) varieties to extend the harvest.

Third, what size, shape, and color appeal to you? Sizes range from the diminutive cherry tomatoes to the jumbo beefsteaks. In terms of shape, tomatoes come in gradations from perfectly round to pear shaped, not to mention the commercial grower's dream, the square tomato. The colors vary as well. Besides the traditional red fruits, tomatoes come in pink, yellowish orange, and white, as well as with stripes.

Fourth, do certain diseases plague gardens in your area? If so, look for varieties that are resistant to various diseases. You will see the letters F (fusarium wilt), N (nematodes), and V (verticillium wilt) after variety names, indicating that they are resistant to these problems.

If you're gardening under special limitations, such as a cool, short season or a cramped growing area, check the catalogs carefully to find tomatoes to meet your needs. The 'Sub-Arctic' series gives an abundant yield of extra-early tomatoes in fifty-three to sixty-one days, even in cool climates. Some tomatoes will set fruit when nights are cold because fruits will form even when seeds won't. 'Oregon Spring' and 'Santiam' are two such varieties, and we suspect that 'Nova' has the same ability, since we have harvested early, seedless tomatoes from it. Wonderful varieties such as 'Gem' are especially well suited for container growing, and some cherry types can even be trained to cascade out of hanging baskets.

Getting Started from Seeds

After slicing a ripe tomato you probably have noticed that the escaped seeds are encased in a slippery, jellylike envelope. This sheath contains chemicals that keep the seed "asleep" so that it won't germinate in the damp, warm environment inside the tomato. Commercial growers get rid of the sheath by shredding the tomatoes, screening out the big pieces of flesh, and letting the seed-studded liquid ferment. The seeds sink to the bottom of this brew, ready for drying and packaging. You can accomplish the same thing with your homegrown seeds by soaking them overnight in a glass of water to which you have added a squirt of dish-washing detergent (the detergent helps separate the sheath from the seeds). In the morning drain the seeds and dry them by spreading them carefully on paper towels. Then store them as described in chapter 1 until the next planting season rolls around.

In most parts of the country tomatoes are started indoors and transplanted in the garden to get a jump on the growing season. Because they grow so vigorously, tomatoes shouldn't be planted much more than five weeks before transplanting unless you have the time and space to grow them in large containers.

When planting time arrives, remember that tomatoes come from southern mountains. They need warm soil to germinate well, but they also prefer cooler nighttime temperatures. A soil temperature of 70°F to 75°F during the day and 60°F to 65°F at night is ideal. Be careful not to let the soil get too hot when germinating tomato seeds. Although they will germinate well at 78°F, the germination rate at higher temperatures drops off rapidly for some varieties. Above 95°F some varieties won't germinate at all, while others will sprout enthusiastically.

Soak the seeds overnight before planting to leach out whatever germination inhibitors may be left in them. This step also increases the uptake of water by the dormant plant embryo, which sleeps inside the seed, setting the stage for germination. When you plant, cover the seeds well with ¼ inch of soil, for tomatoes germinate better in the dark than in the light.

Nurturing Seedlings from House to Garden

Your final product—the mature fruit-bearing plant—can be dramatically affected by how you treat its tiny beginnings. The early growth of the tomato plant, before it sets fruit, is critical to producing an abundant crop. When it's young, the plant puts all its energy into vegetative growth. Once it starts to fruit, however, the balance shifts, and the developing tomatoes compete for the plant's energy. A small plant with few leaves won't be able to provide the energy needed by a large crop of fruits. But a robust, bushy plant can photosynthesize enough to support a generous quantity of big, juicy tomatoes.

Despite their long years of selective breeding by humans, tomatoes still respond best to a day-night schedule similar to that of the mountains—that is, warm days and cool nights. It's best to give your tomatoes what they prefer right from the start by providing them with warm (70°F to 75°F) days and cool (50°F to 55°F) nights. By doing this you will encourage your plants to form flowers early and to produce many blossoms. You also must be careful to give them the proper day length of eight to twelve hours. If you keep them in a room that is illuminated late into the evening, you'll end up with fewer and later-maturing fruits unless you cover the plants at nightfall.

After the cotyledons have expanded fully, carefully transplant each delicate seedling to a roomier pot, at least 4 inches in diameter, to provide plenty of space for vigorous root growth. Set the seedlings deep enough so that the soil comes right up to the lowest set of leaves. Roots will grow out of the sides of the buried stem, strengthening the root system. This new root growth is spurred on by the hormone auxin, which is present in the stem. Light destroys auxin, but when you bury the stem, the auxin is free to go to work stimulating the roots. (Rooting hormone powder that you can buy in the garden store is effective because it contains auxinlike chemicals.)

After this initial transplanting water your seedlings well. A cold frame (see chapter 4) provides the best environment for young tomato plants. There the cool spring nights will alternate with sun-warmed days, and the natural alternation of night and day will match the plant's needs. In addition, exposure to the cold can prepare the plants for the potentially harsh reality of late spring in the garden. Tomatoes can stand temperatures all the way down to freezing quite well if they have been conditioned by cold weather in advance. Scientists found that 'Early Cascade Hybrid' seedlings grown at 68°F during the day and 59°F at night showed no damage even when cooled to 32°F. Tomatoes not accustomed to the cold, however, can be injured if the thermometer drops to 50°F. If you don't have a cold frame, your best bet is to grow the young plants in a south-facing window.

If possible, leave the window open at night when temperatures are above freezing. Remember to be careful not to expose the young plants to light after sundown.

When the risk of frost is over, move your thriving, hardened-off plants out into the garden. Plant them deep, again burying the stem up to the leaves to encourage root growth. If your plants are spindly despite your careful tending, remove some of the lower leaves and bury even more of the stem. Always bury leggy stems at an angle so that as much of the stem as possible is exposed to the richer top layer of soil.

Tomatoes do well when mulched and protected by row covers, especially in cool climates. Experiments in the United Kingdom using slitted polyethylene row covers increased the harvest by 23 to 57 percent over the yield from uncovered plants. If your garden is small but you have a special passion for tomatoes, you can increase production per unit of garden space by planting compact varieties such as 'Sub-Arctic Maxi' mulched with black plastic and grown under row covers. New Hampshire scientists determined that a good system is to space such plants 2 feet apart in staggered twin rows. Early compact varieties probably do better under this system than later, larger types because they finish their vegetative

Tomatoes in the Garden

Planting Tomatoes: The stems of tomato transplants should be buried up to the first leaves so that additional roots will form. Lanky plants should be placed on their sides so that more of the new roots will be in the nutrient-rich upper soil layer.

growth, flower, and set fruit before the roots and foliage of the plants begin to compete with each other. With this system the first ripe fruits will come in earlier than with unmulched, uncovered plants. If you use row covers, however, be sure to keep in mind that tomatoes don't like it very hot, so you must remove the covers if the air temperature gets above 85°F.

In the hot South a reflective mulch of aluminum foil can protect August tomato transplants grown for a fall harvest by keeping the soil from getting too warm. The cooling mulch will increase the survival rate of the plants and help them produce an earlier crop of bigger fruits. It also will help deter aphids, but tomato fruitworms and pinworms seem to be attracted to plants mulched with foil.

Spacing is critical with tomatoes. While a plant of a compact variety does just fine when situated only 2 feet from its neighbors, plants of a large, rambling, late variety won't do at all well when placed this close together. The same New Hampshire researchers who had so much success growing 'Sub-Arctic Maxi' tomatoes intensively failed in growing the late variety 'Westover' in the same way. 'Westover' needed 4 feet between plants in staggered rows a foot apart.

If you choose not to mulch, you must keep your tomatoes weed-free, as they are very sensitive to competition from the roots of other plants. You don't have to spend hours bending over your tomatoes to protect them from weeds, however. Since tomatoes are such vigorous growers, a single weeding performed four to five weeks after transplanting will keep the weeds from inhibiting the tomatoes' growth, as long as your weed problems aren't too serious.

Because tomatoes take up so much space, gardeners are sometimes tempted

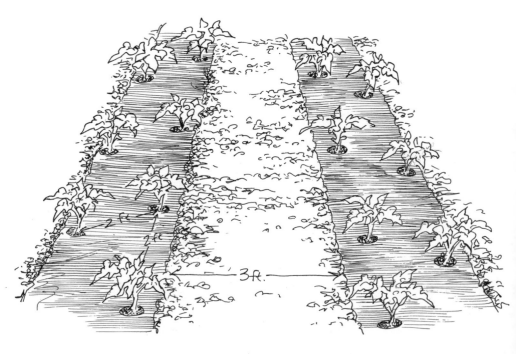

Spacing Tomatoes: Small, determinate tomato varieties can be planted as close as 2 feet apart in staggered rows for a concentrated harvest.

to plant other crops between the rows. Unless you can give up some of your tomato harvest in favor of those plants, resist the impulse to interplant. Researchers have tried interplanting tomatoes with beans, cabbage, corn, cucumbers, and okra, and the tomatoes always lose out. For example, when tomatoes and beans are mixed, the beans will produce abundantly, but the tomato harvest will be reduced by almost a third. The result is an increased total yield of vegetables per unit of garden area but with more of that harvest being beans and much less tomatoes.

Throughout the growing season be sure to keep your tomatoes well watered, but don't overdo it. While their fibrous roots can probe down as deep as 12 feet, most of the roots remain in the top 12 to 18 inches of soil and seem to be quite efficient at water uptake. When your plants have reached the stage where they're producing fruits, avoid watering from above, since water droplets on the developing tomatoes can cause them to crack.

Limited and Infinite Growth

While you were reading your seed catalogs in eager anticipation of the gardening season, you probably noticed that some catalogs featured photos of proud gardeners standing next to giant tomato vines towering 8 to 10 feet into the air. These same catalogs also boasted compact, bushy tomatoes that grow and yield cheerfully in small patio tubs. How can essentially the same plant grow in such dramatically different ways? The answer lies in how tomato vines grow.

The original growth form of the tomato is a sprawling vine. In this type of growth, called indeterminate, the tip of each branch produces a series of three leaves and then a group of flowers (called a truss), followed by another three leaves and another truss, and so on. The tip itself is never transformed into a flower cluster, so the vine just keeps on growing.

In 1914 a new type of tomato plant appeared spontaneously. This plant grew in a way that was quite different from the growth pattern of indeterminate plants. Instead of producing a unit of three leaves and a truss, the stem tips gradually produced more and more flowers and fewer leaves. After reaching a certain distance from the center of the plant, each branch stopped growing and formed a final flower cluster. In the years since the first plant was spotted, this trait has been bred into many different tomato varieties, which are now called determinate. Because their growth is limited and predetermined, these plants never get very large. All their flowers bloom within a limited time, so the fruits ripen over a short period, sometimes within as few as ten days. This trait makes them ideal for gardeners who want to process their harvest. You are assured of a large enough batch of ripe tomatoes to work with at one time instead of having to wait for the more dispersed harvest of indeterminate plants. Determinate plants are perfect for people limited to small gardens or tub growing, and they work well for northern gardeners who must contend with a short growing season.

Kinds of Tomato Plants: Tomato plants come in two basic types—determinate (left) and indeterminate (right). While determinate plants eventually terminate growth by producing a flower cluster at the top, indeterminate ones keep growing and producing flowers throughout the season.

Staking and Pruning Pointers

When you order your tomato seeds, be sure to check whether the varieties you are ordering are determinate or indeterminate. If you buy indeterminate varieties, you must give some thought to how you want to stake and prune your plants or if you even want to bother with any of that. Indeterminate plants will grow and produce without your fussing over them, but there are several advantages to staking that make it a popular practice. Staked plants take up less space and produce considerably fewer rotted or slug-ravaged fruits than do plants allowed to sprawl along the ground. Each plant produces fewer fruits, but since you can space your plants much more closely together, you can obtain a higher total yield per square foot of garden space. It's also easier to harvest from neatly staked plants than from a tangled mass of viny growth, as the ripe fruits are easy to spot.

To stake your tomatoes, drive a strong 5- to 7-foot wooden or metal stake into the ground about 1 foot from each plant. Have some strips of cloth, pieces of old nylon stocking, or special tomato ties on hand to tie the plant to its support.

There are several ways to prune your plants to make them more manageable. You can prune all but the main stem, tying it at intervals to the stake. This is the classic method of pruning, but it leaves the fruits exposed to the sun, thereby increasing their susceptibility to sunscald and cracking. If you allow the first sucker (one of a number of shoots that appear in leaf axils along the plant) and the main stem to grow, you will end up with two stems to tie to the stake. With this double-stem technique you will have more fruits per plant and more leaves to shield the fruits from the sun. You can even keep three main stems if you like, but the process of tying and pruning becomes more time consuming, even though the yield will increase.

Once you have decided which course of pruning you will follow, be diligent in removing all excess suckers, for every sucker will develop into a full-fledged stem if you give it the chance.

Another effective, less labor-intensive way to support tomato vines is to use tomato cages. These cages are available in a variety of designs and materials. Most consist of circles or squares of heavy wire held together by metal spikes that anchor the cage securely. You can make your own cages by forming lengths of poultry fencing into cylinders. Simply set one cage over each plant, and as the branches grow, rest them on the horizontal wires. There's no need to prune your plants when you use cages. Since there's ample foliage cover, you'll seldom have problems with sunscald or cracking. Your garden will have a tidy look because the cages contain the plants' growth, and your harvest will be in good shape because the fruits have been kept off the ground.

If you grow the smaller, self-contained determinate varieties, you must not prune the vines, as pinching off any of the blossoms will decrease your harvest. Instead, let your plants grow naturally, mulching them generously with clean straw or black plastic to protect the lower fruits from rotting when they touch the ground. If you like, you can tie the branches to a short stake to keep the fruits off the ground or contain the plants within cages.

From Flower to Fruit

When your tomato plants begin to produce lots of yellow flowers, pick one so you can examine how it is put together. At the base of the flower you'll see the green sepals and the yellow petals. Look in the center of the flower for the cluster of yellow stamens that are all fused together. Take your fingernail and pull the stamens apart to expose the small, round green ovary that lies deep within the flower. This rather insignificant-looking nugget will one day develop into the juicy red fruit.

Attached to the top of the ovary is the style, with its sticky stigma on top. This modern tomato flower differs quite a bit from the original tomato flower, which had a much longer style and a stigma that stuck way out beyond the stamens. Pollen from the anthers of this early flower couldn't reach the extended stigma, so the flower had to be cross-pollinated before fruit would form. But the cultivated tomatoes that we grow today have been bred to self-pollinate with a short style that barely extends beyond the stamens. Since the flowers naturally hang downward, when they are only slightly jostled, plenty of pollen from the anthers drifts to the mouth of each flower and pollinates the stigma.

Commercial greenhouse growers ensure bountiful pollination by using machines to shake their plants. You can do the trick out in the garden by gently tapping each blossom or by shaking the plant's supporting stake early in the season. Later on foraging honey bees will jiggle the flowers by landing on them and loosen pollen grains in the process. The bees, of course, also can cross-pollinate the flowers by bringing pollen from other blossoms. Most commercial varieties now grown, however, have styles so short that they are completely buried within the stamens, making self-pollination almost a certainty and just about ruling out cross-pollination.

When you were looking at the flower, you probably got small, sticky clumps of yellow pollen on your fingers. Each pollen grain that falls on the stigma is able to fertilize only one potential seed within the ovary by way of the pollen tube (see chapter 2 for more on the mechanics of pollination and fertilization). The ovary houses many young eggs, each waiting to be fertilized by a different pollen grain. After the flower is pollinated, many pollen tubes are simultaneously growing through the style toward the ovary. With most tomato varieties, the more pollen tubes that grow the better, for the more seeds that are fertilized, the bigger the resulting fruit will be. Tomatoes with only a few fertilized seeds may be small and misshapen.

When you see your tomato plants laden with blossoms early in the season, you naturally begin to imagine a plant covered with fruits. But often these early blossoms fall off without even starting to form tomatoes. Unfortunately, a number of factors can lead to blossom drop, and most of them are outside your control.

Speedy fertilization of the flowers within fifty hours of opening is essential for successful fruit set. The young embryos in the seed formed at fertilization produce auxin, which helps the blossoms set. The blossom is joined to the stem by a region of special cells that weaken and separate, causing the flower to fall off if they don't receive auxin within a certain time after the flower opens. Auxin from the seeds keeps these cells alive and healthy, allowing the baby tomato to stay attached to the stem. Temperatures below 55°F slow the growth of pollen tubes so much that auxin isn't released in time to save the flower from falling off. Temperatures higher than 74°F at night or over 104°F during the day also make the blossoms fall off by causing the weakened cell layer to develop too fast. Other factors, such as inadequate light, overfertilization, or a previous heavy fruit set, also can make the blossoms drop off, even if they were successfully fertilized.

The Ripening Process

Forty to sixty days after the blossom opens, the ripe red tomato is ready to pick and enjoy. For the impatient gardener the wait may seem much too long, but the perfect tomato is the result of many complex processes that take time.

Before the tomato is ready to pick, it must undergo a series of changes that transform it from a tiny, hard green ball into a soft, succulent red fruit. About half the ripening process is taken up by the actual growth and enlargement of the fruit. This is accomplished as each cell making up the tomato gradually swells to many times its original size. The result of this cellular expansion is the mature green tomato, a full-size but sour, hard fruit with immature seeds.

While the green tomato appears to be on the verge of ripening, the processes that transform it into its final ripe red juiciness are slow and complex. The first sign of ripening is a whitening of the fruit as the green chlorophyll begins to break down chemically. Ethylene gas is one factor responsible for the chlorophyll break-down. The tomato hastens its own ripening by producing ethylene. Commercial growers often treat tomatoes artificially with this gas to hasten ripening in storage.

All the colors your tomatoes go through before becoming that luscious, deep red are caused by pigments called carotenoids, named for their presence in the bright orange carrot. The carotenoid that gives tomatoes their red color is called lycopene. If you've ever wondered why some tomato varieties are orange or yellow when they are ripe, the answer is that they don't have any lycopene.

Once the change in color is under way, the tomato also begins to soften. A hard green tomato contains a large concentration of pectins in its cell walls. These pectins are much like those present in apples, which are used to firm up jams and jellies. As the tomato ripens, enzymes in the fruit break down the pectins, making the cell walls softer and less rigid. At the same time, the tiny embryos within the seeds are growing to their final size, and the seed coats are developing and hardening.

The last stage in ripening is the most important to us. At this time the sugars and the ascorbic acid (vitamin C) that give the tomato its distinctive sweet-sour flavor are developing. This flavor-enhancing process continues as long as the fruit remains on the vine. Tomatoes picked at the mature green stage and allowed to ripen off the vine lack much of the flavor of vine-ripened fruits, for vitamin C and sugars are destroyed during off-the-vine ripening. This explains in part why homegrown, vine-ripened tomatoes are so superior in nutrition and flavor to typical store-bought ones.

While harvesting your tomatoes, have you ever paused to wonder why the fruits from the same plant aren't all uniform in size? The mature tomato is actual-ly the enlarged ovary of the flower. The thick, flavorful flesh of the fruit is the ovary wall, which contains cavities filled with watery liquid and seeds called locules. The final size of each tomato depends on several factors. Fruits formed on the lower, earlier trusses are the biggest, partly because they were the first to form and did not need to compete with other tomatoes for nutrients. Also, how well pollinated the flower was will affect fruit size, for the more seeds that form, the larger the tomato. The number of locules also is important in determining fruit size. A cherry tomato has only two locules, while a beefsteak tomato has many.

Extending the Harvest

As the expected frost date looms near in the North, many gardeners anxiously cover their tomato vines with plastic to prevent them from freezing. This season-extending tactic is fine as long as the covering is taken off during the day and the weather improves. A plant saved from sudden death by an early frost can go on to produce many more ripe tomatoes during the balmy days of an Indian summer. However, once the temperature starts to drop and stay there, it's a mistake to think that you can keep your plants going by keeping them covered.

As the outside temperature drops, the temperature under the plastic may not get above 54°F. If the temperature remains below 54°F for a week, any mature green tomatoes on the plants will have an inferior flavor when they do ripen. They also will be more subject to rot. If your tomatoes are approaching harvest and the daily high temperature drops below 60°F for more than five or six days, these tomatoes will have the same problem. If you have a few warm, sunny days interspersed between the cold, cloudy ones and the temperature under the plastic rises much over 86°F, this could spell disaster for your ripening fruits unless you rush out and open the plastic or uncover the plant. And the high humidity levels (close to 100 percent) that occur with the high temperatures under the plastic also encourage fungal growth.

Instead of battling the elements for one last harvest of vine-ripened fruits, many gardeners content themselves with house-ripened tomatoes. While the results of indoor ripening often are disappointing, an understanding of the ripening process can help you end up with the best house-ripened tomatoes possible. Whether you pull the vines and hang them upside-down in your basement or pick the individual fruits off the vines, you should never store the tomatoes where the temperature is below 54°F. Temperatures lower than this will damage the fruits so much that they will never ripen normally and will have an inferior flavor.

With this 54°F minimum in mind, you can control the speed of ripening by holding the tomatoes at different temperatures. If you want your tomatoes to ripen slowly, keep them between 54°F and 61°F; the ideal temperature for rapid ripening is between 61°F and 86°F. Unripe tomatoes should not be stored in the refrigerator, where the temperature is usually around 40°F. If you want to extend the ripening period, put some tomatoes in a cool, dark closet and keep others at room temperature.

It is just about useless to pick tomatoes that have not reached the mature green stage, for even if they ripen instead of shriveling up, they will be watery and almost flavorless. But do pick all obviously full-size fruits and any small ones that have begun to whiten. After picking sort out the tomatoes at different stages and store them together. Put the dark green tomatoes in one box and the light green ones in another. Tomatoes require high humidity (85 to 90 percent) to keep their quality so it's a good idea to cover them to keep the circulating air from drying them out. Wrapping also will keep the ethylene gas produced by the fruits close to them and thus hasten ripening.

Hanging Tomatoes: An easy way to ripen tomatoes when it gets cold is to hang the plants upside-down in the garage. Just make sure the temperature doesn't get below 54°F, or the fruits will decrease in quality.

The best procedure is to wrap each tomato individually in newspaper and store the wrapped tomatoes in a single layer in a well-ventilated place such as a fruit box. If you live in a part of the country where the humidity is relatively high, you can lay them in a single layer in a cardboard box and cover them with a couple of layers of newspaper. Never store your immature tomatoes in plastic bags because they will most likely rot before they reach a usable stage.

Tomatoes are susceptible to many diseases and a few pests, but rarely do such problems become serious for the home gardener. In addition, tomato varieties resistant to the most serious diseases are readily available. A few common problems of homegrown tomatoes are more easily dealt with when you understand their causes.

Problems with Tomatoes

Cracking of fruits: It is very frustrating to see your beautiful, plump, almost-ripe tomatoes develop cracks near the stem end. Most gardeners have had this happen at one time or another, and sometimes it cannot be helped. The cracking is caused when water droplets hit a tomato that contains a large amount of sugar. The high sugar content in the cells of the fruit causes the water to be absorbed, swelling and breaking some of the cells. This cellular activity is visible to you as ugly splits on the smooth surface of the fruit. One way to avoid such cracking is not to water your tomato vines from above while the fruits are ripening. Instead, use drip irrigation or soaker hoses.

Unfortunately, there's not a lot you can do if you live in an area where rains are frequent at tomato-ripening time. In that case your best bet is to grow varieties resistant to cracking, such as 'Campbell's 17,' 'Heinz 1350,' 'Marion,' and 'Sunripe.' Paste tomatoes in general are resistant to cracking because they have a lower water content than other tomatoes.

Blossom end rot: A tomato that suffers from blossom end rot looks as if it has been attacked by a virus or fungus. In the early stages of this malady the blossom end of the fruit looks watersoaked. The affected area enlarges, sometimes covering half the fruit, then it becomes black and leathery. Often the discolored spot is sunken in as well, possibly reaching far into the fruit.

Despite the unappealing appearance, this common tomato malady is not caused by a disease organism. It results instead from water stress and is most likely to strike the early fruits of vigorous vines suddenly exposed to very hot, dry weather or to water deficiency. Under such stressful conditions the plants' leaves, in dire need of water, draw it from the far ends of some of the fruits. The fruit cells, deprived of water, shrivel up and form the black area. A lack of sufficient calcium in the soil also may be involved.

Tomato Hornworm: This bizarre-looking caterpillar is the larva of a large brownish moth with white zigzags on its rear wings and red spots on its body.

You can take some simple steps to prevent your tomatoes from falling victim to blossom end rot. Make sure there is enough calcium in the soil by adding bone meal or wood ashes when you prepare it for planting. Avoid using fertilizers that are high in nitrogen, which encourages rapid leaf growth. Finally, water deeply and regularly and mulch to conserve soil moisture during hot, dry spells.

Yellow shoulder: Have you ever seen a supermarket tomato display with the fruits stacked so that their beautiful deep red bottoms are facing up? When you pick up a fruit to examine it, however, you find that the area around the stem end is yellow and hard instead of red and soft. This problem is called yellow shoulder. Some varieties are more susceptible to this disorder than others. 'Celebrity,' 'Duke,' 'Flora-Dale,' and 'Walter' all have the nonuniform ripening gene that can lead to yellow shoulder. Environmental factors also play a role. Low potassium in the soil and high humidity favor the development of yellow shoulder.

Tobacco mosaic virus: This virus can infect not only tobacco plants but also tomatoes and many other members of the nightshade family. Infected plants have yellow mottling of the leaves, which also may curl slightly upward. The virus doesn't kill the plants, but it does reduce their yield. Fortunately, most modern varieties are resistant to this disorder. But because it is so debilitating, it's best to be careful not to take any chances with mosaic.

The virus is spread by various means and often begins when a person who has been smoking touches plants in the garden and leaves behind traces of tobacco. This is dangerous because much of the tobacco used in cigarettes is contaminated by the mosaic virus. If you smoke, take preventive measures such as washing your hands thoroughly with soap and water or dipping them in milk before touching your plants (milk inhibits the virus). You also shouldn't smoke in the garden, and you should ask guests to refrain from doing so as well.

If mosaic virus does appear in your garden, remove the infected plants right away and be careful not to let them or your infected hands brush up against healthy plants. You can add the plants to the compost pile as long as it is properly constructed and heats up well, since the high temperatures will destroy the virus.

Certain weeds, such as catnip, jimsonweed, nightshade, and plantain, can carry mosaic virus. If you have been having trouble with this disease, keep the tomato patch well weeded and be on the lookout for patches of these weeds that may be growing adjacent to the garden.

Tomato hornworm: Because of the poisonous alkaloids in its leaves, the tomato plant is bothered by few leaf-eating pests. The one notable exception is the tomato hornworm, which is a voracious eater of tomato leaves and can devastate a plant in no time. This big, bright green caterpillar can be up to 4 inches long. The white bars along its sides and a pointed "horn" at its tail end make it look quite alarming, but it is harmless to people. It is the caterpillar stage of a large hawk moth.

Several methods of control are available for this pest. If only a few take up residence in your garden, you can pick them off by hand. If you see any with white capsules attached to their backs, however, don't remove them. These caterpillars have been infested by the *Trichogramma* wasp, an admirable parasite, and will soon die and release many more wasps to kill more hornworms. For a heavier infestation, and in the absence of helpful parasites, the bacterial spray *Bacillus thuringiensis* works well. You also can plant dill as a trap plant. Hornworms love to feast on the feathery dill leaves, and they are a lot easier to spot there than on the heavy foliage of tomato plants.

Tomato Frontiers

The prospects for improving tomatoes using wild relatives are very promising. Scientists have uncovered eight wild tomato species, in addition to members of *Lycopersicon esculentum*, that still survive in the wild state. Like wild potatoes, some wild tomatoes have leaves with sticky hairs that can kill insect pests such as aphids. In at least one variety of wild tomato the sticky substance is poisonous and can kill caterpillars that feed on tomatoes. Scientists have isolated the poison and found that it is not an alkaloid like other deadly nightshade family poisons. Since this wild tomato variety readily crosses with the domestic tomato, scientists hope that they can develop a hybrid that has poisonous leaves and good-quality fruits. But even if they are not successful with such breeding attempts, the poison itself might be developed as a natural insecticide for tomato pests.

Since tomatoes are rather particular about the temperatures at which they will germinate and set fruit, scientists are trying to develop varieties that can produce at higher and lower temperatures than present-day tomatoes. A wild tomato from the mountains of Peru offers hope that a more frost-resistant tomato may one day be available. This species lives above 3,000 feet, where it tolerates light frosts. Seedlings of this species will even develop true leaves when grown with eight-hour days of only 68°F and sixteen-hour nights at 32°F. By crossbreeding this species with domestic varieties, a tomato that will survive light frosts may be produced in a few years.

Another possibility for expanding the limits of cultivation comes from the seashore. A wild tomato relative that lives in the Galapagos Islands thrives just above the high-tide line. This wild species is a long way from a domestic tomato, with its ¼-inch sickly yellow fruits. But it can survive irrigation with 100 percent seawater, a great accomplishment for any land plant and a valuable feature to incorporate into crops in a world where much land cannot be cultivated because the soil is too salty or the only water available for irrigation comes from the sea. Successful crosses of this remarkable plant have been made with cultivated tomatoes and have produced a plant that has bright red, cherry tomato–size fruits with a fine flavor. This new fruit will tolerate 70 percent seawater in the experimental plots where it is grown. Despite the promise that this new plant shows, it will be years before it is available to the public. In general, it takes ten to fifteen years

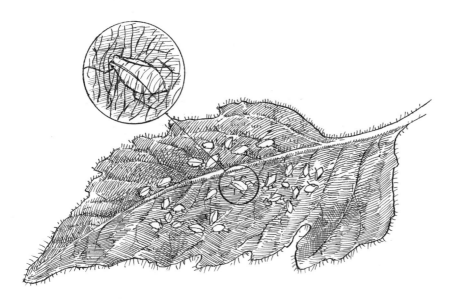

Trapping Aphids: Someday tomato breeders hope to incorporate genes from wild tomatoes with sticky hairs on their leaves into cultivated tomatoes to help control aphids.

to develop a variety that is completely reliable when grown from seed and to produce enough certified seeds for commercial purposes.

Researchers also are experimenting with ways to produce higher yields. One method uses different-colored mulches. It turns out that a red mulch encourages tomatoes to put more energy into the fruit and less into the foliage. As with so many other crops, the role of carbon dioxide concentration in the atmosphere also is being investigated as it relates to tomatoes, as is the potential for biological control of diseases such as fusarium wilt. Since tomatoes are such an important commercial crop, the intensive research into growing the best fruits will almost surely result in exciting developments for home gardeners in the next few years.

Chapter 13

Peppers:
From Sweet Bells
to Red-Hot Pods

VITAL STATISTICS

Family: Solanaceae

Species: *Capsicum annuum*

Soil: Deep, loose, and rich

pH: 5.5 to 7.0

Soil temperature for germination: 60°F to 95°F; 85°F optimum

Air temperature for best growth: 75°F to 85°F daytime; 50°F to 65°F nighttime; lower than 32°F kills the plants

Seed viability: 2 to 4 years

Seed germination: 6 to 28 days

Seed planting depth: ½ inch

Peppers are one of the most satisfying garden crops to grow. They don't take up a lot of space, and the lovely, compact plants with their dark, shiny leaves and colorful fruits are attractive enough to grace the flower bed as well as the vegetable garden. There are peppers to suit every taste, from sweet, fruity bells to red-hot pods that will have you breathing fire. The fruits cover a colorful spectrum, from deep chocolate and dark green to red, orange, and bright yellow.

Most people think of peppers as a tropical crop best suited to southern climates. But the closest wild relatives of garden peppers live in the Mexican highlands, where daytime temperatures aren't terribly hot and nights are quite cool. In the United States peppers are grown as a winter crop in Florida and Southern California, where summers are actually too hot for peppers. Many northern gardeners do not even try to grow peppers because they assume their season is too short and their climate too cool. But with thoughtful variety selection, proper cultural methods, and a little luck, even northerners can harvest a few fat red bells along with many green and yellow fruits.

Although there is no one secret to successful pepper growing, it is critical to keep the plants healthy and growing at every step of their development. This is especially important for gardeners working against the seasonal clock, as a setback to their pepper plants can mean no harvest at all or a disappointing yield of sad, bitter, thin-walled fruits. Rapid, continuous growth is essential.

Many people don't realize that peppers contain even more vitamin C than tomatoes—five to ten times as much by weight. As peppers ripen, their vitamin C content increases, which helps impart that lovely fruity flavor to the sweet varieties. A mature pepper can have up to seventy times as much vitamin C as an immature fruit, so health-conscious gardeners will wait until the fruits are mature to pick them. Besides, they taste better then, too!

Why Some Peppers Are Hot

Like potatoes and tomatoes, peppers are members of the nightshade family (Solanaceae). Despite the great differences in growth patterns, fruiting, and climatic preferences, all garden peppers belong to the same species, *Capsicum annuum*. The Tabasco pepper, from which the sauce is made, belongs to a different species, *Capsicum frutescens*.

The peppery hotness of both tabasco and chili peppers is caused by a group of related chemicals called capsaicinoids. The greatest concentration of these chemicals is in the placenta, the fleshy tissue inside the fruit that supports and nourishes the seeds as they develop. The seeds themselves pick up hotness from the placenta, and the walls of the pepper also contain some capsaicinoids. The degree of hotness is determined by the amount of these chemicals present in the pepper. Although you may not suspect it, even the sweetest bell pepper contains some of them. Scientists have determined the relative content of capsaicinoids in eight varieties of peppers, using a quantitative chemical test to compare their hotness. They ranked the peppers on a scale from 1 to 9, with some interesting results. 'Oakview Wonder' was the mildest, at a rating of 1. Then came 'Roumanian Sweet,' 1.2; 'Hungarian Yellow Wax,' 2.2; 'Anaheim,' 2.8; 'Long Red Cayenne,' 3.5; 'Floral Gem,' 3.8; 'Red Chili,' 5.5; and 'Argentine Wonder,' 8.2. And we think that cayenne peppers are hot!

After classifying the peppers, the intrepid scientists tasted each variety to see if their sensory rating would correspond to the capsaicinoid level. While the tasters perceived no hotness in the three peppers with the least capsaicinoid content, they couldn't even distinguish among the four hottest kinds! 'Long Red Cayenne' burned just as intensely as 'Argentine Wonder.' These differences will show up in cooking, however, so the prudent chef should use a very light touch when adding a firebrand such as 'Argentine Wonder' to a sauce or soup.

Indeed, cooks must use all hot peppers with caution, for some people are very sensitive to capsaicinoids. The first time Diane tried to roast hot peppers to peel them, her hands began to burn as she was washing the fruits. Her husband took over with no trouble and placed the shiny green gems under the broiler while she tried to get the irritant off her hands with soap at the kitchen sink. But her troubles were far from over because as soon as the peppers started to roast, her lungs began to burn and she could hardly breathe. She had to leave the house and stand outside on the porch while her husband roasted, peeled, and cut up the peppers. Once the air had cleared and Diane rejoined her family, they all ate the peppers diced in a delicious salad. Why was Diane able to eat the roasted peppers but not handle them raw or inhale their cooking aroma? Cooking deactivates much of the irritating quality of the capsaicinoids, so Diane could enjoy the cooked peppers with impunity.

Some friends of hers had a similar experience when they naively followed a Chinese recipe calling for twenty-three dried hot red peppers to be fried in hot oil. When the peppers hit the oil, the fumes were so strong that everyone had to leave the house for four hours before they could breathe without coughing uncontrollably!

Remember these experiences if you decide to cook with hot peppers. If you begin to feel even the slightest tingling of your skin while working with them, wash your hands immediately and don a pair of rubber gloves before going any further. And if you decide to try a recipe that calls for frying hot peppers, make sure your oil isn't smoking hot when you add the peppers, turn the kitchen fan on high, and open all the windows.

The pepper's hotness does, of course, serve a purpose. It appears to make the germination of pepper seeds possible. The explanation lies in the capsaicinoids' effect on fungi, which are mortal enemies of pepper seeds. While most seeds will germinate within a reasonable time at fairly low temperatures, pepper seeds are somewhat unusual in that they may take a month to germinate at 60°F. This gives soil-dwelling fungi plenty of time to attack and kill the seeds. And the high temperatures that allow rapid germination of peppers also enable the fungi to grow more quickly.

Fungi also can attack the fruits as they are growing, before the seeds are produced. Experiments with the Tabasco pepper done by a group of Canadian researchers showed that if fungi attack the young fruits before any capsaicinoids are present, the fruits start manufacturing them within twenty-four hours of the fungal attack. This halts the growth of the fungus. Other defensive chemicals in the fruits get into the act and kill off the fungus. The same mechanism is almost certainly at work in our familiar garden peppers (especially the hot varieties).

Peppers begin to accumulate capsaicinoids about twenty days after a fruit has set. The amount increases until the fruit is fully ripe or is picked. Peppers grown at warm temperatures become hotter than those raised under cooler conditions, so if you have an especially hot summer, beware of the potential fieriness of pepper varieties that may have been only mildly hot after a cooler growing season. Long, sunny days and rich soil also contribute to hotness. If hot peppers are picked before they are ripe, they will continue to increase in hotness and color if you store them at room temperature in the light.

Pepper Varieties

Peppers come in a more bewildering assortment than just about any other garden crop. How do you decide what to grow when you have as many as thirty-five choices in just one catalog? You might think the answer is to buy plants instead of seeds. But unless you live in a long-season area, you might as well forget about buying pepper plants that will meet your needs from a garden store because the variety of plants offered commercially is generally dismal. You can usually buy 'California Wonder' bell peppers, 'Cayenne' peppers, and, if you're lucky, 'Jalapeño' peppers as plants. These long-season varieties will not grow well in short-season gardens, so it is no surprise that so many gardeners have given up on peppers!

No matter where you live, you can find peppers offered in seed catalogs that will give you at least a fighting chance of growing crisp, tasty peppers. While 'California Wonder' takes about seventy-five days to reach the picking stage, other varieties of bell peppers such as 'Ace' and 'Canape Hybrid' take only sixty days, a difference of more than two weeks. The key to growing bell peppers in a short season is to buy the earliest varieties you can get. To tip the odds in your favor, plant several varieties and don't be too attached to the idea of nice, blocky green bell peppers. Here in Montana some of the most successful sweet peppers— 'Cubanelle,' 'Dutch Treat,' 'Italian Sweet,' and 'Lipstick'—are not bell shaped at all. 'Cubanelle' is a long, pale green frying pepper that, despite its name, grows quite well when the weather is cool. 'Dutch Treat' is a pretty plant with sweet, aromatic, pointed yellow fruits that form an attractive cluster near the top of the plant. 'Italian Sweet' peppers are long and pointed and have a delightful fruity flavor, even when still green. The walls of the fruit are thin but crisp, and the plants are small and take up little room. 'Lipstick' is a cone-shaped, thick-walled early variety that does well in the North. 'Sweet Banana' peppers also do well in our climate—so well that the plants are covered with long, slim yellow peppers before many varieties have begun to set fruit. 'Sweet Chocolate' is an early dark green variety that ripens into a lovely deep brown color.

Sweet peppers, unless the catalog description states otherwise, turn red when ripe. Don't be misled by catalog listings of time to maturity with peppers. "Days to maturity" means the time from transplanting young plants until the mature green peppers appear. It doesn't include the time it takes to raise the seedlings or the period between the mature green stage and the fully ripened red, yellow, or brown pepper. Sweet peppers take less time to mature than hot peppers, and there are varieties to suit a wide range of growing conditions. Besides the early varieties, there are dwarf and disease-resistant types, as well as giants such as 'Big Bertha,' which can weigh over a pound.

Hot peppers come in many sizes and shapes, too, and it can be fun to experiment with growing something different. Even if the seed catalog lists a long time to maturity for a hot variety, you might be able to grow it successfully in a short-season area. For example, cayenne varieties commonly take seventy-five days from the time of transplanting to reach their ripe red stage, but when picked green, these peppers will ripen quite nicely in the house. 'Ancho' peppers are supposed to take about eighty days, but that is the time to the ripe red stage at which these fruits are dried. That's when they are properly called 'Ancho' peppers. But while the glossy fruits are in their dark green immature stage, they are called 'Poblano' peppers and can add a delightful, mild hotness to Mexican dishes. Some cooks say that 'Poblano' is the only variety to use for *chilis rellenos.*

If your summers are long and hot instead of short and cool, you should consider planting your peppers early so that they will mature before the temperature soars. Peppers also can be planted in late summer for a fall crop in the South. If the temperature is consistently above 90°F, peppers won't set fruit. Since hot varieties can stand the heat better than sweet ones, you might want to concentrate on them. Besides the familiar cayenne and jalapeño, there are many interesting hot peppers that differ greatly in size, shape, and hotness. There is the beautiful, dark green 'Poblano' mentioned above. In long-season areas, this pepper can be harvested green or allowed to ripen into the deep red 'Ancho' that can be dried for use throughout the year. There is the tiny spherical 'Pequin,' which is among the hottest peppers, and the finger-size 'Serrano,' which has its own special spicy flavor. So even if you live where the heat makes growing bell peppers difficult, you can still enjoy growing other varieties of peppers.

Pointers on Seed Storage and Germination

Pepper seeds can last for three to four years if stored in a cool, dry place; however, they seem to be very sensitive to temperature and humidity, and old seeds may be very slow and uneven in germinating. Even year-old seeds may be unreliable if they have been stored at room temperature in their original packet. If possible, you should plant either fresh seeds or those that are not more than a year old unless you have taken care to keep your seeds dry (see chapter 1) and have stored them in a cool place.

Cool does not mean cold. When stored at 41°F, more than 80 percent of pepper seeds will germinate after three years. A storage temperature of 77°F will result in only two-thirds of the seeds germinating after three years. We do not recommend storing pepper seeds in the freezer. While tomatoes often appear around the edges of our compost piles in the spring, pepper seedlings never come up there spontaneously, so we suspect that they may be killed by freezing winter temperatures. It's best to avoid potential problems and store your pepper seeds in an unheated closet or a cool corner of the basement.

Another problem with pepper seed germination is "dirty" seeds. As we already mentioned, pepper seeds are especially susceptible to fungus infection, even though they contain chemicals that give them some protection. If seeds are taken from cracked fruits or those damaged by slugs or other nibbling pests, fungus spores or bacteria may have entered the fruits and reached the seeds. Unfortunately, seeds from some suppliers, especially small firms that specialize in unusual pepper varieties, are sometimes not very reliable. These companies may send generous packets, but you have to plant twice as many seeds to get enough plants for your garden. Perhaps their seeds are not as carefully collected and stored as those from the larger suppliers. In any case be sure that if you save seeds from your own peppers, you take them only from whole, undamaged fruits.

You should plant pepper seeds eight to eleven weeks before you anticipate putting the seedlings into the garden. There is some evidence that eleven-week-old transplants will yield a greater total harvest than eight-week-old ones. Eight-week-old transplants, however, are likely to produce larger early fruits. Some gardeners have little or no trouble growing peppers from seeds. They just plant the seeds ½ inch deep in sterile potting soil, water the soil lightly, cover the containers loosely with plastic, put them in a warm place, and wait for the seedlings to emerge in a week or so. We use this method for fresh seeds from major suppliers, but for older seeds or those from less reliable firms we recommend one of the following techniques.

First, you can germinate pepper seeds between layers of dampened paper towels and then plant them as they germinate. This technique is described in detail in chapter 1 in the box "Germinating Seeds between Paper Towels." Place the seeds in their damp towel sandwiches in a warm place (75°F to 85°F) and begin checking for germination after three days. The first sign will be the emergence of the tiny root. As soon as you see that a seed is germinating, remove it from the paper towel with a toothpick or tweezers (don't squeeze it), plant it ½ inch deep in sterile potting soil, and water it thoroughly. With some varieties, one seed may germinate quickly and the others may take a long time. Germination may be very uneven with old seeds, but at least you will know soon whether they are any good. If no seeds from a particular batch have shown signs of germination after ten days, replace them with fresh seeds of the same variety if possible.

Another simple method used by scientists for sterilizing and germinating seeds also works well for home gardeners. First, boil a pot of water for ten minutes to sterilize it, then cool it with the cover on to keep it as sterile as possible. Place your pepper seeds in a small bag made from a double layer of cheesecloth tied shut with string. Submerge the bag in a solution of 1 cup sterile water (that is cooled to room temperature) mixed with ¼ cup liquid chlorine bleach. Leave the seeds in this solution for ten minutes, swirling the bag around frequently to make sure all the seeds are exposed to the bleach. Then dunk the bag of seeds into a cup of sterile water and swirl it for one minute. Dunk the bag into a fresh cup of sterile water for one minute, swirling constantly. Repeat this procedure for six more rinses in sterile water, then plant the seeds.

Bleach-treated pepper seeds germinate about four days earlier than untreated seeds, and the bleach solution is strong enough to kill any bacteria and fungal spores that may contaminate the seeds. Although no one has proven that the seed coats of pepper seeds contain germination inhibitors, much evidence points in that direction. Perhaps the faster germination of the bleach-treated seeds is due to the destruction of such inhibitors. In our experience even soaking the seeds in a few changes of water before planting can speed up germination by a couple of days.

Anything you can do to hurry along germination is worth the effort with peppers, as they can be very slow to wake up. Peppers can germinate at any temperature from 60°F to 95°F, but you may have to wait three weeks for them to sprout at 65°F. By that time, if the seeds are no good, you could be out of the pepper-growing business for the season. At 85°F pepper seedlings may be poking their heads up as early as a week after planting. As you can see, it's important to find a reliably warm place for your germinating peppers. To keep from cooling down the soil each time you water the seeds, remember to use warm water.

How often you water also is important. If germinating pepper seeds dry out shortly after they've been planted, germination may be thwarted and all you will see is a stalk with the dried-up seed coat on top that never amounts to much of a plant. Inattention to proper watering once the seeds have germinated can have dire consequences, too. The seed coat will trap the cotyledons at the very stage when they should be spreading out. When this happens, you can very gently squeeze the seed coat to remove it from the leaves, but often this process may result in damaged cotyledons. A better solution is to buy a plant-misting bottle and fill it with sterile water. Gently mist your pepper seedlings every day as they are emerging from the soil. This procedure should keep the seed coat moist enough to come off naturally. Also make sure you plant your seeds ½ inch deep so that the old seed must be carried through the soil as the seedling pushes up. This will help remove the seed coat.

Caring for Pepper Seedlings

Although exposure to cool nights makes tomatoes bloom earlier than they otherwise would, there's no early stimulus for peppers, for they start flowering only after nine to eleven nodes have developed. Cool nights do, however, have an effect on pepper growth: they make the plants branch more extensively. Since pepper plants produce flowers at the bases of their branches, the bushier the plant, the more fruits it can yield. The cool nights that increase branching, however, also slow the overall growth of the plants. So if you live in a short-season area, you may want to avoid exposing the seedlings you're growing indoors to cool nighttime temperatures.

If you have a cold frame, the advantages of growing your plants in direct sunlight out-of-doors will more than compensate for the slower growth caused by the cooler nighttime temperatures. While cold frame–grown plants here in Montana are 4 to 5 inches shorter at transplanting time than those grown indoors, they undergo less transplant shock and produce more mature peppers by the end of the season.

To avoid any checks on growth, each pepper seedling should have its own pot. If you've sown seeds in a flat, you should transplant the seedlings to separate pots as soon as they are big enough to handle without damaging them.

Peppers can be grown in smaller containers than tomatoes. One friend of ours grows beautiful plants in ½-gallon milk cartons that have been rinsed, provided with drainage holes, and opened up at the top. These milk cartons can be nestled close together so they don't take up as much room as round pots, and they give the peppers plenty of room to stretch out and establish a healthy root system. When packed tightly together, these straight-sided containers help keep the soil temperature from fluctuating drastically when nights are cool. Peppers are more sensitive than tomatoes to low light intensities, so if you have limited lighting, give your peppers a front-row seat in a south-facing window and put the tomatoes behind them. Peppers grown inside need a slow, careful hardening-off period before being set out in the garden (see chapter 4).

Soil and Growing Conditions

Pepper plants have a fibrous root system. If the topsoil is deep and loose, the roots can reach down as far as 26 inches and as far away from the stem as 40 inches in any direction. This extensive root system allows peppers to make efficient use of water in the soil, so they do not need to be watered as often as less efficient crops such as cabbage. Peppers do need more water than tomatoes, however; grown side by side, peppers will wilt from lack of water before tomatoes do.

There seems to be some confusion about the relationship between pepper plants and soil nitrogen content. Many gardening books warn you not to plant peppers in soil with too much nitrogen. They say that a high nitrogen content will result in bushy, fruitless plants. We believe that this advice is aimed chiefly at chemical gardeners working with highly concentrated sources of nitrogen, for peppers grow best and yield the most fruits earliest in rich organic soil. They appear to be quite sensitive to low nitrogen, responding with pale leaves and few flowers. Since we live in a marginal region for peppers, we pamper them by working chicken, rabbit, or sheep manure into the soil in the fall. Don't get too carried away adding poultry manure, however, as peppers do not like salty soil.

Peppers also are sensitive to low phosphorus levels, but they don't give the same signal of discolored reddish or purple leaves as tomatoes; instead, they produce narrow, grayish green leaves and small, slender fruits. An infusion of a fast-acting fertilizer such as fish emulsion may supply enough phosphorus to revive your plants. But it's much better to make sure they have enough phosphorus from the start by applying bone meal or phosphate rock in the fall or early spring.

When peppers don't have enough potassium, they grow slowly and produce bronze-colored leaves with spots along the veins. The fruits on potassium-starved plants are small and few in number. At the first sign of low potassium work wood ashes into the soil around the base of each affected plant, staying 5 to 6 inches away from the stem.

If your soil isn't deep and loose, dig up an area about 24 inches wide and 18 inches deep for your peppers and add well-rotted cow manure or compost to the soil. Plant your peppers deep, up to the level of the first leaves. Like tomatoes, peppers will grow roots along the buried portion of the stem. If you position them at the same level at which they have been growing in their containers, some plants may fall over from the weight of their fruits later in the season. If your transplants have open flowers or tiny fruit, don't be afraid to pinch them off. If left in place they will drain the plant's energy and can reduce their early yield.

Garden books generally recommend 18 to 24 inches between pepper plants, but different varieties vary greatly in size. 'Italian Sweet' plants may reach only 12 inches in height and can be planted 8 to 10 inches apart, while 'Ancho' forms small bushes that are 24 inches or more tall and 24 inches wide and that need at least 24 inches between plants. Another complicating factor is that some pepper specialists recommend putting two plants in one hole. One friend has tried this method and claims to get a much better yield than with individual plants. A recent study in Florida found that the optimum spacing for commercial production of bell peppers was 10 inches apart, with two plants per hill. In general, peppers produce about the same weight of fruit from a given garden area no matter what the spacing. So if you're growing a variety with inexpensive seeds and don't want to worry about weeding, or if your garden is small and you want to experiment with a number of varieties, space your peppers close together. With expensive seeds or large plants it's wise to leave more room so you can get a generous yield per plant.

Pepper roots are quite temperature sensitive. Soil temperatures that stay around 85°F will stunt the roots, as will soil temperatures of 50°F or lower. If you live in a hot, dry area, use an organic mulch on your peppers as soon as the soil warms up. If you live in the North, clear plastic spread over the ground a few weeks before planting can warm the soil to help the pepper plants get off to a good start. Northern gardeners also would be wise to use a warming mulch after planting. Dorothy always plants her peppers in holes about 8 inches in diameter cut in black plastic mulch. Scientific studies have shown that mulching with black plastic does lead to earlier flowering and early fruit production, and does keep down the weeds. If you have a lot of flat stones around, place a few at the base of each pepper plant. During the day the stones soak up the sun's rays and radiate the heat slowly down into the soil at night. Some gardeners mulch their peppers with aluminum foil, which reflects heat and light up to the branches and increases yields. Make

Mulching Peppers: Flat rocks make
an attractive warming mulch for
pepper plants.

sure to leave a 4- to 8-inch area around the plants free of foil so that water can
penetrate to the roots.

Whatever mulch you use, wait until the soil has warmed to about 60°F before
planting. Loosening the soil as frost-free days approach will help speed the warming of the soil. You may have to wait until after your tomatoes are in before you
plant your peppers, but be patient; you don't want them to become chilled. One
year Dorothy's family had a June vacation planned, and she had to plant her peppers before they left. When they returned, she ran eagerly to the garden to see
how her favorite crop was doing. Much to her disappointment, the pepper plants
looked as though they were the same size as they had been three weeks earlier.
The weather had been cold and rainy, and the peppers hadn't grown at all.

Impatient northern gardeners can try a clever way of protecting their peppers
from cold springtime weather. Southern gardeners who plant in late winter or
very early spring also will find this technique useful. Instead of transplanting your
peppers to open ground, dig trenches 5 inches deep, 10 inches wide across the
top, and 7 inches wide at the bottom. The trenches should be about 2 feet apart.
Transplant your peppers into the trenches and cover them with row covers. The
trenches will hold the heat and protect the plants from the wind. The soil
temperature also will fluctuate less than at the surface, and water will naturally
collect in the trenches and soak in to provide plenty of moisture for the plants.
The scientists who developed this method used drip irrigation lines set 6 inches

deep between the trenches and slitted polyethylene covers. As the plants grew, they nosed their way up between the slits, so there was no need to remove the covers. The resulting crop came in earlier and was 43 percent larger than the crop grown without such pampering.

In the hot South, peppers can be grown as a fall crop. If you are a southern gardener and can spare the space, it's a good idea to solarize your soil before planting (see chapter 4). Experiments in South Texas showed that when pepper beds were covered with clear plastic in the summer, the heat killed the major weeds and infectious fungi but left the helpful mycorrhizal fungi alone. The plastic raised the soil temperature to a depth of 12 inches. Before the peppers were planted in late summer, the researchers sprayed the clear plastic with Kool-Ray, which turned the plastic opaque so it cooled rather than heated the soil. This double treatment increased the pepper yield by 53 percent over that of untreated soil. The solarization treatment alone boosted the harvest by 20 percent.

Pepper Flowers and Fruiting

Tomatoes and peppers may belong to the same family, but their growth habits are quite different. The vines of indeterminate tomato plants grow larger as the tip of each branch develops three leaves, a flower cluster, three leaves, a flower cluster, and so on. The plant just keeps on going until some outside force curtails its growth. Peppers grow and flower in a different way. Only one flower is formed at the tip of a stalk, which is actually a tiny branch of the plant. Then the axillary buds at the base of the flower branch grow to produce more branches. After forming two leaves and a flower, each of these branches stops growing, but its axillary buds form branches that go on in the same way. The result is a bushy plant whose size depends on how long the branches grow between flowers.

When you look at your pepper plants early in the season, you may be encouraged by the sight of flower buds developing low on the plant. Buds mean flowers, which mean fruit. But pepper flowers do not follow the usual pattern of opening—first to come, first to fruit. Even though they are the first to develop, those lower flowers may remain closed until many top flowers have formed and opened.

If you live in an area where the summer pepper harvest extends into October, you might try pinching off the early flowers to increase your total crop. It may seem strange, but if you pinch off the open flowers through early July, you should end up with more fruits and a greater total weight of fruits. The Canadian scientists who found this to be true used the varieties 'Keystone Resistant' and 'Ladybell.' If you are growing other varieties, you might find it interesting to pinch off the flowers of half your peppers and leave the others alone, then keep track of the yield from the plants. By trying simple experiments like this, you can find new ways of getting the most from your garden.

Like the roots, pepper flowers are a bit touchy about temperature. If nights stay hotter than 83°F, the flowers will fall off as mere buds, and you'll get no fruits. The flowers also will fall off if nighttime temperatures stay in the 40s. The largest number of fruits will set when nighttime temperatures are between 54°F and 60°F. But if the temperature stays in this range, you may find your crop consisting chiefly of fruits with few or no seeds. This is often the fate of our pepper crops during a cool summer.

The scarcity of seeds has important consequences for fruit size, since developing seeds produce the hormone auxin, which helps induce the fruit to grow. Fewer seeds mean less of this hormone, which ultimately means smaller fruits. If you're unfortunate enough to encounter this problem, you'll also notice that the peppers are misshapen: instead of having straight sides with lobes on the bottom, they are round or curved along one side.

For reliable setting of normal fruits, the temperature should be between 60°F and 68°F at night. High nighttime temperatures (around 68°F) after flowering will help the fruits grow fast and be well shaped. Fruits that set at nighttime temperatures high enough for normal development but that grow during a cold snap (with temperatures in the 40s) will be longer and slenderer than normal.

If your climate is hot, you can get a good yield of peppers by planting them early or late so that plenty of fruits are set when nights are cool. Planting varieties such as 'Ace' and 'Canape Hybrid,' which are resistant to losing flowers in the heat, also can help. In cool climates gardeners sometimes must wait a long time before they get any peppers. One recent summer our nights were cold all through July, and although our pepper plants bloomed profusely, we didn't see any tiny immature fruits before August.

Picking Peppers at Their Peak

Pepper fruits grow so rapidly during good weather that you can almost see them get bigger from day to day. But don't be in a rush to sample your crop. An immature green pepper is not sweet and fruity like a full-grown one. Just like tomatoes, peppers should be picked when ripe. Many gardening books and articles advise keeping your green peppers picked so that production doesn't slow down, but this advice should be tempered with the knowledge that the longer a pepper stays on the plant, the better it will taste. If you live in a short-season area, you might as well leave your peppers on the plants as long as possible because picking them early won't affect your eventual yield. In longer-season regions you should experiment with picking the fruits at different stages to find out when you like them best.

Left on the plants long enough, peppers will turn red (a few varieties will turn yellow or orange or even almost black). The ripening process is similar to that of tomatoes: the green chlorophyll disappears and is replaced by red pigments

Bushy Pepper Plants: *The growth and flowering habit of pepper plants results in a bushy appearance. After a flower forms, the axillary buds at the base of the flower branch grow to produce more branches.*

called carotenoids. As with tomatoes, about half the pepper's life is spent growing to full size, while the second half is devoted to ripening.

The eventual color of the ripe fruit is affected by temperature. Full color develops when temperatures range from 65°F to 75°F. Temperatures much above 80°F during most of ripening result in yellowish red fruits, while temperatures below 55°F stop ripening altogether. Thus peppers, like tomatoes, should not be left out in the garden under plastic too late into the fall. The fruits won't ripen if the temperature is too cold, and the high humidity under the plastic will encourage fungal growth. Once outside temperatures stay at or below 65°F during the day, you might as well pick your peppers and bring them inside.

Like tomatoes, peppers will continue to ripen after picking. Clean, dry peppers will last several weeks if stored in an unheated place. Dorothy has had good luck storing them in plastic bags in an unheated west-facing storeroom. While peppers keep best at 45°F to 50°F, you can store them in plastic bags in the refrigerator for about three weeks. Humidity is even more important than temperature to pepper storage. While many vegetables need to breathe to keep from rotting in storage, peppers keep best when tightly wrapped and stored in 100 percent humidity.

Storing the Harvest

However you store your peppers, check them every few days for rotting fruits. Remove these immediately, and if they have contaminated any surrounding peppers, wash and dry the remaining fruits before returning them to a clean storage bag.

Peppers freeze very well. You can chop them coarsely or just cut them into quarters, removing the seeds and veins before freezing. Chile peppers, such as the 'Anaheim' and 'Colorado' varieties, can be frozen whole for later stuffing. Drying is another storage option. Thin-walled peppers such as cayennes dry well whole. Thick-walled sweet peppers fare better when chopped before drying.

Collecting and Saving Pepper Seeds

Peppers must be close to maturity for their seeds to be any good. If you are trying to save seeds and your season ends before the fruits are ripe, you can ripen them further at room temperature inside. If the peppers were mature enough at harvest, the seeds will develop just fine as the fruits ripen. Dorothy has had good luck placing green peppers in individual fold-lock sandwich bags and leaving them on the kitchen counter to ripen, where she can keep an eye on them. Once the peppers are fully ripe and have begun to soften, open them up and collect the seeds. Dry the seeds thoroughly on paper towels and store them following the guidelines given earlier in this chapter.

Problems with Peppers

Peppers tend to be afflicted by the same problems that beset tomatoes. This makes sense, of course, since they belong to the same family. We mention a few of the pepper's most frequent ailments here; where the pest or disease is noted as being common to peppers and tomatoes, refer to the section "Problems with Tomatoes" in chapter 12 for some tips on how to deal with them.

Bacteria, fungi, and viruses: As we've already said, fungi are among peppers' greatest enemies. Not only do the seeds often fall victim to a fungus, but mature plants can do so as well, especially if they're grown in a rainy or very humid climate. Fungal and bacterial diseases form sunken, discolored spots on the leaves or fruits, while viral diseases generally cause a mottled leaf color and bitter, bumpy-looking fruits. If your peppers become diseased, pull up the affected plants right away and discard them in the trash or burn them. Like tomatoes, peppers can suffer from mosaic virus, so if you use tobacco, observe the same precautions with peppers as with tomatoes.

Blossom end rot and sunscald: Peppers, like tomatoes, can suffer from blossom end rot. Sunscald occurs when the pepper plant doesn't have enough foliage to cover the fruits. Overexposure to the sun results in discolored spots that become sunken and bleached. Fungi and bacteria can attack through the weakened area, so you should pick and use fruits suffering from sunscald right away. Some pepper varieties are more susceptible to sunscald than others. A variety such as 'Dutch Treat,' which carries most of its fruits high on the plant above the leaves, may not produce a satisfactory crop in a hot, dry climate because of the fruits' susceptibility to sunscald.

Cutworms and hornworms: These voracious insects attack peppers as well as tomatoes. For hornworm, follow the advice given for tomatoes. The best way to protect against cutworms is to place a cardboard collar around each plant when you set it out and firmly press it into the soil around the stem, preventing the cutworms from getting to your plants.

Pepper maggots and pepper weevils: Peppers also have their own unique pests—the pepper maggot and pepper weevil. The pepper maggot is the larva of a small yellow fly with three brown bands across both wings that lays its eggs in the fruit. You can combat this fly by sprinkling talcum powder on the fruits during July and August when the flies are busy laying their eggs. The talcum powder will interfere with the egg-laying process.

The pepper weevil is a small beetle with a long snout. Both the adult and its larva, a ¼-inch white grub with a pale brown head, feed on pepper plants. The grub chews up the buds and fruits from the inside, leaving them vulnerable to diseases and making them misshapen and discolored. The adult beetles eat leaves, buds, and fruits. Pepper weevils live mainly in the South and can be controlled by careful cleanup after the harvest to remove any residue that may harbor eggs. Rotenone also can be used to kill the weevils.

U nfortunately, since peppers are not a major commercial crop in the United States and Canada, little research into pepper improvement is being done by North American breeders. New varieties that tolerate cool climates (such as 'Dutch Treat') or that produce an early crop (such as 'Tokyo Bell') have been developed in other countries. Fortunately for us, their seeds are being sold here as well.

Pepper
Frontiers

Chapter 14

Cucumbers, Melons, and Squash: Rambling Cucurbits

The cucurbit family includes many of our tastiest, most popular, and most colorful vegetables—cucumbers, muskmelons (such as cantaloupe), pumpkins, summer and winter squash, and watermelons. Cucurbits all prefer warm weather, and while northern gardeners have no trouble growing the usual overabundance of zucchini that plagues gardeners everywhere, one or two muskmelons ripening on a vine can be a major source of pride for a northerner. Unlike the members of the cabbage family, which all belong to one species, the cucurbits belong to several different genera and species, some of them more closely related than others. But despite their variety, cucurbits have much the same character and require very similar cultural conditions for success.

The versatile cucurbits came originally from a variety of geographic regions and have been cultivated for thousands of years. Cucumbers have been grown for three thousand years in their native region of India. Watermelons seem to have come from the African deserts, while wild melons are found in the wet tropical regions of Africa. Squash and pumpkins are American natives that have been cultivated for more than nine thousand years; Mexico and northern South America seem to be their original homelands. Cucurbit beginnings in such warm-weather areas explains the preference of these crops for hot summer climates.

The word *squash* comes from the North American Indian word *asquash*. This

VITAL STATISTICS

Family: Cucurbitaceae

Species: *Cucumis sativus*—cucumbers *Cucurbita* species—summer and winter squash; pumpkins *Cucumis melo*—muskmelons *Citrullus lanatus*—watermelons

Soil: Rich and loose

pH: Close to 7.0; cucurbits do poorly in acid soil

Soil temperature for germination: 65°F to 100°F; 80°F to 95°F optimum

Air temperature for best growth: Cucumbers, squash, pumpkins, and muskmelons—65°F to 75°F Watermelons—70°F to 85°F

Seed viability: 2 to 5 years

Seed germination: 3 to 10 days

Seed planting depth: ½ to 1 inch

term means to eat foods when immature, as we do with young zucchini, pattypan squash, and other summer squash. Summer squash are all in the same species, *Cucurbita pepo,* along with pumpkins and acorn squash. While we relish the flesh of these vegetables, the first domestication was probably for their tasty, nutritious seeds. Once selection for large seeds began, the fruits inadvertently became larger, creating new food items. Pumpkins are probably the oldest of the *C. pepo* forms. The American Indians would cut pumpkins into strips and hang them to dry for later use when food was scarce.

Scientists are still trying to sort out the details of the origins of the different members of the *C. pepo* group, but most agree that many different plants were hybridized to produce the fascinating array of fruit shapes and colors. For example, scientists suspect that scallop squash and pumpkins hybridized to form acorn squash.

The probable wild ancestors of *C. pepo* formed inedible gourds rather than tender-fleshed fruits. (The beautiful ornamental gourds we have today probably originated with these ancient forerunners.) Hybridization between pumpkins and ornamental gourds could have produced vegetable marrows, which have woody, mature fruits like gourds. Several squash types are considered to be vegetable marrows, each with its own special shape. Vegetable marrows themselves, which are more popular in Great Britain than in North America, are fat with a slightly triangular shape. The familiar zucchini are narrower, with a long, straight shape, while cocozelle are even longer with a flared base. The crookneck form was probably developed from the original wild gourd in the interior regions of North America, since it wasn't among the squash brought back to Europe by early explorers. Straightneck squash most likely originated relatively recently from the crookneck form, since both crookneck and straightneck varieties have warted rinds (in more mature fruits) and a yellow color (in immature fruits). This is rare in other squash of this species.

Other squash varieties can belong to one of three species. *Cucurbita maxima* includes fine-flavored varieties such as 'Bush Buttercup,' 'Buttercup,' 'Gold Nugget,' 'Golden Hubbard,' 'Pink Banana,' and 'Sweet Meat.' The large crookneck-looking variety 'Green Striped Cushaw' is of the *Cucurbita mixta* species. The rich-tasting butternut varieties all belong to *Cucurbita moschata.*

A Nutritional Profile of the Cucurbits

While cucumbers, melons, and zucchini are not among the more nutrient-rich vegetables, yellow- and orange-fleshed squash and melons are high in fiber and contain large quantities of vitamin A. Winter squash vary widely in vitamin A content. For example, butternut squash provides about 30 percent more vitamin A than does Hubbard squash and almost 80 percent more than acorn. Even so, a half-cup serving of acorn squash contains about half the recommended daily vitamin A allowance. Orange cantaloupes also are high in vitamin A, but green melons (such as honeydew) are not. The seeds of squash and pumpkins, which are delicious either raw or toasted, provide concentrated food in the form of fats and proteins.

If you are weight conscious, you may find the greatest virtue of some cucurbits to be their ability to give you a satisfying "full" feeling while not loading your body with calories. An average-size cucumber has only 45 calories, and a satisfying breakfast of half a cantaloupe (82 calories), a boiled egg (82 calories), and a slice of whole-grain bread (61 calories) amounts to only 225 calories.

Getting Started with Cucurbits

Cucurbit seeds may stay viable as long as five years when stored properly in a cool, dry place. Under poor storage conditions, the seeds will deteriorate quickly and lose their viability in two years, so take good care of them. Hybrid squash and hull-less pumpkin seeds often have a low germination rate, so plant more of these types than you need.

The seed coats of seedless watermelons often stick to the leaves of the young seedlings. This causes a distorted plant that may die or grow very slowly. Since Diane also has had this problem with cantaloupes, cucumbers, zucchini, and several winter squash varieties, she was very interested in research concerning 'King of Hearts' watermelons at the University of Florida. The study showed that among seeds planted with the pointed end up (toward the soil's surface), only 31 percent had seed coat adherence, compared to 94 percent when the seeds were turned down. The young root emerges from the pointed end, so when that end is up, the root has to turn downward, and the foot (a small area of flesh on the young stem that acts like a lever to push off the seed coat) is in the best position to do its job. So when you're planting cucurbits, try to orient the pointed end of the seed up.

Because their seeds are large and packed with stored energy, cucurbits can get off to a good start when planted in very warm soil (the optimal germination temperature is 95°F). If they are planted outdoors in cold soil, cucurbit seeds will rot. While high temperatures allow these warmth-loving plants to germinate quickly, squash seeds may carry the spores of diseases that also grow rapidly at high temperatures. For this reason a lower temperature (80°F or so) is preferable. Muskmelons will emerge in one week at 68°F and in five days at 77°F, while cucumbers will come up in four days if the soil temperature is in the 70s.

In southern areas where the soil may be warmer than 80°F, cucurbits can be planted directly outdoors about 1 inch deep. But in many parts of North America such high soil temperatures are hard to come by early in the season, so planting cucurbit seeds indoors is a good idea. Most studies of cucumbers, muskmelons, and watermelons show that transplants produce earlier and more abundantly than direct-seeded plants. For example, a study in Alabama showed that transplanted 'Chilton' muskmelons produced over 80 percent more early fruit, as well as a greater total yield, than those that were direct-seeded.

Because they grow so quickly, cucurbits should not be started indoors more than four weeks before planting in the garden. Often two weeks is adequate to give fast-growing zucchini or cucumber varieties a head start on the season. These plants normally have a long taproot that can be inhibited by confinement in a small pot. When this happens, the plant develops a fibrous root system and needs more water at the surface than a plant with a long taproot. If you start your cucurbits inside, remember that they may need more frequent watering later than will direct-seeded plants.

Each plant should have its own pot. If you use peat pots, plant the pot along with the seedling so as not to disturb the roots (see chapter 3). Plastic pots are good for starting cucurbits, for when the soil is just damp, the entire root ball will slide out easily with minimum trauma to the roots. Use the larger four-cell plastic pots (the individual cells are 2⅜ by 1½ by 2¼ inches) so that the roots aren't crowded. Plant two seeds per cell, water them, and set them in a warm place. As the seedlings emerge, use a pair of scissors to cut off the weaker one in each cell at ground level, being careful not to disturb the survivor. Then move the pot to a warm, sunny spot such as a south-facing window or a cold frame that is open to full sunlight during the day but closed during the cool spring nights. Cucurbits can be transplanted as soon as the first true leaves unfold, but you might want to grow them indoors or in a cold frame for up to a month so that they have an extra-early start.

Cucurbits also do well when started outdoors in mini-greenhouses. There are

Mini-Greenhouses: Plastic milk jugs provide warm, protective mini-greenhouses for cucurbits. Cut the bottoms from 1-gallon jugs and set them over the planting sites a week before planting to help warm the soil. Then plant the germinating seeds or transplant the young cucurbits under the jugs. Remove the caps on sunny days and screw them back on at night.

several ways to do this, but the basic idea is to provide the young plants with a warm, protected place to grow. One way to make a mini-greenhouse is to cut the bottom off a plastic 1-gallon milk jug. About a week before planting set a jug over each hill where you plan to plant your cucurbits. The jug will warm the soil in the hill. This method has worked well for Dorothy. She germinates cucurbit seeds between damp paper towels in a warm place inside and then plants them in the prewarmed soil under the jugs. Young cucurbits can be grown in these mini-greenhouses (also called hot caps) for a few weeks until they become crowded. On sunny days unscrew the cap of each jug to keep the temperature from getting too hot inside. Screw the cap back on at night to hold in the warmth.

If you want to plant directly in the garden but have a spell of cool, unsettled weather, soak your seeds in water for twenty hours before planting. Scientists who soaked cantaloupe and watermelon seeds found that doing so increased the chances of successful germination when soil temperatures were lower than desirable (55°F to 65°F).

Soil and Growing Conditions

Cucurbits grow very quickly when weather conditions are right, but they need a loose, rich soil to support their rampant growth. The rapid proliferation of cucurbit vines is easy to observe, but the growth of the hidden roots is even more impressive. The taproot of melons and cucumbers can grow an inch a day down to a depth of 4 feet, while the main root of squash and pumpkins can reach down 6 feet into the earth! Cucurbit roots may extend farther than the vines laterally, growing up to 2½ inches in one day. One careful estimate of the total area of a large squash root system was 1,000 cubic feet of soil.

The soil must be loose for such rapid root growth to occur. A heavy compacted or clay soil can prevent cucurbit roots from growing quickly, thus keeping the leafy part of the plant from getting enough of the minerals and water it needs from the soil. The plant will grow more slowly and yield less, and it may produce a late crop, which can mean little or no crop in a short-season area. Soil that contains a lot of organic matter will be sufficiently light and porous for cucurbits, and it will retain the copious amounts of water these thirsty plants require.

Cucurbits need a lot of water during their rapid growth period and also during the production of their fruits. Just think about how watery watermelons and cucumbers are! If watermelons or squash are water stressed, they may produce misshapen fruits or not set fruit at all.

To compensate for poor soil, Dorothy once dug holes about a foot wide and a foot deep and shoveled in 6 inches of manure. Then she filled the holes with soil and planted her squash. The plants really took off at first, but in about four weeks, the leaves began to turn yellow. She didn't know then that squash roots ramble far from the plants. Her plants had outgrown their enriched hills. All she could do was water the plants with liquid fish emulsion and add compost to the soil around them. She did get some fine squash from those plants, but she would have gotten a much better yield by digging up a 2- to 3-foot area around each hill and working in plenty of manure so that the plants' growth wouldn't have slowed when they began to flower.

Cucurbits' need for warm soil can be their downfall, since soil-borne diseases also thrive in warm, moist soil and can attack young seedlings. One easy organic solution to these problems is to use soil solarization before you plant (see chapter 3). This may not totally rid your soil of disease, but it often will delay the onset of problems long enough to allow a good harvest.

Clear plastic laid over the ground in the spring is useful for warming up your soil if it is too cold. If your soil lacks adequate organic matter, dig in fresh or composted manure or shredded compost six weeks or more before you plan to plant.

Planting Cucurbits in the Garden

As you no doubt realize by now, the cucurbits' passion for warmth, water, and rich soil can result in a disappointing harvest if you are caught off guard. But if you are aware of their needs and prepare for them far enough in advance, your cucurbits will reward you with such a bountiful harvest that you'll be giving away cucumbers and winter squash as well as that perennial gardener's gift, the zucchini.

Cucurbits traditionally are planted in raised mounds called hills. They grow best this way because the sun warms the elevated ground, which has more surface area than a flat expanse of soil. Commercial melon growers in Southern California, who raise cantaloupes in the winter, plant the seeds in ridges running east to west. Because of the increased soil surface area, the sun warms the ridges better than it would level ground. Another way to keep the soil warm is to use a rock mulch. Once the plants are up and the soil is warm, place flat rocks all around the plants, leaving a space about 6 inches in diameter around the stems to allow water to get to the roots. The rocks heat up during the day and radiate their stored warmth slowly back into the soil at night, keeping the soil at a more even temperature than if it were left uncovered. Black plastic also absorbs the sun's rays and warms the soil, and it has the additional advantage of keeping the fruits clean.

Cucumbers, muskmelons, and watermelons are more sensitive to cold soil than are squash. For example, cucumbers need a soil temperature of at least 70°F for good growth. If your climate doesn't provide the warm growing conditions that favor growth, plan to use all the season-extending devices that are available to encourage your cucurbits to produce early and abundantly. In the Alabama study mentioned earlier, row covers combined with black plastic mulch resulted in a 38 percent increase in total yield compared with transplants grown without the benefit of row covers or mulch.

Start by hilling up your soil or making raised beds. If practical, install a trickle irrigation system. Trickle or drip irrigation is the most efficient way to water cucurbits because they need a constant supply of moisture. Such a system also helps prevent foliage disease, which can be spread through wetting the leaves frequently with an overhead sprinkler. It also helps keep your harvest clean, since mud isn't splattered on the fruits.

Next, cover the area with black or clear plastic (see chapter 4 for a discussion of the advantages and disadvantages of both). Cut holes in the plastic and place your young transplants in the holes. If you don't use trickle irrigation, be sure to expose enough soil around each plant so that water can penetrate or use a porous mulch such as black landscape cloth instead of plastic. Set each plant about ½ inch deeper than it was in the pot. Then cover the plants with fabric row covers. Leave the row covers on until the plants start to blossom or the air temperature rises above 90°F.

This method takes a little more time and is more expensive than just planting in the garden, but it is the only way Diane has been able to harvest cantaloupes and watermelons in Montana. By carefully cleaning, folding, and storing the black plastic and row covers, you can use them for several years, making them less expensive over time.

Cucurbits also are sensitive to cold water. If you water cucumbers with very cold water and thus reduce the soil temperature, you can actually make them wilt. The tips of the developing fruits may dry out, and the leaves and fruits can become discolored or even die. For this reason, if you must use cold water, always water your cucurbits at mid-morning, when the soil is being warmed by the sun. Cucumbers, muskmelons, and watermelons are more sensitive than squash to cold soil.

As with other crops, cucurbits should not be planted in the same place in successive years. Not only is there the risk of transmitting diseases, but the fast-growing plants pull so many nutrients from the soil that it needs replenishing with a more forgiving crop such as peas after supporting a season's growth of rampant cucurbits.

Cucurbits do not do well in acid soil and should be grown at a pH of 7 or higher. Low pH can cause too much manganese and not enough magnesium to be available to the plants, resulting in leaf injury and reduced yields. Cucurbits also are sensitive to salty soil (see "The Lowdown on Salty Soil" in chapter 5), so resist the temptation to use large amounts of poultry manure to provide the copious nutrients these crops need. If poultry manure is your only source of high-nitrogen enrichment, add it in the fall so that some of the salt will leach out over the winter. If you have problems with salty soil, try growing moderately salt-tolerant cucurbits such as 'Aristocrat' zucchini, but avoid sensitive varieties such as 'White Bush Scallop' squash.

Cucurbit Flowers and Fruiting

Thousands of gardeners have probably had the same experience Dorothy had the first time she grew cucumbers and zucchini. She was thrilled when her plants began to bloom and confident that it wouldn't be long until her family would be eating fresh, homegrown produce. But after blooming enthusiastically, the first batch of flowers on both crops dropped off, leaving no trace of any fruit. Why didn't her plants set fruit? Since she knew something about biology, Dorothy was able to figure out the answer later on, when a different-looking flower with a miniature fruit behind it appeared on her zucchini bushes. She then realized that the plants must have separate male and female flowers. That kind of information is often missing in gardening books, so we'll explain it here in the hope of saving you some needless worry and confusion.

All the cucurbit crops except muskmelons have separate male and female flowers, and the first ones to appear are almost always male. There is nothing you can do about that sequence of events except be patient and wait for the female flowers to appear. In the meantime, you can put some of those early male flowers to good use. Coated with batter and fried, squash blossoms make excellent eating.

Male and female flowers look quite different. The female flowers have an ovary at the point where they attach to the plant—that was the miniature fruit Dorothy spotted. (If you have mixed up your squash seedlings, you'll be able to differentiate between varieties when the female flowers appear.) If you look into the center of the female flower, you can see the sticky stigma waiting for pollen. The male flower lacks the miniature fruit and instead has a cluster of fused anthers covered with pollen. The generously large zucchini flowers offer an especially good opportunity for observing the differences between male and female flowers.

Male and female flowers appear in a regular sequence in cucurbits, but the sequence varies somewhat among the different crops. Long days seem to promote the development of male flowers, which explains why they are the first to appear. The female flowers of cucumbers and summer squash come along after the first few male ones. Once female flowers make their appearance, the plants will produce flowers of both sexes for the rest of the season.

Flowering in acorn squash is quite complicated. The first male flowers to appear do not even open. These are followed by male flowers that do open. Then both male and female flowers appear and open, and you can begin to think about harvesting and eating that squash. After these normal flowers (which can produce fruits) appear, still another type of flower develops. Giant female flowers bloom, accompanied by smaller male flowers that pollinate them to form normal, seeded squash. Finally, at the end of the season the plant produces large female flowers that will develop into seedless squash without fertilization. This progression of flower types is related to day length. Long days (sixteen hours or more) and high nighttime temperatures (above 80°F) lengthen the male phase, while twelve-hour days and lower nighttime temperatures shorten the male phase and encourage the growth of female flowers. While male flowers will predominate in

Cucurbit Flowers: Muskmelons have perfect flowers (right), but all other cucurbits have separate male and female flowers. The male flower (left) appears first and has a cluster of fused anthers in the center. The female flower (center) has an ovary that looks like a miniature fruit at its base. The sticky stigma is in the center of the female flower.

the spring and early summer in northerly regions with long days, both male and female flowers will bloom during the summer, when days are shorter but nights are warm. The shorter days and cool nights of autumn will bring on the large female flowers that need no fertilization. Other environmental factors that encourage female flowers are high nitrogen levels and low light intensities; the opposite conditions encourage male flowers.

If you enjoy eating batter-dipped and fried squash flowers, you can continue to harvest them throughout the season. You need to leave only a few male flowers on the plant to provide adequate pollen for all the females. Be sure to select only male flowers. If you pick and eat the female flowers, you are seriously cutting into your squash harvest.

Muskmelons are like other cucurbits in that male flowers appear first. However, the first *fruiting* flowers of muskmelons (which are perfect flowers with male and female parts rather than female flowers) generally do not appear until the main branch of the plant is 18 inches long. At that time side branches sprout from nodes near the base of the main branch. The first flowers on these side branches will be perfect ones. If these flowers are pollinated, the rest of the flowers on the still-growing side branches will be male ones. In this way the melon plant keeps itself from setting more fruits than it can support. When the weather is good early in the season, most muskmelons will be found near the center of the plants. But when early-season weather is too cool or otherwise unfavorable, each side branch will keep producing perfect flowers until they are pollinated and then set fruit, resulting in fruits farther out on the branches.

Poor weather affects the pollination of all cucurbits. When it is cold, pollen may not be released from the male flowers. For example, pumpkin and squash pollen is not released at temperatures below 48°F. Watermelons and cucumbers require a minimum temperature of 58°F for pollen release, with the most abundant release of pollen at 65°F to 70°F. Muskmelons require a minimum temperature of 65°F (68°F to 70°F optimum).

Cucurbit flowers are most receptive to pollen right after they open. It takes twenty-four to forty-eight hours for the pollen tubes to grow through the style and complete pollination. If you look carefully at the stigma of a cucumber flower, you can see that it consists of three equal parts that meet in the center. If you cut into a cucumber crosswise, you will see three seed chambers, each of which corresponds to one section of the stigma. If one of these sections isn't properly pollinated, the cucumber will be misshapen.

Bees do a very effective job of pollinating cucurbit flowers. Many bees visit the same flower and cover the surface of the stigma with pollen. But it takes a lot of bee visits to pollinate a cucurbit flower well. A cantaloupe flower, for instance, must be worked by ten to fifteen bees, which leave several hundred pollen grains on the stigma, to produce a big melon.

The amount of pollen affects not only the fruits but also the seeds. Researchers at Pennsylvania State University made the puzzling discovery that seeds from abundantly pollinated flowers were likely to germinate faster than seeds from flowers that received meager amounts of pollen. The scientists also found that large pollen loads resulted in larger fruits with more seeds. If you think about how the pollen tube grows down through the stigma, you can imagine that a large pollen load would result in competition among the pollen grains so that only the most vigorously growing grains would fertilize the ovules. With a small pollen load, weaker pollen grains that grow slowly would still have a chance to reach the ovules, and some ovules could be missed altogether.

In another study Pennsylvania researchers found that fruits with more seeds grew faster than those with fewer seeds and that when there was more than one developing fruit, the one with the fewest seeds was likely to abort.

With these facts in mind, you may want to help the crop along by pollinating the flowers yourself if it is cloudy or rainy when your first female cucurbit flowers begin to bloom and the bees are not out doing their job. One way to hand-pollinate is to pick a fully open male flower and rub the anther on the stigma of a female flower. Make sure the pollen can be brushed off the stamen easily. If it's reluctant to come off, the pollen is not yet ready to be released. Another method is to use a cotton swab or soft paintbrush to pick up a generous amount of pollen from one or more male flowers and then carefully dust the pollen evenly over the stigma of the female flower. Move from plant to plant, applying the pollen from one plant to the stigma of a flower on a different plant. The cucumber is the only member of the family that can self-pollinate. But even for cucumbers, transferring pollen from one plant to another is more effective.

You can tell within a couple of days whether a cucurbit flower has been successfully pollinated. If it has, the blossom will wither and the miniature fruit will start to swell. A properly fertilized summer squash fruit will fill out all the way to the blossom end as it grows. The fate of an unfertilized fruit is different. The blossom end remains smaller than the rest of the squash and becomes shriveled.

After about two days, the little fruit stops growing. Such squash should be picked off the vine immediately, or they will drain the plant of energy that could be better used to grow well-fertilized fruits.

One year Diane had to leave her garden right when her zucchini were flowering profusely and a couple of fruits looked as though they might have set. In the midst of all the packing she forgot to tell the person tending her garden to harvest the squash as they matured. When she got back, only one gigantic zucchini was set on the plant. Most plants will continue to produce through the season even if they've set some fruits. But once a zucchini sets fruit, the developing fruit will influence the number and kind of flowers and discourage the setting of fruit by any successfully pollinated flowers that come after it. Diane has found that this process also occurs in other summer squash and cucumbers. Thus it is important to pick your summer squash or cucumbers as soon as they reach the size you like. If you want to grow a giant squash to show your friends and neighbors, wait until late in the season, or that giant may be all you get. And if you need to leave someone else in charge, as Diane did, make sure that he or she knows to check the summer squash and cucumbers every few days and to remove the fruits as they mature.

Cantaloupes and watermelons need to be watched for misshapen fruits. Any fruit that sets will inhibit other flowers from setting fruits—even flowers that have been properly pollinated. If you leave misshapen fruits on the vine, that is all you will get for a long time. The imperfect fruits can inhibit the setting of fruits by other flowers for as long as several weeks. But if you pick off the bad ones, other flowers will set fruits or those from other already pollinated flowers will start to develop.

If you think about the size of a cucurbit vine compared to the size of the fruits it produces, you can understand why it is important for the plant to have ways of limiting the number of fruits it sets. For instance, you might harvest one 50-pound watermelon from a vine that weighs, at most, 10 pounds. A great deal of energy goes into forming each crunchy cucumber, juicy melon, and succulent squash. Scientific study has shown that the leaves of cucumber plants with fruits on the vines photosynthesize at a more rapid rate and send out 40 percent more photosynthetic product (sugars) to the rest of the plant than do the leaves of plants without fruits. For this reason it is especially important to take good care of cucurbit leaves. When you pick the fruits, be careful not to bend the stems (and damage the phloem, which carries nutrients to the fruits) or injure the leaves by rough treatment. Also take care to eliminate any insects that may be munching on your cucurbit leaves. With some crops a few holes in the leaves make little difference in your eventual yield. But with cucumbers and their relatives insect damage can significantly inhibit the ability of the leaves to make enough food for the rapidly developing fruits.

If you want to grow really big melons or pumpkins, pick off all but two watermelons or pumpkins or all but three or four cantaloupes per vine. This will channel all of the food energy produced by the leaves to the selected fruits, thus increasing their size.

Saving Cucurbit Seeds

Many people think that cucumbers will crossbreed with cantaloupes or watermelons, but that isn't true, as these crops belong to different species. You can safely save seeds from nonhybrid varieties of these crops even if they are growing right next to each other. But if you are growing different varieties of the same species, watch out if you plan to save the seeds for planting. Separate the plants by a safe distance so they will not cross-pollinate. Even more caution is necessary with squash, since two of the squash species—*Cucurbita maxima* and *C. moschata*—can interbreed, greatly increasing your chances of seeing weird hybrids from saved seeds. You can never be sure of what will come up if you save seeds from these plants unless you separate them by at least 200 feet. We've seen freaks like giant vining zucchini plants result from such crosses.

One year Dorothy's neighbor grew plants from seeds she had saved from her 'Spaghetti Squash' the year before. The resulting fruits didn't look like 'Spaghetti Squash'; they were bigger and were orange instead of the usual green or creamy yellow. Other friends of the neighbor cooked this strange fruit as they would winter squash and claimed it was delicious. But the squash Dorothy was given looked so strange that she put it in a cold storeroom, meaning to deal with it later. Spring arrived, and she still hadn't faced that squash. It had developed some mold on one side, so she decided to add it to the compost pile. But when she picked it up, she discovered that it was completely dried out and hollow, like a giant gourd! After that she didn't feel quite so bad about not getting up the nerve to cook it. Interestingly, several years after this incident, a new orange spaghetti squash called 'Orangetti' came on the market. This squash has tender, tasty flesh, unlike Dorothy's squash, which had a nice orange color but had reverted to the ancient gourd form without edible flesh.

If you decide to be adventurous and save your own cucurbit seeds, be aware that those of muskmelons, watermelons, winter squash, and pumpkins can be saved from the ripe fruits but that cucumbers and summer squash used for seeds should be allowed to mature on the vine. Remember that by allowing a fruit to mature, you will shut down production of harvestable fruits on that particular plant. Let cucumber fruits mature five to six weeks after flowering for the best seeds. Mature cucumbers should be golden yellow with no trace of green. Summer squash should be large, hard, and gourdlike—a state achieved about two months after the young, edible stage. When the fruit is mature, cut it open and scoop out the seeds. Wash them to remove any clinging flesh, dry them on paper towels, and store them in a cool, dry place.

Cucurbits are susceptible to a great variety of insect pests and diseases caused by viruses, bacteria, and fungi. Not only can the insect pests themselves damage foliage and fruit, but they also can carry diseases from plant to plant. For organic gardeners plagued with pests, the best solution is to grow resistant varieties. Plant breeders have developed cucurbits that are resistant to some of the most common fungal diseases, including gummy stem blight (black rot), fusarium wilt, verticillium wilt, anthracnose, and powdery mildew.

Gummy stem blight causes black or brown spots on the leaves and stems. The spots produce a dark gummy substance that gives this disease its name. Both fusarium wilt and verticillium wilt are caused by fungi that block the phloem and cause the plant to wilt. If you cut the stem of a plant infected with one of these wilts, you will find a yellow or brown ring just inside it. Fusarium wilt often will produce brown streaks on one side of the stem. Verticillium wilt causes yellowing between the leaf veins, while fusarium wilt yellows the veins themselves. Anthracnose often causes dark spots on the leaves; these spots fall out, and the fruits develop sunken areas. Powdery mildew forms white or gray powdery spots on the leaves and stems.

Fortunately, many catalog descriptions list the resistances of the varieties they offer. Some cucurbit diseases exist as different strains (called races in seed catalogs),

Cucurbit Problems

RESISTANT VARIETIES OF CUCURBITS

	Disease Resistance*
Cantaloupes and Muskmelons	
Charentais (cantaloupe)	F, M
Edisto	A, DM, PM
Earlisweet Hybrid	F
Vedrantais (cantaloupe)	F, M
Cucumbers	
Marketmore 80	DM, M, PM, S
Poinsett 76	ALS, An, DM, PM, S
Spacemaster	M, S
Sweet Slice Hybrid	PM, S
Watermelons	
Charleston Gray	An, F, Sunburn
Crimson Sweet	An, F
Sweet Favorite	An, F

* Disease resistance or tolerance: A = Alternaria; ALS = angular leaf spot; An = anthracnose; DM = downy mildew; F = fusarium wilt; M = mosaic; PM = powdery mildew; S = scab.

Note: Disease resistance is not as highly desirable a feature in squash as it is in other cucurbits, so very little breeding effort has been directed toward creating resistant squash varieties.

and you may need to know which strains are common in your area. If you can't find a variety resistant to a problem that plagues you, contact your county extension agent or a seed company representative for advice.

CUCUMBERS

With the possible exception of zucchini, cucumbers are the most popular cucurbit among home gardeners. Just about everyone enjoys cool, crisp cucumber slices in their salads, and pickles are a canning favorite. With their modest-size leaves cucumbers take up less space than most other cucurbits, and gardeners pressed for space can choose between bush cucumbers and the traditional vining kinds, which can be grown on a trellis. Homegrown cucumbers come in a variety of sizes, shapes, and flavors not available in supermarkets. In addition, homegrown cucumbers are tender all the way through, unlike those found in supermarkets, which always seem to be full of big, tough seeds.

Cucumber Varieties

Which cucumbers you choose to grow depends on how you plan to use them. There are special varieties for pickling and others for slicing, as well as all-purpose types. Pickling cucumbers must have a firm flesh that will hold its color and shape well. These varieties bear an abundance of small fruits at one time, so you don't have to wait forever to gather enough for a batch of pickles. They are specially bred not to wrinkle, bloat, or float when soaked in brine. Pickling cucumbers guaranteed not to be bitter include 'County Fair 87 Hybrid' and 'Hybrid Fortos,' both of which are good for eating fresh as well as for pickling. If you like the small, sour pickles known as cornichons, you might want to try growing 'De Bourbonne,' 'Gherkins Pariser,' or 'Vert De Massy.' These cucumbers are picked when very small.

Burpless cucumbers are especially good for salads. They are crisp and sweet and don't seem to develop the bitterness that plagues some of the traditional varieties. That bitter flavor is caused by several different chemicals whose production in the fruit is controlled by a whole group of genes, so it is hard for breeders to eliminate the bitter taste from cucumbers. Diane's favorite burpless varieties are 'Euro-American Hybrid,' 'Sweet Slice,' and 'Sweet Success Hybrid.' 'Euro-American Hybrid' is a very early variety that looks like a regular cucumber except that it is slightly thicker in the middle. In addition to enjoying burpless cucumbers fresh, you can use them for making crosscut dill pickles or any other type of sliced or chopped pickles or relish.

If you want to try something a little different, you might grow 'Lemon' cucumbers. These round, prickly yellow fruits have an especially refreshing lemony flavor that matches their bright color.

For gardeners with limited space or a desire for many cucumbers over a short period, bush cucumbers are just the thing. These attractive plants have short internodes, so they form a compact bush with a cluster of pretty yellow flowers rather than a scraggly vine with widely spaced blossoms. Bush varieties will produce slightly more cucumbers per plant than vine types, and the harvest will be more concentrated, which makes them ideal for pickles. 'Picklebush' has only 20- to 24-inch-long vines, while 'Bush Pickle' needs only 3 to 4 feet of space to produce an abundant crop. 'Northern Pickling' is a very early variety that has performed well in Diane's garden. If you prefer slicing bush cucumbers, you might want to try 'Bush Whopper,' 'Park's Burpless Bush Hybrid,' 'Salad Bush Hybrid,' or 'Spacemaster.'

If you are frustrated by all those early male flowers that fall off without accomplishing anything, gynoecious cucumbers may be for you. These specially bred varieties have an abundance of female flowers that bloom earlier than those on conventional cucumbers. Strictly speaking, the term *gynoecious* refers to plants that bear only female flowers, but some cucumber varieties called gynoecious do have a few male flowers as well. When you receive your packet of gynoecious seeds, you will find colored seeds in the packet along with them. These are seeds of a pollinator variety that will produce male flowers to pollinate your female vines. The female flowers should bloom early in the season, right along with the male flowers on the pollinator vines, giving you an early and abundant harvest. Some gynoecious varieties produce especially heavily and are ideal for pickling. Most major seed companies carry a few gynoecious varieties. Some of the more popular ones include 'Saladin,' 'Sweet Slice,' and 'Victory.' Gynoecious pickling varieties include 'Bush Baby,' 'Conquest,' and 'Pickalot Hybrid.' 'Bush Baby' and 'Pickalot Hybrid' are bush varieties.

Some cucumber varieties have been developed especially for greenhouse culture. They have a special group of genes that direct the fruits to develop even if the flowers are not pollinated. Seeds of these varieties are quite expensive, but if you want to grow your cucumbers in a greenhouse or other place where there aren't enough bees to pollinate the flowers, they are worth the investment. If your greenhouse is cool at night, choose a variety such as 'Corona' that is specially bred to produce even with nighttime temperatures as low as 66°F.

B because cucumber plants are smaller than those of some other cucurbits, they can be grown closer together. If you grow vining varieties on the ground, plant them in hills spaced 3 feet apart with three plants to a hill. Vining cucumbers also can be planted in rows 3 feet apart with the plants spaced at 6-inch intervals. Bush cucumbers can be planted in hills or rows 2 feet apart. They also make pleas-

Growing Cucumbers

ing container plants and are attractive enough to be used as foundation plants along the south side of the house.

One of the best ways to grow vining cucumbers is to train them up a trellis. Cucumber vines have grasping tendrils that grow from the leaf axils. When the tendrils are about one-third grown, they become sensitive to contact and will wrap around anything they touch. The tendrils can react quickly, sometimes beginning to twine within twenty seconds after touching a support. If you plant your cucumbers along a trellis, the tendrils will grab hold and the vines will climb up the supports without further assistance.

Trellising is recommended in humid regions because it allows good air circulation, which keeps the plants drier and thus less susceptible to fungal infections. Trellising also minimizes damage from hail and heavy rain. Trellised vines take up far less space than hills, and heat-sensitive crops such as lettuce can be planted in the dappled shade below the vines.

There are other advantages to growing cucumbers vertically. Trellised cucumbers may bear more abundantly, for all the leaves on a trellis can face the sun more directly. Trellising is good for growing long cucumbers such as the burpless, Japanese, and 'Armenian' varieties. When these types are grown on the ground, the fruits often end up curling around because of contact with the soil. On a trellis they grow perfectly straight because the weight of the developing fruit is pulled down by gravity. The fruits of trellised cucumbers also are easier to find than those of ground-grown plants, and damage to the vines while harvesting is minimized.

All these advantages add up to a larger harvest of higher-quality fruits than the traditional hill-planting method produces. When scientists compared trellised plants of the varieties 'Ashley,' 'Fletcher,' and 'High Mark II' with ground-grown ones, they harvested twice as many fruits from the trellised vines. There was a dramatic decrease in scab and soil rot, as well as fewer misshapen culls. Pesticides were used in this study, but the organic gardener will find that it's easier to spot pests such as cucumber beetles on an exposed, trellised vine than on a ground-hugging one. And if you use rotenone or bug-juice sprays, even coverage of trellised vines is easier to accomplish than with hilled plants.

Yield increases also have been found for trellised gynoecious hybrids such as 'Dasher II,' 'Guardian,' 'Poinsett 76,' 'Raider,' and 'Revenue.' Even though many female flowers are produced in these varieties, some flowers abort and others set fruits that do not develop to a full or marketable size. With trellising many more of the flowers set and develop full-size fruits.

Space plants for trellising 6 inches apart in a straight row and anchor the trellis at planting so as not to disturb the roots. A ½-inch metal reinforcing bar about 6 feet long can be used as a very simple trellis for each plant. Pound the bar a foot into the ground and tie the main stem of the plant to the bar two or three times with old nylon stockings or soft cloth strips. The tendrils will do the rest.

When you pick your cucumbers depends on what you plan to do with them. For the crispest pickles, pick the cucumbers young. Two- to 3-inch fruits picked within two days of pickling will give you the crunchiest results. Cucumbers can grow very fast (they may increase in size by 40 percent in only twenty-four hours), so if you are trying to catch them at a particular size, check the vines carefully every day. Cucumbers for fresh eating should be picked before the seeds have developed very far; about 8 to 10 inches is the usual recommended size. Many of the burpless, Japanese, and Armenian varieties can grow to 2 to 3 feet long and still be crisp. These varieties should be picked before they get larger than 2½ inches in diameter.

Use a sharp knife to harvest your cucumbers. Remember, you do not want to damage the plants inadvertently. When searching through ground-grown vines, be careful not to bend them, or you'll injure the phloem, which brings nourishment to the growing fruits. Always remove any overmature cucumbers that have escaped your notice in previous searches.

Cucumbers should be stored at 45°F to 50°F with a relative humidity of 90 to 95 percent. They will keep for fourteen days under these conditions. The refrigerator is too cold for good cucumber storage, as fresh-picked fruits will keep only about a week there. Cucumbers held at too cold a temperature for too long will develop spots that quickly turn into mushy pits.

Harvesting Your Cucumbers

Much cucumber breeding is being done to produce smaller bushes that bear mostly female blossoms. This is an advantage for home gardeners because you don't have to worry about losing your few pollinator vines to insects or disease. Breeders also are developing cucumber varieties that can germinate in lower soil temperatures. Multiple disease resistance is another breeding goal. Scientists have discovered that although humans prefer cucumbers that are not bitter, cucumber beetles like the bitter fruits. The beetles are likely to leave nonbitter varieties alone, thus sparing them from beetle damage and lessening the chances that cucumber wilt, which is spread by the beetles, will infest the garden. An important but so far not very successful goal of breeders is to develop cucumbers that produce all their fruits at one time so that commercial growers can harvest them all at once. Such varieties could come in handy for home gardeners with limited space and for those who want to make pickles.

Cucumber Frontiers

SUMMER SQUASH

Summer squash is a popular home garden crop because it grows rapidly, yields abundantly, and produces early. In northern areas where melons are a challenge and only early varieties of winter squash can be grown, gardeners can experiment successfully with any of the summer squash varieties, for these adaptable plants grow well in nearly all climates. Here in Montana, where even one ripe melon is the sign of a master gardener, everyone seems to have more zucchini in August than he or she can use or give away.

Summer Squash Varieties

One of the great virtues of summer squash is that all are available as high-quality bush varieties. Instead of rambling vines that spread all over the garden, you can have compact hills of plants that grow predictably. Summer squash come in a delightful variety of shapes and colors, with new varieties appearing almost every year. All have a mild, slightly sweet flavor, but their textures vary from the moist, airy yellow squash to the very firm 'Scallopini.'

Several types of summer squash are an attractive bright yellow color. Crookneck squash have a thin, bent stem end and a warty skin. Their texture is quite loose and a bit watery, but their flavor is good. Straightneck yellow squash are similar to crookneck squash, but some newer varieties, such as 'Gold Rush,' show their zucchini ancestry in their smooth skin and firm flesh. This variety and others, such as 'Butterstick' and 'Golden Zucchini,' have a special B gene that causes precocious yellow coloring in both skin and flesh. This gene also makes the squash grow slowly, which is a boon to gardeners who can't check their gardens frequently. Both Dorothy and Diane like to grow yellow and green summer squash and serve the slices together as a colorful side dish with a summer meal.

Zucchini is the most popular summer squash. Some zucchini have a light greenish gray skin, while others are a dark black-green. In recent years summer squash similar to zucchini but with different shapes have been introduced. 'Gourmet Globe' is round, which makes it good for scooping out and stuffing, while 'Scallopini' has a flattened shape with a scalloped edge, like the pale pattypan squash, but with the dark green color of zucchini. 'Scallopini' has firm but tender flesh and keeps longer in storage than some other summer squash. 'Sunburst' is a brilliant yellow pattypan squash whose color comes from the B gene.

If you love to eat the squash blossoms, try 'Butterblossom.' This variety has been specially bred to produce many large male blossoms. Its fruit also is very tasty.

Growing Summer Squash

There is no secret to growing summer squash. Just give it a rich soil, plenty of sunshine, and adequate water, and within two months of planting you'll be harvesting abundant quantities of squash. Because of the compact, bushy growth of summer squash, hills can be spaced as close together as 3 feet, with three plants per hill.

Summer squash must be watched carefully, for the fruits grow very fast. Within four to eight days of pollination a summer squash is ready to pick, and the warmer it is, the faster it grows. The shriveled petals of summer squash flowers retain moisture and are thus an excellent place for fungal growth to start. Since this can spoil the blossom end of the fruit, you should remove the withered petals when the fruit starts to grow. Many gardeners wait until their summer squash are 8 to 10 inches long before picking them, but the earlier you harvest, the firmer and tenderer your squash will be. Picking the fruits regularly also will keep the plants producing. When harvesting summer squash, always cut the stem cleanly with a sharp knife so as not to damage the fruit or the plant.

Summer squash don't keep long in storage, so try to eat or preserve them as they come in. If you must store your summer squash for a few days, remove the withered petals if they are still attached to the fruits. If the fruits are dirty, wash them, dry them carefully, and store them in plastic bags. Try not to break the tender skin. They will keep up to two weeks in the refrigerator or three weeks at 45°F and 80 percent humidity. Summer squash also can be dried or frozen, although the flesh tends to be limp when thawed. Dorothy gets around this problem by shredding her summer squash, salting it with 1 teaspoon of salt per pound, and squeezing out the excess water after a few minutes. She then flattens the flesh and stores it in fold-lock sandwich bags in the freezer, stacking up the bags after the squash is frozen and placing several of them in a larger plastic bag. Summer squash keeps very well this way and can be used in any recipe calling for shredded squash; just leave out the salt.

WINTER SQUASH

There's something especially satisfying about going to the storeroom in the dead of winter and choosing a colorful, sweet winter squash for the evening meal. And while many people are familiar with eating pumpkin seeds (sold in expensive little packets as *pepitas*), not so many people know that squash seeds taste almost the same after they've been roasted in a low oven. The variety of winter squash is dazzling and no wonder: remember that four different plant species produce these versatile fruits!

Some multipurpose varieties of winter squash such as 'Jersey Golden Acorn' and 'Table Queen' can be harvested early and used like summer squash or at the mature stage for winter storage. 'Kuta' is a pale green all-purpose squash that can be eaten when 2 to 8 inches long or left on the plant and cured for winter storage at a larger size. 'Kuta' is a bush squash, which saves space in the garden, and the compact plants can bear harvestable fruit as early as forty-two days after planting.

'Vegetable Spaghetti,' also called 'Spaghetti Squash,' can be harvested in the summer, but don't expect any fruits before seventy days of growth. The squash can be picked green for immediate use or when mature and yellow for winter storage. It will keep until about New Year's Day. 'Vegetable Spaghetti' is still relatively unfamiliar to many gardeners but is gaining friends fast, as it provides a unique eating experience. It is especially popular with dieters, who bake or boil the whole fruit, cut it in half, and scrape out the spaghetti-like strands to serve as a low-calorie substitute for pasta. It's wonderful, just served with a little butter or margarine and Parmesan cheese. 'Orangetti' is a new variety that has an orange rind and orange flesh, compliments of the B gene, making the flesh much higher in vitamin A than the original 'Vegetable Spaghetti.'

There are many types of vining winter squash—too many to cover here. But a few old favorites are 'Table Queen' (sometimes called 'Acorn') and 'Buttercup,' which has a delicate, dry flesh and a sweet, rich flavor. Hubbard squash—with its hard, warty skin and orange-yellow flesh—comes in several types, and its seeds are plentiful, large, and very tasty. All these types of squash store well, often long into spring.

The popular butternut squash, with its bottle shape and small seed cavity, has an interesting genetic history. It arose as a mutant in a field of a winter variety called 'Canada Crookneck.' The new, plumper form became more popular than its parent, since it had the same sweet orange flesh but lacked the long, fragile neck that could break easily in shipping or storage. It turns out, however, that the butternut form is not stable. Under hot growing conditions 5 to 25 percent of the plants may produce long-necked fruits. Some of these plants produce only the crookneck forms, while others produce both fruit shapes. If you have cool nighttime temperatures (60°F or lower), however, the butternut form persists. Through crosses with a C. moschata variety and further careful selection, some butternut varieties have been developed that do not revert to the crookneck form, such as 'Waltham Butternut.' Fortunately, 'Ponca,' the earliest of the butternut varieties, rarely reverts. So if you have hot growing conditions and want only the butternut form, be sure to grow one of the stable varieties.

For those of you with small gardens and a yen for winter squash, breeders have developed several bush varieties of winter squash in recent years. 'Sweet Mama Hybrid' is a prolific variety with smooth flesh that will keep in storage for four months. 'Bush Table Queen' and 'Table King' are bush varieties of acorn squash, while 'Kindred' is a buttercup variety. 'Table King' plants are about 4 feet in diameter, while 'Bush Table Queen' takes up about 3 feet. 'Kindred' sometimes sends out runners that make it look like a vining squash, but these can be clipped off to keep the plants under control. 'Gold Nugget' is a fast-maturing (eighty-five days) sweet bush squash that forms small, 1- to 2-pound fruits.

Bush varieties of winter squash can be grown like bush summer squash, but the vining kinds need a lot more room. In long-season areas winter squash and pumpkins can be planted among the corn rows to conserve space. This method won't do for short-season gardeners, however, because the vigorous squash vines will take over, robbing the corn of nutrients and sunlight.

Winter squash are traditionally planted in hills spaced 6 to 8 feet apart. The wider the spacing, the larger the ultimate size of the fruits. If you want small squash instead of big ones, plant your hills closer together. Just be sure that the soil has plenty of rich organic matter and keep the plants well watered. More closely spaced plants will need more water than those that are farther apart.

Vining winter squash can be grown on trellises to save space, as they have branched tendrils that enable them to hang on to a trellis even when laden with fruits. If the fruits get really big, they can be supported in slings made from old sheets tied to the trellis supports.

Use your imagination when planting winter squash. For example, their rambling vines can be used to cover rocky, unlandscaped ground. As long as the roots are anchored in rich, moist soil, the vines can spread out anywhere, covering unsightly areas while providing the family with a tasty harvest. Dorothy has a friend who routinely uses vining winter squash to reduce his weed problems. Although the plants must be weeded during the first part of growth, once they take off, the rampant vines will smother most weeds.

Growing Winter Squash

Winter squash should be allowed to ripen fully on the vine before picking. It may take six weeks for the fruit to mature. Wait until the skin is hard (so you can't pierce it with your fingernail) and the stem is tough and woody. Cut the stem as long as possible when you harvest, and *do not* carry the squash by the stem. If the stem breaks off, the area around it will be vulnerable to bacteria and fungi. If the squash are dirty, wash them with water or a solution of 1 part household bleach to 3 parts water and dry them thoroughly. If the weather forces you to harvest some of your squash before they are fully mature, plan on eating those first, as they won't keep for long.

Many sources recommend curing winter squash before storage, but others say it isn't necessary. If you plan on storing your squash in a place with an unregulated atmosphere such as your basement, you are better off curing it first. Cure the squash at 80°F to 85°F for ten days at a relative humidity of 80 percent, then place them in storage. The best storage conditions are a temperature of 50°F to 60°F and low humidity. Depending on the variety your squash should keep for three to eight months. Check them often, and if some fruits of one variety begin to deteriorate, use that kind up as soon as possible. If you notice mold on any of the squash, discard them immediately to keep it from spreading.

Harvesting and Storing Winter Squash

The U.S. Department of Agriculture (USDA) recommends that winter squash *not* be cured. In fact, it claims that curing damages 'Table Queen,' changing its color and causing a loss of flavor. The USDA says that curing has no effect on the storage life and quality of other varieties. It recommends storing Hubbard squash at 50°F to 55°F and a relative humidity of 70 to 75 percent and butternut and acorn squash at 50°F and 50 percent humidity. The USDA also advises growers to remove the stems of Hubbard squash completely before storing and not to store this variety near apples, for they may cause the squash skin to yellow.

Squash Frontiers

Although most cucurbits require a lot of water to produce well, some wild squash can grow with surprisingly little water. Squash breeders are trying to incorporate this trait into cultivated varieties without bringing along the bitterness of wild squash. Seeds of wild squash also are very high in protein. If this quality could be bred into domestic squash, their seeds could be as valuable a crop as the fruits themselves.

PUMPKINS

Although people think of pumpkins as being very different from squash, they belong to the same species as many winter squash varieties, so most of the recommendations for winter squash also apply to pumpkins. Pumpkins, with their tender skin, do not keep in storage as long as some winter squash. Don't worry if you have to pick some pumpkins while they are still green; the skin will develop a rich orange color in storage. Despite the poems about frost on the pumpkin, these vegetables can't take much cold, so both pumpkins and winter squash should be picked before temperatures go below 30°F.

Pumpkin Varieties

Which pumpkins you grow depends on why you are growing them and on how much space you have in your garden. 'Autumn Gold' is a new variety that has the precocious yellow B gene, making it yellow right from the beginning of fruit formation. If you want very large fruit, try 'Big Max' or 'Big Moon.' For pies, grow one of the sugar varieties famous for their fine-textured, sweet flesh. 'Jack O'Lantern' was developed especially for Halloween, while 'Lady Godiva' and 'Naked Seeded' produce hull-less seeds for easy eating. 'Triple Treat' is an all-purpose pumpkin with naked seeds and sweet golden flesh; its round shape also makes it a good candidate for carving. There are a few semibush varieties for the small garden, such as 'Cheyenne,' 'Funny Face Hybrid,' and 'Spirit Hybrid.'

MUSKMELONS

For most of us the word *melon* conjures up an image of a juicy watermelon or cantaloupe. But the melon known as cantaloupe in North America is really not a cantaloupe at all; it is properly called a muskmelon. Our muskmelons have a musky aroma that true cantaloupes and honeydew, Crenshaw, and casaba melons lack. Real cantaloupes (such as the varieties 'Charentais' and 'Vedrantais') are rarely grown in North America because their seeds have only recently become available here.

Despite their differences, all these melons belong to the species *Cucumis melo*, which has three subgroups. The true cantaloupes belong to the group *cantalupensis*, while the muskmelons are in the group *reticulatus*, a word that refers to the netting on the skin. Honeydew, Crenshaw, and casaba melons belong to the third group, *inodorus*, so named because these melons lack the powerful muskmelon aroma. Since the three groups belong to the same species, it should be no surprise that, like cabbage and kale, they cross-pollinate freely. Breeders have experimented in recent years with crossing true cantaloupes with muskmelons because the former have some built-in resistance to mosaic virus and fusarium wilt. Varieties such as 'Chaca' are hybrids of true cantaloupes and muskmelons. These melons do well in many areas, even here in Montana.

Muskmelons are more closely related to cucumbers (*Cucumis sativus*) than to watermelons (*Citrullus lanatus*), which is evident when you look at the plants. The leaves are similar to cucumber leaves in size and shape, and the vines grow in much the same way as cucumber vines. Because of their smaller leaves and shorter vines, muskmelons take up less space in the garden than winter squash or watermelons. And since nothing you can buy in the supermarket matches the flavor of homegrown, vine-ripened muskmelons, you should by all means give them a try.

Muskmelon Varieties

Like so many other crops, muskmelons can now be grown in northern gardens and in small gardens. 'Chaca,' which has rich, juicy, salmon-colored flesh, has a relatively small vine and matures in seventy-five days. Like its European parent, it is resistant to powdery mildew and fusarium wilt. 'Earlisweet Hybrid' and 'Flyer' (a French 'Charentais'-type melon) are ready for picking in seventy days. Diane has had good success with 'Earligold' because the large (about 4 pounds), sweet fruits mature easily in Montana's short growing season. For people with small gardens a few compact varieties with small vines are available. 'Minnesota Midget' matures in only sixty-five days and has vines that grow only 3 feet long (standard varieties spread 4 or more feet). This variety produces an abundance of small (4 inch diameter) fruits.

If you live where the growing season is longer, ask your county extension agent which diseases or strains tend to plague muskmelons in your area and buy varieties that are resistant to those diseases or strains. While many catalogs don't list all the disease resistances of their varieties, you should be able to find out from the seed company which ones are most resistant to common diseases in your area.

Resistance is especially important in muskmelons, for diseases tend to strike right as the melons are ripening. Infections clog the phloem and interrupt the vital flow of sugars to the fruits, resulting in bland, disappointing melons. Try 'Summet' if you have multiple disease problems, as it is resistant to fusarium wilt, downy mildew, and one or more races of powdery mildew. 'Aurora' is a good variety for the South because it is tolerant of gummy stem disease and resistant to downy mildew and powdery mildew. It produces thick-fleshed, 4-pound-plus melons.

When you first start out with muskmelons, it's a good idea to grow two varieties. If they have different maturation times, you will be extending your harvest and also will increase your chances of getting a harvest from healthy plants. If you find that one variety doesn't do well in your garden and the other does, grow the successful one the following year along with a new choice. After a few years you should be reaping abundant harvests of sweet, juicy melons.

Growing, Harvesting, and Storing Muskmelons

Grow your muskmelons just as you would cucumbers. The ideal spacing between plants is 18 inches in all directions. This spacing allows the vines to overlap and shade out weeds. Although each vine will produce fewer melons than if the spacing were wider, your total yield will be greater. To save space, muskmelons can be trained to grow up a trellis if the fruits are tied up in slings so they don't fall off or snap their stems when ripe. Muskmelons also can be planted by the traditional hill method. These plants crave heat, so you should use black plastic mulch and row covers as described earlier in this chapter for the earliest, most abundant harvests.

After your melon plants have set fruit, don't be alarmed if some of the melons shrivel up and disappear when they are about the size of a chicken egg. This is the normal response of the plant; it allows only as many melons to grow to full size as it can support. The nutrients present in the shriveled-up fruits are reabsorbed by the plant and redistributed to the melons that will mature. Whenever you must handle the vines, do so with special care, for they are even more sensitive than cucumber vines.

Most muskmelons are ripe when a crack appears between the stem and the fruit; the fruit is said to have reached full slip when it separates easily from the vine. You'll notice a strong musky odor around the stem end, and the netting will be very pronounced. That is the best time to take the melon inside and eat it.

When the fruit is picked, it begins to respire, slowly using up the sugars stored in its sweet flesh. Refrigerate any fruits that you don't eat right away to slow respiration. They will keep there (preferably at a relative humidity of 85 to 90 percent) for five to fourteen days.

True cantaloupes, honeydews, casabas, and Crenshaws do not slip when ripe or develop the distinctive musky aroma, so it's a bit more difficult to tell when they are ready to pick. When they're ripe, the blossom end feels a bit soft when pressed firmly with your thumb. The skin of honeydews changes from pale blue-green to a lighter ivory or cream color. Hybrids such as 'Chaca' should be harvested at half slip, when the stem just begins to separate from the fruit.

In the future you may be able to purchase a simple hand-held light meter that will tell you whether your melon is ready to be picked. Scientists in Athens, Georgia, developed this special device, and some enterprising companies are looking at ways to make it practical for home use.

Honeydew, Crenshaw, and casaba melons should not be stored in the refrigerator because the cold will damage their flesh. Store them at 45°F to 50°F if possible, keeping the relative humidity at 85 to 90 percent. Honeydew melons can be stored up to four weeks. As they sit in the sun, they often turn light yellow on top. Scientists have found that fruits with this yellowing stand refrigeration better than those without it.

WATERMELONS

Nothing tastes better on a sweltering August afternoon than a juicy slice of cool, sweet, field-ripened watermelon. For many years most gardeners couldn't afford the luxury of providing the large amount of space needed to grow this finicky crop, and the climates where many of us live made growing watermelons a forbidding challenge. But the development of bush watermelons and early-maturing varieties has made this tasty crop at least worth trying in most North American gardens.

There are dozens of watermelon varieties, but once you know what sort of fruit you want and what special conditions your garden offers, you can narrow down choices quite easily. If you have a hankering for the biggest melons, try 'Black Diamond' (also called 'Cannonball' and 'Florida Giant'). In favorable climates this variety consistently produces 50-pound melons. Check with your county extension agent to find out if any diseases are prevalent among watermelons in your area and select resistant varieties.

You can choose between round and cylindrical melons, striped and plain ones,

Watermelon Varieties

yellow and red flesh, and big and small ones. Growing the small "icebox" type weighing 5 to 10 pounds is a real advantage if you don't have a large refrigerator. Yellow-fleshed varieties include 'Yellow Baby,' an early small melon, and the drought-resistant 'Desert King.' If you don't like to spit out a lot of seeds, choose a small-seeded variety such as 'Hybrid Dixie Queen.' Or you might want to try a variety such as 'Extra Early Sugar Baby' that has fewer seeds than other varieties. The ultimate watermelon for seed haters is one of the seedless types, such as 'Jack of Hearts' or 'Nova.'

Seedless varieties were developed by Japanese breeders through a costly, complex process that involves artificially creating a watermelon that cannot crossbreed with other varieties to produce viable seeds. For this reason the seeds are very expensive, often costing 15 cents or more each. While these fruits have no seeds, they do contain some empty white seed coats that can be swallowed. Only small-seeded watermelons are used in breeding seedless varieties because the larger-seeded types would leave a large, empty seed coat that would be as much of a nuisance as a seed.

Seedless watermelons, like gynoecious cucumbers, are sold with extra seeds from a pollinator variety. Plant one pollinator for every five seedless plants, and be sure to mark which plants are pollinators so you will know which melons are seedless come harvest time. (The pollinator plants will produce melons with seeds.)

For gardeners with limited space, bush watermelons such as 'Golden Crown,' 'Sugar Bush,' and 'Sweet Treat' are the answer. These plants need only 6 square feet of garden space, and each vine produces two to four small melons. 'Golden Crown' is a very early variety (it will mature in Montana) and has a bright yellow rind, so the melons look like giant eggs nestled in gray-green foliage nests. Other early varieties are 'Sugar Baby' and 'Yellow Baby.' Watermelon breeders are continuing their search for disease-resistant plants and for varieties that take up less space and produce smaller, more abundant melons.

Growing, Harvesting, and Storing Watermelons

Watermelons need even more room than other cucurbits. They are traditionally grown in hills about 10 feet apart with three plants to a hill, but they also can be grown in rows, with each plant having 6 feet to itself in all directions. Another spacing arrangement is to place individual plants 5 feet apart within the row and to leave 10 feet between rows. Bush varieties can be grown in rows with 2½ feet separating the plants or in hills about 5 feet apart. Just as with muskmelons, watermelons require heat, so if possible use black plastic and row covers as described earlier in this chapter.

Knowing when a watermelon is ripe takes some practice. The fruit needs twenty to thirty-six days after flowering to mature. When you thump a melon, it makes a different sound when ripe than when unripe. If the melon isn't ready to harvest, it will sound solid. But when you knock on a ripe melon, you'll hear a hollow thud. Experimenting with your melons will help you distinguish between the two sounds. Some varieties, such as 'Charleston Gray,' lose some of their glossiness when ripe, and the part of the rind that touches the soil turns yellow.

Try to eat your watermelons soon after they're picked, as they do not store well. If you have to store them for a while, the best conditions are a temperature of 40°F to 50°F and a relative humidity of 80 to 85 percent. Don't expect to keep them for more than two weeks. Your melons will lose their red color in cold storage, but if you keep them at room temperature for a few days, the redness will intensify.

Melon Frontiers

Scientists are continuing to develop smaller watermelons and are experimenting with crosses between different kinds of melon, such as honeydew and true cantaloupe. Increasing drought resistance is another goal, as some of the wild types of watermelon show great resistance to drought. With research being done in these and other areas, such as disease resistance, home gardeners can look forward to having even more success with melon crops in the future.

SEED AND PLANT SUPPLIERS

There are more than two hundred garden seed suppliers in the United States and Canada. Many of them specialize in one type of vegetable (such as Roninger's Seed Potatoes) or in one region of the country (such as Johnny's Selected Seeds for the North). We have selected some of the more generalized suppliers and included a few specialists. For a complete list of suppliers, refer to the *Garden Seed Inventory*, compiled by Kent Whealy, and available from the Seed Savers Exchange (see "Further Reading" for the address). The code in parentheses following each name is used in the list of vegetable varieties to indicate seed sources.

W. Atlee Burpee Company (BP)
300 Park Avenue
Warminster, PA 18991

Wide variety of vegetable and flower seeds; some plants and garden supplies. Catalog free

The Cook's Garden (CG)
Box 65
Londonderry, VT 05148

Specializes in salad vegetables, including many lettuce varieties and unusual greens, but also has some other vegetables. Catalog $1.00

Earl May Seed & Nursery Company (EM)
Shenandoah, IA 51603

Offers a variety of seeds and some plants. Catalog free

Farmer Seed & Nursery Company (FM)
Department 77
Reservation Center
2207 East Oakland Avenue
Bloomington, IL 61701

Specializes in hardy varieties for the North. Catalog free

Garden City Seeds (GC)
P.O. Box 297
Victor, MT 59875

Nonprofit company specializing in untreated seeds for northern climates. Catalog $1.00

Gurney's Seed & Nursery Company (GY)
Yankton, SD 57079

Emphasizes varieties for the upper Midwest, offering seeds, plants, and garden supplies. Catalog free

Harris Seeds (HR)
961 Lyell Avenue
Rochester, NY 14606

Offers a variety of vegetable and flower seeds. Catalog free

Hastings (HS)
P.O. Box 115535
Atlanta, GA 30310

Specializes in varieties for the South. Catalog free

Henry Field Seed & Nursery (HF)
Shenandoah, IA 51602

General seed, plant, and garden supply catalog. Catalog free

High Altitude Gardens (HA)
P.O. Box 4238
Ketchum, ID 83340

Specializes in hardy varieties adapted to cold mountain climates, including 200 kinds of herb plants. Catalog $2.00

Johnny's Selected Seeds (JS)
305 Foss Hill Road
Albion, ME 04910

Seeds for northern climates; especially informative catalog. Catalog free

Jung Seeds & Nursery (JU)
335 S. High Street
Randolph, WI 53957

Long-time company with general catalog of seeds, plants, and supplies. Catalog free

Le Jardin du Gourmet (LJ)
West Danville, VT 05873

Gourmet seeds plus a variety of shallots. Catalog $.50

Lockhart Seeds, Inc. (LH)
P.O. Box 1361
Stockton, CA 95205

General catalog emphasizing varieties for California climates. Catalog free

McFayden Seeds (MC)
P.O. Box 1800
Brandon, Manitoba R7A 6N4
Canada

Specializes in northern varieties. Catalog free

Nichols Garden Nursery (NG)
1190 N. Pacific Highway
Albany, OR 97321

Large selection of herbs and vegetables, including rare and unusual varieties; garden supplies and dried herbs. Catalog free

Park Seed Company (PK)
Cokesbury Road
Greenwood, SC 29647

Flower and vegetable seeds, including southern varieties. Catalog free

Roninger's Seed Potatoes (RO)
Star Route
Moyie Springs, ID 83845

Organically grown seed potatoes and eyes; more than 100 varieties offered. Catalog $1.00

Stokes Seeds Inc. (ST)
Box 548
Buffalo, NY 14240

Very large selection of garden seeds; informative catalog. Catalog free

Thompson & Morgan (TM)
P.O. Box 1308
Jackson, NJ 08527

Specializes in European varieties of vegetables and flowers. Catalog free

Tomato Growers Supply Company (TG)
P.O. Box 2237
Fort Myers, FL 33902

Large selection of tomato and pepper varieties; supplies. Catalog free

William Dam Seeds Ltd. (WD)
Box 8400
Dundas, Ontario L9H 6M1
Canada

Many European varieties unavailable elsewhere. Catalog free in Canada, $1.00 in United States

VEGETABLE VARIETIES

The following list, arranged by chapter in the book, indicates sources for seeds of the varieties recommended. The listings were taken from the 1990 catalogs; seed companies often change their offerings from year to year to reflect the popularity of different varieties and the availability of new ones. In some cases, especially with new varieties discussed under the frontiers sections of the chapters, seeds may not have been available for the home gardener at the time of writing but should appear in seed catalogs soon. Varieties listed with a question mark (?) were not available from any of these suppliers at the time of writing. Varieties listed as *Wide* are widely available. The names of the varieties are sometimes spelled slightly differently in various catalogs, and the word *hybrid* may be added or omitted from the name.

Chapter 5

LETTUCE
Anuenue (JS)
Arctic King (CG)
Bibb (BP, CG, NG, PK)
Biondo Lisce (CG)
Black Seeded Simpson (Wide)
Brune d'Hiver (CG)
Buttercrunch (Wide)
Calmar (?)
Canasta (JS)
Climax (?)
Deer Tongue (CG, GC)
Garnet (JS)
Grand Rapids (Wide)
Great Lakes (Wide)
Green Ice (BP, EM, JU, PK)
Ithaca (Wide)
Mission (PK)
Oak Leaf (Wide)
Parris Island Cos (Wide)
Pirat (Wide)
Prizehead (Wide)
Red Sails (Wide)
Red Salad Bowl (Wide)
Romaine (GY, JU)
Ruby (BP, EM)
Salad Bowl (Wide)
Salinas [Saladin] (TM)
Tom Thumb (Wide)
Valdor (TM)
Valverde (?)
Vanguard (LH)
Winter Density (CG, GC, JS)
Wintergreen (?)

SPINACH
America (EM, ST)
Cold Resistant Savoy (ST)
Dixie Savoy (?)

Fall Green (?)
Giant Winter (WD)
Hybrid No. 7 (FM, NG)
Melody Hybrid (Wide)
Nobel (HF)
Tyee (Wide)
Winter Bloomsdale (HA)

Chapter 6

CABBAGE
Autoro (JS)
Bravo (HR)
Copenhagen Market (BP, EM, HF, LH)
Early Jersey Wakefield (Wide)
Golden Acre (Wide)
Green Jewel Hybrid (PK)
Hybrid O-S Cross (EM)
Jersey Wakefield (GU, JU)
Lariat (JS)
Quick-Green Storage (ST)
Quickstep (JS, TM)
Red Perfection (?)
Ruby Ball (Wide)
Ruby Perfection (JU, ST)
Savoy Ace Hybrid (BP, FM, JU)
Savoy King (EM, NG, TM)
Spivoy Hybrid (PK)
Survivor (ST)

KALE
Dwarf Blue Curled Scotch
 [Vates] (EM, JU, PK)
Peacock Red (?)
Red Russian (GC, NG)
Siberian (GC, HA)

Note: Ornamental types are widely available and are usually offered in the flower section of the catalogs.

COLLARDS
Blue Max (?)
Champion (HS, ST)
Georgia (EM, LH, NG, PK)
Hicrop Hybrid (PK)
Vates (Wide)

BRUSSELS SPROUTS
Achilles (TM)
Citadel F1 Hybrid (TM)
Early Dwarf Danish (GC, HA)
Jade Cross E Hybrid (Wide)
Oliver Hybrid (BP, HS, JS)
Widgeon (JS)

KOHLRABI
Express Forcer (PK)
Giant Purple (MC)
Giant White Super Schmelz (MC)
Gigante (NG)
Grand Duke Hybrid (Wide)
Kolpak (JS)

CAULIFLOWER
Alverda (JS)
Burgundy Queen (ST)
Garant (TM)
Green Broccoli Type Cauliflower (MC)
Predominant (TM)
Snow Crown Hybrid (Wide)
Violet Queen (CG, JS, ST)

BROCCOLI
Bronzino (CG, MC)
Citation (HS)
Early Emerald Hybrid (PK)
Emperor (JS, LH, PK, ST)
Eureka (?)
Green Dwarf #36 (PK)
Green Hornet (ST)
Green Valiant (JS, LH, ST)
Italian [Green] Sprouting

[Calabrese] (CG, PK, ST)
Minaret (JS)
Northwest Waltham (?)
Packman (Wide)
Premium Crop (Wide)
Romanesco (Wide)
Rosalind (TM)
Saga (JS)
Southern Comet (?)
Spartan Early (?)
Waltham 29 (EM, GC)

Chapter 7

ONIONS
Autumn Spice (ST)
Buffalo (TM)
Creole C-5 (HS)
Crystal Wax (BP, PK)
Early Yellow Globe (Wide)
Ebenezer (NG)
Excel 986 (?)
Express Yellow F-1 (?)
Fiesta 61 (HR, LH, ST)
Granex (PK)
Granex Yellow F-1 (?)
Italian Blood Red Bottle
   [Torpedo] (LH, NG)
Keepwell F-1 Hybrid (TM)
Red Bermuda (?)
Red Creole (LH)
Redman (JS)
Sentinel (?)
Southport Red Globe (GY, JU, ST)
Southport Yellow Globe (?)
Sweet Sandwich (Wide)
Sweet Spanish, Yellow Utah
   (EM, FM, LH, NG)
Texas Early Grano 502 (LH)
Top Keeper F-1 (?)
Walla Walla Sweet (Wide)
White Lisbon (ST, TM)

EGYPTIAN ONION (LJ, TM)

POTATO ONION (?)

EVER-READY ONION (?)

SHALLOTS
Dutch (JS, NG, TM)
French (BP, EM, HF, JU)
Frog-legged (LJ)

GARLIC (Wide)
Rocambole (LJ, NG)

ELEPHANT GARLIC (Wide)

Note: Good sources for several garlic varieties and multiplier onions are Kalmia, P.O. Box 3881, Charlottesville, VA 22903 (catalog free) and S & H Organic Acres, P.O. Box 757, Newberg, OR 97132 (catalog free).

LEEKS
King Richard (CG, GC, HA, JS)
Nebraska (JS)

JAPANESE BUNCHING ONIONS
Beltsville Bunching (ST)
Delta Giant (?)
He-Shi-Ko (FM, GY, HF, NG)
Ishikura [Long] (JS, ST, TM)
Kujo Green Multistalk (JS)
Lousiana Evergreen (?)
[Sakata's] Evergreen White (PK)

CHIVES (Wide)

GARLIC CHIVES (BP, CG, NG, ST)

Chapter 8

RADISHES
April Cross Hybrid (NG, PK, TM)
Black Spanish (FM, JU, NG, ST)
Cherry Belle (Wide)
China Rose (EM, HF, JU, ST)
Comet (LH, ST)
Crimson Giant (HF, LH)
Easter Egg (Wide)
Icicle (EM)
Mino Spring Cross (JS)
Miyashiga (JS, NG)
Parat [German Giant] (GY, HF)
Plum Purple (PK)
Saxa (GY, HF)
Sparkler (EM)
White Icicle (Wide)

BEETS
Albine Veredura (CG, ST, TM)
Baby Canning (GY)
[Burpee's] Golden Beet (Wide)
Chiogga (CG, JS)
Cylindra (Wide)
Detroit Dark Red (Wide)
Dwergina (CG, HA, JS)
Early Wonder (Wide)
Formanova (CG, JS)
Little Egypt (ST)
Little Mini Ball (ST)
Long Season (CG, GY, HR, ST)
Lutz [Lutz Green Leaf] (Wide)
Mobile (JS)
Red Ace (Wide)

Replata (CG, TM)
Vermilion (ST)
Winter Keeper (ST, TM)

SWISS CHARD
Swiss Chard of Geneva (PK)
Perpetual [Spinach] (CG)

CARROTS
A+ [A-Plus] Hybrid (Wide)
Danvers Half Long (Wide)
Gregory (TM)
Imperator (BP, FM)
Ingot (JS, ST)
Lindoro Hybrid (PK)
Little Finger (BP, EM, JU, LH)
Minicor (Wide)
Oxheart (GC)
Parmex (JS)
Royal Chantenay (Wide)
Scarlet Nantes (Wide)

Chapter 9

POTATOES
Bliss Triumph (RO)
Butte (GY, HF, RO)
Centennial Russet (RO)
Early Gem (RO)
German Fingerling (JU)
Kennebec (Wide)
Levitts Pink (GY, RO)
Nooksack (GC, GY, RO)
Norchip (?)
Norgold Russet (FM, GY, HF, RO)
Norland (Wide)
Purple Peruvian (GC, RO)
Red Pontiac (Wide)
Russet Burbank (Wide)
Targhee (?)
Yellow Finn (GC, RO)

Chapter 10

GREEN BEANS
Blue Lake [pole] (Wide)
Blue Lake Bush (Wide)
Bush Kentucky Wonder (GY, HS)
Bush Romano [Roma] (Wide)
Commodore [bush] (HF)
Contender [bush] (EM, GY, HF, ST)
Daisy [bush] (HF, GY, HS)
Gator Green [bush] (ST)
Greencrop [bush] (BP, GC, PK)
Hystyle [bush] (HS)
Kentucky Wonder [pole] (Wide)
Legacy [bush] (?)

Oregon Giant [pole] (GC)
Oregon Trail [bush] (NG)
Provider [bush] (GC, HA, JS, PK)
Remus [bush] (PK, TM)
Romano Pole (Wide)
Tendercrop [bush] (GY, HF, NG, PK)
Tenderette (Wide)
Tendergreen [bush] (Wide)
Topcrop [bush] (Wide)

WAX BEANS
Beurre de Rocquencourt (CG, GC)
Cherokee Wax (Wide)
Goldcrop Wax [Gold Crop] (Wide)
Golden Wax (Wide)
Pencil Pod Black Wax (FM, GC, GY, JU)
Rocdor (GC, JS, NG, ST)
Sunglow (?)
Top Notch Golden Wax (FM)

PURPLE BEANS
Royal Burgundy (Wide)
Royalty (FM, GC, JS)

DRY BEANS
Black Turtle [Soup] (GY, PK)
Great Northern (Wide)
Jacob's Cattle [Trout] (GC, JS)
Maine Yellow Eye (JS)
Midnight Black Turtle (BP, GC, JS)
Navy (GC, GY)
Red Kidney (Wide)
Squaw Yellow (GC)

ALL-PURPOSE
Dwarf Horticultural (BP, EM, GY, WD)
Limelight (JS, TM)

LIMA BEANS
Carolina [Sieva] [pole] (HF, HS)
Christmas [pole] (EM, LH, NG, PK)
Eastland [bush] (HR, HS, PK)
Florida (Speckled) Butter [pole] (HF, HS)
Fordhook 242 [bush] (Wide)
Geneva [bush] (JS)
Henderson Bush Lima (Wide)
King of the Garden [pole] (GY, JU, PK, ST)
Thorogreen [bush] (EM, FM, JU, NG)

GARDEN PEAS
Alaska (EM, FM, GY, JS)
Alderman [Tall Telephone] (Wide)
Daybreak (JS, TM)
Green Arrow (Wide)
Knight (GC, HS, JS)
Lincoln (Wide)
Maestro (Wide)
Novella (Wide)

Wando (Wide)

SNOW PEAS
Dwarf Gray Sugar (Wide)
Mammoth Melting [Sugar] (BP, BY, LH)
Snowbird (BP)

SNAP PEAS
Sugar Bon (BP, LH, PK)
Sugar Daddy (Wide)
Sugar Mel (CG, LH, PK)
Sugar Rae (HS)
Sugar Snap (Wide)

Chapter 11
CORN
Bonanza (?)
Country Gentleman (GY, HS, NG)
Crusader (ST)
Earlivee (FM, GC, HA, JS)
Earlivee II (ST)
Golden Cross Bantam (Wide)
How Sweet It Is (Wide)
Iochief (BP, FM)
Kandy Korn (Wide)
Merit (?)
Miracle (BP, FM, LH, NG)
Norgold (ST)
Northern Xtra Sweet (FM, JS, JU, ST)
Precocious (ST)
Silver Queen (Wide)
Sugar Buns (Wide)
Sweet Desire (ST)
Sweet Dreams (ST)
Sweetie 70 (ST)
Sweetie 73 (ST)
Sweetie 76 (ST)
Sweetie 82 (BU, JU, LH)
Tuxedo (JS, ST)

Chapter 12
TOMATOES
Burpeana Early Hybrid (TG)
Campbell's 17 (?)
Celebrity (Wide)
Duke (TG)
Early Cascade Hybrid (FM, JS, NG)
Early Girl Hybrid (Wide)
Gem [State] (HA, JS)
Heinz 1350 (BP, ST, TG)
Marion (PK, TG)
Nova (GC, HA, ST)
Oregon Spring (GC, HA, JS, NG)
Santiam (GC, NG)
Sub-Arctic Maxi (GC, JS, ST, TG)

Sunripe [Hybrid] (TG)
Sweet 100 (Wide)

Chapter 13
HOT PEPPERS
Anaheim (Wide)
Ancho [Poblano] (BP, LH, NG, TG)
Argentine Wonder (?)
Cayenne (BP, CG, FM)
Hungarian Yellow Wax (Wide)
Jalapeño (Wide)
Long Red Cayenne (GC, GY, NG, ST)
Pequin (?)
Red Chili (EM, FM, HF)
Serrano (Wide)
Tabasco (LJ, TG)

Note: A good source for chili peppers is Horticultural Enterprises, P.O. Box 810082, Dallas, TX 75381 (catalog free), which carries varieties such as 'Colorado' and 'Floral Gem' that are hard to find elsewhere.

SWEET PEPPERS
Ace [Hybrid] (BP, JS, ST)
Big Bertha (Wide)
California Wonder (Wide)
Canape Hybrid (HS, NG, TM)
Cubanelle (GC, PK, ST, TG)
Dutch Treat (?)
Italian Sweet (Horticultural Enterprises)
Keystone Resistant (EM)
Ladybell (HS)
Lipstick (JS)
Oakview Wonder (?)
Sweet Banana (Wide)
Sweet Chocolate (CG, HA, JS)
Tokyo Bell (EM)

Chapter 14
PICKLING CUCUMBERS
Bush Baby (ST)
Bush Pickle (Wide)
Conquest (JS)
County Fair 87 Hybrid (PK)
De Bourbonne (CG)
Gherkins Pariser (BP)
Hybrid Fortos (PK)
Northern Pickling (JS)
Pickalot Hybrid (BP)
Picklebush (BP)
Vert De Massy (JS, NG)

SLICING CUCUMBERS
Armenian (BP, HF, LH, NG)
Bush Whopper (PK)

Corona (ST)
Euro-American Hybrid (PK)
Guardian (?)
Lemon (CG, GC, HF)
Marketmore 80 (Wide)
Park's Burpless Bush Hybrid (PK)
Poinsett 76 (GU, LH, JU, PK)
Raider (HS)
Revenue (ST)
Salad Bush Hybrid (Wide)
Saladin (EM, FM, PK)
Spacemaster (BP, GC, JS, ST)
Sweet Slice [Hybrid] (Wide)
Sweet Success Hybrid (Wide)
Victory (ST)

SUMMER SQUASH
Aristocrat [Zucchini] (EM, JU, LH, NG)
Butterblossom (Wide)
Butterstick (BP)
Cocozelle (Wide)
Golden Zucchini (BP)
Gold Rush (Wide)
Gormet Globe (EM, LH, PK)
Scallopini (LH)
Sunburst (Wide)
Vegetable Marrow (GU; bush type from
  ST & WD)
White Bush Scallop (NG)

WINTER SQUASH
Bush Buttercup (FM, JU)
Buttercup (Wide)
Butternut (LJ)
Golden Hubbard (ST)
Gold Nugget (GU, ST)
Green Striped Cushaw (GY, HF)
Hubbard (LH)
Kindred (?)
Orangetti (HF, HS, NG, PK)
Pink Banana (GC, BY, HF, LH)
Ponca (JS)
Sweet Mama Hybrid (EM, FM, LH, PK)
Sweet Meat (GC, HS)
Table King (Wide)
Vegetable Spaghetti [Spaghetti Squash]
  (Wide)
Waltham Butternut (Wide)

DUAL-PURPOSE
Bush Table Queen (BP, JU)
Jersey Golden Acorn (Wide)
Kuta (PK)
Table Queen [Acorn] (Wide)

PUMPKINS
Autumn Gold (Wide)
Big Max (Wide)
Big Moon (PK)
Cheyenne (?)
Funny Face Hybrid (?)
Jack O'Lantern (Wide)
Lady Godiva (WD)
Naked Seeded (CG, ST)
Spirit Hybrid (Wide)
Triple Treat (BP)

MUSKMELONS AND CANTALOUPES
Aurora (HS)
Casaba (LH)
Chaca (NG)
Charentais (JS, NG)
Chilton (?)
Crenshaw (EM, HF, LH)
Earlisweet Hybrid (EM, FM, NG)
Edisto (PK)
Flyer (JS)
Honeydew (EM, JU, LH, NG)
Minnesota Midget (FM, GC, GY, TM)
Summet (LH, ST)
Vedrantais (?)

WATERMELONS
Black Diamond [Cannonball, Florida
  Giant] (Wide)
Charleston Gray (Wide)
Crimson Sweet (EM, GU, JG)
Desert King (GY)
Extra Early Sugar Baby (?)
Golden Crown (?)
Hybrid Dixie Queen (EM, HF)
Jack of Hearts (EM, JU, PK)
Nova (BP)
Sugar Baby (Wide)
Sugar Bush (HF)
Sweet Favorite (JU)
Sweet Treat (BP)
Yellow Baby (BP, HS, PK, ST)

GLOSSARY

Annual: a plant that completes its life cycle in one growing season.

Aphid: a tiny brown or green sucking insect usually found in groups on succulent parts of plants or on leaf undersides.

Anther: the top part of the stamen that contains the pollen.

Apical tip: the region of actively dividing and growing cells at the top of the stem.

Axillary bud: a bud located in the leaf axil (the angle between the leaf and the stem) that serves as a potential growth site.

Bacillus thuringiensis: a bacterium that is very effective for biological control of a variety of insect pests.

Biennial: a plant that completes its life cycle in two growing seasons, growing vegetatively in the first season and then flowering, fruiting, and dying in the second season.

Bolting: elongation of a flowering stem of a plant at the expense of its vegetative growth; generally, a plant at this stage is no longer edible.

Bulb: an underground storage structure composed of a shortened stem surrounded by thick, fleshy leaf bases; the onion is a bulb.

Chlorophyll: the green pigment in plants responsible for trapping the sun's energy and using it to fuel internal chemical reactions.

Chloroplast: a specialized microscopic structure located in the leaf and green stem cells that contains chlorophyll and aids in the manufacture of food for the plant.

Club root: a fungal disease that attacks cabbage family crops, causing grossly misshapen, slimy roots that are unable to gather adequate nutrients from the soil. Affected plants are pale and weak.

Cotyledons (also called seed leaves): special leaflike storage organs present inside the seed that nourish the young seedling. Cotyledons of many plants, such as beans and tomatoes, can be seen as the first "leaves" on the seedling; they usually look different from the true leaves.

County extension agent: a person participating in a U.S. Department of Agriculture–sponsored program in each county whose job it is to advise gardeners and farmers. The county extension agent can give advice about the varieties that grow best in your region and can help you unravel your garden problems.

Cross-pollination: the transfer of pollen from the anther of one plant to the stigma of a flower on another plant.

Damping off: wilting and early dying of seedlings caused by a soil fungus.

Determinate growth: a type of growth in which the shoot tip eventually stops stem formation and usually forms a flower; examples include corn and determinate tomatoes such as 'Nova' and 'Oregon Spring.'

Dicot: a plant whose embryo has two cotyledons; all the crops discussed in this book except corn and onions are dicots.

Downy mildew: a fungus that grows inside a plant, sending out branches through the stomata that create pale patches on the leaves.

Endosperm: nutritive tissue that develops around the plant embryo in a seed. This tissue is used up by the maturing seed in many plants but stays intact in seeds of corn and other cereal plants.

Fibrous root system: a root system lacking one central axis in which the roots branch out in all directions; corn and potatoes have fibrous roots.

Flea beetles: small dark beetles that jump like fleas when disturbed. They often attack seedlings, especially those of radishes and cabbage family crops.

Gynoecious: a plant with only female flowers; this trait appears in some specially bred varieties of cucumbers.

Hardy: a term used to describe plants that are able to withstand temperatures at or below freezing.

Humus: the material remaining in the soil after microorganisms have broken down organic matter; humus helps keep soil porous and crumbly.

Hybrid: offspring produced by crossing two different strains of a particular plant species. Seeds saved from a mature hybrid plant will usually produce plants unlike the parent.

Indeterminate growth: a type of growth in which the apical tip continuously forms stem tissue; flowers form from lateral buds; cucumbers and many tomato varieties exhibit this type of growth.

Leaching: the process by which nutrients are carried down through the soil by percolating water, often out of the reach of plant roots.

Leaf miners: wormlike larvae that make tunnels in leaves between the upper and lower epidermis.

Loam: soil composed of a balanced mixture of sand, silt, clay, and organic matter.

Manure tea: a liquid made by mixing fresh manure with water; the resulting brown liquid is a mild, quick-acting fertilizer.

Monocot: a plant whose embryo has one cotyledon; corn and onions are monocots.

Monoecious: a plant with two types of flowers, male and female; squash and corn are examples.

Mosaic virus: a disease that causes yellowing of leaves. Tobacco mosaic is the most common virus and can be transmitted to the garden by smokers.

Nematodes: a group of worms with many different lifestyles. Harmful soil nematodes are small and suck plant juices from the roots.

Node: a region of the stem from which leaves and axillary buds grow.

Open-pollinated variety: a variety of vegetable from which the seeds can be saved; unlike hybrids, seeds from open-pollinated varieties will produce plants that resemble the parents.

Perennial: an herbaceous plant that lives for three or more years.

Petiole: the stemlike part of a leaf that attaches it to the plant stem.

Phloem: vascular tissue in plants responsible for carrying food from the leaves throughout the rest of the plant; also aids plant structure by providing support for the stem.

Photosynthesis: the conversion of carbon dioxide and water into carbohydrates necessary for plant growth; light energy fuels the conversion, which takes place in the chlorophyll-laden tissues of plants; oxygen is released as a by-product.

Pistil: the female organ of a flower; consists of a stigma, a style, and an ovary.

Powdery mildew: a fungus that attacks the outside of plant leaves, producing hollow tubes that penetrate the plant tissue and suck out the juices.

Root maggots: small wormlike fly larvae that burrow into root crops such as radishes.

Rotation: the practice of alternating crops so that they are not repeatedly grown in the same part of the garden; this is done to alleviate pest and disease problems and nutrient drain.

Rotenone: an insecticide effective against many insects that is derived from plants; it is harmless to warm-blooded animals and degrades rapidly.

Scab: a disease common in potatoes that can affect root crops as well. Scab causes rough patches on the surface of crops. Acid soil helps keep scab under control.

Seed moisturization: a method of allowing seeds to soak up water gradually so their cell membranes won't be damaged.

Stamen: the male organ of a flower; consists of an anther and a filament.

Stigma: the upper portion of the pistil; receives the pollen grains during pollination.

Stomata: tiny openings in the epidermis of leaves and stems through which carbon dioxide is absorbed and moisture is given off.

Taproot: a fleshy main root from which smaller, lateral branches radiate; carrots and beets have taproots.

Tuber: an enlarged, fleshy, short underground stem; the potato is a tuber.

Vernalization: the process whereby near-freezing temperatures speed flowering of plants.

Verticillium wilt: a common disease that can affect a variety of garden crops; the leaves turn yellow, often on just one side of the plant, and then wither and die. Fortunately, resistant varieties of crops such as tomatoes are available.

Viable: a term, when applied to seeds, that indicates they are capable of germinating.

Xylem: the vascular tissue that transports minerals and water from the roots to the rest of the plant.

FURTHER READING

Barton, Barbara J. *Gardening by Mail 2—A Source Book.* Sebastopol, CA: Tusker Press, 1987. A listing of mail-order sources of seeds, bulbs, tubers, and plants. Also a listing of gardening organizations, garden books, and horticultural libraries.

Bennett, Jennifer. *The Harrowsmith Northern Gardener.* Rev. ed. Charlotte, VT/ Camden East, Ontario: Camden House Publishing, 1982. A horticultural classic with straightforward, practical advice on how to cope with the rigors of gardening in the northern U.S. and Canada.

Bubel, Nancy. *The New Seed Starter's Handbook.* Rev. ed. Emmaus, PA: Rodale Press, 1988. Discusses starting garden vegetables, flowers, herbs, and trees from seeds.

Carr, Anna. *Rodale's Color Handbook of Garden Insects.* Emmaus, PA: Rodale Press, 1983. A great help in identifying foes and allies in your garden.

Coleman, Eliot. *The New Organic Grower: A Master's Manual of Tools and Techniques for the Home and Market Gardener.* Post Mills, VT: Chelsea Green Publishing, 1989. An informative guide for both home and commercial organic growers that includes information about green manures, season extenders, crop rotation, and tools.

Logsdon, Gene. *The Gardener's Guide to Better Soil.* Emmaus, PA: Rodale Press, 1975. An excellent handbook that explains important aspects of the soil for home gardeners.

Mangelsdorf, Paul C. *Corn: Its Origin, Evolution, and Development.* Cambridge, MA: Harvard University Press, 1974. A fascinating resource book for anyone interested in the oddball crop.

McCann, Joy L. *Comprehensive Index to the 1989 Issues of Fine Gardening, Flower and Garden, Horticulture, National Gardening and Organic Gardening.* Kansas City, MO: CompuDex Press, 1990. An easy way to find articles about gardening by either subject or author. New editions annually.

Ogden, Ellen, and Shepherd Ogden. *The Cook's Garden.* Emmaus, PA: Rodale Press, 1989. A very helpful book by the experts at The Cook's Garden seed company. Includes recipes and comprehensive seed source charts.

Ryder, Edward J. *Leafy Salad Vegetables.* Westport, CT: AVI Publishing Co., 1979. A technical publication for the serious salad vegetable grower.

Simmonds, N.W., ed. *Evolution of Crop Plants.* New York: Longman, Inc., 1986. An interesting book that explores where the crops we grow today originated.

Whealy, Kent, comp. *Garden Seed Inventory.* 2nd ed. Decorah, IA: Seed Saver Publications, 1988. New edition due in summer 1991. A valuable inventory of all nonhybrid vegetables currently available and where you can buy them. Includes listings for rare heirloom vegetables that should be propagated to preserve genetic diversity. Membership in Seed Savers Exchange, which costs $25 annually, is recommended for all serious gardeners. Send $1.00 to Seed Savers Exchange, RR 3, Box 239, Decorah, IA 52101, for a descriptive color brochure.

Yepsen, Roger B., Jr. *The Encyclopedia of Natural Insect and Disease Control.* Emmaus, PA: Rodale Press, 1984. A comprehensive, easy-to-use reference that discusses the prevention and natural treatment of garden problems.

INDEX

A

Acid soil. *See* Soil, pH level
Air pollution, 42-43, 98, 271
Alkaline soil. *See* Soil, pH level
Allicin, 164
Alliums. *See* Onions
Anther, 53, 340
Apical tip, of plant stem, 36, 38, 49, 340
Auxin, 54
Axillary buds, 36, 38, 340
Axil, leaf, 38

B

Bacillus thuringiensis, 340
Bacteria in soil, 35
Beans, 233-41. *See also* Legumes,
    Lima beans
  growing, 237-38
  harvesting, 238-39
  planting times, 237
  problems, 240-41
  saving seeds, 240
  supports, 223
  types and varieties, 233-37, 337-38
Beets, 184-88. *See also* Root crops
  growing, 186-87
  harvesting, 187
  problems, 186-87
  varieties, 180, 185, 337
Biennials, 49, 340
Blindness, in cauliflower, 132
Blocking off, 76
Block planting, 237-38
Bolting, 50, 51, 92-93, 179-80, 340
Boron, 176-77
Branched roots, 32-33
Broccoli, 136-39. *See also* Cole crops
  air temperature for growth, 138
  growing, 138
  harvesting, 138-39
  planting times, 138
  saving seeds, 139
  storing harvested crops, 139
  varieties, 136-37, 139, 336-37
Brussels sprouts, 124-28. *See also*
    Cole crops
  growing, 126
  harvesting, 126-27
  nutritive value, 127
  overwintering, 126-27
  planting times, 126-27
  soil types for, 125, 126
  topping, 127-28
  varieties, 125, 126, 336
Buds, axillary, 36, 38
Bulb, 340
Bulb formation in onions, 143-44, 148
Buttoning, 135, 137

C

Cabbage, 106-21. *See also* Cole crops
  air temperature for growth, 111
  harvesting, 111
  moisture for, 107
  planting times, 110
  problems, 112
  saving seeds, 112-13
  soil types for, 107
  storing harvested crops, 109, 112
  transplanting, 110
  varieties, 107-09, 111, 336
  winter crops, 110-11
Calcium, 57, 88, 89
Cambium, 177
Carbon dioxide, 46, 255
Carbon in soil, 66
Carotenoids, 45, 46
Carrots, 188-93. *See also* Root crops
  growing, 189-91
  harvesting, 191-92
  problems, 191
  varieties, 179, 188-89, 337
  watering, 191
Cauliflower, 130-36. *See also* Cole crops
  growing, 132-34
  harvesting, 135
  heading, 134
  planting times, 132-33
  problems, 135
  saving seeds, 136
  varieties, 131-32, 133, 134, 336
Chives, 171

Chlorophyll, 45, 46, 340
Chloroplasts, 41, 44, 340
Clay soil, 58, 62, 78, 79, 203
Club root, 106
Cold frames, 72-73, 90-91, 94, 276
Cole crops, 101-39
  nutritive value, 102
  pest control, 103
  problems, 105-06
  saving seeds, 104-05
  stages of growth, 102-03
  starting seedlings, 104
  storing seeds, 105
  transplanting, 104
  vital statistics, 101
  watering, 104
Collards. *See* Kale and collards
Composting, 65-66
Containers for planting, 67-68
Cool places
  for seed germination, 13-14
  for storing harvested crops, 14
Corn, 253-71
  arrangement of plant rows, 265-66
  effect of genetic uniformity on, 28
  effect of weather on, 11
  formation of ears, 260-63
  growing, 267-68
  growing from seeds, 263-64
  interplanting with, 266
  isolation of varieties, 259-60
  little-known facts, 255
  nutritive value, 256
  planting times, 263, 264
  problems, 270-71
  roots of hybrid varieties, 27
  soil conditions, 266-67
  starting indoors, 264
  suckers, 268
  types, 257-58
  varieties, 256-59, 338
  vital statistics, 253
Cortex, of plant stem, 38
Cotyledons, 17-18, 24-25, 340
Cover crops, 60
Crop rotation, 267
Cross-pollination, 340

Crucifers. *See* Cole crops
Cucumbers, 320-23. *See also* Cucurbits
  growing, 321-22
  harvesting, 323
  varieties, 320-21, 338
Cucurbits, 307-33
  flowering, 314-17
  growing conditions, 311-12
  in the garden, 312-13
  nutritive value, 308-09
  planting times, 309-10
  problems, 319-20
  saving seeds, 318
  soil types for, 311
  starting from seeds, 309-11
  varieties, 313, 319
  vital statistics, 307
Curing
  garlic, 166
  onions, 156
  winter squash, 327-28
Cuticle, of leaves, 42
Cutworms, 98

D

Damping off, 71
Day length, effects
  on flowering, 50-51
  on lettuce and spinach, 91-93
  on onions, 143
  on plant growth, 50-52
Day-neutral varieties, 51
Days to maturity, 11-12
Degree days, 11-12
Determinate growth, 340
Dicots, 17, 38-39, 46, 47, 340
Diseases, plant, 41
Drip irrigation, 78-79, 268, 300-01, 313

E

Earthworms, 66-67
Egyptian onion, 160-61
Elephant garlic, 167, 337
Embryo, 17-18, 24, 54
Endosperm, 18, 54, 340
Epidermal cells, of roots, 34, 43
Epidermis
  of leaves, 42
  of stem, 38

Ever-ready onion, 162
Extension agent, county, 340

F

Fertilization and pollination, 54, 224
Fertilizers
  chemical, 62
  organic, 62-63
Fibrous root system, 340
Flowering, 47-54
  of cucurbits, 314-17
  of legumes, 223-24
  of potatoes, 206
  of tomatoes, 281-82
Flowers
  male and female, 26, 53
  parts of, 53-54
  perfect and imperfect, 26, 53
Fruit growth, 54-55
Fungi
  in soil, 35, 71, 82
  on cole crop roots, 106
  problems with mulch, 81

G

Garlic, 163-67
  growing, 166
  planting times, 166
  set storage, 165
  varieties, 165-66, 337
Garlic chives, 171
Genetic variety, 28-29
Germination
  between paper towels, 21, 90, 237,
    243, 264, 296
  light for, 21
  of lettuce and spinach, 89-90
  of seeds, 13-14, 19-25, 71
  testing for, 19-20
Germination temperatures, 20-21, 71
  beans, 220, 237
  beets, 186
  carrots, 190
  cole crops, 101, 104, 110
  corn, 253, 263
  cucurbits, 307, 309
  legumes, 215
  lettuce and spinach, 85, 89
  lima beans, 243

onions, 141, 151, 152
  peas, 248
  peppers, 291, 297
  radishes, 183
  root crops, 173
  tomatoes, 273, 275
Germination time
  for cole crops, 101
  for corn, 253
  for cucurbits, 307
  for legumes, 215
  for lettuce and spinach, 85
  for onions, 141
  for peppers, 291
  for root crops, 173
  for tomatoes, 273
Greenhouses, 73

H

Hardening off, 74-76
Hardy, 340
Harvesting
  beans, 238-39
  beets, 187
  broccoli, 138-39
  Brussels sprouts, 126-27
  cabbage, 111
  carrots, 191-92
  cauliflower, 135
  chives, 171
  corn, 268-69
  cucumbers, 323
  garlic, 166
  kale and collards, 123-24
  kohlrabi, 130
  lima beans, 244
  muskmelons, 330-31
  onions, 155-56
  peas, 248-49
  peppers, 302-03
  potatoes, 204, 208-09
  pumpkins, 328
  radishes, 184
  shallots, 163
  summer squash, 325
  tomatoes, 284
  watermelons, 332-33
  winter squash, 327
Heirloom vegetables, 28-29, 129

History
  of cole crops, 101-02
  of corn, 253-55
  of cucurbits, 307-08
  of legumes, 216-17
  of lettuce and spinach, 85
  of onions, 141
  of potatoes, 195-96
  of root crops, 174
  of tomatoes, 274
Humus, 59, 66, 340
Hybrids, 25-29, 33, 256, 340

I

Imbibitional shock, 23
Indeterminate growth, 340
Indoor planting, 67-71
Inoculant powders, 220
Internodes, 37-38, 40
Interplanting, 266
Irrigation, drip, 78-79, 268, 300-01, 313
Isolation
  of corn, 259-60
  of cucurbits, 318

J

Japanese bunching onions, 170-71
  planting times, 170-71
  varieties, 170

K

Kale and collards, 121-24. See also
    Cole crops
  growing, 123
  harvesting, 123-24
  nutritive value, 122
  overwintering, 123-24
  planting times, 123
  soil types for, 123
  varieties, 122-23, 336
Kohlrabi, 128-30. See also Cole crops
  growing, 129-30
  harvesting, 130
  planting times, 129
  storing harvested crops, 130
  varieties, 129, 336

L

Latitude, 51, 52
Leaching, 340
Leaf axil, 38
Leaf hairs, 43
Leaves, 41-47
  air spaces, 45
  cuticle, 42
  development of, 42
  hairs, 43
  palisade cells, 44-45
Leeks, 168-70
  planting times, 168
  varieties, 168, 337
Leghemoglobin, 218
Legumes, 215-51
  growing, 221-24, 233
  growth conditions, 224, 233
  nutritive value, 217-18
  pole and bush, 221
  pollination and fertilization, 224
  structure of, 223-24
  supports for, 222-23
  vital statistics, 215
Lettuce and spinach, 85-99
  effects of day length and temperature
    on, 52, 91-93
  germination, 89-90
  growing, 87, 91
  nutritive value, 86, 87
  overwintering, 93-94
  pH for, 87
  planting times, 90-91
  problems, 98-99
  saving seeds, 95-97
  soil for, 86-89
  transplanting, 91
  varieties, 93, 94-95, 336
  vital statistics, 85
Light conditions, 44-45
Light
  during hardening off, 75
  for seed germination, 21
Lights, artificial
  for growing seedlings, 73-74
  for lettuce and spinach, 92
  for onions, 151
Lima beans, 242-45
  growing, 243-44

harvesting, 244
  planting times, 243
  problems, 244-45
  varieties, 242-43, 338
Loam, 340
Loamy soil, 58, 78

M

Magnesium, 88
Manure, 66, 80, 86-87, 88, 176, 206, 267
Maturity, days to, 11-12
Melons. See Cucurbits, Muskmelons
Microclimates, 12-13
Moisture, for seed germination, 22, 23, 71
Molybdenum, 134
Monocots, 18, 39, 46, 47, 147, 340
Mulch, 67, 79-81
Muskmelons, 329-31
  growing, 330
  harvesting, 330-31
  varieties, 329-30, 339
Mycorrhizal fungi, 35, 153

N

Nematodes, 167, 186-87, 241
Nitrogen, 35, 48, 57, 59, 60-61, 62-63, 66,
    70, 79, 80, 86, 106-07, 133-34, 135, 138,
    153, 176, 206, 218, 233, 267, 298
Nutrients, 34, 35, 41, 42, 48, 57-58, 59-62,
    70, 79, 80, 86-87, 89, 106-07, 133-34,
    135, 138, 153, 176, 206, 218, 233, 267,
    298, 299

O

Onions, 141-71
  bulb, 142-43
  chives, 171
  curing, 156
  Egyptian onion, 160-61
  elephant garlic, 167
  ever-ready onion, 162
  garlic, 163-67
  garlic chives, 171
  growing, 147-55
  growing conditions for, 153-54
  growing from seeds, 151-52
  growing temperatures, 144
  growth of cotyledon, 25

harvesting, 155-56
Japanese bunching onions, 170-71
kinds, 159-60
leeks, 168-70
nutritive value, 143
overwintering, 152-53
planting from sets, 149-50
planting times, 144
potato onion, 161-62
problems, 158
saving seeds, 157-58
shallots, 162-63
soil temperature for germination, 152
source of flavor, 142
stages of growth, 147-49
storing harvested crops, 157
transplants, 150-51
varieties, 143-47, 150, 337
Open-pollinated variety, 340
Ovary, 54
Overwintering
  Brussels sprouts, 126-27
  garlic, 166
  kale and collards, 123-24
  lettuce and spinach, 93-94
  onions, 152-53
Oxygen, 22, 46
Ozone, 98

P

Palisade cells, 44-45
Pasteurizing soil, 70
Peas, 245-51. See also Legumes
  growing, 248
  harvesting, 248-49
  planting times, 248
  problems, 250
  saving seeds, 250
  supports, 223
  types and varieties, 246-48, 338
Peat pots, 68-69, 77, 243
Peppers, 291-305
  flowers and fruiting, 301-02
  growing conditions, 298-301
  harvesting, 302-03
  hot, 292-93
  nutritive value, 292
  planting times, 296
  problems, 304-05

saving seeds, 295-96, 304
seedlings, 297-98
starting from seeds, 296-97
sterilization of seeds, 296
varieties, 294-95, 299, 338
vital statistics, 291
Perennial, 340
Pest control, 81, 82, 103, 105-06, 158, 164,
  167, 186-87, 210, 241, 250, 270-71,
  287, 305
Petiole, 47
PH level, 63
  for cabbage, 134
  for cole crops, 101
  for corn, 253
  for cucurbits, 307, 313
  for legumes, 215, 220
  for lettuce and spinach, 85
  for onions, 141, 153
  for peppers, 291
  for potatoes, 195
  for root crops, 173, 176
  for tomatoes, 273
Phloem, 34, 39, 40-41, 46, 177, 340
Phosphorus, 35, 48, 57, 61, 70, 153, 176, 206,
  233, 267, 298-99
Photosynthesis, 40, 43, 46, 255, 340
Photosynthetic cells, 45
Phytochrome, 50, 92-93
Pistil, 53, 340
Pith, of plant stem, 38
Plant structure, 31-55
Planting
  containers for, 67-68
  seeds, 70-71
  soil temperatures for. See Germination
    temperatures
Planting depth
  for cole crops, 101
  for corn, 253
  for cucurbits, 307
  for legumes, 215
  for lettuce and spinach, 85
  for onions, 141
  for peppers, 291
  for root crops, 173
  for seed potatoes, 195
  for tomatoes, 273
Pollen, 53, 54
Pollination and fertilization, 54

of legumes, 224
of tomatoes, 281-82
Pollution, air, 42-43, 98, 271
Potassium, 42, 57, 61, 62, 87, 107, 153-54,
  176, 206, 233, 299
Potatoes, 195-213
  deep planting, 203-04
  growth conditions, 207-08
  harvesting, 204, 208-09
  nutritive value, 196-97
  planting sets, 201-05
  problems, 209-12
  seed potatoes, 200-04
  storing harvested crops, 209
  structure of, 199-200
  surface planting, 204-05
  tuber formation, 205-06
  varieties, 197-99
  vital statistics, 195
Potato onion, 161-62
Pots, peat, 68-69, 77, 243
Potting soil, 69-70
Pruning, tomatoes, 280-81
Pumpkins, 328, 339. See also Cucurbits

R

Radishes, 181-84. See also Root crops
  growing, 182-83
  harvesting, 184
  planting times, 182
  problems, 183
  varieties, 181-82, 183, 337
Reflective mulches, 80
Respiration
  effect of cold on, 55
  of roots, 59
Rhizobia, 218-20
Riceyness, 135
Ripening, 54-55
Root cap, 33
Root competition, 32-33, 83
Root crops, 173-93
  food storage in, 177
  growing conditions, 175-79
  nutritive value, 174-75
  planting times, 179-80
  saving seeds, 180
  vital statistics, 173
Roots, 31-35

branched, 32-33
damage during transplanting, 76-77
epidermal cells, 34
fibrous system, 340
grass, interference from, 83
in container planting, 69
respiration of, 59
root cap, 33
root hairs, 34
shapes of, 31-33
taproots, 32
tree, interference from, 83
xylem and phloem, 34
Rotation of crops, 267, 340
Row covers, 81-82, 89, 91, 94, 98, 104, 105,
      138, 152, 243, 277-78, 313

S

Salty soil, 87, 88, 107, 134, 138, 153, 313
Sandy soil, 57-58, 78, 79
Seed banks, 28
Seed coat, 18, 22-25
Seed germination, 19-25, 71. *See also*
      Germination time
Seed moisturization, 23, 341
Seed planting depth. *See* Planting depth
Seed Savers Exchange, 29
Seeds, 17-29
   buying, 26-28
   germination of. *See* Germination
   planting, 70-71
   starting indoors, 67-71
   storage. *See* Storing seeds
Seeds, saving
   beans, 240
   broccoli, 139
   cabbage, 112-13
   cauliflower, 136
   cole crops, 104-05
   corn, 263
   cucurbits, 318
   lettuce, 95-97
   onions, 157-58
   peas, 250
   peppers, 295-96, 304
   root crops, 180
   spinach, 98
   tomatoes, 275-76
Sepals, 53
Shallots, 162-63

planting times, 163
varieties, 162-63, 337
Silt, 58
Slugs, 81, 98-99
Smog. *See* Air pollution
Snap peas, 247, 338
Snow peas, 247, 338
Soaking injury, 23
Soaking seeds, 23
Sodium, 88
Soil, 57-63
   for Brussels sprouts, 125, 126
   for cole crops, 101
   for corn, 253
   for cucurbits, 307
   for legumes, 215
   for lettuce and spinach, 85
   for onions, 141
   for peppers, 291
   for potatoes, 195
   for root crops, 173
   for tomatoes, 273
   pH level, 63
   pores, 58-59
   potting, 69-70
   salty, 87, 88, 134, 138, 153, 313
   solarization, 82, 301
   temperature, 81
   temperatures for planting. *See*
      Germination temperatures
   testing, 60, 63, 88
   texture of, 58-59, 62
   thermometers, 20
   water storage in, 58-59
Soil types, 57-58, 62, 78, 79, 107
   for cauliflower, 134
   for cucurbits, 311
   for kale and collards, 123
   for onions, 153
   for root crops, 175-76
Solar growing frames, 72-73
Solarization, soil, 82, 301
Spinach. *See also* Lettuce and spinach
   saving seeds for, 98
   varieties, 97-98, 336
Squash, summer, 323-25. *See also*
      Cucurbits
   growing, 324
   harvesting, 325
   varieties, 324, 339

Squash, winter, 325-28. *See also* Cucurbits
   growing, 327
   harvesting, 327
   varieties, 325-26, 339
Staking plants, 41, 280
Stamens, 53, 341
Starting a new garden, 60
Stems, 35-41
   apical tip, 36-37
   cortex, 38
   epidermis, 38
   pith, 38
   vascular area, 38-39
Sterilization of seeds, 296
Stigma, 53, 54, 341
Stomata, 43, 46, 341
Storing harvested crops, 14, 55
   broccoli, 139
   cabbage, 109, 112
   carrots, 192
   cauliflower, 135
   corn, 269
   cucumbers, 323
   garlic, 166
   kohlrabi, 130
   lima beans, 244
   muskmelons, 331
   onions, 157
   peas, 249
   peppers, 303-04
   popcorn, 269-70
   potatoes, 209
   pumpkins, 328
   radishes, 184
   shallots, 163
   summer squash, 325
   tomatoes, 284-85
   watermelons, 332-33
   winter squash, 327-28
Storing seeds, 18-19
   cole crops, 105
   cucurbits, 318
   lettuce, 96
   onions, 151-52
   peppers, 295
Structure of plants, 31-55
Style, as part of flower, 54
Suckers, corn, 268
Summer squash. *See* Squash, summer
Super sweet corn, 258

Suppliers, seeds and plants, 335
Supports, for beans and peas, 222-23, 248
Surface planting, of potatoes, 204-05
Swiss chard, 185-86, 187. *See also*
    Root crops

T

Taproots, 32, 341
Temperature, air
    effect on maturation time, 11-12
    for flowering, 48-49, 51
    for pollination and fertilization, 54
    for storing harvested crops, 55
Temperature, air, for growing, 11
    beans, 238
    broccoli, 138
    cabbage, 111
    cauliflower, 134
    cole crops, 101
    corn, 253, 258-59, 265
    cucurbits, 307
    kohlrabi, 129-30
    legumes, 215
    lettuce and spinach, 85, 90
    lima beans, 244
    onions, 141, 144
    peas, 245
    peppers, 291, 302
    potatoes, 195
    radishes, 182-83
    root crops, 173
    seedlings, 74
    tomatoes, 273, 276, 282
Temperature, soil, 81
    for germination. *See* Germination
        temperatures
    for sprouting potato sets, 195
Tip burn, 89, 112
Tomatoes, 273-89
    harvesting, 284
    limited and infinite growth, 279
    planting times, 275
    pollination and fertilization, 281-82
    problems, 285-87
    pruning, 280-81
    ripening process, 282-83
    staking, 280
    starting from seeds, 275-76
    transplanting, 276-79

varieties, 274-75, 278, 338
    vital statistics, 273
Topping, Brussels sprouts, 127-28
Transplanting, 36-37
    cabbage, 110
    cole crops, 104
    kohlrabi, 129
    lettuce and spinach, 91
    seedlings, 76-77
Trellising
    cucumbers, 322
    winter squash, 327
Tuber formation in potatoes, 205-06

V

Varieties, 12-13, 336-39. *See also* individual
        vegetables
Vascular area of plant stem, 38-39
Vascular cambium, 39
Vascular system, 46
Vernalization, 49, 51, 129, 341
Viability
    of cole crop seeds, 101
    of corn seeds, 253
    of cucurbit seeds, 307
    of legume seeds, 215
    of lettuce and spinach seeds, 85
    of onion seeds, 141
    of pepper seeds, 291
    of root crop seeds, 173
    of seed potatoes, 195
    of tomato seeds, 273
Viable, 341

W

Warm places, for seed germination, 13-14
Water for flowering, 54
Water storage in soil, 58-59
Water stress, 44
Watering, 33, 78-79, 88
    cole crops, 104
    corn, 267-68
    cucurbits, 313
    during hardening off, 76
    for transplanting, 77
Watermelons, 331-33
    growing, 332-33
    harvesting, 332-33
    varieties, 331-32, 339

Weeds, 21, 22, 60, 154-55, 179, 267
Weeds, rhizomatous, 83
Welsh onions, 170-71
Winter squash. *See* Squash, winter
Withee, John, 29
Wood ashes, 62, 87, 153-54, 176, 233

X

Xylem, 34, 39-40, 46, 177, 341

ABOUT THE AUTHORS

Diane Bilderback and Dorothy Patent.

Dorothy Hinshaw Patent and Diane E. Bilderback are long-time organic gardeners. As residents of western Montana, they have become experts, by necessity, on gardening under less-than-ideal conditions. The authors share a substantial background in plant and animal sciences. Patent has a B.A. in biology and a Ph.D. in zoology and has written numerous books. Bilderback has a B.S. in botany and has been involved in botanical research.